Engendering Blackness

Inventions Black Philosophy, Politics, Aesthetics
Edited by David Marriott

Engendering Blackness
Slavery and the Ontology of Sexual Violence
Patrice D. Douglass

Stanford University Press
Stanford, California

Stanford University Press
Stanford, California

© 2025 by Patrice D. Douglass. All rights reserved.

No part of this book may be reproduced or transmitted in any form or by any means, electronic or mechanical, including photocopying and recording, or in any information storage or retrieval system, without the prior written permission of Stanford University Press.

Library of Congress Cataloging-in-Publication Data

Names: Douglass, Patrice D., author.
Title: Engendering Blackness : slavery and the ontology of sexual violence / Patrice D. Douglass.
Other titles: Inventions (Series)
Description: Stanford, California : Stanford University Press, 2025. | Series: Inventions : Black philosophy, politics, aesthetics | Includes bibliographical references and index.
Identifiers: LCCN 2024043900 (print) | LCCN 2024043901 (ebook) | ISBN 9781503630819 (cloth) | ISBN 9781503641617 (paperback) | ISBN 9781503641624 (ebook)
Subjects: LCSH: Enslaved women—Violence against—Philosophy. | Women, Black—Violence against—Philosophy. | Slavery—Philosophy. | Rape—Philosophy. | Philosophy, Black.
Classification: LCC HT871 .D59 2025 (print) | LCC HT871 (ebook) | DDC 306.3/62082—dc23/eng/20241209
LC record available at https://lccn.loc.gov/2024043900
LC ebook record available at https://lccn.loc.gov/2024043901

Cover design: Bob Aufuldish / Aufuldish & Warinner
Cover art: Lathan D'Agostino & Leo D'Agostino, *A Painting for Mom*, 2018, Acrylic, Private Collection
Typeset by Newgen in 10/14.75 FreightText Pro

The authorized representative in the EU for product safety and compliance is: Mare Nostrum Group B.V. | Mauritskade 21D | 1091 GC Amsterdam | The Netherlands | Email address: gpsr@mare-nostrum.co.uk | KVK chamber of commerce number: 96249943

For Lathan and Zoë, my reasons

Contents

Acknowledgments ix

Introduction 1

One Slavery, Racial Sexuation, and the Death Drive 25

Two Suspended Absences and the Substrates of Naming the Female Slave 62

Three Aborting the Slave Mother 96

Four On Historicizing Sex and Sexual Sense Making 145

Five Manning Black Gender 194

Six Toils of Flesh 233

Conclusion After/Wards: Notes on Representing Slavery and the Ontology of Sexual Violence 262

Notes 271

Bibliography 307

Index 323

Acknowledgments

I can recount the exact moment this book became possible. It was an answered email from Jared C. Sexton. I, a disillusioned activist, reached out to see if he'd be willing to meet to discuss my proposed graduate school project. This was in November 2008. His response was almost instantaneous, letting me know he thought my project was "crucial in fact" and would meet with me to strategize my graduate school applications. We met and talked about that project. This was my first conversation with someone about antiblackness that flowed without pause or the need for me to overexplain my reasoning. Before this critical moment, racism and white supremacy were the primary analytics used to think about Blackness. Dr. Sexton, along with Frank B. Wilderson III, were shifting the focus to antiblackness, which is why I reached out seeking his guidance on my project. This book differs from that project (although semblances appear in the conclusion). However, *Engendering Blackness* began with the generosity and acknowledgment I received from Dr. Sexton in his email response. He let me know I had thoughts worth pursuing in an intellectual register and that he would help me along the way.

Jared, thank you for answering that email. Your response exemplified the kindness and patience you have extended to me throughout the years. You have modeled an astute quality as a thinker that I continue to aspire towards. Thank you for being available at every transition I have made. You always make yourself available to answer messages and generously offer keen advice.

Thank you, Frank B., for your unwavering support. As a mentor, you have guided me to ensure my thoughts stay in the ship's hold and never cave to the desire for flight. You have shepherded me into rooms, spaces, and conversations, allowing my work to expand in ways I could have never imagined. You also continue to imagine my potential as a scholar and encourage me to dream bigger. You have pushed me to be a reflective thinker, a marksman on the page, and someone who understands that power exists in how one poses the question. As a mentor, you have steadfastly trusted me to take ownership of my journey. Above and beyond the academy, I thank you for embodying a genuine commitment to Black feminist practice by supporting me as a mom, especially when I struggled to see a future in this career. You encouraged and welcomed me to bring my children into many spaces, and never once questioned my commitments as a scholar for doing so. Your guidance has strengthened my relationship to the text, made me a better teacher, and truly taught me the power of what friendship can be and look like in the academy. Your ethics as a person and politico are unquestionable and an example for many. Thank you is incapable of capturing the essence of my appreciation for you. I am grateful to know you.

Thank you to the Institute for Citizens and Scholars for funding my ability to take time away from teaching to dedicate energy to researching and writing. Your Career Enhancement Fellowship mentoring structure allowed me the space and time to work with David S. Marriott, whose guidance expanded how I imagined this project's stakes.

While journeying through my career as a professor, I have had the privilege of returning to a student's seat to learn from and think with David. David has guided these ideas to a place that has strengthened their reach and claims. You set a high bar for erudition and possess a tremendous breadth of knowledge. Thank you for believing in this book and me.

Graduate school was a paramount time in my intellectual life. I had the privilege of working and thinking with a cohort of brilliant peers and friends. Our dedication and investment to theorizing afro-pessimism and the structural predicament of Blackness brought us together and has kept us together. Our time at the University of California, Irvine, marked a unique and generative moment as we collaborated in classrooms, directed readings, Skype meetings, apartments, over meals, and on walks to carve out an understanding of a burgeoning theoretical field. This all before afro-pessimism had the uptake and response it has today. Thank you to Jaye Austin Williams, Darol Olu Kaye, John Murillo, Nicholas Brady, Jerome Dent, Ryan Sinclaire

Davis, Letty Garcia, Christopher Chamberlin, Ahkila L. Ananth, Sara-Maria Sorentino, Jasmine Montgomery, and Linette Park for journeying with me to explore what afro-pessimism can and does make possible for thought.

Thank you to Jaye for supporting me through difficult decisions and continuing to show up for me in unwavering ways. You are the purest example of kindness, grace, and understanding.

I want to extend many thanks to my intellectual community and interlocutors who have imparted me with advice, listening ears, a deep sense of shared investments, invitations to collaborate, academic support, and many needed laughs: Axelle Karera, Cecilio M. Cooper, Mlondi Zondi, Tyrone S. Palmer, Sam Tenorio, Omar Ricks, Danae Martinez, Zakiyyah Iman Jackson, Sora Han, Rei Terada, Sabine Broeck, Franco Barchiesi, Christina Sharpe, Calvin Warren, Carsten Junker, Marie-Luise Löffler, Cedric Essi, Zamansele Nsele, Ra'il I'Nasah Kiam, Felice Blake, Kenyon Farrow, James Bliss, and Brittnay Proctor-Habil.

Axelle, you are a true example of friendship in the academy. Thank you for encouraging me to advocate for myself and to see my true potential.

To my Duke University community, thank you for being warm and welcoming intellectual interlocutors and dear friends. You all made my three years in Durham worth a lifetime of memories: Joseph Winters, Frances Hasso, Cecilia Marquez, Esther Lee, Mark Anthony Neal, Jarvis McInnis, Gustavo Silva, Ttitsi Jaji, Anne-Maria Makhulu, J. Kameron-Carter, Adam R. Rosenblatt, Gabriel Rosenberg, Priscilla Wald, Jasmine Cobb, Kathi Weeks, Ranjana (Ranji) Khanna, Riikka Prattes, Pedro Nicoli, and Sarah Wilbur.

Thank you to Joseph for being one of the first people to welcome me to Duke. Thank you for the coffee-table meetings where we theorized and imagined the contributions of Black studies.

Thank you to Cecilia and Annise Weaver for our weekly Zoom calls, which kept life bearable amid the pandemic. Escaping the terror of reality to check in about very important matters like reality television was the balm I needed to keep going.

Frances, thank you for meals, advice, encouragement, hugs, and gifts for the children. Your kindness and generosity have provided me with such warmth.

I am grateful to my colleagues in the Department of Women and Gender Studies at the University of California, Berkeley. A very special thank you to

Eric A. Stanley for supporting me throughout the years. Thank you first for helping me apply to graduate school by sharing your statements with me and providing feedback on mine. Thank you for being an amazing colleague and a good friend. Thank you to Mel Y. Chen and Courtney Desiree Morris for being warm and supportive colleagues.

I am thankful for the current (and recently former) cohort of graduate students and thinkers who share my work and believe in the paths I am working to carve out. Thank you to Jordan Mulkey, Brendane Tynes, Kevin Rigby Jr., Jon Jon Moore Palacios, Leah Kaplan, Taija McDougall, Rebecca A. Wilcox, Da'Shaun Harrison, Tea Troutman, Ebony Oldham, Sarah Haugh, Chloé Samala Faux, Jocelyn Burrell, Justin James, Tapji Garba, Marcelle-Anne Fletcher, Josh Falek, and Patrick Teed.

Thank you, Charlie Pollard-Durodula, for the countless hours you spent helping me propel this manuscript to the finish line. Your keen sense of detail, supreme work ethic, and investment in this project have been a lifeline. I cannot thank you enough for filling in and completing so many tasks to help this manuscript take shape. You are a gem!

Erica Wetter, I could not have imagined a kinder and more supportive editor. Thank you for believing in this project and supporting me along the journey. Most of all, thank you for providing the space to write the book I wanted and needed.

I want to thank Caroline McKusick and the other Stanford University Press staff for helping to finalize this manuscript for publication.

Thank you, Tamara Nopper, for editing this entire manuscript for clarity and rigor. Your editing strategies and political commitments have made this a better book.

Thank you to my reviewers for making this a stronger book than I initially conceived. Thank you for pushing me with your prompts and questions so I could see my moves differently and pose other ways of seeing and doing.

Thank you to the Dean of UC Berkeley Social Sciences, Raka Ray, for supporting this project with the Abigail Hodgen Publication Award.

I sincerely thank Joshua Mitchell, Kenneth Leblue, and Lydia Kelow-Bennett. Before *Engendering Blackness* was an idea, you each held me as I journeyed on various thought explorations to arrive at what this book has become. In your ways, you have shown up for me as emotional and intellectual support but, most importantly, as friends. I cannot express my appreciation for you in words.

Thank you to my friends who keep me grounded and continue to cheer me on from outside the walls of the academy. I appreciate your care to learn more about what I do while also providing a space of respite for me to maintain a full life outside of my profession: Mecca, Lucia, Whitney, Raquel, Katrina, Gloria, Mei, Ruby, and Jasmine.

To my parents, thank you for raising me to ask questions and to never settle for insufficient answers. Thank you to my brother Michael and nephews Zion and Eli for always being proud of me. Thank you to my husband Leo for sustaining me through this entire process. You have listened to me rehearse my arguments countless times, traveled with me as I presented, and helped calm my uncertainty when things felt too hard. Thank you most of all for being my balance in life. Thank you to Lathan and Zoë, my babies. You each were born at different stages of this project, and each helped to propel the work to the finish line. Thank you for being the light you both are and being curious about what Mommy is writing. Special thanks to Lathan for keeping me on task and never failing to ask, "How is the book coming along?" Or to express honest encouragement by letting me know my book is long overdue to my editor. The two of you have brought much-needed levity to this journey. Thank you for being my world!

Engendering Blackness

Introduction

Despite the physical chains being severed, the ontological strictures of slavery continue to illustrate the constraints of reinvention for Black people. Specifically, the slave's sexual captivity still overdetermines the impossible mattering of Blackness after over a century and a half of freedom in the United States. As the most refracted violence of slavery, sexual violence is found everywhere, in all things—from employment disputes, revisions made to the fugitive slave acts, the distinction between federal and state law, to literature, Hollywood film, and critical theory. The marking of the slave as sexually open, and thus violable, situates the merger of the experiential, structural, and psychic. The performance of the violation, the language of (non)injury, and the conceptual frameworks deputized to articulate the matter of what occurred are effectively muted by the disarrayed nature of this violence. This is not disrupted by formal emancipation but is obscured by the assumption of distance.

    The sexual captivity of slaves is not a new topic. It is frequently mentioned as a horror of the transatlantic slave trade. Yet there are competing theories about it. While diverging on key points, these theories share a commitment to finding a logical reason for sexual violence against slaves. In the process, they neglect that the curious arrival of Blackness in the modern world, as both person and property, cannot be assuaged by reason. The slave is a reasonless object, insofar as slavery is unethical in the first instance of violence. Though even the use of reason in the previous two sentences is improper. Blackness and opacity are not reasons but living dead conditions that escape ontological capture. Furthermore, the attempt at constructing reason for sexual violability denies the modern slave is irrevocably Black, and that there is no reason for the captivity of the slave except its Blackness.

Thought attempts to reason away or ignore the antiblack violence betraying the relation between cause and motive. Such that what appears, without persuasive motivation, is rendered speechless in the pursuit of reason. Given this position, how does one approach history without constructing reason? Is violence able to labor without recourse to meaning? What if the sexual violation of the slave occurred for no other reason than the fact that it could? What if Black sexual violability is an intractable fungible thing? If the sexual violations of the slave were illogical, then what are the implications for *us* now?

Taking up these questions, *Engendering Blackness: Slavery and the Ontology of Sexual Violence* argues that the cause of the sexual violability of the slave is the opacity of its condition. Sexual violation of the slave occurred for no other reason than the fact that it could. As my book asserts, theorizing sexual violability as the status of the slave requires a paradigmatic analysis that questions what authorizes this condition, how it is embodied, and how the many experiences are socially and politically accounted for. Such a paradigmatic analysis interrogates how gender and sexuality crystallize the limits of theorizing the slave as partially or situationally conscripted by violence.

Returning to the archive of slavery and its political philosophical interpretations, this book centers on the Fanonian insistence that all antiblack violence returns to the question of sexuality and the sexual. As Fanon writes, "Is the lynching of the Negro not a sexual revenge? We know how much of sexuality there is in all cruelties, tortures, and beatings."[1] *Engendering Blackness* details how interrogating sexual violence serves as the most essential commentary on how every violation made operable by slavery is sexually sutured.

Yet interrogating sexual violence is not the same as addressing gender and sexuality. A focus on gender and sexuality serves to obfuscate and minimize the saturation of violence over the slave. Gender is a coffle. Sex is the marketplace of flesh. Too often, gender analyses and sexual theories take up the slave as an empty signifier for the fortification of the Human—the modern philosophical and scientific social construction of a being that is actionable and willful because it is not a slave or an animal. Gender and sexual theorizing, then, serve to distill the purported true function of sexual captivity to connect the slave to existential and political concerns beyond slavery. What this all means for Blackness is a question that lacks a definitive elaboration.

Slavery and Gender

In the scholarship on slavery and gender, the work of Angela Y. Davis is deeply influential. Similar to Fanon, Davis heralds the dire necessity of apprehending the import of sexual violence under slavery on contemporary Black revolutionary politics. Writing from her jail cell, she penned "Reflections on a Black Woman's Role in the Community of Slaves." This essay was a critical response and dedication to her comrade, and imprisoned intellectual, George Jackson, who was assassinated in San Quentin prison a mere few months before its publication in *The Black Scholar*.[2] In a dedication to Jackson, Davis writes, "As I came to know and love him, I saw him developing an acute sensitivity to the real problems facing black women and thus refining his ability to distinguish these from their mythical transpositions."[3] These "mythical transpositions" emanate from the belief that Black women are inherently matriarchal.

Davis takes pains to situate Jackson's perspective of Black women within the political climate of the era. She turns to the 1965 Moynihan Report, a sociological document about the problems of Black family life, as evidence of the pervasive misappropriation of Black women's power and position in the Black community and American society writ large. The report, written for the federal government by Assistant Secretary of Labor Daniel Patrick Moynihan, depicted Black family structure—particularly Black matriarchy—as a key determinant in poor social outcomes for African Americans. Jackson, according to Davis, treated as credible the Black matriarch trope, a "cruel" image "because it ignores the profound traumas the black woman must have experienced when she had to surrender her child-bearing to alien and predatory economic interests."[4] She argues further that rape was the most "terroristic texture of plantation life" that slave women were unguarded from, and that the matriarchal ascription could never be applicable under these conditions.[5]

The sheer force of slavery, Davis argues, annulled the category of woman for Black women slaves and "rendered her equal to her man."[6] This transmutation of gender was a byproduct of a system predicated upon the relinquishment of "the myth of femininity" in order "to extract the greatest possible surplus from the labor of slaves."[7] About fifteen years later, a similar point was made by Hortense J. Spillers, who argues, "in the historic outline of dominance, the respective subject-positions of 'female' and 'male' adhere to no symbolic integrity."[8] Despite the theoretical equivalence that Davis and Spillers draw between Black women and men, they each cautiously relieve Black women of the feminine expectation while not alleviating Black men from the lures and power of patriarchy. The question remains: if Black women are rendered equal to Black men in terms of subjugation, why not similarly relieve Black men of their relationship to gender? Why are Black men not situated through their own plantation sexualized terror?

Spillers does suggest that the Black male is uniquely situated because he "has been touched, therefore, by the *mother*, *handed* by her in ways that he cannot escape."[9] However, the assumptive logic turns toward the Black female, or the *mother*, as an essential truth or structural orientation in a manner that does not question the violence that makes the female an incontestable form of violable intelligibility. If, as Davis (and by extension, Spillers) presupposes, gender is annulled for the female slave for her to "function as a slave," then how does the category of slave, irrespective of gender, expose the outer limits of notions that rest on sex and gender as always already clarifying forms of differentiation?

Interrogating how gender is theorized in relation to slavery and sexual captivity helps us understand how a focus on Black women serves to elucidate the conditions of others in relationship to the economy and patriarchy, but not to grapple so much with the ontological strictures of slavery and Blackness. Consider what Davis delineates as the implications of sexual captivity for politics. She argues that "the brutal force of circumstances" assigned Black women "the mission of promoting consciousness and practice of resistance."[10] At the root of the symbiosis between force and resistance is how the structural architecture of slavery is wedded to the permanent capture and control of Black women's sexual function as well as their gendering. "Reflections" thus presents a double bind that continues to plague many Black feminist projects.

As a field, Black feminist historiography has an acute awareness of the contradictions of extending the category woman to female slaves, and Black women more generally, without caveat. However, this understanding does not result in the field abandoning the use of woman as a qualifier for slave or Black. Rather, the scholarship redoubles the category of Black woman as a primordial figure whose affection and response to violence and violation are, to use Davis's term, their own mythical transpositions. Within Black feminism, the Black woman operates as an uncontested figure of truth whose violation produces the conditions of possibility for autonomic resistance to centuries of unflinching violence. As my book addresses, inquiry should be critical of how and why the Black woman's continued existence is thought to resolve or at least clarify the history of sexual violence under slavery.

To this end, *Engendering Blackness* argues that the investment in maintaining gender as an ironclad alibi to explain why the slave is saturated by sexual violence does more to mystify the structure than to reveal its truths. Davis's privileging of the Black woman as the revolutionary or insurgent against slave sexual captivity has had a profound impact on Black feminism that cannot be understated. For example, the Combahee River Collective asserts in their field-defining statement that "Reflections" clarifies that "Black women have always embodied, if only in their physical manifestation, an adversary stance to white male rule and have actively resisted its inroads upon them and their communities in both dramatic and subtle ways."[11]

My point is not to disagree with Davis's claim that "to say the oppression of black slave women necessarily incorporated open forms of counter-insurgency is not as extravagant as it might initially appear."[12] Instead, I am asking what is occluded when we rest analyses on the gendering of female slaves as the content of their violations and, in turn, their resistance? I do so to interrogate how Black feminism remains deeply enmeshed within ascriptions of Black women as fundamental revolutionary actors in a manner that does not question the gender binary and its relationship to slavery and sexual violence. As *Engendering Blackness* shows, taking up gender to humanize the female slave inadvertently serves to reify and strengthen the binary as an essential organizing factor of emancipatory practices and imperatives. Additionally, Black feminism continues to orbit around a silence regarding if, and how, Black women's sexual beingness can be severed from her sexual violability, even in the midst of her radical action.

Black feminism is stratified by disagreements about what Black sexuality is or can be in the midst and afterlife of an existence constituted by sexual violation. Evelyn M. Hammonds contends that psychoanalysis might move

Black feminists closer to dislodging Black female sexuality from perceptions that it is "inherently abnormal, while acknowledging the material and symbolic effects of the appellation."[13] She concludes that through psychoanalysis, Black feminist projects can expose the essential nature of the Black female other within a paradigm where sexual difference and sexuality are made palpable yet exclusionary. Here, Hammonds is countering the Black feminist tendency to read sexuality and desire as pronouncements of an untouched site of Black women's interiority. Additionally, she wants to register violation but not subsume Black women's sexual practices and existences within a fixed and overdetermined relationship to it. Hammonds's contentions with why Black feminism is stunted by dualistic thinking about sexual agency and sexual violation harken upon a structural predicament: the contradictions between how far violation extends beyond physical captivity into notions of self-possessed desire. Hammonds is correct that if theory can contend with the psychic and material imports of sexual violation, then Black feminism "could begin the project of understanding how differently located black women engage in reclaiming the body and expressing desire."[14]

Before Black feminist theory arrives at the place Hammonds so desperately demanded of the field thirty years ago, there must be crude assessments of how sexual violence under slavery poses a fundamental challenge to how violation is understood on a paradigmatic scale by Black feminists, white feminists, queer theorists, and other scholars of race, gender, and sexuality. While sexual violence does not stop Black sexuality from emerging, slavery does structurally impair the capacity to delineate violation without falling back on the schemas of difference and intelligibility made possible by the psychic and material effects of that same violence. This centrifugal trap of lacking a language that is not implicated within the problem that one is attempting to name, or at least describe the texture of, can be approached from various vantage points. However, *Engendering Blackness* interrogates this structural predicament by grappling with how gender fails to theorize the antiblackness of sexual violence and violation.

While the rampant sexual injury, and denial of such occurrences, for female slaves plays a particular role in the historiography of slavery, I am eschewing employing this gendered framing as my point of entry into this debate. I do so because the narrative of the particular femaleness of slave sexual violations grossly undertheorizes the magnitude of slave sexuation.

The argument here contends with the fact that *all slaves* were sexually violable. Which is to say, the sexualized violations of male slaves and children are not secondary to a paradigm that is particular to the reproductivity of female slaves. Rather, the structure is constitutive of the sexual captivity of slaveness/Blackness.

As historian Thomas A. Foster has argued about the sexual violation of male slaves,

> The study of enslaved men has not covered sexual assault not only because of the legacy of slavery, which characterized black men as hypersexual (and therefore always willing sexual participants) but also because of the historical and enduring understandings of sexual assault.[15]

He notes that early American law, and white feminist discourses, framed rape as a category of injury and experience only available to white women perpetuated primarily by unknown Black men assailants.[16] This trope of white gendered victimhood and Black male sexual prowess and supposed power pervades much of the white imaginative history of slavery and beyond.[17] This spectacle serves to both punish Black men and to obscure the realities of the sexual injuries and vulnerabilities they experienced. Yet, like the female slave, the question of sexual consent and agency for the male slave was incomprehensible, making sexualized violations a common experience for slaves regardless of gender.[18]

By excavating the history of Black women's hyper-susceptibility to rape by white men, many Black feminist historians did the crucial work of displacing the misappropriated victimhood of white women in discussions of interracial rape. This critical work illuminated that under slavery and beyond, Black women have been subjected to systematic sexual brutalization at frequencies and intensities far greater than those experienced by white women. However, by granting primary attention to the experiences of Black women, these works dedicated less conceptual labor to examining how the plantation operationalized sexual violations against all slaves.

My purpose in critically examining Black feminist historiography is not to render it obsolete, but to grapple with its tensions. Indeed, the work of Black women historians makes this book possible, namely by having prioritized giving attention to Black women's enslavement and sexual captivity. Such work was necessary to challenge not only the tropes of Black women's dominance, as Davis sought to counter with "Reflections," but the racial politics of how white feminist scholars theorized rape.

Feminist philosophy and legal theory have substantially reconsidered sexual violence, namely the question of rape. Challenging the perception of rape as separate individual acts, these fields shifted the public conversation from considering rape a private matter to clarify how sexual violence is structured by the ethics of a gendered society. Though as fields of thought, there is not a uniform approach to theorizations of sexual violence as public political concerns, these theoretical enterprises collectively expose the faults within legal, political, and social understandings of rape. By reasserting discussions on gender, the feminine and masculine, consent, power, the state, the public versus private, capitalism, and the question of sex and sexuality in rape, they often provided limited insight into how to grapple with slavery and sexual violability of slaves. The challenges of Black feminism to the racial lens of feminist philosophy and legal theory, although steeped in gender categories, have helped make clearer how the sexual violability of slaves still requires a theoretical vocabulary.

Without a critical introspection into Blackness, analyses of sexual violence reduce its severity and scale to the act of rape, while also subtending the problem to the constitutive order of Human gendering. Even the most radical feminist logics that understand patriarchy as foreclosing all semblances of feminine choice fail to acknowledge that sexual violability for the Black is predicated on the force of violence that is absolved of questions of consent. The inconceivability of Black agreement to a violent sexual order undergirds the preconscious and unconscious investments held out for the transformative power of Human gendering, even in its dispossessed or degraded forms. The capacity to imagine the possibility of consent even in place of its absence is completely nullified for the slave. A structure of consent cannot dissolve a paradigm of sexual force. This is not to suggest Blackness is occluded in most analyses of sexual violence. Rather, the slave functions as the most pervasive rape analogy. However, when Blackness is engaged in rape theory it is used to extend and buttress an assumptive logic about the centrality of Human sex/gender in determining the form and matter of sexual violations.

In this respect, my book moves forward on the premise that the full weight of violations must be attended to, and that gender cannot be the point of departure for theorizing sexual violence and slavery. To understand the full weight of violations, our analyses cannot be limited to a preoccupation with Black women's sexual captivity. Nor can it, as Black queer and Black trans theories underscore, operate with the biocentrism often anchoring gender categories.

With respect to the genealogies of Black queer and Black trans theories, the point is to challenge what we assume as gender and how and where it is assumed to emerge. The body or the fantasy that genitals are the space where the ascription of gender arises is eschewed here. The call is to not assume gender integrity unless such can be proven to exist in the objects of analysis. Here, gender expands beyond self-definition and the usage of pronouns in reference to self or others. The description of slaves as gendered subjects does not determine that the structure and discourses of gender are explanatory of their conditions. Rather, "The slave system defined Black people as chattel. Since women, no less than men, were" (re)produced as socially dead, such that "they might as well have been genderless as far as the slaveholders were concerned."[19] Gender does not reveal the antagonisms of social death, in the same unrelenting manner that social death reveals the veil gender places over what cannot be explained about Blackness. Though I would hesitate to describe this as a chicken and egg argument. Blackness, theoretically, scandalizes gender. Gender is the possession of the Human. Blackness exposes its outer limits. In sum, I begin with Blackness, as it is dynamized by gender imposed under violent erasure. Sexual(ized) violence as a paradigm cannot be disarticulated from Blackness.

The push here to sexualize the paradigmatic order of slavery does not surmise, as Michel Foucault stated, "that there is no difference, in principle, between sticking one's fist into someone's face or one's penis into their sex."[20] Rape, or sexual assaults, carry a tremendous psychic weight because of the Human virtue of owning one's sex and sexuality. The act of dispossessing one of the possessive rights of the sexual encounter fundamentally erodes an essential quality of Humanness. The slave/Black is held captive to a paradigmatic ordering of violence predicated on the dispossession of the body reduced to flesh, which, as Spillers has argued, is pornographic in nature, though broadly expansive beyond acts, permeating psychic registers.[21]

Racial Sexuation and Afro-Pessimism

Engendering Blackness is a critical expansion of afro-pessimism, which is a theory of antiblackness, ontology, and violence. Offering a radical return to the Fanonian treatise on Blackness, afro-pessimism contends that slavery is a paradigmatic relation rather than a historically situated experience. Although one can point to 1865 as the formal end of slavery in the United States, Blackness, as the slave of modernity, maintains a captive relation with the Human and its world. This position contends that the Black is not Human, nor is it a subject of the Human world. Nevertheless, antiblackness is essential to the overdetermination of the Human as a universal signifier of common struggle and community. As Frank B. Wilderson III argues,

> through chattel slavery the world gave birth and coherence to both its joys of domesticity and to its struggles of political discontent; and with these joys and struggles the Human was born, but not before it murdered the Black, forging a symbiosis between the political ontology of Humanity and the social death of Blacks.[22]

The argument taken up here maintains that the Human is a political ontological category constructed and maintained through a violent relationship with Blackness. Reading the captive condition on its own terms without equivocating towards Humanness and its various forms of subject differentiation (gender, sexuality, class, etc.) allows for an unflinching attunement to the scales of violence as force. Violence here is more capacious than physical acts, as it engulfs Blackness within a totalizing ontological erasure. Afro-pessimist interrogations clarify Fanon's insistence that "ontology—once it is finally admitted as leaving existence by the wayside—does not permit us to understand the being of the black man."[23] Questions linger about the import of afro-pessimist frameworks on studies of slavery. How does manhood relate to "the unbearable hydraulics of Black disavowal" that Wilderson describes as saturated in gratuitous violence?[24] Is the violent thrust of the world that afro-pessimists describe rooted in a type of masculine violation reserved for cis-men or masculinist appeals towards reading violence as a singular truth? What is gender to afro-pessimism?

My book is a response to, and disavowal of, the assumption that sits at the heart of these questions. The afro-pessimist is demanded by other Black studies, feminist, and queer theorists to disavow the objectification that the archive reveals, and to assert that the truth of the structural predicament of the slave is one of denied entrance into Human community. Thus, there is great effort to amplify the social life of the slave in contradistinction to emphasizing the totalizing condition of social death. As a theory, social death contends that the slave is natally alienated, generally dishonored, and subjected to gratuitous violence.[25] Yet social death is not disproved by the social life of the slave.

Prioritizing the focus on social life instead of social death is meant to produce a more nuanced reading of slavery not fully shrouded in violation. The desire here is to render the racial slave more than their violating conditions and thus, a Human suspended by abjection rather than a *true* slave who is totalized by objecthood. Recognizing the social organization of gender and sexuality within communities of slaves is meant to illuminate social life, and thus counter slavery as a totalizing condition. This position, however, is belated insofar as it fails to question why gender and sexuality demand forceful implementation within the social arrangements of captive life. Why is the theoretical project of most area studies to forcefully insert the significance of slave gender and sexuality within a history where its subjective qualities are vaguely present, rather than to question the explanatory power of those identificatory terms for the captive condition altogether?

We can consider, then, how the pressure placed on afro-pessimism to prove the gender of its theory is an anxiety shored up in response to the deadening of subjective differentiation for the slave in the archive. The flattening of the slave's structural positionality is not imposed, as often attributed, by the afro-pessimist insistence on reading slaveness, and by extension Blackness, as social death. Instead, studies of slave social life, I argue, offer additional damning content about the pervasiveness of social death in the face of varying forms of slave attempts at alternative forms of kinship relations, community building, and resistant strategies. Simply, afro-pessimism is not the foreclosure it is purported to be. As a theory it pushes past the limits of compulsory Humanism, exposing "a meditation that does not so much reiterate an analysis of gender difference and its politics as it poses the question of the very possibility of engendering and embodiment."[26] Where thought arrives on the other side of this investigation is to contend with the unthinkable ways that slavery continues to possess the frameworks deployed to apprehend the meaning and redress of violation or to confront the impetus to avoid engaging the violence of Humanism altogether.

Engendering Blackness develops the concept of *racial sexuation* to elaborate a more expansive framework for understanding the implications of sexual violence as a structural component of modern racial slavery.[27] Racial sexuation connotes how the slave is suspended within a terrain of sexual violence as a permanent status of ontological obsolescence. It indexes a condition of (non)being that is always sexual(ized) and violating—an indeterminate status that is propelled into structural relations by force through proximity and repetition, and most essentially, through fantasy and desire. I employ terms like sexual violability or sexually violable to symbolize the manner in which racial sexuation is realized through grotesque and mundane forms of sexual brutality, how sexual violations were structured as a permanent potential for the slave (even if each slave did not individually experience such), and, more critical to the argument laid out here, that every violence of slavery, sexual and non-sexual, arguably works in service of preserving and perfecting the slave as gratuitously sexually available in a manner inconceivable for non-slaves. Everything relating to Black slaveness is sexually violent because all violence is oriented by the sexual.

My study of slavery, then, offers a theory of antiblack sexualized violations rather than a historiography of such. What does it mean to theorize about, rather than to accumulate facts on, sexual violations and slavery? This argument contends that the latter disposition, of itemizing the sexual violence endured by slaves, forecloses the perceptual capacity to grasp that structural antiblack sexual violability is not a fact of the past that is offset and refigured by emancipation. Though the sexual violations experienced by slaves are shocking beyond what most can conceive as possible to endure, the spectacle of its extreme performances is not explanatory on its own. In addition, I challenge the notion that documenting events, actions, and responses is adequate to grasp the structural predicament that authorized such totalizing violence. This position firmly resists the desire to assume the sexualized suffering of the slave does not overdetermine and dictate our ways of knowing/mattering/being in the present, and our imaginings of the implications of the past and any conceivable futures.

The point is to interrogate how the sexual violation of the slave is far more central to the orientation of the modern world—not simply the contours of Black life—than previously theorized. This is evidenced by the fact that there are no formulated logics available to make sense of and redress what occurred drawing from the analyses available to the assumed past or the present. How do you affect material or imaginative Black freedom from the very mechanism that made and decayed slaves? What form of reparations can rise to the level of adequacy to deal with the magnitude of such a demand? Are there any definitive terms, political prescriptions, or narratives that can provide a Black grammar of suffering that attends to the viscous history of the sexual mores of slavery?

Humanism and Black Differentiation

This book contends that engaging Black sexual violability is imperative for understanding the lures and complications of differentiating Blackness with respect to types, intensities, and forms of violence. Gender is the primary form of Black differentiation called upon to apply reason to sexual violation. Moreover, as my book addresses, the emphasis on political condemnation of, and resistance against, sexual violence helps to reinforce a belief in Black differentiation by both gender and politics. It is through gender that scholars attempt to connect the sexual captivity of slavery to struggles associated with Human categories, like woman, mother, victim, and worker. In these accounts, to draw attention to slaves' sexual violability is to help us better understand the antiblackness of who is authorized to mother, patriarchal relations, who is understood as vulnerable to rape, the (un)gendering of Blackness, and the political economies of slavery. As I discuss, just as social life brings into greater focus social death, so too does the emphasis on Black political resistance or efforts to link slave sexual violability to conflicts and struggles that are associated with the Human and non-Blackness. Ultimately, such efforts evade grappling with the ontology of sexual violence, which is a philosophical and conceptual imposition of Human gendering and sexual ordering as a total and explanatory structure.

The engendering of Blackness through sexual violence exposes the realm of racial sexuation that makes Human gender possible and holds the slave/Black ontologically captive to the Human's multiplicities. What sexual violence and slavery reveal is that the sexual(ized) force that conditioned the life of slaves served to mark violation as a permanent status for Blackness while also wagering the value of being Human as an otherwise to this status. In this respect, the sexual violability of the slave, as potentiality, and the acts and fantasies of these violations inaugurate a grammar of the value/meaning/matter of what it means to be Human, as an ontology that is distinct and structurally protected from the gravity of capture, dispossession, and loss that constitutes Blackness.

Thus, the title of this book sits in tension. The ontology of sexual violence demarcates a structural logic of accounting for sexual violence that forecloses the ability of thought to grapple with Blackness, which emanates from sexual violence. This position challenges the perception that the sexually violent experiences endured by Black people from slavery into the present are but one component of racialization. Instead, I contend that sexual violence operates as a modality of force that (re)inaugurates the conditions of slave capture that ushered Blackness into modern coherence by the marking of peoples as Black through an identification of their perceived sexual otherness and fecundity. Racial sexuation as a modern predicament is what made and propelled Blackness into thought as the amorphous and violable condition that reason incessantly attempts to capture, even centuries after the first slave ships set sail for worlds unknown to the captives onboard.

In this respect, *Engendering Blackness* interrogates how, across assumed disparate moments in time and throughout seemingly distinct realms of thought, the world relegates antiblack sexual(ized) violations as dissolvable conflicts that can be relieved by adjusting the slave/Black to appear perceptually as Human. I argue that this is a constitutive component of slavery, which, to use Saidiya Hartman's terms, renders Blackness a condition of fungibility and accumulation, and thus sexuated as formable to any matter other than its own. The dispossession of Black gendered and sexual capacity is positioned to graft the logic and language of suffering from forms of symbolic integrity it is fundamentally denied. As Hartman demonstrates, law and social customs rendered the slave unrapeable, as consent for the slave was inconceivable. However, to expose what this status may mean, historically and for the present, rape and sexual consent are taken up as the language to describe this non-dispossessed dispossession. What appears here is that the slave is speechless about violence and violation as constitutively produced as its distinct possession or experience. Conversely, the slave is (re)figured to orient a structure of recognition that extends becoming Human as the essential redress for its condition. However, the violence of the Human is obscured by a structure of desire and incorporation that disallows thought to perceive its essential role in creating and extending the paradigm of racial sexuation. In short, the Human is not freedom from sexual violability for the slave; it is its making.

I want to caution against the impulse to respond to the sexual violation of the slave as a form of domination to maintain the hegemonic control of the master. This position undermines the long-documented forms of resistance taken on by slaves to fight back against sexual brutality.[28] Despite ample daily, well-orchestrated, and carried out sexual refusals, the structure of racial sexuation remained intact. This by no means is an indictment of the slave. Nor does it render their resistance meaningless. Rather, it is to argue that racial sexuation orients a structure of coherence that determines the relation between the slave and the master prior to, and in excess of, action. Using archival examples, this book illustrates how mundane, casual, and unremarkable the many sexual acts imposed upon slaves often were. Instances involving the dismemberment and mutilation of sexual organs, physical and mental torture, forced coprophagia, murder, feticide, infanticide, and the neglect of children reside so abundantly in the archive that the excessive nature of their presentation is confronted with a structural aphasia. At the level of analysis, it becomes impossible to account for the sheer magnitude of violent acts captured by the historical record as well as the many instances not captured by the archive at all. The question remains: what did all this sexual terror do? Arguably, the sexuation of the slave extends beyond the corporeal, economic, and temporal operations of the plantation into the psychic and Humanistic impulses of what constitutes life and movement within.

The psychosexual life of antiblackness is perfected in ways that undermined the assumed importance of the plantation as key in structuring political ontological distinctions. The plantation is rendered the penultimate space of unrelenting antiblack sexual brutality. In this respect, the plantation concretizes the violent antiblack arrangements of political ontology, though too often the assumption is that violence is the plantation or more intensified in the close physical proximity to the master. However, passive reflections on the plantation as the beginning and end of the Black captive condition are part and parcel to the entombing nature of racial sexuation.

The types and degrees of violence preserved as the domain for the Black, which do emanate from slavery, are confined not to the plantation nor to the temporal limits of the formal institution. Fantasies and desires about the fungible and disposable nature of Blackness are germane to the paradigmatic order of the after/life of slavery and, thus, are not contained by any singular institutional form.

This engagement refuses a moralistic approach about right or wrong treatment of slaves. One could argue that the weight of this history shows how frequently slaves were mistreated and sexually abused, thus opening up analyses to discover or reify alternative ways of existing outside the frame of such brutality, a gesture often made by those seeking to amplify social life. However, the aim of this book is more provocative. Instead, I posit that there is no just way to treat a slave insofar as their conditions as slaves is unethical at its core. The point is not to reify slavery by privileging discussions of its performances, by way of good and bad actors in history. Instead, it is to always hold in thought that slavery had no ethical right to exist. Or, as Wilderson puts it, making sure the analysis stays within the hold of the slave ship. If slavery is sexually unethical in spite of, and beyond, the sexual behaviors of its actors, and Blackness extends from this unethical arrangement, what does all this mean for the present? Engaging the institution of slavery from this vantage point exposes the ethical dilemmas that undergird the impulse to remark upon Black sexual violability as an object of history or to parse Black differentiation. In other words, it highlights how the refiguring of Blackness across time is fundamentally tethered to unethical arrangements of sexual force.

The concern here is not to reproduce a desire to prove that slaves were not actually slaves, to say that slaves were humans temporarily suspended by violence and not objects of their condition. Rather, the point is to raise the question, if sexual violence figured all parts of slavery, what, then, is a slave? How does the slave's sexual status permeate Blackness in the after/life of slavery? Furthermore, what can gender and sexuality *be* under these conditions?

The blood of the violence congeals over us regardless of how slaves identified themselves, gendered, sexual, and otherwise.[29] Thus, I am interrogating the lens that weighs upon the historical, to wager how slavery structurally positions Blackness and Black people in the present tense. Slavery, as a paradigm of violence, has implications for all Black people, not simply those that can find their pronouns and genders in the archive. Furthermore, the point of the project is to expose the sociodicy of Human gender and desire as the "severing of the captive body from its motive will, its active desire," such that "[t]he captive body, then, brings into focus a gathering of social realities as well as a metaphor for *value* so thoroughly interwoven in their literal and figurative emphases that distinctions between them are virtually useless."[30] The metaphor of value in the case of sexual violence and slavery is that of the narrative schema of Human differentiation as freedom for Blackness. The up from slavery story would hold that the ex-slave's or new Black's capacity to perfect gender articulation or sexual agency, like the Human, is what unravels the ontological strictures of a condition oriented by sexual violation. Is the question of silence fundamentally redressed by acknowledging the structural harms that were once denied recognition? What, to the slave, is sexual violence if not a permanent obliteration of its potential for reinvention? How does racial sexuation lock the Black in a recidivistic relation to suffering?

On Reading Sexual Violence and Slavery

What constitutes sexual violence under slavery? Is it produced at the level of penetration, fleshly lacerations, the marking, tearing, or the pulling apart? The morphing of the body into an unseen thing through action or fantasy? Is sexual violence, as Walter Benjamin has argued, law-making, law-preserving, divine, or mythic at its roots?[31] Can some sexual violence rise to a level of obscenity such that it fails to register as violent under the purview of most schematics of suffering? How do some forms of violation suture a paradigmatic order, which, like air, is so pervasive that announcing its presence serves as mere redundancy rather than explanation? The interplay between these questions, resting firmly on the last, tethers the concerns *Engendering Blackness* interrogates with respect to the violent acts and fantasies that occur at the intersections of Blackness, gender, and the sexual. The contextualization of the structural predicament presented here extends in the broadest sense, spanning the realms of the corporeal, as well as the social, political, temporal, legal, symbolic, and psychic. The book's six chapters clarify that fantasies of the slave are expressly unbound, making the (a)temporal possibilities of the sexually deracinating effects and affects of the slave estate continually palpable.

Chapter 1, "Slavery, Racial Sexuation, and the Death Drive," lays out the theoretical premise advanced throughout the book. Challenging the association of sexual violence under slavery as primarily a means for plantation reproduction and economic gain, I posit that racial sexuation helps us grapple with sexual violence beyond physical acts and the life of the plantation. Doing so takes seriously how the slave is saturated, both materially and psychically, by its inability to escape sexual capture. By reading nineteenth-century abolitionist accounts alongside slave narratives, antebellum law, and contemporary political writings, this chapter interrogates how structures of feeling and demands for evidence necessitate that the slave's sexual violability enters into thought by rousing the obscene as the essential requirement to extend empathy and seek redress. To this end, this argument deploys death and fantasy as analytics, in addition to sexual acts, to expose how sexual subsumption for the slave pervades the archive, memory, and narrative in a manner that disallows the slave to be untethered from its sexual status. As I discuss, this structural positioning is not undone by slave death, sympathetic literature, through self-obliterating acts of slave resistance, or by alternative historical frameworks extended by post-slavery Black subjects. This chapter also takes up the concept of the death drive to elucidate the paradigmatic necessity of refashioning the slave in new sexually violent terms under the auspices of affect and uncovery. The death drive clarifies how the sexual function of the slave is not resolved by obscene exposure. Instead, the sexual demands of the archive, memory, and narrative clarify the permanent relationship between rousing slave sexual injury to buttress desires for Human incorporation and expansion.

Chapters 2 and 3 are dedicated to examining Black feminist theory's essential role in the study of sexual violence and slavery, and in unearthing the unseen gratuity of slavery's sexual terror. Despite the critical historiography and groundbreaking interventions of Black feminists, the scholarship is still plagued by limits in terms of the theorizing of sexual violation. These chapters consider the pitfalls of decades-long Black feminist engagements with the sexual status of the female slave and the slave mother. Each chapter considers how the field is marked by a resistance to engaging sexual violence and violability as the constitutive element that gives rise to how the female slave is named and claimed as a subject of injury and endurance. On these grounds, Chapters 2 and 3 argue in distinct yet overlapping ways that the subjective qualities that Black feminism afford the female slave and slave mother to refuse their overdetermination by sexual violence are premised upon assumptive logics that uncritically deputize biocentrism to orient its political stakes. These chapters ask, how might Black feminist theory approach sexual violence and slavery differently if it relinquishes its possessive investments in Black cis-womanhood and the slave mother as an uncontested extension of birthing?

Chapter 2, "Suspended Absences and the Substrates of Naming the Female Slave," grapples with the vexed attributions ascribed to the suffering of the female slave. Using a runaway slave ad designed to capture a female slave named Sarah, this chapter begins by resting with the complexities of how the female slave is underwritten by pejorative sexual inscriptions that morph her body through contradictory terms. Rather than arguing that Sarah is misnamed in this ad, I contend that removing the violating terms like wench by replacing it with woman is an uncritical gesture that fails to address how the notion of the slave as wench makes the perceived redemptive qualities of woman possible. To rename the slave fails to consider that all naming is implicated within the structure of violation that renaming is seeking to escape. From this provocation, the argument developed in this chapter considers how deputizing the Black woman as the figure that resolves the crude attributions associated with the female slave relies on biocentric assumptions about gender and injury that do not ameliorate violence, but silently impose its necessity for reinvention. I argue that Black feminism is guided by an assumptive logic that perceives the Black woman as an essence that must be restored for the female slave, who is marked by a sex designation rather than gendered integrity. I term this gesture *a theoretical politics of dissemblance*, which I draw from the work of Darlene Clarke Hine, to examine how the investment in renaming the female slave within the confounds of a gender binary places emphasis on Humanizing the slave. In the process, renaming obscures how far sexual violence extends into the structure of naming, especially, and most critically, within alternative classificatory schemas—like womanhood—that are assumed to offer credence to the slave as not totalized by its violability. By turning to Sylvia Wynter's reading of William Shakespeare's *The Tempest*, as well as the novel *Corregidora* by

Gayl Jones, Chapter 2 concludes by grappling with the profound limits of deploying the concept of Black woman as an inherently revelatory structural location. Lastly, I argue for a Black feminism that shifts beyond binarism to consider how the sexual and gender antagonisms that pervade Black history and embodiment should be deployed to erode structures of coherence, rather than latch onto them as assumed revolutionary potentials.

Chapter 3, "Aborting the Slave Mother," meditates on various terms used to describe birthing slaves, such as slave mother, radical insurgent, breeder, and mammy. This investigation is staged by taking a critical look at how Margaret Garner, a runaway slave who was arrested for committing an act of infanticide, is figured in Black feminist theory. This chapter asks if Garner's act of killing a child she birthed was an act of insurgency, as it is often described, or if Garner's case helps to clarify why the slave mother is an oxymoronic association. I argue that the idea of the slave mother as a female birthright allows Black feminist projects to project and imagine a fantasy of Black existence prior to and free of sexual captivity. Additionally, this fantasy of motherhood as a sentient right creates the staging metaphor for how the loss and injury of sexual violability are charted. As I delineate, the slave mother is a conceptual ruse that inhibits theory from grappling with sexual violence as a totalizing inscription where language of loss is also made vacant for the slave by racial sexuation. The chapter turns to an interview given by a former slave on what it meant for her to be held captive as a breeder to tarry with how slave breeding and being a slave collapse into one another, illustrating a lack of distinction between the two. At the same time, there is a profound psychic and national value placed upon the conceptual labor of slave caregiving. To this point, Chapter 3 considers how Aunt Jemima, as a national mammy figure, exemplifies the constricted terrain that maps slave caregiving along an axis of biological mothering and structural expectation. I examine the proliferation of Aunt Jemima as a post-emancipation longing for a plantation return alongside legal battles to compensate a family who claimed their foremother's likeness and recipes were stolen by the corporation Quaker Oats. This chapter then asks critical questions about what it could mean to dislodge the mammy from her maternal expectations, as well as the significance of a Black family's inability to prove their maternal claim to a Black mother confounded by competing economic, discursive, and psychic demands. As the Aunt Jemima case is but one in a long trail of historical and contemporary battles to prove or disprove Black maternal connection in the American legal system, Chapter 3 also considers *Hudgins v. Wrights*. In this 1806 case, a female slave by the name of Hannah and her daughter petition the courts for their freedom on the grounds that they are wrongfully enslaved. They argue that they were mistakenly held captive because they are descendants of a native woman, Butterwood Nan. This case opens critical perspectives about racial ontology and motherhood. Additionally, *Hudgins* provides an angle to consider how slave paternity should not be figured as insignificant despite legal, structural, and even Black feminist, privileging of *partus sequitur ventrem* as the essential marker of slaveness. The chapter ends by turning to colonial Maryland to consider the vexed issue of slave paternity. I argue that laws of heredity pertaining to male slaves serve to divert attention from the female slave as a supreme type, to instead consider the formation of New World gendering as the grounds for white feminine self-making.

Chapter 4, "On Historicizing Sex and Sexual Sense Making," interrogates how queer theory and white feminist philosophy engage sexual difference, sexuality, and slavery. Recently, there has been a turn in queer theory to contend with questions emerging from Black studies in a manner that marks a new moment in the field. With the proliferation of queer theory texts turning to racial Blackness to investigate the structure of queerness, this chapter asks, on what grounds is this alignment staged? By critically examining recent literature, I consider the claim that queerness provides a vantage point to resolve some of the opacity that plagues the structural predicament of Blackness. Rather than moving forward on the assumption that queerness and Blackness orient a similar structural alignment, I argue that Blackness is its own stimulus to sexual anxiety that demands singular exploration. This is not to suggest that Blackness and queerness are antithetical. Instead, this chapter shows how, in emergent nineteenth-century discourses on sexuality, queerness and Blackness occupy fundamentally distinct ontological alignments. Queerness is theorized as a deviation from normative human sexual development, yet still contained within the category of the Human. Contrarily, Blackness is repeatedly positioned as antithetical to all forms of Human sexuality and marked as a sexual singular vector that has the potential to erode the Human altogether. Turning to case studies on masochism, where subjects present queer sexual fantasies involving slaves, this chapter discusses how, even in the same psychic spaces, queerness and Blackness are suspended as structurally divergent. In these fantasies, Blackness is absent of a sexual subjectivity, operating instead as a sexual phantasm to heighten the imaginative potentials of queerness. Resting on this provocation, this chapter considers how queer theory and feminist philosophy repeatedly deploy the slave as a phantasm to strengthen and broaden their theoretical claims about universal suffering within a sexual paradigm. I also examine feminist legal theory works on rape as well as the sexual contract to argue that attempts to think slavery through analogy nullify slave suffering by deputizing slavery to extend arguments that subversively challenge whether the slave's sexual status constitutes a paradigmatic singularity.

Chapter 5, "Manning Black Gender," addresses a set of provocative claims and contentions regarding gender and injury that arise from the field of Black male studies. This chapter deploys a personal account from Black male writer Courttia Newland about his experiences with sexual and gender violence to mediate how theory might respond to his queries about the role history plays in authorizing his sexual vulnerability to white women. I antagonize what Black male studies offers Newland's observations. I interrogate how Black male studies takes up gender and sexual injury for Black men and boys by abandoning prior scholarship produced by Black queer theorists and Black psychoanalytic theories on gender and sexuality. In this respect, this new iteration of Black male studies moves forward on the insistence that Black men like Newland have been crowded out of conversations on gender and sexual violence by the supremacy granted to Black women by Black feminism.

As I show, this argument is propped up by a series of conjectures about theoretical moves made by Black feminists that cannot be proven true. Additionally, and most central to the point here, I posit that how Black manhood is theorized and extended by this field is conceptually hobbled by its insistence on wagering this category as an innate material reality versus, more appropriately, as a psychosexual condition. By bringing Black male studies in conversation with Black queer theory and Black feminism, Chapter 5 theorizes castration, rape, and physical brutalizations of Black men and male slaves as evidence towards the impossibility of advancing a theory of suffering under the auspices of negated manhood or emasculation. By examining James Baldwin's short story "Going to Meet the

Man," the antebellum case *Humphreys v. Utz*, which involved the castration of a male slave, and Frederick Douglass's brutal interactions with the slave breaker Edward Covey, I argue that strict adherences to binary distinctions of Black gender and its suffering are haunted by the untenable division between slave genders that were imposed through endless acts of sexual torture and mutilation. Furthermore, an attunement to the hyper-susceptibility of Black males to sexual violence must contend with the stark inconceivability of gendering as a mode of differentiation to account for how the experience of antiblack sexual violations are structurally imposed rather than binarily construed.

Chapter 6, "Toils of Flesh," engages the most pervasive dramatizations of slave sexual brutality, major motion pictures. This chapter offers a close reading of the 2013 independent British film *Belle*, directed by Amma Asante, and the 2013 biographical drama *12 Years a Slave*, directed by Steve McQueen. I examine how the aestheticization of slavery in both films is dependent upon staging freedom for the protagonist in oppositional tension to a slave who is the sexual captive of the film narrative and visual scope. Each film clarifies that sexual openness as a predicament is an unbound stasis that is repeatedly gestured towards, then disavowed, as a staging grounds for announcing the buoyancy of Black freedom from the plantation. *Belle* operates on the unspoken consensus that the protagonist Dido Elizabeth Belle (Gugu Mbatha-Raw) was granted freedom from slavery by the moral benevolence of British aristocrats, most namely her father, Sir John Lindsay (Matthew Goode), who appears only briefly in the film. Her mother, Maria Belle, a slave in the West Indies, is a haunting reference throughout the film, but she is never shown. The narrative labors to herald Dido as a champion for racial and gender freedom in a repressive society but does so by making her body a spectacle of sexual violence. *12 Years a Slave* dramatizes the autobiography of Solomon Northup, a once free Black man, by offering a visual backdrop to his capture and enslavement. Solomon (Chiwetel Ejiofor) labors and longs for his freedom while he is held captive on the Epps Louisiana plantation. I argue that to maintain that Solomon is a "wrongful" slave, his circumstance is juxtaposed against the sexual predicament of the female slave Patsey (Lupita Nyong'o). Despite the narrative and visual efforts to prove Solomon is an illegitimate slave, I contend the film's most pivotal scene, when Solomon is commanded to whip Patsey, illustrates their structural alignment as each sexually constricted by the force of slavery. Additionally, this chapter argues that the lure of the slave film, as a genre, is less about adjudicating history and more so bound to the reproduction of the enjoyment of gazing upon antiblack brutalization, where the bloodied and raped slave is tethered to the physicality of the Black actors on screen.

The conclusion, "After/Wards: Notes on Representing Slavery and the Ontology of Sexual Violence," closes *Engendering Blackness* by interrogating the prison-industrial complex (PIC) abolitionist movement. I query how the vestiges of slavery are imagined and articulated into political platforms and dreamwork. The conclusion maintains that the sexual status of the slave haunts the assumptive logic of the PIC abolitionist movement. I argue that a movement based on the failed promises of emancipation must take seriously the slave's imperative posture and that its emancipatory demands not be usurped into a Humanist agenda, lest it replicate the freedom slavery has always extended to the slave. Sexual violence under slavery makes expressively clear that subtending the psychic dimensions of the plantation to materialist claims produces a conceptual hobble. Advancing a universalist movement based on access to expanded rights and freedoms for all upholds Blackness as ubiquitous content in broader social and political struggles. I argue that this political positioning must account for how the slave's freedom dreams become a universal claim. *Engendering Blackness* concludes on an emphatic note by maintaining that the longue durée of abolition cannot delink from the paradigm of racial sexuation that slavery bestowed upon us that undergirds our capacity to speak, think, or imagine Blackness into any realm. If politics does not confront the sexual violability of the slave with direct force, we stand to carry its violent fetters into other worlds.

One

Slavery, Racial Sexuation, and the Death Drive

> "There is no slavery without sexual depravity."[1]
> – Gilberto Freyre, *The Masters and the Slaves: A Study in the Development of Brazilian Civilization*

W. E. B. Du Bois begins his magnum opus *Black Reconstruction in America* with a set of compounding statistics. He announces that Reconstruction begins with the "dramatic" onslaught of four million newly freed slaves. Du Bois attempts to estimate the sheer volume. "By their own reproduction, the Negroes reached 3,638,808 in 1850, and before the Civil War, stood at 4,441,830."[2] Most striking is the announcement that "at least 90% were born in the United States, 13% were visibly of white as well as Negro descent and actually more than one-fourth were probably of white, Indian, and Negro blood."[3] What Du Bois's accounting illustrates is that, despite marking Black reproduction as "their own," the perceivability of racial mixture indexes a structural relation of racialized sex that is particular to the Negro and sets precedence in sexual relation to others.

How to explain or, at least, recognize this structural relation? The widely discussed law of hypodescent, popularly known as the one-drop rule, partially explains the inability to (dis)appear slave sex when coupled with non-Blackness. However, what determines the permanence of the one-drop rule necessitates a confrontation with why slave sexual capture cannot be undone. The sexual act possesses the slave. The utterance of the sexual act (re)captures the slave. The attempt to depart from the violation illustrates that this condition is essential to anchor the psychic freedom of not being a slave. In the end, the violation and the slave remain inseverable.

What Du Bois unwittingly stages in the opening pages of *Black Reconstruction* is a commentary on the banality of slave sexual vulnerability and openness under modern racial slavery. He, of course, is not naïve to the sexual force of slavery. Indeed, he observes that "in America without a slave trade, it paid to conserve the slave and let him multiply."[4] The implications of conservation and multiplication on Reconstruction, and postbellum life more generally, cannot move forward by treating rape, breeding, and mass-reproduction as mere ubiquitous facts of a complete historization of sexual violence and slavery. The vast and violent practices of transatlantic slavery, such as an instance Du Bois notes "in the West Indies to kill slaves by overwork and import cheap Africans," also contribute to and buttress the perceived fecundity of the slave.[5] Du Bois instructs the reader to consider death as a claim on the nuanced maneuvers of the plantation. Here, death is not a limit but a placeholder for reproduction and replication.

In this respect, reproduction references the biological creation of new slaves *and* the means through which the uses of the slave expand unendingly through the unbound creation of physical and psychic registers for the slave to occupy. A slave can always be replaced by any other slave. Replication indexes the inessential nature of the individual slave in this calculus, where the category and status are structured as void of any essential quality of being or individual differentiation that can upend the desires of the slave estate. Like reproduction, replication is unending. Death then marked the continuation of the sexual logic insofar as another slave or African was summoned to reproduce and replicate the ontological void of breeding new flesh for capture.

Du Bois exposes—through first addressing Black sexual reproduction to then attempt to displace it by focusing on the multiplication of "wealth and land" and the constitution of the Black worker— an unintended conceptual quandary. The calculus Du Bois presents historicizes sex and slavery as a teleology of forced labor relieved by emancipation. At the level of conscious consensus, slavery as an institution was invested in its preservation and proliferation. The examples from the United States and the Caribbean offered by Du Bois highlight the necessity for the replicability of the slave. However, while it is through death the sexual predicament of the slave can be thought, death also signals a rupture. Du Bois invokes death and turns back toward slavery as a logical pronouncement of sexual goals and aims. Death clarifies how the rampant maiming, torture, and murder of slaves and free Black people in the antebellum world harken upon a structure that is less finite and conceivable. It helps illustrate the intractable and unruly ways that the sexual force of slavery extends beyond the sexual acts that served the plantation model.

This prognosis does not collapse the experience of sexual violation and the deathly disregard as equivalent. Rather, the structural disposability of the slave necessitates a consideration of how sex intersects with violence that cannot be adequately explained by a focus on reproduction. While reproductive capacity is a widely recognized description of slave experience and usefulness, deathly disregard clarifies that the totality of the sexual paradigm is less tethered to the physical proliferation of the plantation. Which is to say, in absence of the plantation—in both the antebellum and postbellum contexts—the slave occupies a structural position within the racial order that collapses its sexual capacities into the unconscious demands and preconscious investments of Human sexuality.

This chapter expands the framework of sexual violence beyond penetrative acts and other forms of sexual domination to posit all forms of violence as sexual. It does this by tarrying with attempts to define the slave as embodying a true violable form and logical sexual necessity. I make the provocative claim that there is no truth of sexual violence as every violence related to political ontological distinction returns to the sexual question. This argument interrogates how theorizing sexual violence as a technology of rape and breeding made operable towards the expansion of life forms (the slave, the plantation, the master's/mistress's sexual prerogative) orients a conscious and well-accepted consensus regarding the centrality of reproduction in orienting the plantation. Reproduction in this sense highlights the vibrancy of the plantation as a longstanding experiment in making racial distinction real through the deployment of sexual violence. Contrarily, this chapter considers how racial sexuation, rather than the reproduction thesis, accounts for the unconscious structures binding all forms of violence waged against slaves as sexual violence. Sexuation is the process by which slaves were made vulnerable to sexual acts, and other acts that may not be perceivably sexual, to bar the slave from entrance into the Human sexual order. This denial from being part of the Human sexual order is part of racialization, in this case, equating Blackness with slaveness. As an analytic, racial sexuation unearths how racial sexual classification is sutured solely and primarily by repressing the essential nature unbound violence plays in differentiating Black non-being from Human ontology.

When confronting the archive and its interpretations, attunement to violence and violation reveals how the slave operates as a postulate for the supremacy granted to Human ontology. Undertheorized and uncontested is how the hyper-visible and repeated sexual violation of the slave is structurally positioned by a forced relation with Human violence, which is displaced onto the slave as its possession. Basically, racial sexuation is the structure upon which Blackness, and thus slaveness, assumes the form of a violable object deprived of a violating referent. This is the precondition upon which Black violation is always assumed and anticipated. Conversely, the Human is driven by a violent relation to the slave that deploys it as the uncontested redress for the very violence of its making.

Citing the presuppositions that undergird the 1662 Virginia Act, Jennifer L. Morgan indexes the relationship between the psychic structure of slavery and the architecture of the plantation. This act held that all offspring born of slave mothers were also slaves—*partus sequitur ventrem*, the offspring follows the belly. Morgan writes,

> Regardless of the rate of reproduction among the enslaved—which remained low in all early American slave societies—the ideological solidity of those slave societies needed reproducing women. Building a system of racial slavery on the notion of heritability did not require the presence of natural population growth among the enslaved, but it did require a clear understanding that enslaved women gave birth to enslaved children.[6]

What sutured the reproduction of slaves was a fantasy about their sexual fecundity, which is referenced here as "ideological solidity." Unlike ideological solidity—which implies the sedimentation of a set of ideas, ideals, and practices—fantasy is the register that situates slave affectability and articulations of its affection.

The fantasy of sexual violability persists, as Morgan illustrates, in absence of the material experience or performance of slave sexual acts or violations. Sex, and its violating quality, for the slave, is both physical and metaphysical. Just as the quality of being a slave can be reduced to the space of the belly, contrarily, as in the case of the Maryland law of 1664, where "All children born of any black or other slave were to be 'Slaves as their Fathers'," the penis was also constituted as a voided terrain of sexuality that could reproduce the embodied status of being a slave.[7] If "'sex' is historically subordinate to sexuality," as Foucault has argued, the historical matrix of sex and slavery underwrites another component of history.[8] Sex reduced to the belly or the penis is *not* sexuality but rather a disembodied state of (non)existence. In this sense, slave sex is historically subordinate to the violating quality of a fantasy, which precedes and exceeds the law and its abolition. Though the Virginia and Maryland laws placed concern on different reproductive capacities, both were subtended by a metaphysical drive that presupposed that to be a slave is to always be a slave in reproductive perpetuity. While the implications of each law allowed for the prolonged life of the institution, carrying indisputable material implications, the unconscious dimensions buttressing the institutionalization of slave sexual violability were not bound by the rise nor the fall of the institution.

The psychic terror of *partus sequitur ventrem*, or the Maryland inverse, brings to the forefront the theoretical imperative of parsing out a distinction between the psychic and the material. The fantasy and the act are separate, albeit often intersecting, structures of affection. In the absence of the act, as Morgan shows, the fantasy does not erode. Rather, the fantasy is preserved by the unconscious, which proceeds identification and particularizes which identifications of violation enter into being. The sexually violating nature of slavery includes the uncharted acts and conditions that are present and absent in the historical archive *and* the pleasurable fantasies of uninhibited access, which are timeless. The (mis)representations of sexual violence in the archive, secondary texts, as well as the social and cultural underscoring of the structural significance of this history, "constitutes, at the same time, both its irrefutability and its insufficiency as witness."[9] If representations of slave sexual violations are themselves acts of witnessing or remembering and contained within the boundaries of memory, how is one certain "that they are actually speaking of the same entity?"[10] When is the time and attribution of the violation's affects and effects? When is the time? Is it prior to, during, or post the act? Is it the fantasy of the act's possibilities, the material effects of the act's occurrences, or in the affects produced by the terror of remembering?

Sexuating Death in Archival Memory

By returning to the archive of slavery one can home in on the structural inability to wager the sexual, and other violent torturous acts against slaves, as distinctive points of inquiry outside of the vocabulary afforded by Humanness. Take, for example, the narrative renderings of slavery provided by Reverend William T. Allan. His statements appear in *American Slavery As It Is: Testimony of a Thousand Witnesses*, a collection of slavery narratives from whites, curated by Theodore Dwight Weld and the Grimké sisters Sarah Moore and Angelina (who was married to Weld), to support the call for abolition. Allan's statements were later re-printed, in part, in another abolitionist text, William Goodell's *The American Slave Code in Theory and Practice*. Among the many brutal tales collected in each volume, Allan narrates his and other's experiences as witnesses to violent acts perpetrated against slaves. Although a son of a slave owner, Allan describes himself as rarely having the occasion of visiting plantations, and that his "personal knowledge of slavery, was consequently a knowledge of its *fairest* side."[11] Yet given this self-proclaimed limited exposure to, and distance from, the physical plantation, each of his stories were saturated with brutality and violence. The latter suggests his knowledge of slavery is deeper than his conscious identity, as one opposed to and removed from the plantation, desires to disclose.

His narrations spare no details as he reports witnessing whippings and howling screams of slaves. Nothing is quite "fair" about the heinous gratuitous violence described. He notes, most egregiously, that a notorious overseer by the name of "Tune," upon becoming "displeased with one of the women who was pregnant, made her lay down over a log, with her face toward the ground, and beat her so unmercifully, that she was soon after delivered of a *dead child*."[12] In recasting these stories—ones including a Black child dead before taking their first breath—as the commonplace and natural occurrences of the plantation spectacle, Allan affectively distances himself from slavery. This implied distance permeates Allan's capacity to approach this unending trail of violence, which is knowledge he holds precisely because of his proximity to enslavers, as collateral waste. Each story is cast as an additional mark in the ledger, "retired to a place more distant, in order to get away from [the slave's] agonizing cries."[13]

Unlike other abolitionist testimonies that attempt to assuage the brutality with moralistic language, Allan provides little to no affective registering of the incidents he details. What appears in Allan's accounts, and across the many tales collected by Weld and the Grimké sisters, are sets of practices or principles that lack traceability to a single origin or problem, yet all are riddled with sexualized violations. While nineteenth-century abolitionist literature may differ from the official record by its extension of sympathy to slaves, in form it too contains fragmented accounts of endless violent acts. This point says less about abolitionist efforts than it does about the nature of slavery, as sympathy cannot override or annul brutality.

In the case of Allan, his testimonies are broken and incoherent stories. The reader is left to discern the importance or significance of what is said. The overarching call is to abolish slavery. The question then becomes, what should be abolished and by what means? The formal legal institution, the concentrated array of violent acts, or the cultural fantasies that are buttressed by and exceed the instrumentalization of the physical plantation itself? At one point, Allan states that one of his uncles had "killed a woman—broke her skull with an ax helve: she had insulted her mistress! No notice was taken of the affair. [stating], further, that slaves were *frequently murdered*."[14] Each account lacks even the slightest meditative pause. As Allan moves with ease from example to example, each violent act appears without the imposition of meaning. These narratives provide raw accounts that are open for interpretation. It displays crude examples without narrativizing gestures from the speaker. As such, his accounts differ from ones like Angelina Grimké, who imparts humanizing sympathy onto the story she tells. She writes:

> A slaveholder, after flogging a little girl about thirteen years old, set her on a table with her feet fastened in a pair of stocks. He then locked the door and took out the key. When the door was opened she was found dead, having fallen from the table. When I asked a prominent lawyer, who belonged to one of the first families in the State, whether the murderer of this helpless child could not be indicted, he coolly replied, that the slave was Mr.----'s property, and if he chose to suffer the *loss*, no one else had any thing to do with it. The loss of *human life*, the distress of the parents and other relatives of the little girl, seemed utterly out of his thoughts: it was the loss of *property* only that presented itself to his mind.[15]

Grimké imposes Humanity onto the lost life. In doing so, she attempts to distinguish life from property, the Human from the slave. Perhaps a valiant gesture, this narrative account assumes that the integrity of the Human does, or at least should, extend to the slave girl at the center of the story. However, what is Humanity, if the violent actor is granted the right to kill without question? What undergirds Grimké's assertion that the act of violation does not bar nor degrade the claim of Humanity for the slave girl, is the belief that the slave girl is Human like her murderer, the slaveholder.

However, the question here is does the brutal violent act bar or degrade the Human claim for the slaveholder ontologically? This does not seem to be the contested concern. Yet, how can we assume an essential similarity, at the level of Humanness, with such incongruent conditions and relations of power between the slave girl and the slaveholder? How do we attend to the question of the Human, without placing faith in the fact that the girl's Humanity is suspended temporarily by the institution of slavery but is nonetheless there like a divine inscription of natural law? The assertion of Human life, loss, and value onto property fails to ask critical questions about those terms. Does the violent act itself serve as a dividing line between what classifies one as Human and as slave/Black? Is Humanity the essences of all sentient beings, that is denied by the violent act in its marking of differentiation? Or does the integrity of violence itself serve as the equation between what can be accounted for within the diversity of the Human and what is distinguished as the objectifying quality of Blackness?

If we refuse to assuage the brutality with the extension of Humanity as a form of naturalness or essence, what appears? The flogging of the thirteen-year-old-girl represents the cruelty of fantasy as it relates to the slave, that one can imagine and carry out such torturous proclivities that are boundless in form and execution. Furthermore, the death drives of slavery, which are totalizing ontological erasures articulated through the practices and fantasies of racial sexuation, invade upon the presuppositions of relationality, exposing a series of ruptures. Imposing "the distress of the parents and other relatives of the little girl" as a sympathetic gesture to draw her into the Human community cannot belie this death drive. Being a slave is the antithesis to patriarchal kinship, bearing the reproduced into a structure that requires their maturation and severance from kin prior to the event of birth. The mattering of the slave's death placed by Grimké is one of innocence, as the criteria for concern, mis-attuning to the reality that at the age of thirteen, this slave likely already entered the phase of life where she served as a breeder. Regardless of her status as a breeder, her position, determined by racial sexuation, was of always being available to be one at the whim of the master.

The imposition of childhood here contradicts the reality of the sexual positionality or violability for the slave. Childhood, care, and filial relation operate in this context as veils of sympathy that presupposes that these categories are extended ab initio. However, the right of the slaveholder to assess the value of the loss after the death of this slave girl illustrates the violent material and fantasy of captivity. Contrarily, Grimké extends a counter fantasy that the cultural materiality of slavery's violence can be unwritten through projections of desire for an otherwise existence. However, the gesture of this fantasy, regardless of its good faith premise, extends the death drives of slavery when the terms of distinction—child from adult, kin from kinless, or man from slave girl—are metaphysically differentiated from slavery. In the assessment of Grimké or the slave owner, the slave is taken up as a pure possession of the act of interpreting its value with respect to violation and naming. The slave girl thus continues to be affected through the articulation of what constitutes her violation, which is always already a reductive prescription. Additionally, the account given by Grimké affects the slave by demonstrating that the Human is both a limit and a telos. Which is to say, the unpunished violence of the Human is what murders the slave girl. However, the slave girl is offered up in memory by attempting to make her a benefactor of the very ontological category that authorized her death and captivity, i.e., Human. The repetitious grasp of the violence of the Human and the benevolence of its extension of perpetual reinvention reduces inquiry into violence and slavery to that of a moral concern.

Many who condemn slavery will remark on the ineffectiveness of moralizing when it comes to slavery. Yet for many, this critique will serve to direct our attention to what are often framed as materialist analyses, that which can be explained through a focus on the political economy. Yet the turn away from the moral to the materialist can also evade dealing with the death drives of slavery. In both moralizing and materialist analyses, the category of slave—which is always sexually constituted—is evacuated and essentially left unattended. Thus, we are left with a limited lens for identifying and locating the violence. If we face the slave as a category on its own terms without morally equivocating towards Humanness or reducing it to an outgrowth of the economy, what might be revealed about violence and, most crucially, about the sexual nature of violence, that structures the (non)ontologies of slave and the Human?

Suspending a desire to embrace Humanness and the Human as a recourse to suffering is essential to theorizing violence and the fantasies of its making.

Returning to the accounts provided by Allan, he briefly details four separate incidents of murder. The incidents are reprinted in *American Slave Code* by Goodell, in a subsection titled "Facts Illustrating the Kind and Degree of Protection Extended to Slaves." Two of these stories involve negro women, while the other two are about negro men. Each incident occurred in antebellum Alabama. The stories are presented in the following manner:

> (1) A man near Courtland, Ala., of the name Thompson, recently shot a negro woman through the head, and put the pistol so close that her hair was singed. He did it in consequence of some difficulty in his dealings with her as a concubine. He buried her in a log-heap; she was discovered by the buzzards gathering around it. (2) Two men, of the name Wilson, found a fine-looking negro man at Dandridge's Quarter, without a pass, and flogged him so that he died in a short time. They were not punished. (3) Col. Blocker's overseer attempted to flog a negro. He refused to be flogged, where-upon the overseer seized an axe, and cleft his skull. The Colonel justified it. (4) One Jones whipped a woman to death for grabbing a potatoe [sic] hill.[16]

The terse nature of Allan's accounts does not diminish the significance of these examples. Instead, such sparse details enhance the explanatory potential of these accounts, as they are not buffered by extenuating details that may draw attention away from the slave at the center of the violent act. The focus here cannot extend far beyond the deceased and the fantasies and desires that buttressed their murders. These deaths are presented in crude and abrupt terms. The violators, conditions of their captivity, if any (or any other assumed relational points of access), cannot take privilege in providing explanation for the violence, as such details are sparse. In this respect, the deathly act and the sexual fantasies or desires that resonate in the reasoning for such acts become the sole sites of exposure. The casual maneuvering of these scenes of sexual and/or deathly subjection demonstrates the embeddedness of violation with the constitution of slaveness.

Although Allan's testimonies are devoid of moral sentiment, his accounts illustrate that the sadism of his recollections are the property of the plantation. His testimonies also reveal his violent fantasy and memory. The event of violence encapsulates the psycho-reality *and* reality proper. How can we determine the scales of reality and fantasy in Allan's accounts? In a sense, we can surmise through evidence that there is a plausible realness to what he presents. For example, Goodell subheads a section of *American Slave Code* with "the submission required of the slave is unbounded," charting how the unthinkable pervades slavery such that what is represented in law, defined practices, and the official record are not the sum total of antebellum violence.[17] There maintains a great sense of un-representability that extends beyond the material and is encapsulated in the psychic dimensions of violence, making what is perceived and understood murky and unstable.

A sexual insurrection or resistance foregrounds and subtends each murderous act as the stories are presented by Allan. The first story is recalled with far more detail. We are told that the negro woman was killed because of her "difficulty" in being kept as a white man's concubine. Rightfully, one might assume that her refusal to be held as a sexual captive led to this woman's brutal murder. The second story, however, does not present itself as clearly. Though, the noting of the deceased being "a fine-looking negro man" is an implication of the emergence of sexualization in catalyzing his murder *and* in the recollection, memory, and recasting of the story. How are the attributes of fine-looking as a fantasy of transgressive action located in this death? Whether he was being propositioned for sex or his physical appearance led to his being singled out to prove his freedom, "fine-looking," which was a common antebellum colloquialism used to describe light-skinned Black males, resonates beyond banal reference.[18] Thomas A. Foster argues that "the sexual abuse of 'nearly white' men could enable white women to enact radical fantasies of domination over a man."[19] By extension, sexual abuse and fantasies of domination were also enacted onto "fine-looking" negro men by white men, as these desires are not bound by heterosexual proclivities.

However, the final accounts, numbered three and four, lack sexual pretext. These two examples involve torturous violence—attempted flogging, a strike of an axe, and whipping—leading to the death of the negro and the woman. Allan narrates each as a transgression of an imposed order. The negro refuses to submit to a flogging by his overseer and is killed for his resistance. The woman, presumably a negro female, grabs a possible source of food and is killed. Can these examples, like the other instances detailed by Allan, be read within the matrix of sexual violence begat by slavery? Do flogging, bludgeoning, and whipping classify as sexuating acts? How is racial sexuation distinct from but interconnected with the sexual?

There is a sado-masochistic relation between the torturer and the slave tortured to their death. In most systems, torture functions on a relay between the tortured and the torturer, what Elaine Scarry identifies as the motive and the betrayal.[20] This interplay prompts and justifies the physical pain inflicted onto the body by a weapon designed to extract a wanted response from the victim. The justification and means of torture are initiated by the voice, a question and answer, that exposes the body to pain.[21] Contrarily, under slavery, torture rendered the slave's consent or contestation as irrelevant. The slave is the embodiment of authorization, such that the "interactions occurring between body and voice in torture" are removed not from the violent event but from the fantasy of the act.[22] The primacy of interrogation typifying the justification of physical pain is voided under slavery. As Allan recollects, the speaking slave is absent. This is not to suggest that in his examples the slaves never expressed complacency, opposition, guilt, or pained agony. There are no means for this to be known. This point intends to highlight how responsive actions from the slave are removed from these recollections, placing focus solely on the violence and the slave as transgression and pure violation.

Flogging and whipping, which apply pressure and pain to the body using rods or lashes, excised vocalizations from the slave.[23] However, these vocalizations are not in service of admissions of guilt of action (though they can verbalize such), but guilt of existence. That the slave exists under the confines of ontological captivity indexes that the slave is exterior to, by way of racial sexuation, the Human community. Racial sexuation positions the body as the reproductivity of kin and kinship in contradistinction to the Human slave. There is no existence external to this matrix, one predicated upon actionable being versus objectified matter.

Referencing BDSM, which is relevant to thinking about torture, pleasure, and sex, Ariane Cruz aptly asserts that "it is the contract that binds, not the collars, cuffs, or chains."[24] In the case of slavery, sexual acts, individually carried out or repetitiously orchestrated, are irreducible in binding the slave sexually to the master. The constitution of the slave as *the* zero-degree fantasy of sexual availability and violability authorizes the potentiality and actuality of all material and psychic violations. To say this otherwise, the slave is not made a sexual object through and because of acts of sex, but the slave is ontologically a sexual object and their sexual violability is repeatedly revealed and animated through every interaction. The slave is affectable because sexual openness is its ontological unmaking. The slave emerges in the world as a necessity for the recognition and the claiming of being, through the voiding of any prior constitution of relationality external to the essential master over slave relation. Though the master too is produced of a fantasy that is genuflected through desires for distinction. Which is to say, there is a historical embodiment of the master as white men and a psychic fantasy of their power. The psychic dimensions can be performed and carried out by anyone; historically this was mostly the mistress but also everyday non-slave peoples and even other slaves.[25]

Death animates the sheer vulnerability and the unending nature of the multiple uses of the slave, which is set into motion by the sexual question. Physical pain and lacerations, as well as death and decay, open other orifices into the slave, offering additional conduits of pleasures or drives in search of satisfaction or gratification. Relating death to sex is not meant to resonate these terms in the sense of necrophilia. Thinking back to the Du Boisian examples, tethered to the death drives are reproduction and replication, which push the slave beyond the perceivable limit of the Human capacity for suffering. Rampant sexualization and torture ingratiate the structure of slavery, increasing its impulses to arouse not just the pleasure of genitals but also the unbound capacity to expand upon the subjects with access to the sadistic fetishes of antiblack differentiation. The infinite quantifications of dismemberment, disfiguration, penetration, fondling, and death are not satisfying, at neither the level of the individual act nor their innumerable possibilities or presentations.

Racial sexuation thus exceeds the purview of the sexual, whereas death is a component feature. The sexual involves the pleasure of the genitals or the gratification of sexual impulses. Racial sexuation attunes to how force and violence position the slave prior to any enactment, such that when and if the act occurs there is a structure of identification that proceeds the event that brings into autonomic coherence the slave as the extremity of conceptual analogy. Furthermore, in absence of the sexual act or arrangements, death animates the slave as an object of ontological absence, because slave death recasts its inescapable sexual quandary.

Returning to the question of sexual violence and its interrelation with death in the accounts provided by Allan, the distance between these stories is lessened at the point where the rendering of the slave as sexuated object becomes the precondition for their violation, as well as the context under which the violation is veiled. The obscurity lies in the fact that the assumptive premise of sexual violence renders "the subordination of all the component sexual instincts under the primacy of the genitals."[26] With respect to the slave/Black, genital phasic focus is too narrow a frame to grasp how death meets their sexual affectability. To be shot in the head then buried in a log-heap and flogged to death indexes something excessive to the gratification of genital pleasures. For "fine-looking" references the scopophilic nature of sex and the sexual. Scopophilia does not purely resonate in the act of violence but also in the context of memory, recollection, and archival gazing. There is pleasure derived in locating oneself, to see one's subjectification, becoming, and renewal as distinct from the torture imposed upon the slave. Additionally, "consequence of some difficulty," "refused to be flogged," or "grabbing a potatoe hill" highlight that in Allan's calculation, the deadly act is disciplinary rather than gratuitously imposed. However, "in discipline, punishment is only one element of a double system: gratification-punishment."[27] In each circumstance a real or perceived resistance is acted upon. What constitutes the transgression is less marred in structurally hardened predeterminations but is reproduced as real through the relationship between desire and action. Sexual violability derives meaning in these accounts from the sexual classification of the slave *and* the means of violation and torture used to subject them to death. In this respect, sexual violence is a means of sexual classification and declassification, the act of violation, and the repetition of the scenes and fantasies of flaying, branding, flogging, lacerating, cutting, and mutilating flesh and organs.

As a conceptual logic, sexual violence with regard to slavery comes into being through identifications of acts in relation to subjects that cohere with certain rubrics of intent and action. However, the purpose of the argument here is to expand the framework of sexual violence and slavery such that the slave/Black is understood as a sexual captive insofar as its reproductive function served as the conduit upon which the Human continually reconstitutes itself through memory, meaning, and becoming. Reproduction extends beyond the function of organs into the terms of multiplication and conservation, where violation under slavery and in desires that meet the archive are sutured by an auto-erotic pleasure of engaging the obscene, demonstrating that the slave never dies but is a moving surface upon which objectification and violation persist. In short, reproduction here is not about the biological.

Despite the violent acts Allan recollects as being relational to slavery, the physical site of the plantation is noticeably absent. A deeper analysis of slave as a category is vital to understand how and why "slave" is being read onto the deceased in the stories. In no account is slave called upon to name or locate the negro at the center of the story. Furthermore, the plantation is not presumed as an absolute, as being "without a pass" presupposes possible freedom from slavery or possible transgressed captive status, but neither is definitive. However, Allan recounts these stories, which are reproduced in print for the purposes of abolishing slavery; the violence resonates with the speaker and the researching abolitionists as culminating under the auspices of violations and violence beget by the plantation.

It is worth noting that in nineteenth-century Alabaman law, slaves and "free persons of color" were governed by the same legal statutes and codes, which is where the incidents archived by Allan occurred. The law at this time was similarly disinterested in marking a difference between the conditions of life for the slave and for the conditionally free Black. However, rather than privileging the law as the mechanism that determines truth and thus brackets understanding, I want to interrogate the ontological assumptions at the heart of the law, Allan's recollection, and the reproduction of those memories in books designed to support the undoing of the plantation system. Additionally, law begets contradictions between its intents, its actions and, most centrally here, its fantasies, and the embodied realities of legal classification. For example, section three of the nineteenth-century law governing Slaves and Free People of Color in Alabama stated the following:

> Any person who shall maliciously dismember or deprive a slave of life, shall suffer such punishment as would be inflicted in the case the like offence had

been committed on a free white person, and on the like proof, except in the case of insurrection of such slave.[28]

What constitutes an act of malice when performed against a slave? For the slave, what qualifies as lacking the quality of insurrection? The use of malice and insurrection in the law governing slaves and free persons of color in Alabama is exemplary of a certain logic pertaining to slave/Black injury and redress. In each of the cases described by Allan, the violent perpetrators were not punished despite the law's insistence that such actors be punished in the manner of anyone committing a similar offense against a white person. The interweaving of moralist language into the law allows the presuppositions of fairness to overdetermine the metaphysical impositions of violence, which in the words of Justice Roger B. Taney in *Scott v. Sanford*, the negro "has no rights which the White man was bound to respect."[29]

Under these conditions, Black desire is preconditioned as a violation or insurrection against the ontological order of structural positionality, unless in the case where the Human subject contends that slave desire is permissible. Which is to say, the claim of desire or injured status is not the ontological propriety of the slave but of an onto-epistemological order that superimposes questions of consent and collective good (read morality) onto the slave as a foreclosure. Furthermore, the law imparts ritualistic fantasy where, written into slave law, is the obsolescence of its use and value for the slave, as it references the slave as a passable indexicality towards the Human as the fundamental juridical, and thus redressable, body. What is malice or malicious intent when such would need to be determined as the mens rea of the very ontological positionality that is responsible for slave capture and for determining the use and integrities of such a category? How can a slave be wrongfully violated, when violation is the ontological foreclosure placed upon the African, which allows for the modern emergence of slavery as a racial system of sexual ordering and differentiation?

In the law, as in empathetic abolitionist accounts, morality serves to disinherit the slave from articulating its affectability outside of the psychic and metaphysical prescriptions of Human ontology. Which is to say morality disinherits violation and violability as potential and self-obliteration for the slave. The same goes for materialist accounts, which also evade the death drives of slavery. The slave cannot *be* and this non-ontological status is exposed through the gratifying ritual of gazing upon its inescapable terror and death.

Blood, Sex, and Resistance

In the many examples of violation provided in this chapter thus far, corporeal death is the suture binding them together; the young slave girl who is flogged, the woman killed with an axe helve, the slave baby beaten from the belly, the negro woman who resists forced concubinage, the fine-looking negro man at Dandridge Quarter, the negro who refuses to be flogged, and the woman who grabbed a potatoe hill. Saidiya Hartman raises the question of death in her discussion of the murder of a slave girl she calls Venus. Although the archive says very little about this girl, Hartman sought to imagine the possibility in thinking with, and through, death and the unnamed. "The archive is, in this case," Hartman concludes, "a death sentence, a tomb, a display of the violated body..."[30] It is here that I want to rest, on death and the display of the obscene.

Sexual bondage, William J. Anderson writes, "is another curse of slavery—concubinage and illegitimate connections—which is carried on to an alarming extent in the south."[31] Narrating his twenty-four years as a slave in his 1857 autobiography, he describes his master as a man who partook in many pleasures. In a drunken splendor the master would retreat to "the field to whip, cut, slash, curse, swear, beat and knock down several, for the smallest offence, or nothing at all."[32] His violent jubilee coupled sexual assault and torture. Anderson recounts the ritualistic manner in which "he divested a poor female slave of all wearing apparel, tied her down to stakes, and whipped her with a handsaw until he broke it over her naked body."[33] The master would go on to produce a child with this slave. These lascivious enjoyments were not all his own. Despite having a slave husband who was "permitted to visit her but very seldom," she was sold to "other men, both white and colored, [to] cohabit with her."[34] There was nothing uncanny about the master's behavior given that "he always kept a colored Miss in the house with him."[35] To Anderson these "are some of the *real* 'dark deeds of American Slavery'," so presumably inconceivable that he asks the reader to read these words "remembering that I give no fiction in my details of horrid scenes . . . the half can never be told of the misery the poor slaves are still suffering in this so-called land of freedom."[36]

Anderson guides the reader to grasp the intimate proximity between his master's desire for blood and sex. There is a boundlessness to his power that exists at the convergence of carceral technologies of violence—the whip, cut, slash, curse, swear, beat and knock down—and sexualization, contracting out slave sex infinitely for his own enjoyments and capital gains, and for the limitless pleasures of others. The master possesses a fantasy that has the force to produce reality for the slave. This is orchestrated by the death drives of slavery that foreclose ontology for the slave. There is no way out of or space exterior to the capture of fantasy. This is where fantasy and reality intersect and blur. The slave (re)presents a set of confounding and often contradicting fantasies that do not reproduce it as a being with the capacity for subjectivity, even if the fantasies for such are spoken by the slave. What is fantasy besides a (re)presentation of the paradigm of violence that necessitates that the slave must exist?

Anderson provides an account of slavery that brings together sex and torture as two intersecting and distinct forms of antebellum pleasures. Goodell remarks that slave sexual status "in their almost interminable varieties, corroborate the preceding, and illustrate the almost innumerable uses of slave property!"[37] The whip upon naked Black flesh, the brothel, and the laceration of flesh, conjoin a broad and innumerable spectrum of pleasure and enjoyment. Is the whip distinct from the penis in enacting fantasies of sexual conquest and mutilation? Is the scopophilic drive to gaze upon bleeding tortured flesh as tantalizing as one's sexual climax?

The production of fantasy does not pause, as death of the drive gives way to the production of others, because the drive is never satisfied. By the abolition of slavery, sexual violence was a perfected lynchpin of the peculiar institution. The quotidian nature of breeding, rape, force concubinage and coupling, and sexual torture produced a structure where these occurrences were almost unremarkable. The legal, social, and political ramifications for sexually violating a slave were mild, only finding fault if the injury could extend as a violation of their owner, not the slave. As Jacques Lacan argues, the drive is not reducible to the biological function as "it is not the food that satisfies it, it is, as one says, the pleasure of the mouth."[38] The fact that "no object of any Not, need can satisfy the drive," arguably can be taken up to unsettle the insistence on the slave serving a quintessential sexual function, as in biological reproduction. If sexual violation or torture renders the slave pure passability, as in an object taken up for the desires and subjectification of other beings, fantasies, and desires, then one can see how the death drives of slavery are without aim and do not render the slave a definitive object but as a thing that is taken up in service of an endless array of paradoxical satisfactions. The slave is acted upon and acts upon such that the flesh is never finished but embodies a moving surface of motility and resistance. As Anderson heeds, "the half can never be told of the misery of the poor slaves."[39]

Matrices of sex and sexuality that crystallized in the nineteenth century are often attributed to what Michel Foucault theorized as biopower or biopolitics. The conditions of colonialism and slavery are loosely and commonly referenced as biopolitical arrangements given the sexual entrails that emerge under each structure. Biopower, as described by Foucault, constitutes

> *institutions* of power, ensured the maintenance of production relations, the rudiments of anatomo- and bio-politics, created in the eighteenth century as *techniques* of power present at every level of the social body and utilized by very diverse institutions. . . . Operated in the sphere of economic process, their development, and the forces working to sustain them."[40]

Under a biopolitical order the rule of the nation-state is no longer predicated on the sovereign's rule to order death and regulate life, "take life and to let live," but now functions through the proliferation of life.[41] This political, social, and economic order creates "a new body, a multiple body, a body with so many heads that, while they might not be infinite in number, cannot necessarily be counted."[42] The biopolitical investment in man-as-species unwrites the necessity for disciplining individual bodies, as discipline reproduces docile bodies, which can be "subjected, used, transformed, improved," rather than optimized.[43] Silvia Federici similarly argues that discipline, in the European context, eliminates irrationalities by a "transformation of the individual and social body into a set of predictable and controllable mechanisms."[44]

Old world European torture tactics and tools are imported in the New World through practices that were embedded in the structures of slavery and colonialism. There is a profound distinction between the use of what may appear to be identical forms of torture when those mechanisms transfer from the European to the slave. Seemingly non-sexual forms of violence—branding, flaying, hanging, whipping, copagraphy, and flogging—become sexuating death drives when applied to the New World Black slave. The transmutation of torture in the context of slavery is predicated on a fundamental divergence between discipline, regulation, and normation. Discipline, as Foucault and Federici illustrate, is a set of corrective practices that regulate a body into predictable submission insofar as normation imposes a repetition of anticipatory relations between the object, the aim, and the satisfaction of a goal.

Unlike normalization, which is the process of making something normal, normation is consistent performance of the norm. Under slavery, consistency and expectation are absent from torture but also from the constitution of the slave. In this sense, the slave is brutalized using a series of violent tactics and acts that do not conform to a norm. In fact, the insistence that such is or should be true when evaluating this condition elides a focus on the inconsistency and infinite nature of violence and its unbound relation to the slave. What is distinct here is that the individual, everyday persons (as well as masters), rather than a distinct and identifiable sovereign structure, are empowered by and make this structure operable. The plantation economy did not possess sovereign reign over the violence of slavery. Instead, the capacity for violation that is embedded in its structure is endemic to the social constitution of a world in which slaves function and are made to function as essential to structures of identification.[45]

Pleasure is derived in this system from unpredictability and supreme heterogeneity because of the limitless nature of access. This relation differs from biopower, insofar as the essence of biopower is the expansion and optimization "of concrete arrangements that would go to make up the great technology of power of the nineteenth century."[46] While the nineteenth century marks both the sedimentation and dispersal of a set of centuries-old practices that institute racial slavery in the New World, it does not fundamentally mark a distinct shift in the production of drives that seek gratification from repetitious torture and Black sexual violability.

In this respect, biopower is inadequate for analyzing the structural predicament of the slave. Binding Blackness, torture, sex, death, and slavery excises discipline from the modalities of violence since discipline "individualizes bodies by a location that does not give them a fixed position, but distributes them and circulates them in a network of relations."[47] Contrarily to the process of biopower, the convergence of disciplinary power and man-as-species does not ontologize the slave into a population. Torture, sex, and death do not impart upon the slave a new bodily constitution. The slave is reproduced and replicated as the slave. Which is to say, although the slave is affected by and resists the constraints of its predicament, it continues to (re)emerge as devoid of ontological capacity. If biopower replaces the individual body with populations, "to ensure, sustain, and multiply life, to put this life in order," the slave is but a culmination of matter, as in a mass, that exists in disarray awaiting form or substance. This is a procedure Calvin Warren describes as onticide, wherein it "uses the technique of erasure (sous rature) in relation to features of human difference that exclude blackness but are necessary to articulate the fracturing of fungible commodities."[48] On the other side of slave sexual violation is not territorialized sexuality but the openness of its violations made operable to the ends of asserting the supreme nature of the sex of Human beingness. The slave thus is the marked sexual substance upon which Human sexuality announces potentiality and the structure of its violating potentials. Those potentials and potentialities are cartographic schemas of intelligibility that the slave is denied given the porous and unbound essences of its violating quality.

Torture with respect to the slave is a structure of sexual impulses. A discourse on sexuality, which is the context of biopower, inadequately prescribes form and meaning to the slave's condition, as sexuality is capacity. The fantasy of the slave is structured by the slave reproducing and infinitely perfecting the violence of its (un)becoming. "The disappearance of torture as public spectacle" in Europe sets the stages for the transformation of power "from *a symbolics of blood* to *analytics of sexuality*."[49] However, these same antiquated disciplinary tactics and technologies are taken up as the quintessence of the racial schematization of slavery, which is premised upon ontological sexual division. Antiblack fantasy marries the "handsaw" and "the naked body," a coupling that disavows for the slave a transference from blood to sexuality. This relation marks blood and sex as ontological foreclosures by perversely wedding the public *and* private spectacle of its violation—excess, repetition, destruction—to the reproduction of fantasies of life and capacity, which is the discourse of Human sexuality. Slavery is not a complete project as it is refigured by a cultural imaginary that deputizes slave violation in service of the fantasies that underwrite the structures of identification that constitute desires for Human incorporation.

The archive of slavery (re)presents slaves in an array of violation, disregard, sexual openness, and death. Unlike the torture archive of Europe, which employed similar tactics of discipline to control certain behaviors or subject sensibilities, death carries a prevalence in slavery that is not comparable to the European condition. Flogging, branding, whipping, or any other tactic for the slave do not mold slaves into docile or regulated bodies, but instead mark the sheer deathliness of their entire condition. The slave and the violation are inseparable. Theory can either turn back on or away from the violation but cannot discern the slave as a sentient being for which violation does not void the capacity for bios; unless, however, a considerable amount of force is asserted to conceive the slave otherwise.

Yet some desires seek to challenge what is posited as historical reality by contending that resistance be read in positivist terms. Conversely, the argument here holds that resistance for the slave is its own death drive, a self-obliteration. Slave resistance as only deathly possibility is disregarded by historical retellings that insist on maintaining the slave as a worldly necessity. By giving the slave a positive quality, resistance becomes a modality upon which the totalizing violating quality of being held as the slave of a master is suspended in favor of moralistic rationales that privilege arrangements of life within the paradigm of slavery as antithetical to the structure. However, this position does not ontologize that slave into bios because it cannot will the impossible. As such, logical framings of slave life are taken up to stave off confronting the immanence of slave death. Yet the irrational nature of the archive, the nameless or unnamable attributes of violent acts and the deathly automation of slaveness, do not carry historical truth but affect the psychic capture of the slave each time the violations are confronted or gazed upon. Thus, there is no real slave embodiment; the slave is mere fleeting fantasy. Attempts to hold onto it as an immutable embodied subject redoubles obscene desires to make the slave operable as a single being.

A theory that begins with death, rather than life, can perhaps move the needle closer and back to the point of racial sexuation. Death is pertinent here because on the other side of death, the slave does not emerge in a new or renewed relationship to violence, though the form and function may change. Death does not inaugurate meaning, matter, or life for the slave. Rather, death highlights how the slave functions within a paradigm of fantasy and desire that solidify its sexual condition because its excitation is purely retrospective.

Achille Mbembe critiques Giorgio Agamben's refiguring of Foucauldian biopolitics by instead presenting a theory of death.[50] Necropolitics centers the "subjugation of life to the power of death," rather than the proliferation of life, which reproduces death, as central to the organization of colonial sovereignty.[51] While Agamben thinks of the camp as "the new biopolitical nomos of the planet," Mbembe challenges this positioning as an anachronistic association. He contends that a return to the plantation is necessary to understand how it figures as one of the first sites of "biopolitical experimentation," which then makes the violence of the camp possible.[52] The plantation is taken up in this argument as a spectacle of carnal physical violence. Likening the whip and death, Mbembe notions that each is an "act of caprice and pure destruction aimed at instilling terror."[53] The slave here is subjugated by the violence of unrelenting deadly institutional force.

What is unclear in Mbembe's assessment is what separates the slave from the institution of slavery itself. Is the slave terrifying or is it the institution? Or perhaps it is both? Although the text does not wager an explicit position on these questions, the subsequent moves taken on to develop necropolitics seek to elide the force and power of slave death by engaging other subjective possibilities. In this vein, to detract from the terror of being reduced to a "thing" where "the slave's life is possessed by the master," Mbembe turns to song and dance as proof of slave Humanity.[54] He writes,

> In spite of the terror and the symbolic sealing off of the slave, he or she maintains alternative perspectives toward time, work, and self. This is the second paradoxical element of the plantation world as a manifestation of the state of exception. Treated as if he or she no longer existed except as a mere tool and instrument of production, the slave nevertheless is able to draw almost any object, instrument, language, or gesture into a performance and then stylize it. Breaking with uprootedness and the pure world of things of which he or she is but a fragment, the slave is able to demonstrate the protean capabilities of the human bond through music and the very body that was supposedly possessed by another.[55]

The prefacing of this section with "in spite of" performs a terrorizing yet familiar gesture in studies of slavery that assert that the impacts of violence can be suspended temporarily such that pure and uninhibited forms of life emerge in its absence. The move to the anthropological, that is, to offer examples of Black life and sociality, can be an effort to evade, even if temporarily, the death drives of slavery. However, I and other critical Black theorists would suggest that these forms of Black social life emerge because of the violence, not in spite of it. For example, Jared C. Sexton critiques this gesture by pointing to Mbembe's own anachronistic viewpoint, stating "Uncritical, and ultimately romantic, ethnographic claims, like those Mbembe draws upon, about the slave's capacity and capability for 'stylization' are theoretically untenable since the publication of *Scenes of Subjection* . . ."[56] Sexton returns the engagement back to the work of Hartman to upend the enjoyments of the slave as a fundamental challenge to the slave's existence.[57] What Sexton clarifies is that this disavowal is still silent about how music, performance, and the appearance of Black joy meet deadly force with equal or greater resistance. Displacing death, whipping, and thingification with slave jubilee may seem farcical; however, it is a far too common assertion that pushes away from violence rather than turning to violence and death to see what else may be exposed. What is in fact quite terrifying is that slave music and performance are the only weapons a theory of death can imagine as an oppositional positionality to structural violence predicated on "caprice and pure destruction."[58]

Sexton takes up Mbembe's discussion of necropolitics, arguing that without a concentrated and rigorous pause on slavery and violation, the depth of violence that saturates the slave is grossly underestimated. This critique is sutured by a critical engagement with what Mbembe fails to consider, which, for Sexton, is the sexual suffering of the female captive. Sexton argues that the female captive is the zero degree, unlike the *homo sacer* who is reduced to bare life but possesses the capacity for bios. He writes, "her suffering is therefore imperceptible or illegible as a rule. It is against the law to recognize her sovereignty or self-possession."[59] Sexton employs Hartman to upend slave performance as resistance, by placing critical attention on the case of Celia, a slave.[60]

In the 1855 circuit court case *State of Missouri v. Celia, a Slave*, Celia, a nineteen-year-old female slave, was charged and convicted of murdering her master who repeatedly sexually violated her from the time she was purchased at the age of fourteen.[61] Her sentence was death by hanging. Sexton reads Celia as exemplar of how, "before the law, even the potentiality of slave resistance is rendered illegitimate and illegible a priori."[62] While Sexton is correct in refocusing the analysis on death and liminal life on the sexual violence of slavery, centralizing the focus on the sexual predicament of the female captive in relation to law only skims the surface of the problem. He argues that the possibility of her resistance is a legal oxymoron in response to the will of the master, as well as that of "the whole of the free population."[63] This fact is indisputable. However, the law as an authorizing modality is made operable by desires, phobias, and fantasies about the slave that exist in excess of the legal capacity to make something real and/or (im)possible.

Despite legal refusal to recognize or authorize the right of the slave to resist within its structure of reason and (im)morality, slave resistance was central to the matrix of sexual violence. Resistance is less about what is or is not allowed in the moralist sense of the law's own ego fantasy or ideal. Rather, resistance for the slave was always happening as the slave was acted on, acted upon, and acted against its condition. Refusal was anticipated. It was as essential to the paradigmatic remaking of the sexual death drives of slavery as was the sexual act itself. Which is to say, slave resistance breeds its own fantasies of sexual violence *and* refusal, which extends the psychic life of the violation beyond the event. What is centrally more damning than the legal denial of the right of the slave to possess motive will and desire is that resistance for the slave occurred en masse. However, the truth of this did not and does not upend or change the slave as an available sexual object or the structural operation of its quotidian implementation. Though it may have staved off the threat of the act of violence—such as Celia killing her master did stop the occurrences of forced copulation—in the archive, Celia is nevertheless figured and refigured through fantasied projections as the sexually violated slave, who killed her master, and then was executed by the state for her crime.

Celia is but one example where the curious romanticization of resistance is called into question as always inducing a positive change in the force of violation. When Frederick Douglass recalls the events that catalyzed the beating of his Aunt Hester by her master, the scene is figured by her refusal to submit to the master's demands on her sexual being and forced submission to sexual violation. Douglass describes that Hester defied orders by going out one night and being absent when "my master desired her presence."[64] Furthermore, she refused to heed to the command of never allowing him to catch her in the company of Ned Roberts, a male slave on another plantation. Her sexual refusals and liberties are responded to with a whipping. The ritualistic nature of the beating involved the spectacle of the whip as well as the overt sexualization of the scene. Douglass describes Hester as being stripped "from neck to waist," leaving her breast bare for her merciless beating. Here, the laceration of the flesh is its own forced penetration and the witnessing of the scene serves to reinscribe slave sexual will and agency as extensions of the master's prerogative.[65] The whipping of Hester, however, is split between the historization of the event and infinite nature of fantasy. Sexualized brutality and the refusals that catalyzed her beating are not contained within the historical content of Douglass's portrayals. Instead, the reverberations are maintained by fantasies that continue to give the meaning of these events new form and signification beyond the scope of retelling and teleological boundaries of legalized slavery. Each time sexual openness, refusal, and force are reflected upon, they produce fantasies of their meanings and implications that extend the psychic and material effects of violation.

Attempting to rewrite the slave out of the veil of racist historiography, which contends the slave was a docile and accepting object of domination, counternarratives impose the slave as a priori resistant. The latter framing, while more politically left or radical in its assumptive logic, is still short-sighted in its understanding that resistance becomes its own fantasy object that is not external to slavery but indicative of its relation. Whether or not the slave resisted their sexual conditions as an affective refusal of their sexual status is a moot point. The slave most certainly resisted in a variety of ways.[66] Celia resisted until her death. A non-event in the sense that the psychic permeability of the act and its fantasy do not erode in response to refusal and self-defense, resistance re-entrenches the permanency of Celia as an object of sexual access and violent retreat. Resistance is not antithetical to the condition but serves as an anchor that holds the slave captive to a form that must act against the very thing that the resistant act is taken up to disavow. The relation is recidivistic rather than linear. Simply, the modality of resistance is not inherently freeing. To say the slave resisted is not an expressive act of breaking its chains, although such assertions are commonly made. The force of the sexual act and the fantasy of resistance as an erosive potential are bound up as relational rather than as canceling gestures.

In the case of Celia, Hartman concludes, "*Missouri v. Celia* illustrates how difficult it is to uncover and articulate the sexual violence of enslaved women exactly because the crime surfaces obliquely and only as the captive confesses her guilt."[67] This evaluation of the case illumines that in confessing her guilt for resisting, the act of sexual violation is uncovered. Meaning, it is the resistant act that produced the possibility of the appearance of the sexual violation of Celia in the legal archive. The courts upheld the desires of her master as lawful and just, which is sedimented into the archival documentation of the case. Perversely, there is no record of the sexual act outside of the omission of resistance that brings the sexual nature of the repeated offenses to the surface. Had Celia not resisted, the record of her sexual violation would not exist. Which is another way of saying that the sexually violent act does not exist, in this case, without the act of resistance. They are tethered. This is not a positivist association. Rather, it is a reading of resistance that interprets it as its own sexual death drive, which reveals the concealed nature of the sexual act. However, it does not abolish the paradigm of racial sexuation despite its deadly consequences.

What Celia, Hester, and other cases like theirs animate is that slave resistance, the acting back against the sexual act, does not set in motion a paradigmatic redress of the act. Rather, these instances become substance in a web of materiality and matter that speak to the infinite nature of sexual violence under slavery, and the various ways it appears or disappears in the historical record. The invocation of the sexually violable slave excites and incites new psychic potentials that excise the slave from death, serving them up as evidence that there were other ways to imagine their being. Predicating thought on the legality of sexual violation or resistance attunes focus to slavery as social and political constraint yet profoundly disregards the psychic significance of the slave as an empty signifier. At the most primal stage what drives the fantasy of what makes a slave is its unrestrained embodiment of sexual functionality and its ability to fight back against this designation. Through its sexual violability the slave reproduces a matrix of sexuation for which it regains no possessed integrities of sexual makings— no kin, no body, no history, no future, no ontology.

The death of Celia was not a necropolitical event nor an attribute in the nineteenth-century record of biopolitics because death or sexual life are not the focal points here; rather, racial sexuation is. Racial sexuation prefigures where and when the slave enters the frame, in absentia of the act. *Missouri v. Celia* directs attention to the normation of death and sexual violence under slavery, where Celia is sentenced to be "hanged by the neck until death on the sixteenth day of November 1855."[68] Prior to her condemnation to death, was Celia living, in the ontological sense of the term? What is death in this context? Death as constituted by racial sexuation is a predicament of absent life, as in bios, reproduced by the ontological void of sex/gender primacy for the slave. When death appears, it exposes that the slave never possessed a body. This absence of bodily form, as a metaphysical and individualistic substrate, is located precisely in sexual violability. Celia had her cabin visited on multiple occasions by her master. She was also paired with another male slave, who resided in her cabin and witnesses the master repeatedly entering.[69] However, the placement of Celia in these sexual relations is produced by a fantasy of Black sexual availability, not an isolated treatment of Celia as an individual. What positions Celia in a condition of sexual violation, forced resistance, and death is infinitely reproduced and replicated for slaves on end.

The act of hanging Celia upends the notion that, upon the exit of the last breath, "when death arrives on the scene the body is what vanishes."[70] The terror of being a slave is the recognition that it is not alive, as it is absent of bios. That is what makes slavery incomprehensible, the ability to reproduce and replicate the slave as devoid of a body or bios, which is to say that the slave exists solely as its violation and subsequent response. Bios, in the Greek constitution, refers to the life that is shaped by action and speech, a life that is biographical and coherent. Though it is undeniable that slaves made life out of their conditions, the disruptions that were constituent of slavery disallow these life forms to institute permanence or a quality that can rewrite the slave's relationship to violation. As former slave Henry Bibb once commented,

> Licentious white men can and do enter at night or day the lodging places of slaves, break up the bonds of affection in families, destroy all their domestic and social union for life; and the laws of the country afford them no protection.[71]

White men here mark a material and symbolic signifier; slavery extends a relation where the white man is not static, but the slave is, par excellence, statically broken, destroyed, and protection-less.

Myths of Origins, Ends, and Limits

Revisiting the archive of slavery to meditate on the scope and dimension of sexual violence is motivated less by representing history appropriately and more with grappling with the aftereffects and aftershocks of sexual violence and slavery. The representations of such are not contained in documents of the past but are reinvigorated to the ends of many uses and meanings into the present tense. Such that the historiography of slavery is not contained pre-emancipation, but represented within a milieu of meaning and matter that continues to revise and refashion slave violation into the present. So long as slavery is cast in representation or is made excitable, the slave is possessed for the purposes of transmuting its violating quality into meaning that continues to render it void. Rather than reading this history teleologically, as in a pre-event, event, and post-event linear substance, the relation between the slave and sexual violability is understood as an ongoing structure of suffering and transference. When slave sexual injury is excited, we are not gazing upon history insofar as we are immersed within the meaning making and violent structures of present ontological (un)makings. The archive is a continued project.

Meditations on slavery that contribute to the memory and memorialization of history do not halt in 1865. Contrarily, there is a pervasive casualness and intentionality behind deploying the history of the sexual status of the slave as cultural relics bolster understandings of present political predicaments. Writing against the conservative outcry to preserve confederate and colonial monuments, Caroline Randall Williams interrogates the desire for historical preservation of unliving things by telling the story of interracial sexual violence in her Black family lineage. In a 2020 *New York Times* opinion piece, "My Body is a Confederate Monument," Williams writes against expressed concerns with incidents of defacement and toppling of statues.[72] She interrogates erasure and competing truths about histories that are concealed in the valorization of cold hard sedimented memorialization, placed upon "monuments of stone and metal, the monuments of cloth and wood" or statues and archives.⁷³ She begins on a provocative note, stating firmly, "I have rape-colored skin. My light-brown-blackness is a living testament to the rules, the practices, the causes of the Old South."⁷⁴ Black skin, body, and blood, to Williams, are "truth" and "proof" of the survival of her ancestors and speak back against the honor conferred onto those who sexually violated their slaves and continued to sexually violate Black people post-slavery. In this analysis, the Black body forces antiblack desires that celebrate the Old South to see and "acknowledge your emotional investments in a legacy of hate."⁷⁵

Commenting in a similar respect but expanding the framework to the North, Tiffany Lethabo King describes the repeated defacement of a Christopher Columbus statue on the North End Waterfront in Boston as "the act of defacing or bloodying the statue of the conquistador in 2015 (and over and over again) short-circuits the idea that conquest is a past sin committed for the greater good."⁷⁶ The particular incident King interrogates involves the defacement of the Columbus statue with red spray paint that read "Black Lives Matter." She understands this act of defacement as participatory in an arrangement of responses to the continued celebrations of conquest and slavery. Another more contentious incident involved the bloodying and toppling of the Silent Sam statue on the University of North Carolina, Chapel Hill, campus where Black activist and History graduate student Maya Little was criminally indicted for involvement in organizing within this movement.⁷⁷ Here the statue and the power it represents is persistent in relations of violence as further carried out through the torment, criminalization, and delegitimization of Little as a political actor.

In "My Body is a Confederate Monument," Williams points to the livingness of these histories in the terms of embodiment, which demonstrates how her genealogy is one of Blackness as the embeddedness of racial sexuation that persists in "emotional investments" not distinct from the past. This history figures her and the criminalization of Little as both pushed to reframe the visuality of Southern space. For Williams, Black bodies are the "truth" of immorality that made slavery and its celebrated figures. In arguing for the rightful removal of the many confederate and colonial monuments that litter the U.S. landscape, she ends her piece on the emphatic note: "I am quite literally made of the reasons to strip them of their laurels."⁷⁸ Williams contends that the issues around monuments are moral ones, and monument supporters can be persuaded to shift perspectives by gazing into the obscene, the forced sex that reproduced her. Yet there is an irreconcilable antagonism at play in this framing. Is her body a confederate monument or an object locked within a forced sexual relation that must continue to announce itself in attempts to prove its very existence? What if the laurels that she "quite literally" upends are laurels not despite sexual force but because of it?

In searching for a language of redress, Williams draws on an assumed universal code of reconciliation and response, where one can be redeemed by looking more honestly at slavery's brutality. But the tension is not one of morality, persuasion, or ignorance. It is a metaphysical predicament regarding ontology. Her body is the result of a web of violent conditions that obliterates the potentiality of Black being rather than obscures it. Retelling these stories seeks paradigmatic signification. However, truth does not require repeated force that must rely on the scaling up of obscenity as an attempt to produce a shift in valuation. This history cannot produce a master narrative no matter how many times the endless stories of sexual violation are told.

Memory in this context performs its own assumptive veil that believes the act of revelation or remembering is forceful enough to push back against the unimaginable. As Williams uses the obscene to produce a definitive pause on the sexual terror of the slave, does her deliberate centering of sexual harm and racial perversity reshape the narratives of slavery? Does removing the veil over the sexual violence that pervaded slave narratives produce a fundamentally different way of remembering or addressing violation? The death and sexual terror that are emblazoned within Black embodiment cannot be represented, in the sense that representation sediments forms of subjective knowing. This is to say there is not a logical history of sexual violence and slavery that "rape-colored skin" exposes. Simply, it is a history that is entrapped in its own endless necessity for spectacle, to display the obscene as the ineluctable raw material for boundless becoming or disavowals. Which is to say, it is not a singular history of slave rape but one that reproduces Blackness such that her body is indistinguishable from the structural authorization of unlimited sexual access and its paradigmatic disavow. Essentially, Williams produces a neo-slave narrative that is preceded by a barrage of antebellum and postbellum texts that have produced a similar ineffectiveness to structurally make the slave's sexuation a present form of matter.

In a 1995 essay, "The Site of Memory," Toni Morrison toils understandings of the American slave narrative.[79] Though the range of autobiographies engaged is broad—from Olaudah Equiano to Harriett Jacobs to Frederick Douglass to Henry Bibb, and more—Morrison finds that a shadow is cast over each autobiography by the structural conditions of their productions and publications. Although accounts like Equiano's "gave fuel to the fires that abolitionists were setting everywhere," she writes, "popular taste discouraged the writers from dwelling too long and too carefully on the more sordid details of their experience."[80] Thus, the descriptive textures of slavery's violence, both spectacular and quotidian, are brushed away with silence. Morrison quotes Henry Box Brown's autobiography in stating,

> I am not about to harrow the feelings of my readers by a terrific representation of the untold horrors of that fearful system of oppression . . . It is not my purpose to descend deeply into the dark and noisome caverns of the hell of slavery.[81]

One can ascertain that under these conditions, of not arousing the disdain of white sympathetic readers, that much of the inner contours of slavery remain unseen.

Yet, modern racial slavery is positioned in most social and political thought as a categorizable set of violences that are both recognizable and containable. This appears in definitive statements that assert what slavery was and how we can find the evidence to prove the facticity of such. It also animates the efforts to locate social life and resistance among slaves as a counter to death drives. Thus, the premiere authority on slavery is placed upon the slave narrative to speak truth to the form and function of the peculiar institution, as there is a perception that telling and retelling the story chips away at the structure. As such, theories of slavery continuously grapple with a limited selection of first-hand accounts to help make sense of its most obscene and violent iterations, which, as previously stated, these texts understandably are limited in their discussion of such, given the historical conditions under which they were written and the vexed nature of their production with respect to their publishers and assumed audiences. This is by no means an indictment of these writers, but one of the worlds into which they, as former slaves, were positioned to write.

The limitations placed upon these narratives are structurally produced and upheld by maintaining ancillary focus on the candid, yet censored voices of former slaves. These voices, Morrison notes, "over and over . . . pull the narrative up short with a phrase such as, 'But let us drop a veil over these proceedings too terrible to relate.'"[82] Respectfully, slave narratives, and other first-hand accounts of slavery, are critically important materials for theorizing the aphasia that meets the brutality of slavery. However, these narrative accounts must be held in conversation with theories of the larger paradigm of slavery that condition the possibility of their emergences, reception, and how the replication of the brutalities they do and do not reveal are wagered in the present tense as to "immure us to the pain by virtue of their familiarity."[83]

The duality of exposure and secrecy presented by these accounts are most silent around an elaboration of many things. But sexual violence is the most pivotal and often veiled silence. In *Incidents in the Life of a Slave Girl*, Harriet Jacobs illumines this silence not as a choice made by Black people, but one violently imposed by whites:

> The secrets of slavery are concealed like those of the Inquisition. My master was, to my knowledge, the father of eleven slaves. But did the mothers dare to tell who was the father of their children? Did the other slaves dare to allude to it, except in whispers among themselves? No, indeed! They knew too well the terrible consequences.[84]

What Jacobs reveals is the vexed nature of silence given that the taboo here is not preconditioned by a religious or moral sentiment adverse to exposing the interracial sexual encounter but one produced by the racially antagonistic drive of whites to maintain access to, and power over, Black sexuality without remark. The relation between gratuitous sexual availability, produced by violent means, and the lack of remarkability of such a condition prefigures the complications for thought and actions that pervade present engagements with the peculiar institution. Morrison highlights Lydia Maria Child's introduction to Jacobs's autobiography as evidence of the particularly vexed feelings about exposing the sexual proclivities of slavery. Child writes, "I am well aware that many will accuse me of indecorum for presenting these pages to the public," going further to reinforce that Jacobs is intelligent despite these exposures. "This peculiar phase of slavery," Child states, "has generally been kept veiled; but the public ought to be made acquainted with its monstrous features."⁸⁵ Despite the honesty Child puts forth here, little is revealed in the text, as Morrison notes, about the interior life of slaves that is less interested in responding to, appeasing, or informing an outside subject.

What is fascinating about Morrison's pausing on sexual violence and the comments provided by Child is the timeless feature of slavery's aphasic relationship to sexual violence. While Morrison highlights the repeated raising of the veil in eighteenth- and nineteenth-century texts, I argue that the aphasia and occlusions continue to pervade conversations about the sexual terrors of slavery. This is the historical silence Williams sought to write against by honestly invoking the obscene. Contrarily to "My Body is a Conservative Monument," a 2019 *Washington Post* article, "Two Centuries ago, University of Virginia students beat and raped enslaved servants, historians say," illustrates this problematic of continued occlusion.⁸⁶ Highlighting two recently published books, *Thomas Jefferson's Education* by Alan Taylor and *Educated in Tyranny: Slavery at Thomas Jefferson's University* by Maurie D. McInnis, the article intends to weave together a scandalous narrative about the interwoven history of a respected institution of higher education, slavery, and the sexual abuse of slaves. However, the first sentence of the article exposes its fissure. It states, "The two young, white university students had a secret," revealing the subjects of the story are not the slaves who were sexually abused.⁸⁷ The morality of the white students and the larger institution are what the spectacle presumes to unearth. Although sexual subjection, slavery, and Thomas Jefferson are no shock to anyone familiar with the vexed history of Sally Hemings and the Hemings family. The following scene is the only detailed account of sexual abuse provided:

> It was September 1826, and the men—both scions of wealthy Southern slaveholding families—were suffering from the same sexually transmitted disease. Conferring, they identified a possible culprit: an enslaved black woman whom both had raped. They also thought of a solution. Joined by several classmates, Turner Dixon and George Hoffman attacked the woman, "[accused] her of giving them a venereal disease . . . stripped her naked and beat her" . . . Her name is lost, but her age is known: 16.⁸⁸

The 16-year-old slave girl, who is inappropriately referred to as a woman, is left bare by the acts that produced her sexual subjection and, I argue, by the retelling of this story. Her sexual assaults, exposure to a sexually transmitted infection, and merciless beating fade into the backdrop. An exposé into the lives of the two white students unfolds thereafter, leading into a discussion of the sinister foundations of the University of Virginia (UVA) and its relationship to Thomas Jefferson. Although the name of the 16-year-old is lost, she is not lost. Sexual violations like the one she was made to endure play a particular role in the psychosexual after/life of slavery. The maneuvering of these violent sexual acts, demonstrate a profound reliance on the (re)animation of slave sexual violations. Telling the story is assumed to perform a type of care work, "as in an antidote to violence;" by presuming that mere reference of the violated is redemptive.[89]

Paraphrasing UVA professor Alan Thomas, the *Washington Post* article states, "While shocking today, the incident was unremarkable for its time and place."[90] However, it seems given the handling of this story that something continues to be "unremarkable" about the sexual violations of slavery. Is the problem of telling the story of the 16-year-old slave girl a problem of history? Does omission in the archive occlude deeper understanding? Or is slave sexual violability a psychic continuum that is called upon to perform an essential form of subject making and fact-telling? How does the spectacle allow the casualness of this occlusion to repeat itself without end? How is the sexually violable slave still made available?

What is at play in the narration of the 16-year-old girl's sexual and physical assaults is a fundamental belief in a temporal disconnect between the event of violation and the moment of its retelling, just as was the case with Allan's nineteenth-century accounts. However, I argue that placing a temporal distance between the violent sexual act and the (re)use of the violation demonstrates a particular and peculiar crux about slavery. As much as racial slavery is narrated as an historical event, something from another space and time, the ways that slavery is called upon demonstrates how sexual violations—one of its most pervasive and broadest structural conditions—are paradigmatically irreconcilable in the present. We do not have the terms to wish them away with ease.

The *Washington Post* article focuses on the spectacle of the sexually abused slave to simply allow the implications to evaporate. Taylor explains this as a sort of common code of conduct, stating, "Throughout the first half of the 19th century, male students studying at Southern universities regularly mistreated, beat and raped the enslaved men, women and children who catered to their everyday needs."[91] Despite the initial shock produced by the invocation of sexual abuse, the article seeks to assuage the effects of what is revealed. Taylor states further, "These men are 16 or 17 years old, they've been raised on plantations and been trained from youth that it is their job to command people and abuse them if there is any resistance to their command." And "For a student to lash out and hit an enslaved person, that was routine in this world."[92] Offering these observations in neutral terms explains away, rather than antagonizes, the manner in which we come to understand sexually violent acts and allows this story to be read as an unfortunate consequence of history. Furthermore, the use of the term resistance here suggests that sexual abuse occurred with respect to an intelligible structure, albeit improper of intent and action. That slavery's sexual subjection, although immoral, functioned by identifiable means to rear, command, and punish slaves. However, the imposition of mens rea and actus reus here makes it such that when intent and action are not apparent the violation disappears or, at least, is read as tertiary rather than integral to the matrix of sexuation. When action and intent are wedded to the formal systems of the peculiar institution and its individual actors, the transfer and implication of the (non)injuries perpetuated against the slave become positioned as the concerns of a distant past, in a space of the other time, a concern of yesteryears.

Returning to Morrison's remarks in "The Site of Memory," she offers strategies for moving the veil aside. There are ways to tell the interior stories of sexual violence and slavery without caving to moral or affective tones and gestures or assuming that nothing can be known beyond the violent act. Understanding that slavery is a collective story, Morrison offers that, in addition to our own knowing, the writer can "also depend on the recollection of others."[93] This is where memory enters the frame. Though Morrison cautions that resting on memory and recollection alone is not enough, as she makes clear, "Only the act of the imagination can help me."[94] This means she attempts to "explore two worlds—the actual and the possible," because "the act of imagination is bound up with memory."[95] We must imagine, with the fragmented archival remnants, what existed, how it existed, and under what conditions did it produce the coherence of what stands because of it. It is the expansive nature of how we remember that locates the specifics to the path or paths forward. As Morrison makes clear, "all water has a perfect memory and is forever trying to get back to where it was." Thus "still, like water, I remember where I was before I was straightened out."[96]

So then, what is redress of this condition? Some may argue that the formal end of the institution is that. However, the dedication Morrison offers in *Beloved*, to "Sixty Million and more," summons the intractability of loss set forth by the Middle Passage and its innumerable refractions. Holding the magnitude of this reorganization of worlds must stay present in memory and imagination and serve as a starting point to contest conjectures that imply that any aspect of slavery and its after/lives is banal. This chapter as well as the chapters that follow are oriented by a suspicion that the sexually violable slave provides clarifying content for the annunciation of the modern world, yet what constitutes the extent and vestiges of sexual violation for the slave is a murky and highly contested terrain.

Two

Suspended Absences and the Substrates of Naming the Female Slave

"She is a lusty wench . . ." These words were written by George Somerville to describe a female slave who ran away from a plantation, owned by a George Fox, near a copper mine. Sarah, Somerville claims, had taken, among several articles of men's clothing, "a molatto boy, about 6 or 7 years old." Upon the successful return of Sarah, Somerville guarantees a reward of ten pounds, along with "all reasonable charges" necessary to ensure her return. One cannot begin to imagine with certainty the world Sarah inhabits. Yet try to imagine what it may have meant to inhabit the category of a "lusty wench." Is she this by action or by her structural position as a slave in temporary flux between freedom and captivity? Sarah is suspended by her absence and by her racial sexual marking. Lusty connotes an insatiable appetite for sex. Wench equivocates slave femaleness with sexual laborer, in a manner that inextricably binds the terms such that one cannot exist without thinking of the other. Wench, a medieval term used to connote a child or a woman, is ushered into the slave archive as a racial gender marker to overdetermine the sexual uses and availability of female slaves.[1] In this sense, lusty and wench are redundant statements. Or, perhaps, lusty is employed to illustrate that Sarah has a more forceful sexual appetite than the natural proclivities of the everyday sexualized female slave. Under this designation, Sarah is sex exponentialized. Somerville insists the reader, capturer, or sympathizer understand that what Sarah has to offer is the raw pleasure and angst of sexual deception.

Sarah oscillates through gender and sexual narratives, as both sexually loose and available, to potentially passable as a male slave, having taken men's clothing. Her gender is confounded by competing desires and forces

> TEN POUNDS REWARD.
>
> January 24, 1778.
>
> RAN away, on the evening of the 14th inftant, from George Fox's plantation, near Dr. Stevenfon's copper mine, in Frederick county, a likely molatto wench, named SARAH; fhe took with her a molatto boy, about 6 or 7 years old; fhe alfo ftole and carried off a man's furtout coat, and a ftraight bodied ditto, both light colour'd, three mens white fhirts, a fum of money, a bed and beding, and many other articles.— She went off in company with Valentine Lind, by trade a taylor, who had been employed in that neighbourhood; 'tis fuppofed they have one or more horfes with them, and may poffibly attempt to pafs for man and wife.—She is a lufty wench, fpeaks good Englifh and Dutch, has plenty of good clothes with her, and a large fum of money.————Whoever apprehends faid woman and boy, and brings them to the copper mine, or to the fubfcriber in Baltimore, fhall have the above reward, and all reafonable charges, paid by
>
> GEORGE SOMERVILLE.

Figure 1. "Ten Pounds Reward," *Maryland Journal and Baltimore Advertiser*, published January 27, 1778. Source: Collection of the Maryland State Archives. Reprinted with Permission.

that suspend her in time and space. The function of her gender, like the function of her sex, is determinable by whomever orchestrates her capture. Is marking her a lusty wench authorization to sexually violate her upon contact, designating carnal knowledge as her truth, or is it for visible assertion that upon seeing her you know her as sex personified? Any further details about Sarah are unknown, though there are some assumptions that can be inferred. She is potentially a mother, having stolen away a mixed-race child whose conception is only perceivable through the context of forced copulation.[2] The existence of the child exposes that to be a lusty wench has reproductive and future consequences that the slave carries. The child is representative of the stain of racial mixture borne under the violence of captivity, and the ubiquity of sexual violence that engulfs plantation life.

Sarah is only one of many slaves who traffics through the remanences of archival documents as a wench or named for her sexual availability to others. Cultural historians approach suspended absences, like Sarah, by producing a rhetorical tradition that seeks to locate the agentic subjectivity of the slave that power excises from the archive. By suspended absences, I mean historical objects that are only spoken of, but do not speak on their own behalf to identify themselves other than the pejorative names they are given by others who possess power over their existences. The counter gesture seeks to provide proper names to the unnamed or maligned.

Sarah is emblematic of a milieu of female slaves that are unknowable beyond their sparse violated presentations in the historical record. The intention of counternarratives is to recognize and represent female slaves as Black women who are cultural and political agents within the history of slavery. This political approach to reading history pushes against the objectification of the female slave as lusty wenches or seductresses by nature. However, the desire to apply agentic logics as counter forces of redress to the existence of Sarah and others like her critically underscores the level of violence waged against them. Sarah is not simply silenced by the historical record. Nor is the demand to determine her status as property solely represented by Sommerville or her master. Sarah is situated at the nexus of a continuously unfolding *history*, comprised of slavery and its afterlife, which situates the Black slave, gender, and sex within a rupture. She does not possess a name all her own nor does she have a fixed gender. This is precisely the problem. However, it is not a problem of history but one that continues to reemerge each time the female slave is spoken into existence, or one attempts to engage her suffering. Each engagement with the female slave, whether in the historical record, mundane discourse, or even Black feminist historiography, illustrates her as lacking a substance, yet she is serviceable towards the naming and recognition of conditions of existence that she is structurally barred from. Naming the female slave otherwise does not upend this relation; rather, it glosses over it. History and contemporary theory continue to reveal an unbearable truth, which is that the female slave is not a woman or an inevitable historical revolutionary martyr, but a suspended absence upon which her status as pure violation cannot be undone. Does Sarah possess her own story where the power of the master class pauses or ceases to confound her existence? Or does Sarah possess a name that disembowels the structural presence and permanence of the master's prerogative?

I would argue that the female slave is not written improperly, despite the harsh connotations of the terms written onto her existence, because the pejorative is what constitutes being a slave. Attempting to write the female slave as a counterforce within the sexual paradigm of slavery relies on dialectical inverses to unwrite pejorative terms that are used to classify the slave as inherently sexually open. Feminist legal theory has spent a considerable amount of time grappling with how the adjudication of rape under the law and in cultural discourse writes the victims/survivors wrongly, where the character of the rape victim/survivor is maligned in order to extend the life of sexual violence and its justifications.[3] What continuously appears in these reengagements with history is the racial violence that undergirds and buttresses the language and concepts used to describe agency as contradistinction to passivity, complacency, or objecthood are themselves racially coded. To counteract the structural designation of the slave as a wench or seductress by noting her status as a wife or charting her subversive act to repulse unwanted sex does less to undo the antiblack prescripts of slavery as it does to reinforce them. When individual action is levied as evidence to unwrite how individual slaves were misclassified by the archive, what is uncontested or left unattended are the ontological constrictions of racial sexual classification. Sexual deviance or violability are not wagers on slave actions but constitutions of their (non)ontology. Rather than repulsing the pejorative in favor of more seemingly palatable connotations, which themselves are written in racial sexual violence, moving with and through the pejorative to psychologize the labor they perform in racializing sexual choice and agency provides clarity on the deployment of sexual violence as the modality through which slaves are named and unnamed.

Thinking through the preconditions of naming, this chapter tarries with how the female slave transmutes into the Black woman in Black feminist projects. I argue that in these works, the violating sexual quality of slavery is undertheorized in service of offering Black womanhood as a transformative subjective quality. This heroic image of Black womanhood seeks to undo the deracination of unrapeability through the deployment of the Black woman as the revolutionary subversive subject of the plantation, par excellence. While such gestures attempt to challenge the devaluation of the female slave in philosophies and theories of the violence of modernity, this position inadvertently redoubles the erasure of the particularities of sexual violence under slavery. Notably, as I detail, this theorization favors a reliance on terms such as rape, injury, motherhood, and woman, which are structurally antithetical to the condition of being a slave.

Historically, to rape a slave was not recognized as an offense under law or in social customs.[4] The interest here is with how the female slave is made to occupy the quintessential exemplar of rape. Black feminist theory and historiography have sought to contend with the unthinkable dimensions of a suffering that is refused the ascription of injury in the historical record. What sits at the merger of Black feminist investigations is charting how the slave experienced their sexual injury in contradistinction to the structural refusal to name forced copulation as a violation. The arrival of the female slave in the position as the meaning of rape exists primarily in a manner that retroactively represents her as the historical figure of an experience she was structurally barred from claiming. These recuperative projects seek to preserve or locate the spirit of the female slave; her interior dimensions, feelings, affects, and responses to her exclusion from the right to name her injury.[5] In these discussions she is both affected by sexual violation yet transcends the structural designation of being held captive to her sexual objecthood.

This investigation is less interested in adjudicating the terms of history, where sexually violating slaves was legally and culturally permissible. Rather, the interrogation centers on how the female slave becomes the meaning of rape. Given that sexual force against a slave was unremarkable, how does her unrapeability translate to possible injury and subject making? What we see is resurrecting the female slave as able to be raped (which is a particular legal and political framework) requires a leap of judgment. In the instances where rape or gendered violation are read onto the female slave as injury, her status as a slave, an object of force, is subdued or subordinated to the perception that there is a natural state of sexual integrity available to all sentient beings that supersedes the racial sexual ordering of slavery.

It is important to note that the gestures taken up here are not intended to deny the pervasiveness of forced copulation and other forms of sexual force for the millions of slaves held under bondage. The intention is to home in on how attempts to evacuate the obliqueness of this condition do not undo or unwrite the structure that made the slave the antithesis to sexual choice and freedom. By turning towards the unrapeable status of the female slave rather than repulsing this designation, we can see how the terms granted to the female slave as agency and freedom from, and against, rape reinscribe the ontology of sexual violence as it coheres for the non-slave. Which is to say, the gestures that articulate rape as ontologically possible for the slave inevitably reinscribe the very terms of gender, volition, and sexual capacity that were inaugurated by the racial strictures of slavery. To be raped or unrapeable, then, are not dialectically oppositional but rather circulate within a structure of being that sustains and upholds the antiblack sexual violence upon which they cohere.

Black Feminist Theoretical Dissemblance

In a 1994 article entitled "The Occult of True Black Womanhood," Ann duCille wonders what will Black feminist studies look like in the face of the postmodern draw to oversaturate various milieus with Black women as a supreme form of otherness.[6] She likens the over theorization and marketing of Black women, in the academy and beyond, to what bell hooks termed "eating the other" or "the commodification of otherness."[7] For duCille, her primary concern was to interrogate how Black women were being engaged and defined from outside of the field of Black feminist studies by people other than Black women.

duCille was responding to the 1980s and 1990s retreat from the racially distinct power movements of the 1960s and 1970s and the push to universalize subjects in theory. What resulted was a multiculturalist propensity to engage conditions of suffering as amalgams devoid of specificity for the purposes of performing theoretical sophistication and reach. Feminist theory, as well as other fields, were implicated in this maneuver. For duCille, contemporary theoretical approaches were in tension with Third Wave feminisms, where theories by Black and other feminisms of color unapologetically centered race in feminist discourses on gender and sexuality, which was set in motion by 1970s women of color feminist activists.[8] This particular move against the subsumption of race into generalized discussions about gender and sex is an ongoing attempt at carving out a distinct space for the discussion of racialized gender and sexuality and its attendant violences.

In the thirty-year span since the publication of "The Occult of True Black Womanhood," Black feminist theory has enacted a response and position to duCille's concerns. The field has taken up Black womanhood or the Black woman as its political signifier, such that, to speak of Black feminist issues signifies to the listener or reader that the primary subject of concern is the Black woman and the object of inquiry is the particularity of her suffering. This focus speaks back against eating the other such that Black womanhood is not tangential to other disciplinary concerns, but a serious field or condition of inquiry situated on its own terms. In this respect, Black feminist theory contends with the status of the female slave in a manner that seeks to locate her elided or erased gendered Humanity both in and outside of the historical archive.

While Black feminist scholarship's centering of Black women made crucial interventions in feminist and race theorizing, this chapter takes a departure from this work by exploring the plight and fantasy of the female slave while refusing the category of womanhood as constituent of this condition. Identifying the female slave as distinct from the category of woman or from the imposition of Black womanhood is not to suggest that woman is not a descriptor used in the historical archive to identify slaves. In fact, some gendered terms or descriptors used to describe female slaves included girl, female, wench, slave, and, at times, woman. However, the argument here parses out a conversation on gender and gendering by refusing to assume that the female slave is gendered ab initio as a woman based on assumptions that align with biological organs. The complications of this argument are that female and woman are both terms that exist within the biological assumptive framing of binary gendering. Such that the female is not natural or untainted by sociogenic principles embedded in beliefs about gender as locatable at the level of the physical body and in perceptions about inherent forms of difference.

Additionally, Black woman is not intended to be read equivalently with the category of woman. Black as a qualifier fundamentally changes the quality of woman. However, as will be discussed later, Black woman is a retroactive ascription placed upon the female slave post-emancipation. When applied to the slave, Black woman performs a labor of retelling and reimagining that demands its own interrogation. The female slave is not primarily Black in the archive, but is also African, negro, negress, or slave. While these terms overlap and bleed into one another, it is important to maintain their distinctions. Despite the Black being the slave of modernity, slave signifies on its own terms. By refusing the conflation of two undefinable affectable categories, the point is to consider how they are structured by converging and competing forces. It is also to ask, how does the female slave become the Black woman? Essentially the distinction between these two categories lies in a question of capacity.

In her groundbreaking book *The Invention of Women: Making an African Sense of Western Gender Discourse*, Oyèrónké Oyěwùmí argues that "the distinction between sex and gender is a red herring."[9] The argument that sex is biological and gender is socially constructed is an untenable argument when considering how biology is manufactured by the structures of power and fantasy that give gender meaning, matter, and form. Engaging biology as fixed, immutable, and/or universal disavows that biology is mutable, and thus shifts and reinforces its assumptions based on the social constructs and violence of race, as well as gender and ability. While social constructionist theory has prevailed in discussions around the convergent and divergent uses of sex and gender, it is critical to foreground violence, *and particularly antiblack violence*, in theorizing the modern preoccupation with these distinctions in feminist theory, as well as in general discourse. In this respect, the female slave as the conceptual framework that guides this chapter is less insistent on considering femaleness in relationship to the physical body of the slave. However, this position is a priori embroiled with inescapable flaws insofar as every slave spoken of in this context is, based on genitals, sexed as female by the plantation system. Nonetheless, in the context of racial slavery, what female unearths is a designation of an object that is categorizable by its utility and quantifiable arrangements rather than as a psychosexual stage of potentiality toward womanhood as a form of ontological becoming. Rather, the female slave is permanently fixed as oppositional and distinct from woman as a subject constitution. The female slave is a stasis. Femaleness for the slave is rendered legible not on its own terms but through the forced affixing of the violent injuries attributed to womanhood, like rape, onto the slave as explanatory of its suffering. Woman is a violable subjectivity insofar as her ontological pursuit of self-possession seeks to dislodge her from being property for and of man. Her injury is located at the crux of self-possession and property status, where man forcibly dispossesses her consent, will, and agency by acting upon her subject based upon his possessive desire for power. Yet capacity for property status does not make her a slave, as property and slaveness are not inherently the same. Rather, property marks many relations and "proprietary claims and powers are made with respect to many persons who are clearly not slaves."[10]

The interrogation of womanhood and femaleness that informs this chapter is preoccupied with Blackness and slaveness as they are dynamized by gender imposed under pure violation. The intent of this position is to wager how slavery, as an arrayed condition, is productive for unthinking the primacy of gender with respect to sexual violence and rape. The imposition of the slave into the sexual and the violent erodes preconceived perceptions of what constitutes the arrangements of history, but also has implications for how our engagements with history may impact the present. Furthermore, the argument here refuses to hold stridently to gender categories in an attempt not to reproduce biocentrism.

To be clear, the call is to not assume gender integrity, unless such can be proven to exist in the objects of analysis. Rather, it is to consider how, according to some gender theorists, gender can, even under oppressive conditions, be a space for freedom or self-making. Yet while non-slave bodies might be a target of gender and sexual violence, they are not inherently sites of containment for what one's body can and should be and do for others. More, to be marked as non-slave is to be gendered as having a capacity and relation to slaves. The description of slaves as gendered subjects does not determine that the discourse and narrative of gender is explanatory of their conditions. As Sylvia Wynter has argued,

> If the Black–White Distinction functioned to fix the Major Referent and optative identity for all groups and races, the gender-distinction, man/woman functioned to replicate the representation of "natural Difference" which bonds the order, enabling it to function as a sociodicy, i.e., an order whose empirical everyday praxis justifies the ways of the order to itself. Both the Black-White and the Gender distinction as well as the related "naturalness" of heterosexuality to the "unnaturalness of all forms of nonheterosexuality, served to *substantialize* the order's *discourse of justification*."[11]

Gendered categories are both reinscribed as natural and as the logical terms to make sense of their violent arrangements. Which is to say, gendered categories are upheld as the predicating reason for injury, *the why*, and the explanatory reason for the violence, *the because*. However, relying on gender, its terminology and conceptual frameworks as the order of all things, as a form of primacy for thought, reifies it as the essential sociodicy of violence. While this may be the case for the Human, the Black slave disfigures the gender canon with respect to violence. Simply stated, one cannot definitively assert that gender functions as the why *and* because of the sexual perversity of slavery (though it may texture the analysis), it does not impart reason. The sexual(ized) violations of slavery, as a structure of violence rather than an experience, betrays rather than reifies the sociodicy of feminist frameworks. The assumptive logic of the feminist project is that gender degrades the subject upon and after arrival. The Black feminist tradition presented here asks how natal alienation, general dishonor, and gratuitous violence dispossess the slave of *being*, structurally occluding the possibility of the arrival of a subject. As such, there is no slave gendered subject, insofar as the slave is a violent projection and captive possession of Human gender ontology.

Over the past two decades, the literature written on race, gender, and slavery centers Black women as the predominating lens of analysis. With the exception of a limited number of recently published works, the female slave as a category has largely been abandoned by Black feminist elaborations in favor of the use of enslaved Black woman or simply enslaved woman.[12] Although even in cases where the female slave is concretely theorized, the term is also deployed interchangeably with enslaved woman. The unspoken or silent contention present in the privileging of the Black and/or enslaved woman over female slave involves perceptions about dehumanization, where designating female slaves as Black women is an attempt at a humanizing or re-humanizing gesture that stakes a claim on her gendered subjectivity as inalienable and innate. Framing slavery as such contends that violation for the slave harkens on denied Humanity that is reclaimed through a possessive investment in gendering through naming. However, this guarding of "woman" as the slave's gendered Human right is rooted in a biocentric association wherein genitals are taken as the content of proof upon which the politic is staged. Which is to say, gender in this respect is a claim on the perceived biological instantiation of what it means to be a woman that is then particularized through the racialization of the slave, which is maintained at the level of bodily experience. The historiography of Black womanhood is propped up by reading slave gendering as a marked bodily constitution that is degraded in a hegemonic struggle for power and recognition with the master, mistress, and male slave. What lies beneath this assumptive logic is that in order to grant the female slave credence as a speaking and acting subject, her suffering must be mimetically ciphered through the representational schemas of the contractual schisms of cis-centrism, such that patriarchy, rather than her Blackness, becomes the essential quality of her (un)gendered or unnamed suffering. Additionally, theories of slavery and gender that speak against cis-binarism are not immune to having to contend with a structure that forcefully upholds gender as a fact of the body while denying how gendering is made real through racial social sexual relations that are oriented by antiblackness.

Marking Black womanhood as the essence of the female slave that must always be returned to is emblematic of what I call a *theoretical politics of dissemblance*, which is a term drawn in part from the work of Darlene Clarke Hine. "By dissemblance," Hine argues, "I mean the behavior and attitudes of Black women that created the appearance of openness and disclosure but actually shielded the truth of their inner lives and selves from their oppressors."[13] Hine is interested in how certain puritanical ways of being are performed by Black women to counteract narratives of their inherent sexual perversity that were used as justification for their sexual violation in antebellum and postbellum life. Additionally, Hine charts how a "cult of secrecy" around sexuality was also a tactic employed by Black women to help secure jobs in the unskilled and semiskilled labor markets to move their labor out of domestic spaces where they were subjected to wanton sexual violations in the intimate spaces of white homes. Hine theorizes dissemblance as a complicated arrangement of racial, class, and gender responses and associations that are enacted by Black women to ascend racial, sexual, and social statuses and ascriptions. In a sense, dissemblance can be understood as a practice through which Black women attempted to contest their social conditions to enter new and, seemingly, more safe spaces. However, what emerged in the context of secrecy around sex are various new forms of exclusion where Black women created women's clubs and social societies to support their new senses of self and social stature.

Evelynn M. Hammonds interrogates dissemblance and secrecy as not only means to an end for self-protection but also ways Black women themselves created exclusionary practices that, through silence, center Christian heteronormativity as the predominant form of Black sexual presence. For Hammonds, these practices in essence leave Black women's sexuality underdefined. Additionally, as Hine and Hammonds make clear, these practices leave the contexts of sexual violation and violence that Black women are up against veiled behind a politics that cannot tell nor confront the contours of the very thing it is resisting. Additionally, these silences, as Hammond critically argues, demonstrate how black women's sexuality is a belated and reductive consideration where the complexities and potentials are crowded out by the automatic assumption of compulsory heterosexuality.

Dissemblance is theoretically rooted and socially performative. The former emerges most clearly in theoretical spaces centrally concerned with the pain constitution of the Black woman. Hammonds argues that in Black feminist theory, the theorists themselves inure a relation to Black women and their sexuality that imparts an extension of dissemblance and silence. She contends that "the goal should be to develop a 'politics of articulation' that would build on the interrogation of what makes it possible for black women to speak and act."[14] Black feminist theory is sutured by a double bind where its approach to exposure can symptomatically reveal its entrapment to a theoretical politics of dissemblance. This dualism appears through a performed refusal to contend with the obscene, as a way to protect Black women, or the category of Black woman, from being overdetermined by pejorative and perverse ascriptions of her sexual beingness. To say this otherwise, the impetus to hold Black womanhood as separate or distinct from its inhabited conditions reinforces understandings of gender and sexual difference that extend the very logics of violence this political gesture seeks to escape from. Imbued within the structural predicaments of womanhood, despite its Blackening by terminological associations, is that the cult of silence is parasitic upon slave sexual openness to announce its distinction and ontological right within the Western epistome. However, in order for woman to be distinct from man it must also be distinct from slave, which makes up the triumvirate of modern racial gender violence. What distinguishes woman from slave is precisely how each category is made intelligible or is obliterated by sexual violence.

The entrapment of Black feminism within the triumvirate of woman–man–slave is that its theoretical politics of dissemblance reveals that its move toward a claim on womanhood does not resolve the slave—because it cannot disintegrate its historical presence. Rather, the qualities of womanhood that are upheld in theory partake in a theoretical politics of dissemblance by refusing to ask, with respect to the above provocation by Hammonds, "what makes it possible for the black woman to speak and act" that is impossible for the female slave? Some might argue that the distinction between the categories is simply semantic and that across time, female has become supplanted with woman/women as a casual progression emblematic of a shift in political language. However, what has also occurred with this shift is a deputization of womanhood to the ends of forms of speech and action that challenge the absence of these qualities in the historical record for the female slave. Which is to say, the female slave as a fixed recipient of violation is countered by presenting the Black woman of history as a speaking and acting willful agent. Again, the question remains, what makes the agentic Black woman possible?

With respect to the woman–man–slave relation, theoretical dissemblance is eerily silent about gender intelligibility as a form of violent subjectivity. Gender is not a given but is a form of structural making and integrity between the dualism of woman–man, which is clarified through how each of these categories violently relates to the slave. Lastly, if womanhood is taken up as a category, politic, or term against femaleness as a state of pure violation or nascent form, then what makes the woman cohere demands interrogation.

Zakiyyah Iman Jackson argues that Blackness is not figured solely by a relation to the subhuman but is made to occupy multiple inflections of the Human in simultaneity. Jackson identifies this as ontological plasticity, wherein "the enslaved, in their Humanity, could function as infinitely malleable lexical and biological matter, at once sub/super/human."[15] Countering femaleness with womanhood as a resistant strategy against dehumanization is a maneuver that attempts to resist what Jackson puts forth here, which is that antiblackness is contained in each formulation of the Human, which the predicament of the slave clarifies. I would argue that the shift from taking stock of the violence of slavery—what is the violating quality of female slaveness—to projecting the willful capacity of the Black woman as resistant historical actor is a conceptual leap that intends to impose or center the Human as a particular freedom from the violence of ontological obliteration.

While the Human is free from gratuitous violence, it is also parasitic on Blackness simply because it cannot rid itself of the slave. Black womanhood, as imagined by historiographic accounts of slavery, is a morphological imposition of the superhuman into theories of slave gender. The female slave is evacuated in service of the buoyancy of the Black woman as an unrelenting and infinitely resistant Human designation. The violation of the female slave is not refigured or proven inessential to the Black woman but is repositioned as a different type of permanence. In this respect, the female slave as the zero degree of abstractive matter is not resolved, because it cannot be. Rather, she is morphed into the supreme political actor, a super Human type. As such, the enslaved Black woman is a phantasmic figure of superhuman resiliency against the toils and strife of daily domestic and intimate violation all while resisting the sexual architecture of the plantation and the sexuation of her existence indefinitely. All of this demonstrates Jackson's point about ontological plasticity.

Aware of the entrapments of the category woman, Jessica Marie Johnson offers the black femme as an alternative model, stating, "Invoking black femme instead of (black) women or womanhood remembers the slipperiness of the category of woman in a multilingual world of slaves."[16] Using this analytic to theorize the forms of self-possession taken by "women of African descent" against sexual and intimate violence in New Orleans, Johnson contends,

> Black femme freedom points to the deeply feminine, feminized, and femme practices of freedom engaged in by women and girls of African descent. In the practice of refusal, whether in rejected labor demands or sexual advances, and even refusal to concede to officials in manumission disputes, black women and girls claimed ownership over themselves. Their claims superseded that of their owner; it even rejected claims of their bodies and labor by their husbands. Black woman created black femme freedoms by stepping into the fray on each other's behalf.[17]

Johnson is expressively careful in her prose to not over assume or assert womanhood or the woman as the signifier in this arrangement. Black femme is privileged here as an actionable response to violation rather than as an identity that rests on ontological grounds. Despite this refusal to center womanhood, the figure of the black femme is represented as someone who still must fight endlessly and overcome gargantuan vectors of force such as possessing the capacity to superseded or overwrite the labor demands and sexual claims of the master. Claiming this fight as the action of freedom continues to maintain a single-axis existence for the female slave or manumitted former slave and reproduces objecthood and terror but by other means. If freedom from sexual captivity is indexed by the female slave's capacity to fight back, then sexual violence is not destabilized as the primary modality of her condition. Rather, sexual violence is silently acknowledged as unbending such that the female slave must be armored against its force in perpetuity. It is an exhausting and morally astute positionality to assume. One that never rests. Furthermore, it is more of a fantasy of undoing than it is a paradigmatic undoing of the racial sexuation that produces the ontological absence of agentic gendering for the slave.

Examining infanticide, abortion, and marronage as forms of resistance and revolt in the seventeenth and eighteenth centuries, Jennifer L. Morgan argues,

> Enslaved women carried a set of experiences that attuned them in particular ways to the perverse logics of early modern Atlantic slavery: these experiences began on the slave ships, where their relative freedom of movement exposed them to the sexual violences of Europe an crewmen and at the same time enabled them to be conduits of information and occasionally of rebellion, and continued in slave sales, when women's fecundity became part of the calculation of their value and, in the case of those with children in arms, also part of their anguish.[18]

While Morgan does not overemphasize resistance as fundamentally subversive and paradigmatically transformative, this argument still maintains that from violation, and particularly sexual violence, Black women acquired "critical perspectives on the new world they were situated within."[19] Morgan essentially maintains that through violability a subjectivity for Black women arose that is attuned to the emergence of a New World order situated in the crises of race, capital, and kinship. Sexual violence thus imparts an unattended positivist consequence of a New World racial and gendered subjectivity that contains the information to unwrite the violence of its emergence. At the same time, one must wonder, is this subjectivity or a fantasy projection of an object that is violated in perpetuity toward the advancement of its kind and the broader world? Which is to say, how is the belief that the slave becomes a perfected subject by way of slavery a fundamentally different logic than the one advanced by pro-slavery advocates who believed that the treatment of slaves assisted them in becoming better, more productive Humans? Instead, it seems what Morgan illustrates—which is a deeply held Black feminist association between violation and subject insight—is a subjectivity that cannot emerge despite deep desires for it to be. If the Black woman is tethered to sexual violence and its consequences that are refracted and amorphous, there is no coherent collective knowledge that can be contained and expounded upon as a result of this condition.

Simply, sexual violability for the slave is a static condition that cannot be written or thought against by approaching the archive from a different lens. Rather, theorizing objecthood as the permanent status of the female slave over the leap towards subjectivity as an assumed given would render more damning conclusions about how our current reliance on gendering as an explanatory model of suffering, perseverance, and power is reproduced as desirable out of an ontological angst of becoming the transmutation of nonexistence that was inhabited by slaves. In this respect, Black feminism is bound up in anxiety about female slaveness, or sexual objecthood, because it is an inescapable relationship to violability. It is an unavoidable anxiety that is either embraced or disavowed by theory.

The forceful shift to rewriting or retooling the female slave into gendered categories such as the enslaved Black woman or into an agentic selfhood such as femme-ness falls critically short of conceptualizing the racial violence that subtends slavery and gender. In theory, the Black woman is positioned as the superhuman savior, where her volition is served up as the antidote to the real and fantasied enactments of violence and violation. According to this calculation, what makes the Black woman distinct from the female slave is that her will and action are assumed as a tactfully political and supremely intentioned slight against the structure of slavery, where her existence is not confounded by her condition but resists it always and unendingly. The catch is that there is no other way to enter gender than to enter by way of relations of violence. Entering gender, as in entering its representational folds, does not unwrite violence as much as it stakes a quiet claim on authorizing or accepting its permanence. Allegiances to gendered categories are not enacted through benign performances or the implementation of cultural or daily rituals and customs. These boundaries are possessed by a claim to the usages of violence as a right of self-making rather than one of totalizing sexual dispossession.

Ontological Absence Follows the Slave

In her re-engagement with William Shakespeare's *The Tempest*, Wynter situates her argument in "Beyond Miranda's Meanings: Un/Silencing the Demonic Grounds of Caliban's Woman" as a departure from, and critique of, Luce Irigaray's "purely western assumption" of the term woman as a universal position silenced by patriarchal discourse. This insistence of a universal woman is emblematic of the core split between womanism and feminism more generally.[20] Written as an afterword to the edited volume *Out of Kumbla: Caribbean Women and Literature*, "Beyond Miranda's Meanings" ponders if the labors of womanism demonstrate the impossible metaphysical emergence of its subject of concern. Which is to say, womanism as a thought pursuit may reveal the absence rather than the presence of the Black woman.[21] Wynter argues that the question of sameness and difference is paradoxically exposed by the imposition of womanist concerns. For Wynter, the topos "race" unearths a totemic schema that challenges gender difference or patriarchal order as the mimetic order of Human relations. "The *physiognomic* model of racial/*cultural* difference" ushered in a paradigmatic shift from premodern sex-gender attributions, or sex-anatomical difference, to a system of white racial power that subsequently stratifies gender along racial lines. *The Tempest* animates this order, clarifying the illusive nature of paradigmatic violence with respect to race. Wynter argues that "race" as a qualifier imposed against feminist modes of thought presupposing gender as universally constituted inserts a contradiction into the frame of thought. Like feminism's insertion of gender into previous epistemological frameworks that subsequently assumes the presence of racialized gender as a form of "positive knowledge," it adds to and complicates the universalist tendencies of thought.

The Tempest sets the stage for the interrogation of racially distinct gender positions. The play is allegorical and revealing as "one of the foundational endowing texts of both Western Europe's dazzling rise to global hegemony, and, at the level of human 'life'."[22] Arguably, the fantasy that grounds the narrative and the desire for its production and replication are structurally enabled by the same conscription of power and violence that produce the possibility of race and gender in the New World. In the play, the relationship between Miranda and Caliban concretizes a psychic gender power relation that mirrors an almost complete simulation of the libidinal subscripts of the Maryland slave law of 1664 that will be discussed at length in Chapter 3. Miranda is the representative figure of white womanhood. She is granted power over the native population by her father Prospero, the white patriarchal colonizer. Caliban, the native, is marked by nascent manhood, which Wynter recasts as the most primal native, the nigger. Wynter foregrounds this relationship to demonstrate a series of problems for Western feminist thought. The first of such demands is that thought contends with Miranda's power, rejecting the universal Western feminist notion that Miranda is silenced. While white women may experience silence in the face of white male patriarchy, they are granted power over the racial other. Wynter acknowledges that one need not be figured as "rational," like Prospero, to possess power. Having the capacity for rationality in a racial order, like Miranda, is power. Secondly, under these conditions, Miranda is figured as the desired form of beauty for Caliban. For Wynter, Miranda is the idealized form of beauty, with "features of straight hair and thin lips is canonized as the 'rational' object of desire, as the potential genitrix of a superior mode of human 'life,' that of 'good natures.'"[23] Miranda's form is juxtaposed against what Wynter identifies as "the most significant absence of all, that of Caliban's Woman, of Caliban's physiognomically complimentary mate."[24]

For Wynter, the ontological absence of Caliban's woman creates a cesura for Western feminist thought, and the point where Black feminism unsettles the demonic grounds of thought. Wynter writes,

> It is within this latter 'real' imperative that the absence of Caliban's woman as Caliban's sexual reproductive mate functions to ontologically negate their progeny/population group, forcing this group to serve as the allegorical incarnation of 'pure' sensory nature ... As such too, as Caliban's women, are reduced to having no will or desire that has not been prescribed by Prospero/Miranda in the name of the existential interest of the population group for whom the 'images' of Prospero/Miranda, stand. Given that the idealization/negation of both groups is effected precisely by the dominant group's imposition of its own mode of volition and desire (one necessarily generated from the raison d'être

of its group—existential interests) upon the dominated; as well as by its stable enculturating of the latter by means of its theoretical models (epistemes) and aesthetic fields, generated from its increasing hegemonic and secularizing systems of meanings.[25]

Wynter precisely details the violence of white filial order, as resonating in epistemic, aesthetic, and ontological form. However, the extent of violence, I argue, is more totalizing than Wynter accounts for here. Wynter lays forth a racialized gendered schematic of white supremacy, where whiteness is positioned as superior to all other beings, objects, and things, or the epitomizing of whiteness and white life as Human life. Thus, whiteness is idealized, desired, justified in its dominance, given theoretical privilege and pristine aesthetic form. Wynter identifies this as an increasing hegemonic hold. In Gramscian terms, for hegemony to develop, consent (in the form of Caliban's betrayal of his physiognomic mate), coercion (in the form of Caliban's woman desire to be Miranda), and force (through Prospero and Miranda's power) must take concretized form. However, what does Black ontological resistance mean in the absence of totalizing white domination? When the Black breaks free, or is emancipated from chains, presenting to the world its own aesthetic fields, theoretical models, reproductive desires, raison d'être, what, then, constitutes Black gendered relation?

The complications of thinking ontological absence unfold infinitely. When the question is posed, why doesn't Caliban's woman exist, inquiry into that question reveals that no Black gender exists under these conditions. By these conditions, I mean ontological erasure. By attending to the question of Black female absence, extended interrogations arrive at a point to suggest even the most overrepresented presentations of Black gender are not presence. They are projections of Human libidinal desire. Black presence and/or absence remarks upon the necessities of Human life. Caliban reaffirms the all-encompassing power of Prospero, contained within the sexual capacities of the captive relation. Miranda's position is, however, more challenging to apprehend. Miranda represents the locus of sexual desire; however, this is not her most possessive quality. Miranda also writes and produces the master narrative for what it means to suffer, making her logic—which is what Wynter contests in the work of Irigaray—the component of proof necessary to elevate one from flesh to an intelligible injured/able to be injured body.

To say this otherwise, Miranda completes the script of Human life. Her sexuality is inessential to this problem. She is the perfection of the Nietzschean principle "Man, the bravest animal and one most inured to suffering, does *not* repudiate suffering in itself: he *wills* it, he even seeks it out, provided that he is shown a meaning for it, a *purpose* of suffering."[26] Miranda gives female form the value of womanhood, even if that form is presented in a semi-deracinated state. In a war of positions, Caliban's woman is needed to expose Miranda's lie, that she, like Prospero, is also empowered. This amounts to nothing more than a hegemonic recoupling. However, this exposé does not unhinge Black gender from a zone of non-being. The emergence of Caliban's woman, if, in fact, *she* can emerge, is not the redress of the originating violence of her obsolescence.

Wynter sounds the call to move beyond Miranda's meanings. She asserts that the essays she is responding to in her afterword assert womanism as a response to Black erasure in feminist literature, and thus "enabled the move, however preliminary, on to the 'demonic' and now unsilencing trans-'isms' ground of Caliban's woman."[27] In this respect, revealing the trans inhabitations and speech registers of Caliban's woman begins the process of offsetting Miranda's power. However, Wynter pushes this call further by stating, "This terrain, when fully occupied, will be that of a new science of human discourse, of human 'life' beyond the 'master discourse' of our governing 'privileged text', and its sub/versions. Beyond Miranda's meanings."[28] When this demonic terrain is "fully occupied," a rupture or break will orchestrate a new narrative or narratology of human life, which expands the frame to include the trans-"isms" ground of Caliban's woman. This final moment in the text offers an impending teleological optimism situated in a revelation of truth and power. As time moves forward, and Black feminists, or womanists, completely occupy the demonic ground of Caliban's woman, a representational and Humanist shift will usher in a new epoch of human relation.

In their work on Blackness and political demonology, Cecilio M. Cooper invites Black studies to take up a demonological approach to thinking how Christian theologies saturate the logics of the field's understandings. Thinking against and through the field's interpretations of gender matter(ing), Cooper offers a counter demonological conscription of Blackness and gender, where a primary gender position or degree of signification is nullified or canceled out such that no singular sex-gender position quantifies nor qualifies the condition. Cooper argues,

> Blackness spirals out in too many directions to be definitively domesticated—in other words, territorialized—as mere matter orbiting one sex-gender structural position. Matter is among blackness' potential incarnations rather than its only predestination. Blackness is the agender chaotic fullness that precipitates femaleness, maleness, epicene, and any other prospective sex-gender particularity. Blackness is an inimitable cosmological medium for sexuated (re)generation itself.[29]

Rather than centering Black femaleness or maleness—which, curiously, scales up in theoretical equivocation to Black woman or man—Cooper theorizes Blackness as "agender," which opens up space to think beyond teleological inscriptions of transcendence or mutation of the epistemic or epochal violation. Cooper's theorizing helps us construe Blackness as such that its post or prior inscriptions are immutably fixed yet chaotic and (re)generative via its sexuation into the Atlantic world. Blackness, rather than gender particularity, is figured as quaquaversal, which overdetermines its shift into another terrestrial terrain or threshold of conceptualization of matter(ing). Which is to say, the violation of Blackness cannot be contained by the unearthing or demonological uprooting of a singular sex-gender positionality as the true terrain of matter or meaning. Caliban's woman as a representational figure of Black womanhood or Black femaleness figures but one example of a multitude of ontological absences and erasures.

As complex as Wynter's argument is, the explanatory power of this proposition rest upon a set of truisms about gender and Blackness that remain uncontested after the epistemic rupture that is being privileged. Black womanhood factors as the tabula rasa of the racial gendered order given its silenced position in the present epistemic order. As David Marriott has argued in the context of other works by Wynter,

> this rupture can only appear *out of order* to the narratives it interrupts, and so bound to those narratives as content. Further, that breakthrough is meaningful—to humanity, to history—only when a breakthrough is adduced to have reordered codes that cannot themselves be historicized.[30]

Caliban's woman cannot be historicized as the essential element of an onto-epistemological privileging of her mattering.

Katherine McKittrick argues in her engagement with Wynter, "the *place* of black women is deemed unrecognizable because their ontological existence is both denied and deniable as a result of the regimes of colonialism, racism-sexism, transatlantic slavery, European intellectual systems, patriarchy, white femininity, and white feminism."[31] For McKittrick, the stakes of unsettling the demonic grounds—which are arguably distinct from Wynter's calculus—are about marking the geographies of Black women's existences such that if "Caliban's woman is inhabited," it opens up the terrain to be "part of a larger human geography story."[32] In this respect, the demonic exposes what already stands before in the sense that the project is one of uncovering or uprooting what is unseen and unsaid about Black women's existences and potentials. These untapped possibilities are carried forward into a new epoch that is shifted given the reordering of Black women's significance. However, the terrain of Black womanhood is not contested by McKittrick, which is an inherited stance from Wynter. The geographic coordinates of mapping new Human relations are established upon biocentric conscriptions of and investments in Black womanhood as the racialization or Blackening of sex-gender, which is codified as radicality based purely on scopophilic assertions of her capacity for existence.

What arises as a limit-point for Wynter's calculation on ontological absence is the placement of the physiognomic Black female as the privileged site of contradiction. This recognition of the absence of a Black physiognomic female form is too narrow to account for the innumerable absent presentations of Black gender. In fact, Wynter's position is broadened and challenged if Blackness is inserted as that which is ontologically absent rather than a Black physiognomic representation of womanhood. She is not Caliban's woman, because she is not. If womanhood is constituted by Miranda "as the only symbolically canonized potential genitrix,"[33] Caliban's woman cannot possess this status. Caliban's woman is not womanhood awaiting emergence but gender under erasure. *She* is allegorical. Provocatively, the same can be said for Caliban, who is nothing more than a projection of white libidinal investments. He too is allegorical. Caliban is not imbued with the capacity to possess anything, even himself. Is it a misaligned gesture to *name* the missing element, Caliban's woman? Does Caliban, his "woman," repressed queers, gender in drag, or trans actualizations even possess bodily form? Or are they phantasms of fantasies, desires, and phobias that can also speak back—what some call resistance—but are trapped in the violence of their antiblack unmaking?

Gendered form, as in physiognomic representation or positionality, does not matter here. However, there is something particular and distinct about Blackness that does. Whereas ontology is a concern with being, physiognomy is a particular representation of presence. The concern this book places on historicizing and politicizing Black female gender as the quintessential attribute of gendered sexual violence is that it crowds out and seemingly rationalizes the myriad ways that gender violence performed against the Black slave escapes reason. This reliance on the corporeal schema, to use Frantz Fanon's words here, and biologically heterosexual couplings unwittingly presupposes Caliban and Caliban's woman role in *The Tempest* as degraded beings.

However, *The Tempest* enacts a grand-scale fantasy. While Caliban's woman is perceptively absent at the level of physiognomic progenesis in a matrix of racial sexual ordering, she is overrepresented at the level of violence. Caliban's place in the ontological arrangement positions him at the helm of patriarchal desire. Locating Caliban solely as a desiring benefactor of patriarchal promises occludes an unflinching engagement with Caliban's violation. *The Tempest* allegorically remarks upon the peculiar status of Black gender through and by way of opaque violation, which gives the play its coherence. Only under these circumstances can *The Tempest* be deployed as theorical armor to imagine Black procreation as metaphysically barren, when the material realities of slavery and colonialism speak an entirely different tune. *The Tempest* writes its own script of truth based in the Western metaphysical imposition that holds the Black as a fungible object to the projection of an all-empowered Human world. This affects the problem. The problem is not how Caliban and Caliban's woman are physiognomically made and unmade, present or erased, but that they can be made operable for many desires even if or when those desires are competing.

Developed as a theory of species in the seventeenth century, physiognomy—the judgment of facial features, the bodily form, and biocentric essentialisms—is how ontology or the lack thereof is mapped onto the terrain of the body granting features intellectual and affective visuality. Johann

Caspar Lavater later interpreted physiognomy into a science of racial sexual difference that was located on the face. Contrary to phrenology, which maps the texture of the skull, physiognomy takes stock of facial features, using approximation of distance between various poles of the face, shapes of noses, lips, eyebrows, chins, cheekbones to determine the virtue and intellectual capacity of people along racial lines. Regarding the negro, Lavater expresses many views and concerns about their featural and intellectual inferiority. He ruminates,

> The most beautiful complexion may become jaundiced, may be lost; but the negro cannot be washed white. I shall not become a negro, because, to imitate him, I blacken my face; nor a thief, because I assume the appearance of a thief.[34]

Lavater invites the physiognomist to use the visual as a conduit to think beyond what of the face may be fleeting, with aging and other circumstances of choice or imposition, to consider "what would be visible, under various other circumstances."[35] On these terms, the concern of this scientific exploration is with the question of ontology as a racial demarcation where the surface levels expose the depths of existential matters. For the negro, who is marked as an agender species, the appearance is immutable, that of a thief, one for whom mimesis is its only form, which is rather Black formlessness. The negro can only take from but cannot be the proper physiognomic subject. However, in commentating on gender, Lavater contends that "even single bones in the female are more tender, smooth, and round; have fewer sharp edges, cutting and prominent corners."[36] The form of non-negro female gender is a terrain of its own marked by lesser degrees of physical intensity.

The physiognomist's gendering of featurism is also a container for reproduction. As Mary Olmstead Stanton argues in her nineteenth-century study on how to read faces, "Love or amativeness, is the fundamental faculty of the human organism."[37] The appropriate measure of amativeness produces "love of the opposite sex, procreative energy, physical passion, conjugality, manliness and womanliness, sexual perfection, energetic individuality, fecundity, base of mentality."[38] Stanton lays bare physiognomy as fundamentally invested in the facialization of heterosexual desire and sexuality. She argues that attractiveness, or the science of attraction, connotes how the face offers a mirror into the internal function of the organ systems and the soul of the individual. Intellect or morality as a scientific measure operationalizes the sexual beingness of the superior race(s) by deploying their sexuality to territorialize sexual features as mechanisms for policing the racial sexual boundaries of gender. Amativeness thus only has value or meaning insofar as its gendered classificatory schemas are buttressed by what it means to be overdetermined or underdetermined by its deployment. In the case of excessive amativeness, one "tends to immodesty, unchastity, and to unbridled licentiousness, lust, prostitution, obscene language and slight regard of sexual ethics."[39] Inversely, a

> deficient amativeness makes the character narrow, unsocial and unlovable, with no power to attract the opposite sex . . . Those deficient in love of the opposite sex are wanting in magnetism, and often exhibit a morbid, shrewish, suspicious manner, and angularity of body.[40]

Despite the inclusion of various poles of sexual (dis)functions, physiognomy is not a science of, or for, the wayward or homosexual subject, who in nineteenth-century American discourse is conceived in relation and contradistinction to the negro. Siobhan B. Somerville notes that "it was not merely a historical coincidence that the classification of bodies as either 'homosexual' or 'heterosexual' emerged at the same time that the United States was aggressively constructing and policing the boundary between 'black' and 'white' bodies."[41] In defining the parameters of physiognomic heterosexual mating, modern physiognomists are explicit in crowding out the use-value of this science for the darker races. Simply, the negro is not a physiognomic subject but an object deployed for the purpose of racial distancing. As Stanton argues, "The fusion of white with black is detrimental in every way, while the crossing of dark Caucasians with negroes or Indians almost always creates low, criminal, and brutal types."[42] Physiognomy is a science of locating virtuosity, which, given its mimetic character, Blackness is ex nihilo matter except as a commentary on the extremity of its comparison.

Despite introducing physiognomy with a critical articulation of the embeddedness of racial othering within its deployment "as the primary 'totemic operator' of the principle of Sameness and Difference" from the nineteenth-century onward, in Wynter's theoretics, the "primacy of the anatomical model of sexual difference" continues to overdetermine the relationship of power and conscription Caliban "possesses" in relationship to his so-called woman.[43] If the project of moving beyond Miranda's meaning is sutured by Caliban and Caliban's woman as signifiers of "'native' human subordination" on the premise of their physiognomic relation, then the urgency of their ontological predicament is elaborated on the basis of their epidermal genital schema that is referential to the statuses of Prospero and Miranda.[44] Under this schematic, Caliban occupies the position of the "native" sovereign head who, like Prospero, can and will be supplanted with the reason of a racial sexual genetrix, his woman the figure of the demonic grounds. Caliban's woman as a radical transformative demonstrative figure is buttressed on an assumptive premise of Caliban and his suprapositional racial sexual ontological presence.

The demonological approach offered by Cooper, however, forces a pause on this point. The erasure or obscuring of the sexual for Caliban brings into focus the following convention offered by Hortense J. Spillers, that the Black male "must regain as an aspect of his own personhood—the power of 'yes' to the 'female' within."[45] This, I submit, is not a statement about identity, but one about proximate distance to sexual violence and violability. Spillers provides the preconditions for eroding the metaphysical presuppositions of the gender binary. Distinction, or "symbolic integrity," does not apply to the socially dead. In the case of slavery, not only does the gender binary fail to apply to material realities of the slave's existence, but the sexualized conditions of the slave put tremendous pressure on the assumed explanatory power of gender as a framework. How might a *"black descensus,"* a term elaborated by Cooper, lead interrogations of Caliban's role in the native/Black racial sexual order to entirely different conclusions that may "dissolve sex-gender coherence" for Blackness writ large, not just for the anatomical physiognomic cis-Black woman?[46] How does Blackness conscript Caliban such that his replicated racial sexual epistemological understanding buttresses him with the credence of mutated empowerment that grants primacy to the cis-anatomical model as explanatory of his assumed possessive potentials? How might we understand the sexuality of Caliban's woman as disimbricated from Caliban? Under what conditions does her sexuality emerge?

Genital Fantasies

"Genital fantasies" is a term Gayl Jones offers in her 1975 novel *Corregidora*, about the sexual perversity of white enslavers. Jones animates the dizzying dysfunction of the protagonist, Ursa Corregidora, a blues singer who obsesses about bearing generations to undo the sexual taint of slavery that bore her maternal lineage. Ursa is introduced in violence by way of an assault or an accident, which pushes her or assists her in falling down a flight of stairs. The details of this encounter are unclear; however, what is evident is the exchange with her husband Mutt results in Ursa suffering a miscarriage and a subsequent hysterectomy. The politics of this seemingly personal loss weighs heavily on Ursa, and arguably the reader. She seeks to make sense of and rectify her place in the world as someone who cannot bear children while carrying a deep neurosis to do so as a means to remedy her family's history of racial sexual terror. Ursa's reproductive foreclosure clarifies how the desire to deploy Black sex to undo the structural predicaments of slavery and sexual violence is an impossibility.

The surname Corregidora was branded onto Ursa by a Portuguese enslaver who owned and fathered multiple generations of her maternal lineage in Brazil. Corregidora, described as a whoremonger, owned Great Gram, with whom he fathered Gram, with whom he fathered Mama who birthed and mothered Ursa. This relation is ever so complex and vexing, as Ursa explains, "Their survival depended on suppressed hysteria. She went and got her daughter, womb swollen with the child of her own father. How many generations had to bow to his genital fantasies?" Ursa is painfully aware that these fantasies live longer than the mortal lives of their creators. Through her own life events she comes to understand the inescapable structural force of how slavery made her through haunting sexual possessiveness. The text repeats that the evidence of slavery was buried such that no one can "say nothing" about what occurred. Yet, as Mama explains to Ursa about the spectacular nature of violence exhibited towards slaves, "all them beating and killing wasn't nothing but sex circuses, and all them white peoples, mens, womens, and childrens crowding around to see . . ."[47] In explicit candor, Mama opens the line of thought to think about the sexual implications of all forms of violence enacted upon Black bodies. The sexual and gendered (mens, womens, and childrens) realms of being are locked within the emergence of identity through the libidinal economy of phallic and phobic associations with Blackness.[48]

After leaving Mutt and struggling through another failed marriage where she is unseen and disregarded, Ursa returns to the scene of her first marriage, however this time on different terms. She is no longer attempting to disassociate from her maternal past but embraces the terror of its paradigmatic grip over her existence, twenty-two years after the push-fall. Ursa and Mutt reunite not on romantic terms as lovers but by way of the mutual nonexistence of their self-possessed sexuality. The point here is not to look past the bodily and mental harms Mutt perpetuated against Ursa but to think of the hysteria of her inability to bear generations with Mutt as an impossibility bestowed upon them before that fateful night. There is nothing to idealize by marking these two as bound through a condition beyond their individual actions. Ursa is drawn to Mutt because there is a structural misalignment, a paradigmatic necessity as to why they cannot coexist. To make generations means to bring forth life that is free from a condition of gratuitous violence; such would necessitate producing heirs who have access to the preconditions of gender arrangements and subjectivity bestowed by a kinship structure, "our father's children," as opposed to "mama's babies and papa's maybes." It would mean transgressing the limits of slave law into the symbolic structure of the white patriarchal law. Neither Ursa nor Mutt, pre the push-fall nor post the event, have the capacity to circumvent a paradigm of sexual (non) relation set forth by the auspices of the peculiar institution.

In the end, Ursa and Mutt come together. Her blues performance is where Mutt finds her. He reconnects by reminding Ursa of his great-grandfather, gesturing to suggest his loss of Ursa gave him the same feeling his great-grandfather had when he lost his wife. "After they took her, when he went crazy he wouldn't eat nothing but onions and peppermint . . . I tried it but it didn't do nothing but make me sick."[49] Mutt, however, had the option to return, so he did. Ursa had no choice but to be found.

The thoughts that led Ursa to accept a physical reconnection with Mutt are revelatory and haunting. Ursa wants to know what drew Corregidora into this perverse generational narrative:

> It had to be sexual, I was thinking, it had to be something sexual that Great Gram did to Corregidora. I knew it had to be sexual: "What is it a woman can do

to a man that make him hate her so bad he wont to kill her one minute and keep thinking about her and can't get her out of his mind the next?" In a split second I knew what it was, and I think he might have known too. A moment of pleasure and excruciating pain at the same time, a moment of broken skin but not sexlessness, a moment just before sexlessness, a moment that stops just before sexlessness, a moment that stops before it breaks the skin: "I can kill you."[50]

With these thoughts of sex stifled by death, or more aptly social death, Ursa begins removing the value judgments she inscribed on her sexual making. Finding that what Corregidora had done was implicated in all of the consensual Black sexual relations in her life; her mama and daddy, as well as she and Mutt.

Ursa and Mutt embrace following the repetition of the words "I don't want a kind of woman that hurts you," to which Ursa responds, "Then you don't want me." Mutt shakes Ursa until she falls crying. She relays that, "I don't want a kind of man that'll hurt me neither."[51] A sexual embrace occurs in this moment, where it feels good to avow a disavow in moving forward that such could not be true. They are hurting one another in the truth of speech and the context of the embrace. Blackness hurts. It is hurt. It is (en)gendered that way.

In the final scene of *Corregidora*, when Ursa and Mutt come together in hurt and an act of fellation Jones presents a moment steeped in the nonrelationality that haunts and violates them. What occurs between them over the course of their relationship is a metacommentary on the belief that there is a primary and innate sexual relationality between Black men and Black women. The haunting to make kin or bear generations for Ursa, which is a paradigmatic burden placed on her by slavery, exposes the relation between the female slave and male slave, Caliban and Caliban's woman, as a force produced by a shared relation to sexual violability. Ursa's biological and ontological barrenness propels her into the realization that Black genitals cannot combine to make Humans but instead conjoin out of obligation to make more slaves. The heritability of this predicament does not stop with emancipation but is buried in the evidence "they" did or did not leave behind, as Ursa ruminates, about how the sexual thing that was done is immutably rooted in Blackness. While the "they" references white men like Corregidora it is not confined to his racial sexual positionality and thus expands to include others, like Miranda from *The Tempest*, or even Black people themselves.

By drawing on *Corregidora* as an example, I want to contextualize the complex genital fantasies at play in acts of mutilations as well as fantasies of sexualization, sexual aggressiveness, and punishment. *Corregidora* is situated within a tradition of Black feminist writing that rejects one-for-one descriptions of gender that reduce Black gendered violability to that of patriarchy alone. Blackness has the explanatory power to reveal endless accounts of the itemization of the flesh through deracinating forms of sexual(ized) violence in ways isolated gender categories fail to apprehend. While sexual violence can be, and has been, largely theorized as a terrorizing facet of Black life under slavery, the concept of genital fantasies gestures towards marking sexual violence as a paradigm of relations between Blackness and the making of Human kinship and differentiation, rather than an individual violator. Christina Sharpe argues that,

> In *Corregidora* we are made to see that more complex elaborations of slavery "as the ghost in the machine of kinship" of post-slavery American subjectivity are long overdue and that the spaces for witnessing through particular kinds of disavowal, repetition, reoccupation, and reanimation are already long past.[52]

Corregidora amplifies the contradictions of what the content of the novel can and cannot do in terms of retracing history. As readers and theorists, we are left to wallow in the inconsistencies that arise from being pushed to imagine a history that is simultaneously present and absent, silent and pervasive.

The intention here is to not assert *Corregidora* as a pure rendering of slavery. It is worth considering how *Corregidora* succeeds and fails, not by the fault of Jones, but by the narrative constraints of attempting to write a story so grandiose it structurally cannot be told, not even in the realm of the imaginary. In this respect, what are the stakes of grappling with the implications of sexual violence and slavery for Black existence when it must be imagined unsuccessfully? Can we confront the force of racial sexuation if it renders Blackness illegible and gratuitously open for intrusion and reconceptualization? Is it possible to stay with the inconclusiveness of the previous two questions without retreating into the recourse of possibility and alterity as optimism? Additionally, what is Black sexuality without slavery? Can Black sex exist without the stain of violation?

Genital fantasies, as Jones articulates, provide a context for considering the vexed relationality between Black women and Black men. Ursa and

Mutt's relationship starkly highlights Black sexuality and relation as violation born from their fraught gendered embodiments thrust forward from slavery. Black gender is confounded by a psychic structure upon which fantasies of its lack are redoubled to entrench ideas of binary gender as just, legitimate, and essential forms of sexual coexistence. As such, Black women and men are perceived as inverse gendered conditions; however, all Black genders are reproduced in forced relations steeped in violent subsumption. Genital fantasies and the violence of their operationalization are not the possession of singular actors or binary relations, such as man–woman. Rather, the inability for Black gender to emerge is present in all interactions or invocations of Blackness as a gendered substance. What I mean by substance is something that is less a form or matter but relegated to a thing or an object inhabiting multiple permutations. Thus, the violence that conditions the (en)gendering of Blackness is situated by the overdetermination of gender as an essence based in a biologically rooted sociogenic principle of sexual mutuality, which always returns to a Human homeostasis parasitic on Black exclusion for its terrain of intelligibility and subject making. The excising of Blackness from the Human condition of gendering and its conflicts is buttressed and maintained by the gratuity of Black bodily mutilations that are explored throughout this book and described as a structure of racial sexuation.

Blackness was ushered into the New World as the stained and marked flesh of sexual openness and violability, a condition that prevails regardless of sex or gender designations or attempts at self-making. Which is to say, perceivable womanhood or manhood for Black people does not make up the essential quality or differentiation of sexual suffering. Instead, the attempt at fixing violation within those categories leads to a neurosis that turns back on itself and leans on binary expectations in an attempt to make sense of suffering that cannot help but to fall outside of the assumptive logics of cis-gendering.

Black Feminism Beyond Binarism

The framing of the primary intervention of Black feminist theory as redeeming the status of the "silent and suffering Black woman" is an interpretive ghettoization that some Black feminists have spent well over half a century theorizing against.[53] The foregrounding of some, rather than all, Black feminists here is to acknowledge that there are divergent approaches, intellectual schisms, and various methods of thought encapsulated under the rubric of Black feminism.[54] This point does not challenge or change the argument offered in this chapter, but maintains that Black feminist theory is and has been operable towards other modes of analyzing sexual force that do not uphold Black cis-womanhood as its historical makings, present assumptions, and theoretical longings. I contend that contemporary Black thought has entered a vexed relationship with the deification of, rather than critical engagement with, Black feminist theory and its predominate anchors, Black women, transmasculine, non-binary, and queer people.

Theory, especially when produced by highly regarded thinkers, is left unmoved and seemingly considered untouchable. From my position, Black feminist theory is a critical analysis of the world, and not a practice in perfecting theoretical replication. How does one think with, through, and against vectors of Black feminist thought as a political commitment towards undoing the hold of the slave ship? How does one perform this work while also being mindful of the conditions of gender that may render some thought more disagreeable because of the positionality of its producers? I will say that no single theory or theorist, including me, has their pulse situated completely on the problem. Though some shatter previously held perspectives in a manner that produces new portals and entry points for critical analysis. Lastly, one can find value in thought, while maintaining that aspects require additional critique to respect that there may be other ways of seeing that serve to further disrupt the opacity of antiblackness.

Nonetheless, privileging *the* contribution of Black feminism as the refashioning of Black womanhood anew misaligns fleshly form for structure. Although the status of the Black/slave female, most specifically in the contexts of slavery, colonialism, and their afterlives, amplifies the contradictions of prevailing discourses of racial, gendered, and sexual violence, this figure should not be held as the permanent fixture or truth of Black feminist thought. Black feminism need not be a placeholder to perform demonstrative concern for Black women as sympathetic, additive, and inclusive subjects who are misaligned or forgotten. Interrogations that ask how the Black woman came to *be*, rather than presuppose an inherent naturalness to her to levy arguments against erasure, precondition the possibility to deterritorialize orders of thought. Which is to say, Black feminisms contain a potential disruption to knowledge, the capacity to critically move with, through, and against questions relating to ontology as it relates to sex/gender emergences and foreclosures. This serves to disimbricate theory from a reliance on womanhood as critical emphasis while not discounting the importance of the labors of critical analyses that substantiate and/or undo the assumed value of form and meaning.

The conceptual necessity of writing a radically different script on Black gender serves to embody antagonistic agitations as productive for thought. What would it mean to lead with the unknown rather than to refuse it? Reflecting upon the matter of the female slave does not necessitate that theory hold onto gender categories as fixed presuppositional renderings of "real" forms. Black feminist theories that contend with fungibility and the fluid status of Black gender must in many ways provide space for the expansion of gendered (im)possibilities in the order of thought. This must occur beyond the inadvertent or intentional upholding of cis-binarisms, as the (un)spoken given and assumed locus from which the policed boundaries of Blackness emanate. Appearances of Black people and discussions of Blackness in the historical record in fact suggest quite otherwise: that the prolonged fixation with and mutation of Blackness disallowed Black people to exist uncontested in cis-gendered identities.[55] In this respect, the pliability of Black feminist theory represents the embrace of a fungible order of thought that is malleable in attending to the (dis)appearances of relational, competing, and unnamed fleshly forms. Thus, when the technologies of violence shift from slavery, to reconstruction, Jim Crow, mass incarceration, and unbridled fascism, what constitutes the violence of Black gender cannot presuppose a form. Furthermore, there should be a weariness about projecting womanhood or manhood as biocentric constitutions, lived experiences, or possessed identities in thought. Rather, if we are to attune to suffering, Black womanhood and manhood demand disaggregation from the order of things. That is, these categories should not be privileged as sacred but understood as conditions that are produced from violence. They also carry the potential to obscure violence when elevated in thought as incontestable through the desire to extend care and protection to conditions that have been so often violated. What emerges here is that the polarity of gender, in its binary form, will not allow thought to erode its contended importances. If categories like Black woman and Black man are figured in the order of thought as erosive rather than redemptive, Black gender theory, or Black feminism, functions to provide a more expansive and nonexclusive discussion on Black engendering. In this respect, asking what the conditions of Black suffering are, from a Black feminist perspective, has the potential to move with a very different current.

Three
Aborting the Slave Mother

The last chapter ended with a critical examination of Black feminist approaches to gender and slavery. This chapter considers the status of the female slave through an interrogation of three tropes with which she is associated: the slave mother, the breeder, and the mammy. For each, I consider how the female slave lacks symbolic capacity for representational singularity. I also clarify how the womb is a voided maternal space where intelligible subjectivity cannot emerge given the possessed form of Black exteriority that exceeds the relations of plantation sexual arrangements. Lastly, this chapter ends with a mediation on the first U.S. anti-miscegenation law to consider the paternal status of the male slave as essential to the inheritability of captive status and the reproduction of gendered, sexual, and racial desires in the New World.

Like the case of Sarah, the escaped female slave in the runaway slave ad discussed at the beginning of Chapter 2, there are many suspended absences in the archive deputized to elicit coherence in the face of unspeakable violation. One of the most circulated and wagered upon suspended absences is the case of Margaret Garner. On January 30, 1856, the Cincinnati Daily Gazette published the following: "We learned the mother of the dead child acknowledged she killed it and that her determination was to kill all the children and then destroy herself rather than return to slavery."[1] The slave mother was Garner.[2] Having escaped a plantation in Kentucky, Garner, a twenty-two-year-old pregnant female slave, crossed an ice bridge into Ohio along with four other adults and four children. Upon facing her (re)capture, Garner brandished a knife and slit the throat of her two-year-old daughter

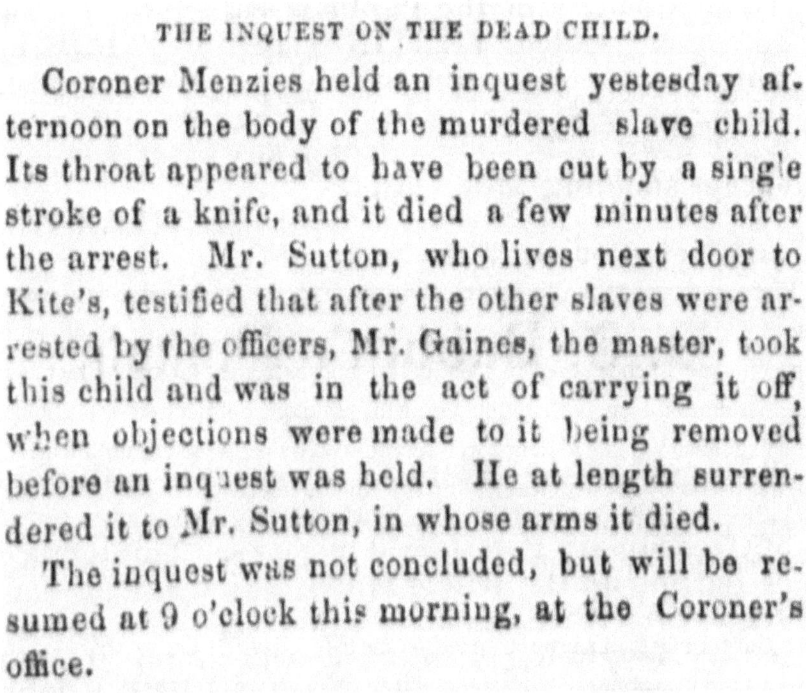

> **THE INQUEST ON THE DEAD CHILD.**
>
> Coroner Menzies held an inquest yesterday afternoon on the body of the murdered slave child. Its throat appeared to have been cut by a single stroke of a knife, and it died a few minutes after the arrest. Mr. Sutton, who lives next door to Kite's, testified that after the other slaves were arrested by the officers, Mr. Gaines, the master, took this child and was in the act of carrying it off, when objections were made to it being removed before an inquest was held. He at length surrendered it to Mr. Sutton, in whose arms it died.
>
> The inquest was not concluded, but will be resumed at 9 o'clock this morning, at the Coroner's office.

Figure 2. "The Inquest on the Dead Child," *Anti-slavery bugle*, February 2, 1856. Source: *Anti-slavery bugle*. (New-Lisbon, Ohio), February 2, 1856. Chronicling America: Historic American Newspapers. Lib. of Congress. https://chroniclingamerica.loc.gov/lccn/sn83035487/1856-02-02/ed-1/seq-3/. Public Domain.

Mary, then turned the knife towards three other children.[3] By admission she killed one child. But given the chance, she would have killed them all.[4]

In Garner's case, infanticide does not just kill the slave child, it is also a metacommentary on motherhood as aborted slave potential or signification. The coroner performed a partial inquest on the death of Mary the afternoon after she died. Testimony about the events of the previous night were gathered from a neighbor, Mr. Sutton. He attested that Mary was retrieved by her master, Mr. Gaines, shortly after her throat was slit by Margaret. It is unclear who contested Gaines taking possession of the child; however, there were contentions expressed about his doing so. As people disputed whether the child should be removed before a formal investigation of her death was carried out, she died in the arms of Mr. Sutton. This all occurred shortly after Margaret was arrested. She was never questioned about the events of that fateful night despite her actions being central to the inquiry and her relationship to the child.

The inquest into the death of the child excludes Garner from the fact inquiry.[5] Despite having produced Mary, Garner is denied right to the child by her action but most centrally, by her status as property. Under these conditions, she is not a mother of the children, if mother is a proper noun connoting kinship as right and personal possession. While it might be obvious to conclude Garner acted in a deliberate and extreme fashion against her captive status, even, perhaps, engaging in a uniquely political act, infanticide for female slaves is a violent force reproduced by the absolute nullification of her power and resistance. Killing the child is referential to the individual desires of Garner and of the female slave as captive fertility, writ large. The crux here is captive fertility is as much a statement about birth and rearing as it is about death and killing.

Garner exists in a liminal space, as she is faced with a choice that lacks a clear moral response: return the children to slavery or kill them. There are no easy answers to this ethical quandary. Her structural predicament as a historical figure, who pushes thought beyond assumed limits of what is understood as right, wrong, or just a reaction, is repeatedly called upon to scandalize thought with regard to the utility of violence for the slave mother. It is largely perceived that Garner's children were the offspring of forced sexual copulation. This evidence is based on an account given by Luce Stone Blackwell, an anti-slavery activist who addressed the court on behalf of Garner. Blackwell emphasizes the particularly light complexions of the faces of Garner's children and speculates she may have been impregnated multiple times by Archibald Gaines, her master.[6]

The story of Garner, one pivotal to the enactment and publicity surrounding the Fugitive Slave Act of 1850, was rediscovered by Toni Morrison, as an editor at Random House, and became the inspiration for her Pulitzer Prize winning 1987 novel *Beloved*.[7] Arguably, Morrison is singlehandedly responsible for the presence of Garner in post-1980s Black feminist thought.[8] The reasons for this are as much about the particulars of the life of Garner and the event that lodged her into the historical record as it is for the many things that cannot be said about the value of her life and legacy. As Morrison notes around the time of *Beloved*'s publication, "One doesn't know the actual experience of being a slave. You only know about it. It is abstract."[9] Thus Garner, a real person, becomes both a fiction and a fantasy representing the investments of Black feminist thought to contend with the unknowable constraints of gender for female slaves. As we reflect on Garner's commission of infanticide, her ultimate return to slavery on a plantation in Mississippi and uneventful death from typhoid fever should also be considered.[10] While we know little about her life upon being returned to slavery, the same can also be said about her motivations to kill the child(ren).[11]

Garner becomes a powerful referent given the historical content her story provides for *Beloved*, as well as many theoretical works. While Sethe, the protagonist in *Beloved*, is not a literal representation of Garner, they share the same ethical plight of committing infanticide. Critical introspections about Sethe have been written at length.[12] Despite inspiring so much discourse, Garner is less a subject and more an object of history whose voice is nearly absent in the archive. Her story is reproduced by way of abbreviated transcriptions and inferences that are based on how she is presented in the historical record via newspaper articles, court proceedings, and trial witness accounts.[13] In the literary analysis, Sethe and Garner are frequently treated as similar to the extent that extrapolating the qualities of sameness are assumed rather than engaged. In likening the predicament of Sethe and Garner, Sharon Holland notes,

> Sethe establishes herself as mother when she claims the "right" to kill—to possess this body in the literal sense of the word. She becomes a "mother" when she kills her daughter, when the local papers recognize her as the author/mother of both the act of infanticide and the birthing of her baby. Because of the violence of this assertion and the myriad of questions it produces, it is no wonder that Morrison resurrects the spirit of the Margaret Garner story to challenge the boundaries of language and the limits of mother-love.[14]

We can ask, what about Garner and her story challenges and places limits upon the crux of slave mothering as acts of love? To kill and attempt to kill the child(ren) is a fervent reaction; a peculiar act of mother-love.[15] Taking a dagger to the neck of a nursing baby and bashing the other children with a shovel are no passive acts. Yet analyses of her deathly act are so frequently supplanted with focus on the question of motherhood where Black feminist theorists argue, "The most extreme version of a Black mother's radical refusal of racialized kinship might be seen in the case of Margaret Garner."[16]

In this calculation, Garner's actions as refusal, radicalization, and repulsion of circumstance determines her slave mothering as radical potential. Deadly force as a choice is disappeared. Violence is posed as a fact of the encounter—between Garner, her captors, and the children. This reading positions violence as a purely affecting experience for the slave, situating the slave as an inherently anti-violent actor who is a passive receptacle of violence unless extreme circumstances arise. While this might generate some sympathy towards Garner and other female slaves, the significance of the use of violence by Garner as a metacommentary on the impossibility of motherhood are nullified when the context of its usages is directed to another end point. Violence in this respect is merely considered a breaking point, an extreme response as opposed to more damningly the truth of Black (non)existence being revealed. The implicit passivity granted to Garner by marking infanticide as shocking radical spectacle rather than as commonplace practice is ill attuned to the historical record, where blood and carnage are tantamount to the most ordinary and mundane. Speaking for herself, Garner suggests infanticide a common act of slave necessity. In a news clipping recalled by Morrison, Garner's brief statement includes "I will not let those children live how I have."[17]

Slavery makes the use of violence by the captor *and* the slave an ordinary and routine response. Slavery is violence and the only response is violence. Violent acts do not make the slave a martyr or more sympathetic figure as violence is the predicament of the condition. The extent to which the slave is positioned to react and respond by way of violence is infinitely dispersed. Which is to say, the extremity of slavery preconditions the extremities of slave responses. Under this pretense, acts that are morally reprehensible by contemporary standards, and thus are labeled extreme, were not more radical or oppositional to the institution of slavery.[18] Like Newton's third law of motion, where force is applied, the force is returned. The vexed nature of this is that the master does not solely spill blood or force "carnal knowledge" upon others.[19] If we can contend that slavery is a paradigm of violence, then we must also contend that the worst of its actions are not distributed along an even axis vis-à-vis the master onto the slave. The slave enacts violence too, in direct response to its condition and ordinary circumstances. So is with the case of Garner, where one child dies by deliberate actions, another child dies by happenstance. In the latter circumstance, Garner is noted as delighting in "an expression of joy" at the news of the death of her other daughter Cilla, following the decision by the courts that Garner was a rightful slave and should be returned to slavery following her fateful escape.[20] In this sense the children continued to die and their deaths brought forth for Garner a monstrous satisfaction and gratification.[21]

In critical texts, Garner is committed to a passing allegorical reference that connects the fiction of history, i.e., *Beloved*, to the gruesome content of the archive. Although the full extent of her intentions is unknown, speculation about her desires is debated in nineteenth-century pro- and anti-slavery political writing, as well as in post-1980s Black feminist literature.[22] In the latter, Garner is positioned as a representative model of unimaginable strife and perseverance in the Black feminist tradition. She represents a hero and an insurgent. As Alys Eve Weinbaum argues, "Garner's act of violent insurgency ought to be understood as part and parcel of a sustained and polyvocal black feminist mediation on sex and reproduction in bondage."[23] The murder of the child is seen as a final act, a definitive moment of response to the unethical nature of slavery and its sexual arrangements.

Yet Sara Clarke Kaplan argues, "The violent disruption of the logics and structures of slavery initiated by the enslaved mother's infanticidal act is an instance of insurgent potential, not a promise of political transcendence."[24] Insurgency here is not a heroic act from which political possibility is entrenched on the other side, but, as Kaplan goes on to assert, "Margaret Garner is sent downriver to die."[25] Death here is a crucial touchpoint. The act is deathly as is the descriptive quality of slavery. Kaplan moves thought closer towards thinking death as an inescapable drive of slave reproductivity rather than as an insurgent politic of becoming. Nonetheless, Kaplan holds onto the mother as a descriptor to make sense of the act. Infanticide is given texture and made representable through the "enslaved mother" as its own political prescription, where the proclamation by Spillers of "claiming the monstrosity (of a female right to 'name')" is projected into a future potential.[26] The female slave is called upon in her sexual and reproductive violations as the one who "reconfigures normative conceptions of kinship, of maternal love and social death," thus providing the content for "making new possible modes of being."[27] In this argument the insurgent is extinguished to reposition the mother as the possible and violence as a step towards freedom and world-building. Both insurgency and mother are made operative through reclaiming the act of violence and interpreting infanticide as a politic of retribution and reparation.

In the poem "the mother," Gwendolyn Brooks animates a crisis of abortion by drawing out contradictions in mourning lives that never were. She writes,

> If I poisoned the beginnings of your breaths,
> Believe that even in my deliberateness I was not deliberate.
> Though why should I whine,
> Whine that the crime was other than mine?—
> Since anyhow you are dead.
> Or rather, or instead,
> You were never made.
> But that too, I am afraid,
> Is faulty: oh, what shall I say, how is the truth to be said?
> You were born, you had a body, you died.
> It is just that you never giggled or planned or cried.[28]

Throughout the poem, death is an uncertain landing point. As such it appears as contention and disavowal as the speaker tries to name the consequences of the act of aborting. To make death real, as in give it a feeling, then life must be imagined and also ascribed a texture, an affect. But this affect, these emotional associations are the possessive fantasies of the speaker. The child is a delirious thought. The absent child is a figment of guilt and anxiety about an action that assumedly halted a becoming. A thwarted emergence, the relationship between "the mother" and child overdetermines the act of abortion to produce a substance to authorize the performance of grief and sadness. The speaker emotes that "you were born," although the poem begins by asserting "abortions will not let you forget." The antagonism here is that an abortion is not a birth; as such, the speaker is not a mother. As the stanzas progress, the abortion is supplanted as fluctuating forms of death and loss. The speaking subject is possessed by the question, a mother of what? In response, the form of a mother, like the child, is imagined through guilt, projection, and, ultimately, nothingness.

Motherhood for Garner, like "the mother" of Brooks's poem, is also a figment of imagination. Her motherhood is claimed not despite of the extreme act of infanticide but through the very act of killing the child and the attempt to kill the others. As Garner is symbolically deployed by Black feminism as a figure of motherhood pushed to its limits, this excavation and reimagination leaves the children untheorized. Which is to say, the children in Garner's story are objects to the point of asserting her motherhood up against a violent structure that renders the category of mother a white racial form of becoming. Just as the poem is not about the child, readings of Garner as a heroine are not about the children. These readings forcefully revise motherhood as a primal condition to assert the slave not as a "breeder," but as a formidable mother, even in the midst of deadly childless desires. This point is evidenced by the fact that the fantasy work about what makes Garner a mother is not projected around the lives and lost life potential of the children. Arguably the mother–child relation could be elaborated through the fugitive act, an attempted flight towards freedom, but its potential significance is thwarted by death and clarified by the joy Garner expresses at seeing the death of another one of her children after she killed Mary. Corporal death becomes the substance of her motherly necessity, the extreme potential of her mother-love, serving to retool the racial constriction that maternal capacity is voided for the captive, even in flight. The oxymoronic nature of naming Garner a mother, as a possessive claim of radical possibility, abandons inquest into how social death is the context of her conceiving offspring through forced copulation. It also reveals a theoretical refusal to engage female slaves' desire to rid themselves of the imposed burden of children.

More, analyzing Garner's actions and words as motivated by motherhood suggests a disavowal of kinship as a racially sexuated designation paradigmatically denied to slaves. The "childless mother," observes Brigette Fielder, is a space of structural reinvention, which, "despite kinlessness or the 'loss' of one's mother (though a real and affectively valid experience of antiblack violence), extending toward larger generational scales reveals a kind of racial prescience."[29] The terrain of being a slave, which is constituted by endless, or mindless, multiplication and reproduction, is retooled into a category of productive excess, what Fielder terms "kinfullness," to the point of making kin differently and challenging racial sexual force.[30]

Reading Garner's infanticide as an act of kinfullness offers up an extreme counterexample to dispossess the force of the peculiar institution. The dispossessing violence that forced pregnancy and birth onto slaves, in a manner akin to automation, stripped the birthing slaves of the power to determine the status of the offspring. While this, and the sexual violability of female slaves are widely recognized by Black feminist scholars, explaining Garner's murder of the child on the grounds of her being a mother runs the risk of disavowing the paradigmatic arrangements of slavery. Asserting slave motherhood requires that the stakes of this motherhood ascend to revolutionary proportions capable of offsetting and upending the ironclad structural nature of the female slave's sexual violability.

Is the infanticide committed by Garner an act of insurgency and heroism meant to secure her freedom from sexual violability, the freedom of her children from the same fate, and/or as a symbolic placeholder for a future possibility where similar acts may stave off or undo further captivity? This is a question about impact and temporality. A revised question asks is Garner a symbol of the past or a force necessary for the advancement of a different project altogether? Given the gravity of infanticide, it is curious that feminist scholars conclude it to be an act of heroism—which is an estimation of bravery—rather than one of desperation or nihilism.[31] Given that Garner killed a slave child likely born of sexual violation, heroism or insurgency, as political philosophical determinants, imposes a hopefulness upon the act such that sexualized violability morphs into an action toward agentic subjectivity or recuperated motherhood. This rendering of Garner does not, ultimately, disavow the force of sexual violability and openness, but it does cement forced copulation as essential to her mothering or mother-love. Indeed, the "mulatto" children that give Garner her claim to motherhood are also proof of her violation. To put it bluntly, if sexual violence is what made the children, it is also the context upon which motherhood for Garner is performed and claimed.

At the center of her reclaimed becoming—a mother pushed to infanticide—is still an unreconciled relationship to her sexual vulnerability and how that sexual status extended into the absent life potentials of the dead baby and the other children. To claim Garner as a slave mother, violence is refashioned as her potential rather than her unmaking. Killing the children, then, is the essential quality of her intelligibility as a racialized, gendered subject. Situating Garner through the symbolics of motherhood is an attempt at coherency. The mother as a conceptual framework gives her act a political impetus or meaning. Without adherence to the category of mother, her act is simply one among many in a saturated terrain of slavery and its violence.

As argued in Chapter 1, sexual objectification does not require inaction or docility. The complication and the burden of this analysis is that racial sexuation constitutes the condition of the slave regardless of the response. This is what Black feminist projects often seek to disavow, that acts of force from "below" can be meaningless in the face of a structure that anticipates response and revision. It is curious how infanticide, the act of aborting the child(ren), somehow intensely preserves Garner as a mother. The killing of the child(ren) also presumably aborts the slave ~~mother~~ or makes an honest statement about the incapacity of the slave to exist as kin. It is revealing that in most Black feminist accounts of Garner's murderous refusal to see the children returned to slavery, the mother has not been aborted. Arguably, Black feminism cannot refuse the slave mother because the term is bound with the field's consideration of slavery. The mother is the most pervasive theoretic deployed by Black feminists to articulate what plenitudes of affection and kin existed prior to slavery, the severity of loss for the sexual captive, and the possibility and potentials of future Black relationality that break the sexual bonds of the plantation.

Social Death and the Womb

Social death, slavery, and gender as a relation was animated as a contested milieu by the introduction of afro-pessimism as a field of thought. While there are competing ideas of what afro-pessimism is, the theory was first elucidated in detail in Frank B. Wilderson III's *Red, White, and Black: Cinema and the Structure of U.S. Antagonisms*.[32] Afro-pessimism is described as produced by "theorists of Black positionality who share Fanon's insistence that, though Blacks are indeed sentient beings, the structure of the entire world's semantic field ... is sutured by anti-Black solidarity."[33] While Black positionality is of particular concern to afro-pessimists, slavery, for Wilderson, is the harbinger that grants the world its violent antiblack orbit. Of the many responses to this structural analysis of Blackness and violence is the repeated question of whether afro-pessimism does not or cannot account for gender. This question is belated in many respects, as Wilderson repeatedly addresses gender throughout the text.[34] Nevertheless, social death brackets how gender is explored by afro-pessimism and serves as the analytic to theorize the structural antagonism between Black women and white women. Wilderson argues,

> Civil society's phallic wound is a laceration between, on the one hand, the open access to Black women's "sexuality"—marked by their open vulnerability to the violence of the slaveocracy—a sexual access so open that it spreads across boundless space and endless time. This sexuality has no coordinates and as such it cannot provide the White male with the satisfaction of access: there is no woman's "body," thus there was no sexual "event." On the other hand, on the other side of the phallic wound's laceration is the White "woman," the antithesis of a sexual access so open it is meaningless: White "woman's" sexuality is so meaningful as to be inaccessible, forbidden (until marriage).[35]

The use of scare quotes throughout this passage points to Wilderson's most searing arguments; the terms situated between these markings are obsolete. Sexuality for Black women exists under erasure, where she is devoid of a body. Womanhood for the white woman serves to shield her deputized position within the white racial order as structurally enabled. Patriarchal violence against her may be disabling, but it is not disempowering.[36] Contrary to feminist arguments that a woman's sexuality is subordinated to that of the phallus, racial slavery imparts upon white women proprietary claim to the violence of the phallic wound, as Wilderson charts here, but also the violence of the maternal or the domestic. Deploying the phallic wound as white racial power, for which gender is an obsolete distinction, pushes back against the feminist insistence that patriarchy binds all women in relations. The sexual openness and vulnerability of Black women should make clear that the essential violence of the phallic wound is antiblackness. The coherence of the white "woman," whose sexuality is deemed "meaningful as to be inaccessible," is derived from the sexual accessibility of the Blackness.

Slavery provides the context for this argument to take shape, as does the theorization of the racial and gender dimensions of slavery provided by Black feminist scholars like Saidiya V. Hartman and Hortense J. Spillers. However, there is a conversation here, as the above passage is the result of Wilderson carefully parsing the work of Spillers. The female slave as a "condition of mindless fertility" is where afro-pessimism critically contends with Black feminism, by way of Spillers, to consider how antiblackness levies a distinction between the symbolics of white maternity and motherhood up against the Black female as "hyperbolically sexual."[37] For Spillers, loss or dispossession are identified in exact terms, motherhood as the consecration of the uterine function. "Robbery," or theft, observes Wilderson, is "the metaphor Spillers uses to epitomize this coherence."[38] Spillers states that being "robbed of the benefits of the 'reproduction of mother,' is, consequently, the very negation of femaleness that accrues as the peculiar property of Anglo-American woman."[39] The mother breeches womanhood and femaleness or gendering and (un)gendering. To say this otherwise, the mother is the link between freedom and captivity.

In an examination of Black transness as operable fungibility, C. Riley Snorton expresses contention with Wilderson's engagement of Spillers. By "posing gender as contingent on blackness," Snorton argues, social death "becomes incapable of perceiving un/gendering as a mode of violence that makes black fungibility palpable."[40] Afro-pessimism theorizes Blackness as an essential antagonism to the structuring logic of civil society and positions gender and sexuality as contingent riders for the slave, which is to say, gender and sexuality are important but inessential for contending with the truth of the paradigm of slavery. In this respect, the slave is captive because it is Black, not because of its relationship to a sex/gender paradigm. This assessment, according to Snorton, is flawed given how the transness of Blackness deploys fungibility as indexical to flight as an evasion of capture or ontological determinism. Snorton arrives at this critique of Wilderson by way of the question of freedom, noting that for afro-pessimism, "Black freedom is thinkable only in terms of categories of being."[41] Whether freedom is explored through social death and political ontology or un/gendering embodied against totalizing violence, each position is unclear as to what continues to reproduce the necessity of its articulation with respect to gender. Why is political ontology unable to evade an engagement with gender? Likewise, why is the palpability of Black fungibility, and, might I add, Black accumulation, entangled with the violence of un/gendering?

Although Wilderson and Snorton may diverge on the question of gender and its utility, they converge when considering the significance of the mother.

Each of their theories is inaugurated by the absent Black mother, lending coherence to their claims. Which is to say, the absent Black mother is the staging ground of coherence for the enunciation of an ensemble of questions pertaining to a structure of Black non-being or freedom. Regardless of what each theory assumes about the meaning of Black maternal erasure, the paradox of fertility without maternal capacity allows the gravity of Black suffering to enter a realm of meaning. Wilderson takes up Spillers's theorization of white motherhood as the violent juxtaposition to slave female's sexual vulnerability. Snorton, on the other hand, turns to early twentieth-century Black autobiography and social theory to consider the paradoxes of Black maternal figures, where "her figuration . . . is the palpable experience of the phenomenon known as black sociality, which occurs even under the conditions of social death."[42] In either case, social death is the crux of the mother's functions, by which the Black mother is made obsolete or is made the progenitor of vexed sociality. Spillers provides the anchor by which the mother is deployed conversely as the centripetal force of antagonism or palpability. In respect to the latter, Snorton argues,

> The black mother's gender is vestibular, a translocation marked by a capacity to reproduce beings and objects. But one should not mistake her figuration for the real. As Du Bois relates in his damning of Reconstruction and its inevitable demise, the inhabitation of the structural position of blackness produces black gender as "mother-like," a concept he invokes to describe how inhabiting blackness produces not a gender in a dominant symbolic sense but a figuration of gender that is inextricably linked to a metaphysics of time.[43]

While the Black/slave mother may not constitute the real, the *fantasy* of her power remains ironclad over the relationship between the transfiguration of objects into beings or the movement between slavery and freedom. However, it is less the Black/slave mother's existence or life that marks this transition. Instead, it is her death, loss, or disappearance that stages the breeding grounds for how slaveness enters into perceivable Black personhood contained by a deep sense of longing. Death or incapacitation of the mother marks a rupture. Whether positioned as foreclosure or possibility, the dissolution of the mother is paramount to the staging of gendered life inside, outside, or in excess of slavery. When social death is employed as an analytic to assess the sex/gender function of the slave, we can arrive at a more definitive statement about what the sexualization of the slave as mother achieves. A theory of social death tells us that the slave loses its mother by way of natal alienation. This association is guided by an unspoken assumption, that the mother is omnipotent. The assertion that the mother existed prior to slavery, such that the slave can lose her, or that the matter of the mother carries the kinship and constitutive anchor that grants her value outside of a slave society, requires a faith-based associative logic.

In reading autobiography and Black theoretical works, Snorton highlights the corporeal death of the mother as a symbolic moment of impasse and transformation. Likewise, in Snorton's theoretical text, Black maternal death provides the context for revisioning and declaration. As Snorton ends a section with definitive points on the meaning of Black maternal death in the autobiographies *Up from Slavery*, by Booker T. Washington, and *Autobiography of an Ex-Colored Man*, by James Weldon Johnson, these symbolics become the grounds upon which the palpability of Black transness is enunciated as possibility. He asserts, "This reconstitution of Blackness signaled a return to the scene of 'female flesh ungendered' to create blackness anew."[44] By "this" he means "Blackness, as a condition of possibility that made transness conceivable in the twilight of formal slavery."[45] The interest here is not with assessing the truthfulness of this logical framing but rather it is curious about how and why the Black/slave mother continues to animate Black feminist and gender theory with respect to the question of what is (im)possible with respect to Black life and social existence.

In many respects, Black feminism carries forward the drive of the questions regarding the mother and mothering. Hartman notably titles her second monograph *Lose Your Mother: A Journey Along the Atlantic Slave Route*. The text looms the anxiety and fracture surrounding the notion that "to lose your mother was to be denied your kin, country, and identity. To lose your mother was to forget your past."[46] But is the mother a link to the past or an anxiety about the present? What, in fact, is the past if the severance of the slave from all prior relationality, which constitutes natal alienation, is total, thus making the loss utterly unimaginable? When Hartman arrives at Elmina armed with ambivalence, angst, and sorrow, the propulsion of these affects is from the current condition of her life and, most importantly, from a rift that severs what she perceived should be the relationality between her as a Black American and those who reside on the Continent. "When the children of Elmina christened me a stranger, they called me by my ancestors' name."[47] She *is* a stranger, and her ancestors are not indicative of the real but are of her desire to rupture slavery's hold on the present. What may have existed prior to the epochal rupture of transatlantic slavery is impossible for her to know. There is simply no way to recover the knowledge systems or referents that could confirm if the mother was there in another space and time. This is a reference to the mother as symbolic power and privilege, not as a biological function.

Spillers argues, "Motherhood as female bloodright is outraged, is denied, at the *very same time* that it becomes the founding term for human and social enactment."[48] As the defining term of the female slave's dispossession, motherhood also determined freedom prior to her individual bondage or the paradigm. The loss of the mother is often read along teleological lines, in which the slave is a disruption to a prior plenitude of existence that is ruptured by captivity. Slavery's valuation is retroactively (re)produced and placed upon African relational bonds that are granted a singular association or lineage. In this respect, Africa, as a generalized space, is fantasized as the maternal. How the slave is conceived prior to its captivity inadvertently reproduces it as the embodiment of precisely the type of sexuality empowered by the plantation arrangement, the mother as the predominating body of kinship and social relationality. The calling upon Africa as the pre-event to mark slavery as the crisis event of motherhood sutures and advances a politic not from the past, but of modernity.

To note, Hartman disavows positivist associations of reclamation and restoration of a prior African topology. She writes against a more salient Black feminist tradition, which defines the mother as the figure of loss and dispossession, where slavery is "the four-hundred-year holocaust that wrenched tens of millions of Africans from their Mother, their biological mothers as well as their Motherland, in a disorganized and monstrous fashion."[49] Arguing that a finite Africanness is a fictive kinship, Hartman states, "The vision of an African continental family or a sable race standing shoulder to shoulder was born by captives, exiles, and orphans in the aftermath of the Atlantic slave trade."[50] Here, Hartman suggests the African mother is not lost, but imagined. If the mother is the glue that binds and reproduces the kinship of Human community, it is contended as that which must also bind captives as kin in resistance and opposition to their gratuitous violation.

The mother then is a politic made operable and palpable by slavery in that "racial solidarity was expressed in the language of kinship because it both evidenced the wound and attempted to heal it."[51]

Contrary to Hartman, but also with similar awareness of the past as irreconcilable loss, Alice Walker imagines the mother as a pristine creator. She asserts, "Guided by my heritage of a love of beauty and a respect for strength—in search of my mother's garden, I found my own."[52] Walker is honest that her mother, the past, is her own present desire or dream making. She locates it centuries ago in a generalized fictive homeland, stating, "And perhaps in Africa over two hundred years ago, there was just such a mother."[53] The word "perhaps" guides the remainder of *In Search of Our Mothers' Gardens*, where "perhaps" clarifies the mother is as uncertain as she is a fantasy.

Overall, motherhood as a politic is perceived as a counterhegemonic strike against the denied access of female slaves to determine the status of their offspring. Despite the primacy given to the maternal, the political anxiety to define the female slave as a mother is not animated by the real, but by a projected fantasy. The angst about the power of the mother is an anxious relationship to the idea that the female slave is void of any sustainable meaning on her own terms. To say this otherwise, motherhood as female birthright is its own projected fantasy, where life is confined to the reproductive function of the female body. The birthright of the female slave cannot be denied if it was never her possession, unless, of course, the assumption is that motherhood as a birthright is fundamental to sentient beingness. Rather, the denial is a relation that reanimates the fall into obsolescence by simply attempting to think of the female slave as a violable subject. Her violation is perceivable insofar as she is believed to be dispossessed of "the founding term for human and social enactment," which was established precisely because she could not possess it.[54] The female slave is racially sexuated into a structural position where voided motherhood is a permanent relation. She cannot break free from this bond because this term holds her condition captive in language. The female slave was never a mother. The slave cannot find the mother. The search for the mother is the search for slavery. As Spillers has so aptly noted, "'mother' and enslavement are indistinct categories."[55]

From this vantage point, slavery does not make the slave lose their mother. Rather, slavery bars the slave from *embodying* the mother as an antidote to the violence that distinguishes some uteruses as affectable organs and others as the wombs of ontological making. Conversely, the mother indexes the violence of womanhood as an antiblack configured space that (re)produces the plantation mistress as distinctly not a female slave and thus inaccessible as hyperbolic sexual openness. The desire for the mother is (re)produced and incessantly driven to underwrite the sexual stain of female slaveness and transmute it into the sexuality of womanhood. By this I mean, the mother functions as a drive to rewrite the slave outside of affectable femaleness into womanhood, which embodies variations of capacities for consent, volition, and recognition. Every time the concept of the slave mother is approached, it is foreclosed by violence that cannot be articulated within the frame of its announcement. The slave mother cannot be satisfied. Rather than a search for truth, this drive is catalyzed by a generalized anxiety about the nothingness of her fertility. Nothingness has no meaning. This is not the same as suggesting that it lacks form, implication, or emotion. Instead, mindless fertility signals unending meanings, where the fertility of the slave is granted an overproduction of valuation to the effect of producing an illogical referent incapable of identifying the violence as an event, or events, that are generative of a coherent causal and effectual relation.

Black feminism, then, has tasked itself with locating the arrival points and departures of an existence that cannot be represented because it does not exist outside of the anxiety and fantasy that constitute the existence of its own field. This is to say the moralization of sexual injury becomes the (in)stability of a field of thought as it repulses the notion that pure violation can constitute the status of any being. This political refusal buttresses itself repeatedly by imposing positivist action upon the female slave that inadvertently illumines an aphasic essence to her existence and the unrepresentable descriptive quality of her victimization by an unbending history.

In this sense, aborting the slave ~~mother~~ means both acknowledging how the transference of the womb or belly is a critical part of the history of slavery, while also not subtending all other forms of transference as insignificant in relationship to womb/belly, as the incontestable pinnacle of slave-making. The Black womb/belly is also a disregarded ripped apart piece of flesh, even as its reproductive capacities are tethered, at times, to higher (economic) valuations. Secondly, it is also a call to decenter the feminized body as the primary site of violation, in its physiognomic sense. This point is not a call to transfer the focus to another gland, another form of tissue, another organ, or even to the masculinized body, but to proceed to think flesh without a body in a way that centralizes fungibility and refuses the persistent tendency of thinking the Black ~~body~~ as unrealized Human gender capacity.[56] The value of each capacity attributed to the body must be questioned, so as to not superimpose meanings and significations onto Black flesh that are derived from its gendered deracination. Flesh without a body, in the order of thought, concedes that the womb is the "literal" organ of some Black bodies as well as the psychic possession of the slave estate. The inability of the slave to claim its organs, reproductive and other, as an internal property of its being, symbolizes that without organs there is no body, just flesh. The womb/belly, when figured in this sense, as internally dispossessed, brings to the fore the ontological absence of the slave as a metaphysical presupposition that underwrites Black gender structurally. The womb, the loins, the heart, and the blood (or any other organ, tissue, serum, or gland) of the slave are externally possessed and configured with many meanings, uses, and absences. Attempts to cohere a meaningful body against theft and interior dispossession must contend with how gender is perceived to resituate and reinvest organs into "real" and "literal" types of being. Thus, claiming the womb as a site of potentiality or mothering and care for Black women may push against sexual dispossession, while performing the reification of the body as the site that confers gender becoming and its assumed appropriate capacities.

Given these provocations, what is the place of the womb in theory? Is it to reveal that the womb is always strong and all revealing? Or is it to announce that the womb, like the flesh, is fungible? In some instances the womb is revelatory and other instances arbitrary, and can oscillate between or occupy multiple poles of signification. The womb, like Jackson's articulation of trophallaxis in her consideration of what she terms "blackfemale," represents a transference of information, though this does not imply value. Jackson argues, "trophallaxis is the giving of soma to an Other" where "pendulous breasts provided evidence that the indeterminate and contested (yet inferior) ontology of the blackfemale with respect to the discourses of species and sex/gender issued from nature itself."[57] The womb in Black feminist theory has played a central role in theorizing and accounting for the extremities of violence and also is held as a site for radical alternative potentials through marking motherhood as an inalienable right of birthing. In this sense, the material intensities of Black womanhood are taken up as psychic drivers and indicators of the value, lack of value, or revaluation placed upon biocentrism. However, I argue the mediation of material and lived experiences is tethered to psychic drives that do not prove that the Black woman is "real," which itself is constituted as an effect, but that *she* is a condition.[58] As such, the (un)naming of this condition is explanatory of many things, but is not the truth of the captive relation between antiblackness and gender. The attempt to cohere speech around the material aspects of Black women's lives as the remedy to the violent erasure of Black gendered and sexual realizations is an inadequate, or partial, inquiry into the gamut of what (does not) appear(s). Furthermore, it reifies assaults against the body as the truth of flesh. *She* transfers information through the womb/belly, though what is transferred may be the absence of relationality or may be no transmission at all.

Breeding Blur

A short excerpt lifted from the book *Unwritten History of Slavery*, a collection of 100 interviews of former slaves conducted by Ophelia Settle Egypt and Charles Johnson, was published on the website "This Cruel War."[59] The excerpt is titled "Voices of Slavery: They Were Saving Me For a Breeding Woman."[60] The name This Cruel War was a popular nineteenth-century political and colloquial reference to the Civil War, often used in songs, personal letters, and media to illustrate its intensity and dividedness.[61] The website of this name is described as an archive providing "an evidence-based exploration of the causes and ramifications of the American Civil War."[62]

"They were saving me for a breeding woman" is accompanied by an 1825 painting that features a split image of a white man embracing and kissing a female slave, and white man preparing to whip a male slave.[63] Adorned with the painted caption "Virginian Luxuries," the image highlights the luxuries of white life, the capacity for unbridled access to antiblack sex and violence. Arguably, the painting does not separate sexual violence from the spectacle of physical violence. Both encapsulate the psychosexual dynamics of slavery. The image conjoins them as the quotidian indulgences that make white life pleasurable.

"This Cruel War"—which was once easily locatable online by searching breeding and slavery—is significant insofar as it illustrates how narrative

Figure 3. Virginian Luxuries, Unidentified Artist, probably New England, ca. 1825, oil on canvas. Source: The Colonial Williamsburg Foundation. Museum Purchase. Reprinted with Permission.

attempts to articulate the essence of sexual violence under slavery by deploying a logical framing that enacts the assumption of a scandal. The slave narrative is deputized as an answer or antidote to the aphasic nature of permanent sexual force and vexed reproduction inherent to slavery. The title "They were saving me for a breeding woman," which is a statement made during an interview, is meant to produce a type of shock and, possibly, titillate. What does it mean to be held as a breeding woman? What do the conditions of this type of life reveal about the brutality of sexual violence and slavery? How does the narrator *feel* about this status? One enters the text, accompanied by these or other sets of assumptions and questions, deputized by the drive to uncover evidence about the sexual demands of the peculiar institution. The inquisition is sutured by an affect like that argued by feminist philosopher Susan Brison regarding rape, which hinges upon the claim that "imagining what it is like to be a rape victim is no simple matter, since much of what a victim goes through is unimaginable."[64] The reader of "This Cruel War" is encouraged to want to know more about the subject who is figured as a breeder, reduced primarily, and perhaps solely, to her capacity to bear offspring without a mother's claim. The excerpted title figures the text as a documentary excavation to learn more about how, as Brison suggests, "sexual violence and its aftermath raise numerous philosophical issues [about] the disintegration of the self-experienced by victims of [sexual] violence."[65]

The original slave interview, however, does not take the reader to a place and time where breeding can be located as a type of disorientation that splits the narrator between an assumption of a reproductive selfhood and the conditions of captivity. Nor does it offer an analysis of breeding as an actualization of sexual violation. In fact, there is no singular nor individualized experience(s) of sexual violence described. In the moment the narrator announces the desire of her master to keep her as a breeding woman, she goes on to say, "but by the time I was big enough I was free."[66] The narrative moves on to describe slavery and its afterlife as enmeshed in a spun web of violence that is localized around racial sexuation as a paradigmatic arrangement rather than a schematized set of events. In her account, white men and white women were both imbricated in the array of violence that conditioned the lives of slaves.

Throughout the text, the narrator provides episodic scenarios of violence. The narrative does not carry a logical throughline—cause, effect, and aftermath—with respect to violence, sexual or otherwise. Yet there is no dearth of violent examples provided, making violence and life indiscernible. The narrator begins with detailing how, upon marrying, a white man would be given by his father "a woman for a cook and she would have children right in the house by him, and his wife would have children, too."[67] Noting that once the wife caught slave children in the home, "the wife would be mean to them and make him sell them."[68] The text details how female slaves were having so many children, that in many instances it was hard to discern force from desire, stating, "Now, mind you, all of the colored women didn't have to have white men, some did it because they wanted to and some were forced."[69] While the narrator was never used as a breeder on the plantation, she was born of breeding. She stated, "My mother was born in Mississippi and brought here. My father was born in Maryland. He was an old man when he come here, but they just bought them and put them together."[70] But, as the narrator expresses, there was nothing extraordinary about her. "They would buy a fine girl and then a fine man and just put them together like cattle; they would not stop to marry them."[71]

I offer "They were saving me as a breeding woman" as an example to ask why is the sexually violated slave called upon to speak about sexual violation as interiority? Borrowing from Fanon, I would suggest what is offered here is not "a feeling of inferiority," or interiority for the matter at hand; it is a description of nonexistence.[72] There is an antagonism at the heart of the structuring logic of the "This Cruel War" post. The title is foregrounded to pose rape as the violent context of the speaker's existence, while subsequently eschewing focus from the fact that the entire narrative is steeped in violence, both sexual and otherwise, of which the narrator is a witness and not the recipient. Rather than approaching this narrative as a commentary on the gratuity of slavery's violence, as a theoretical articulation, it is taken up as a personal (re)presentation. Institutional force is rendered banal, as the tale is turned inward on the slave. How can the female slave deploy and possess a logic of suffering that is predicated on surfacing the content of who I am, by presenting a violence structurally conditioned upon what we are? As Fanon contends, "I am not a slave of the 'idea' others have of me but of my own appearance."[73] If we are to understand Black narrative (dis)appearance as both epidermalization and representational incapacitation, how might we understand the problematic positioning of this isolated narrative?

As presented by the excerpt of "They were saving me for a breeding woman" published on "This Cruel War," breeding is conditioned by what Wilderson has argued is "objective vertigo," which is "a life constituted by disorientation rather than a life interrupted by disorientation."[74] Humans do not breed, they reproduce and create kin.[75] The imposition of sexual force scandalizes the symbolic integrity of Humanness. Breeding is an acknowledgment of the non-Human status of slaves, a condition in waiting that does not require actualization. A slave need not be explicitly identified as a breeder to be held captive as such. This marks the separation between the structural dimension of slavery and the lived experiences of slaves. Seemingly, all slaves were kept as breeders unless conditioned otherwise by early death, by biological inabilities, or the desire of whites to employ their labors for other means. Slavery made this determination for slaves without recourse to consent or comprehension from the slave.

Breeding is not something that happened as a finalized event or spectacle. The eventualizing of sexualized violence refigures the condition of forced copulation and reproduction into the singular narrative of *the* breeding woman. By eventualizing, I mean materializing acts of violence into a proper name is to grant it the credence of historicity. The attention given to the status of being a breeding woman grants the speaker, who is nameless, a form of subject recognition. The title gestures around the shock of her individualized terror. It positions her as a victim of sexual violence, in the subjective sense, such that violence is done to *her* as a prior constituted being. However, there is no *her*, in the singular constituted arrangement of self, that can be found in a community of slaves. She carries no symbolic integrity outside of the desires for meaning placed on her story. The narrator never reads her life nor the brutal lives around her as a historical event demanding pause or even redress. The website imposes these meanings upon her words. This is not to say concentrated focus, redress, or liberation were not her desires beyond the parameters of the interview. This is a fact we cannot know because, structurally, we cannot find her, she is presented without a name. Furthermore, rather than approaching this story as it is presented by "This Cruel War," as a reclamation of lost or denied presence, a subject with no name, I argue it emerges within a web of structural entanglements with the ontological absence of the speaker. All we know is she is free from captivity, in the legal sense, at the time she is speaking. The narrator speaks as if the story lacks time referents and a central subject. Furthermore, the register of speech does not segment slavery from the present, or the present from slavery. Her speech flows in a way that makes the break between the two unimaginable or, at the very least, indiscernible. Nothing subsides or is drastically reimagined once slavery comes to a legal end. The world keeps moving on, and sexual violations, beatings, murders, births, and rearing are not privileged as spectacular. In fact, they are all banal renderings of slave existence.

"This Cruel War" epitomizes the assumption of the given-ness of Black subjectivity by foregrounding the speaker as someone deracinated by a cruel or heinous event. Life beyond breeding, however, is not an extension of what Lauren Berlant might term "cruel optimism," which is "when something you desire is an obstacle to your flourishing."[76] As Berlant explains, all attachment is optimistic, if we describe optimism as the force that moves you out of yourself and into the world in order to bring closer the satisfying something that you cannot generate on your own but sense in the wake of a person, a way of life, an object, project, or scene.[77]

Optimism in this sense is based on the good faith assumption that cruelty is conditional for human subjects. That cruelty enters the frame "when the object/scene that ignites a sense of possibility makes it impossible to attain the expansive transformation for which a person or people risks striving," which is intensified

> insofar as the very pleasure of being inside a relation have become sustaining regardless of the content of the relation, such that a person or a world finds itself bound to a situation of profound threat that is, at the same time, profoundly, confirming.[78]

What Berlant sets up is an understanding of what they term "the historical present," which illustrates how human capacity for transformation and transcendence is tethered to a sense of what it cannot generate on its own, which is found in the object or the thing outside of itself. As Patricia Clough argues,

> the turn to affect points instead to a dynamism immanent to bodily matter and matter generally—matter's capacity for self-organization in being in-formational—which, I want to argue, may be the most provocative and enduring contribution of the affective turn.[79]

Affect theory's proliferation of form into matter is the Human claiming that its own enslavement is the result of a forceful wedding to the object/(non) Human racially black other. The social body of Humanness, if we are to think the social as the site of relationality, is parasitic on the historical stillness, or repetition, of antiblackness. Tyrone Palmer argues,

> Despite its pretenses toward universality, affect as force is tethered to the logics of raciality that create and sustain the World. In contrast to an unmarked affect as universal relationality essence, "Black affect" might then be the name we give to those fleshly intensities that register the catastrophic violence that produces and subsumes Black existence.[80]

Blackness is formlessness, a position of the unthought, that is captured by its structural inability to inaugurate its history as the condition of (im)possibility for the formulation of being. This is why the gesture to grant Blackness a subjectivity, which is the coherence of form, is not Berlant's articulation of cruel optimism. It is not cruel because it is not an intention, and not optimistic because it is not a feeling. It is the predicating necessity of Black ontological absence. Human desire, which affect theory emerges through and from, claims formlessness as its rightful transcendent property. The epidermalization of Blackness renders it both banal and matter of fact. Freedom from Blackness is a dynamic matter that is as provocative and enduring as it is violent. Thus, affect theory cannot think Blackness, because it mimes Blackness as its Human capacity. It performs this gesture explicitly through what the Black cannot do, which is to dislodge its present reproductive understanding from the history of its undoing.

Given this, what affect *is* discernible for breeding? How does theory contend with antiblack sexualized violence if it is banal? What if sexual force is not spectacular but the regimenting of life processes? Can Black gender and sexuality be dislodged from the (re)production of its objectified form? Is the terroristic nature of the sexual violence the casual way breeding is usurped into narratives of kinship and maternal worlding that make it increasingly unclear what the stakes of contending with violation are?

I want to turn to *Kindred*, the 1979 science fiction novel by Octavia E. Butler, as a critical commentary on the stakes that emerge when assuming the slave had conditional access to kinship that could destabilize the heritability of the instability of breeding. Dana, *Kindred*'s protagonist, is faced with the imperative to see that everything the world touches is conditioned by the psycho/sexual after/life of slavery. Yet, the longue durée of the sexuating paradigm of antiblackness is precisely what Dana cannot see. She is engulfed within a structurally imposed aphasia. The antagonism of unbound antiblack sexual violations is not assuaged for Dana by the logic, reason, and causal associations she is able to apply to all other violent things. Making several physical returns from the 1970s to the nineteenth-century antebellum South, Dana is guarded by a political imaginary of slavery—from its after/life—that perceives how undoing and circumventing the violence of slavery entail reason, rationality, and the refusal to *be* understood as a slave. Despite her refusals to situate herself as a slave among other slaves, Dana is both formed and deformed by the sexual subjections that proceed and condition her arrival within the after/life of slavery.[81] Which is to say, sexual violation produces and reproduces the status and stasis of her (non)being, a condition that she interprets as subjective possibility and potential. She is driven by an anxious desire to vindicate her ancestors, who are white and Black, from the hold of property relations, and to know more about the relation that brings them together as "kin."

If life, as in bios, emanates from kinship, what Dana uncovers on her returns is anything but the productive interrelation of kin. What she is confronted with on her return is not a familial excavation, but what John Murillo describes as "a choice between never having existed or not *being* 'while' existing. . . . Reflect[ing] that Dana belongs irreducibly to this untimely force, and to the mastery of what it is an appendage."[82] To this effect, everything Dana encounters, I argue, is guided and oriented by the sexual order of slavery. The text is scaffolded by sexual violence. Everything encapsulated within and between the moments of overt sexual terror is part and parcel to that same matrix of sexuation.

Dana, curious about the interracial underpinnings of her coming to being, reads her ancestors Rufus Weylin, a slave owning white, and Alice Greenwood, a free-born Black woman, as consenting lovers. Although understanding her interracial roots indicates her desire to know slavery, what drew her back in time was not this desire. Instead, the novel places Dana in a direct and continual encounter with Black sexual dispossession. This forced engagement for her is sustained over time, but on trip after trip to the "past," Dana fails to reconcile the sexual violations she is confronted with. From the sexual assault of Alice's mother by slave patrollers to the sexual assault of Alice by Rufus, Dana finds herself ill-equipped to anticipate or remark upon these violations. Sexual violability as a non-ontological status for the Black troubles all of her conceptual logics. As a rational-thinking post-slavery subject, a liberal individual and the rights-bearing subject, Dana cannot contend with the making of slaves as the antithesis to the Human subject she imagines herself to be. Dana cannot accept that sexual violence is what determines her status in the world, without consideration of her will and action. She does not have the language for it, she simply cannot see it. That is, until she was confronted with the inevitability of her own sexual violation. In the midst of Rufus attempting to sexually assault her, a conceptual break occurs. In this moment, Dana's awakening was as "cold and nonliving" as it was totalizing and disorienting.[83]

Kindred is instructive for considering the antecedents of Black reproductive antagonisms. Though Dana is fictive, what Butler is able to tarry with in her science fiction book is not. Through Dana, Butler exposes how, like science fiction, the archive is an imaginative project. How one arrives at the archive is only as powerful as the questions one carries with them on the journey. *Kindred* confronts an affect about post-emancipation encounters with slavery. The naivete represented by Dana as a twentieth-century Black subject, and her thoughts and actions, are unhinged. Slavery meets its after/life, and its after/life is propelled forcefully into captivity. Fantasies about a fundamental epochal shift between these teleologies are severed. What emerges instead are many contradictions, which are contradictory because of their similitudes. Thus, I employ Dana here allegorically. She demonstrates how the occlusion of post-emancipation Black subject potential is haunted and upended by the sexuating power of antiblackness and the violent acts of slavery that are irreconcilable. *Kindred* places the sexual dispossession of the slave in stark contrast with the inability to think and act against this status in a manner that structurally upends its gratuity.

In the final scenes of *Kindred*, Dana faces an imperative: to understand, as a necessity for resistance, that everything that proceeds, exceeds, and concedes her existence is structured by slavery, not as a war of maneuver between slavery and freedom, but as a paradigm of racial sexuation that preconditions thought and action. Dana's final moments in the antebellum South propel her to see that she, too, is a slave. Emancipation has not fundamentally augmented this hold. She then remarks, "A slave is a slave. Anything can be done to her."[84] Her passivity with respect to violence was tethered to the perception that formal emancipation restored kinship and authorized Human potential for the slave. Dana states, "I could accept him as my ancestor, my younger brother, my friend, but not as my master, and not as my lover."[85] However, the loss of kinship for the slave is not simply degraded by the legal institution of slavery. Instead, the paradigmatic power and value of kinship is granted meaning and matter because the Black is paradigmatically barred from possessing the symbolic integrity of filiation and affiliation within its structure. The persistence of interpreting the sexual violation of the slave as a passive rather than a constitutive element of parsing out slave/Black from what it means to be Human cannot be underscored. In the end, Dana is dispossessed of a limb so that she may never forget the overarching reach of sexual violation into the after/life of slavery. Thus, if the sexual violation of the slave is not forcefully imposed within thought, it may be hard to discern its prevalence, and when and where it enters within the matrix of violation.

The Mammy as Reproductive Negation

After over 135 years, the highly contested image of Aunt Jemima no longer markets the popular American breakfast brand. The brand's new name Pearl Milling Company pays homage to the mill that first produced, in 1889, the grains for the pancake mix.[86] Aunt Jemima embodies the American fixation with the iconography and materiality of the mammy, a representational figure from slavery deemed asexual despite her real, ongoing interracial sexual violation. In racist cultural fantasies, the mammy willfully abandons her own offspring in service of her undying care of the Master, the Mistress, and their progeny. She indexes the inherent discord between how representation overwrites and fictionalizes the reality of antiblack violence. Nonetheless, it is antiblackness that makes the need and love of the mammy figure so powerfully possessed. As Omar Ricks argues,

> The "Mammy" archetype may have originated in the slave domestic sphere, but it is more than just another name for "domestic worker." It's more complex than that, so much so that critiquing the "Mammy" should never be the same as critiquing the representation of domestic workers.[87]

Aunt Jemima is not loved because she is perceived as an asexual caregiver who serves up breakfast to American families. Her fiercely possessed adoration, which made her removal a hotly contested battle of capitalist and cultural desire, exists precisely because of the fantasy of Black sexual openness, which prefigures her inability to speak back against her captivity. The smile she adorns as she is made into the literal form of a syrup bottle or the recognizable pancake box lady is emblematic of being made the figure of enjoyment of one's own dispossession and endless suffering. The family of one woman behind the Aunt Jemima image is seeking reparations. Despite removing the racist representation, the brand is pushing back, demonstrating the change as more an empty symbolic gesture than a confrontation with the material effects of exploiting an image of a Black woman for well over a century.

Kaplan remarks on the legal case brought by the descendants of Anna Short Harrington, a South Carolina Black woman who, starting in 1935, portrayed Aunt Jemima for Quaker Oats for fifteen years.[88] Kaplan notes that the case was short-lived, filed in August 2014 and dismissed in February 2015 on the grounds that if the descendants "had legitimate standing as executors of Harrington's nonexistent estate, the court ruled the statute of limitations had long expired."[89] The question of legitimacy is vexed in this case and with respect to the legacy of Aunt Jemima, as multiple Black women were hired to portray her fictional likeness. Thus, the claim by Harrington's descendants that her recipes were used for profit and brand proliferation by Quaker Oats would also be difficult to establish. Nonetheless, what this lawsuit signals is a question about whose (fore)mother is Aunt Jemima? Kaplan argues the failed lawsuit is "instructive in what it reveals about the quotidian operation of the law in regard to Black personhood/property."[90] In this sense, Aunt Jemima is locked within a legal perpetuity that wagers yet never settles the claim of freedom from reproductive insignificance and captivity. As a symbol, she is an amalgam of Black women and their offspring, many and no one at all; as her labor can be adjudicated as the rightful property of bodies not her own.

The legal contestations over Aunt Jemima and her legacy symbolize the peculiar dynamics of mammification. Which is to say, she embodies being made a reproducer of offspring who are without clear claims to her as a mother in the sense of kinship. Does Aunt Jemima have kin? Though many are affectively bonded to her image and the nostalgia of her referent, her role as a mammy figure in the American cultural imaginary took on many forced and choice caregiving roles. Who can claim her, and why, is an American riddle steeped in sexual and gender violation and captivity. The removal of her image from the marketing of breakfast products is, as Kimberly Juanita Brown argues, "not so much 'liberation' as it is subterfuge."[91] Her visual absence does not resolve the irreconcilable antagonism of her existence nor does it restore a subjectivity for her that is unsaturated by the capitalist consumption of her flesh, fantasies of her physical form, and longings for her bonded care. As much as she is legally enmeshed as

Figure 4. Betye Saar, *Liberation of Aunt Jemima*, 1972, Mixed media assemblage 11.75 x 8 x 2.75 in (29.85 x 20.32 x 7 cm). Source: Collection of Berkeley Art Museum and Pacific Film Archive, Berkeley, California; purchased with the aid of funds from the National Endowment for the Arts (selected by The Committee for the Acquisition of Afro-American Art). Courtesy of the artist and Roberts Projects, Los Angeles, California. Photo Benjamin Blackwell

the property of a corporation, as a mammy, she is legally construed by a history of heritability that foreclosed her claims to the forms of maternal personhood that her descendants sought on her behalf through the courts. This is maintained even as she has disappeared from the product she was long associated with.

Despite the importance of removing this longstanding racist iconography, this gesture does not signal the emancipatory dreams encapsulated in artist Betye Saar's 1972 mixed-media assemblage "Liberation of Aunt Jemima." Saar credits the heightened contempt following the 1968 assassination of Dr. Martin Luther King, Jr., as inspiration. Ironically, the removal of the Aunt Jemima image from the breakfast brand coalesced with the 2020 uprisings that occurred around the world in response to the police and extrajudicial murders of many Black people in the United States.[92] Though each renewed focus on Aunt Jemima emerges from the demands of Black riotous moments, they are result of antagonistic political genealogies.[93] One of the genealogies is the confrontation with antiblackness, as it sutures Black gender and sexuality, and the other is the drive to preserve capital and the psychic hold of Black captivity.

"Liberation of Aunt Jemima" presents an amalgamation of Aunt Jemima's multiple inflections as America's mammy. Created in response to an open-call for Black art from the Rainbow Center, a Berkeley, California, community center—which was once situated in close proximity to the Black Panther Party headquarters—Saar presents Aunt Jemima in revolutionary form. As a cast-iron mammy figurine, she brandishes a rifle in one hand, a broom in the other, and is gleefully charting her revenge. Her liberation has multiple targets, each represented by different textural elements in the piece. In the center of the frame, there is a photo of a Black woman holding a white-child under one arm, with the assumed neutrality of the image disrupted by a Black power fist rising from below to overshadow the scene. In addition, photos of Aunt Jemima, as they appear on breakfast tables, are tiled in the backdrop, repetitiously signifying the mass-commodification of her image and a sense of haunting. Some of the pictures are captioned with her name, while others are not. Some are fully exposed, while others partially visible. Her face and smile strike a deep resonance of a longing for reckoning and the dissemblance of her pained constitution. The entire composition is nestled on a fluffy haze of Southern unspun white cotton.

For Saar, the significance of the "Liberation of Aunt Jemima" is embodied in its use of images; she states, "I used the derogatory image to empower the black woman by making her a revolutionary, like she was rebelling against her past enslavement."[94] Saar treats the degraded image, and its infinite replications, as unfettered proof to support the intensity of the counternarrative. Aunt Jemima's liberation is essential and requires force, hence the gun's symbolism. The imagery of the assemblage is powerful given its ability to foreground Black insurgency without yielding to questions of its legitimacy. In referencing her choice image, Saar notes, "I take the figure that classified all black women and make her into one of the leaders of the revolution—although she is a pretty strong character anyway."[95] While, in Saar's estimation, Aunt Jemima is but one of many leaders, she stands alone in this rendering. The implication of her solitary revolutionary presence could result in directing her iconography toward another means, performing a type of mammification of her revolutionary type, rather than a reification of her revolutionary prescription. To say this simply, Aunt Jemima is not owned by Saar and her artistic intent. Though this usage conveys a powerful signification, the production of this assemblage does not possess the force to release Aunt Jemima from captivity. As such, her image can be replicated towards the reification or deification of whatever people want her to be—a revolutionary or marketing symbol. What keeps her image entombed, however, requires an interrogation that begins with "Liberation of Aunt Jemima," but must disturb the referent that holds the assemblage in place by producing Aunt Jemima as an archetype, and suturing her labor to a deep psychic possessive investment in her existence.

While the image of Aunt Jemima is important, the iconography that situates her reclamation and liberation is vexed. Whether iconography is deployed for sinister or positive purposes, the icon is always deployed deceptively, as it drives attention towards its particularities rather than to its unspoken foundations. This paradox emerges in maddening hallucinations for Pierre Delacroix, the protagonist in Spike Lee's 2000 film *Bamboozled*. Delacroix, a Black television executive, is haunted by his collection of late nineteenth- and early twentieth-century Black figurines and objects. As a willing participant in the production of a new-aged minstrel show he considers subversive, Delacroix becomes unsure if he is a casual collector of historical objects, or if he, too, is an object held captive by the same racist fantasies of the Black imago that gives these collectibles their lure and taint. What, then, is the object, the racist figurine, if it contains the power to signify Delacroix and Aunt Jemima as captives?

Considering Saussurian semiotics, the sign is relational and weighs on the signifier and the signified for meaning. The signifier grants meaning. The signified announces the meanings produced from the signifier. If Aunt Jemima is the sign, we can argue that she is, in fact, arbitrary or relational to a set of significations that render her coherent at a certain register. Thus, she is made to stand in for something else entirely. She is phantasmagoric. What, then, is the signifier and what is signified by her manifestation? As revealed in Saar's discussion of how "Liberation of Aunt Jemima" came to be, the target context, or the signifier, is slavery, not Aunt Jemima. She is but one of many signs that amplify the paradigmatic order of slavery, the signifier, as predicated on physical, psychic, and libidinal captivity, the signified. It must be considered how slavery produces the possibility for Aunt Jemima and also the possibility for her arbitrariness, for her to representationally serve multiple purposes. If we focus on Aunt Jemima as a subject, her pained constitution seeps into opacity because it becomes about the liberation of an individual fixture, and not a confrontation with a set of constituting violences. However, if we focus on her pained constitution, we see that her icon is a ruse because she is but one minor figure in a broad array of capture.[96]

Charles Sanders Pierce's contribution to semiotic thought complicates this scenario. For Pierce, the concept of the interpretant elaborates an additional role of the signified. The interpretant demonstrates that the sign and the signified can function interchangeably and, in fact, are coterminous. However, holding slavery as the signifier in the articulations of semiotics by Saussure and Pierce demonstrates how Aunt Jemima and the mammy, the signs, the signified, and/or interpretants, cannot refract into subjectivity. Which is to say, neither articulation can make them the Human subject of slavery. The investigation exposes that the production of these categories includes an additional vector, namely who or what produces the slave, which is referentially absent in these arrangements. The semiotic closure is produced through relational exposure or a reciprocal loop that locks each into a captive form of signification with penetrating focus. The mammy is as much of a productive violence as Aunt Jemima, even as she takes on specific form.

However, they are both meaningless despite many attempts to make them meaningful. Whether their coupling is approached synchronically, as simply relational terms without a larger referent, the mammy is to Aunt Jemima as Aunt Jemima is to the mammy. Or diachronically, relationally based on a historical condition, Aunt Jemima exists because she is made to be a mammy, which is a figure produced from slavery. Weighing on either figure to tell us something about the gravity of slavery, as meaningful and independently sutured significations, leaves more stones unturned than it offers definite conclusions on the use-value or function of either. Why, and from what, do these figures need liberation?

Well, according to Saar there is something particular about slavery. But what, exactly, is that? Saar also contends that the mammy is but one of the many leaders. Who are the others? How are they constructed? We can expand the discursive field to then think about these two figures through the category of the female slave to broaden the conversation. Though the question still remains: if we continue to expand the frame of signification, that is, by adding more particular identificatory sutures to our rhetorical strategies, can this deeper introspection guide thought to consider the signifier, as in slavery, as the coeval that proceeds and anticipates the discursive frame?

Contextualizing Aunt Jemima by examining the legacy of the mammy figure in U.S. history is to ponder the conditions of Black womanhood and opens thought to think about labor distinctions. The mammy is structured both materially and psychically. The mammy, as assessed by Barbara Christian, "was always presented as docile, loyal, protective of the white house and, the big house, an indication that, that she understood, the value of the society."[97] She also reveals the scandal that props up the valuation of the sex/gender divide:

> If the mammy were to be a sexual being, which of course in reality she was, but if she were to be that in myth, and in fiction and so on, she would become a threat to the mistress of the house, she would become a threat to the entire system. She, because she would then be capable of being desired by the master of the house.[98]

Her sexual status reveals that the devaluation of her sex is libidinally constituted to carry out the psychic pleasures of epitomized white femininity. However, materially, the mammy is hypersexualized through her sexual vulnerability to interracial forced copulation, while laboring in close proximity to white people.

The mammy is emblematic of the sexual bifurcation of Blackness. This designation places Blackness at the helm of conflictual desires, where sex as a self-determining or performative self-making is submerged by violent cultural fantasies of Black sex. Mammy is a desexualized figure where her sex and sexuality are muted, yet she is surrounded by offspring. Dorothy Roberts argues against perceiving this relation as purely historical, noting, "The sexual exploitation of enslaved women and girls, and the degrading mythology that supported it, continues to affect black female sexuality today."[99] This mythology is as antiblack as it is historically configured. Which is to say, the tropes of Black female sexual embodiment are as rooted in slavery as they are in prevailing social structures that breed on the mythos of Black sexual fungibility. Roberts addresses how the Black female embodies the extremities of sexuality and asexuality, such that they fail to emerge as sexuality at all:

> the asexual Mammy and hypersexual Jezebel work together to suppress Black women's own liberated sexual ethics that reflect their perspectives, values, and humanity. Slavery's stereotypes linking natural Black femaleness to sexual promiscuity and Black respectability to sexlessness leave a crippled cultural language of Black women to define an alternative sexual ethics.[100]

What is referred to here as stereotyping more aptly exists as tropes which transfigure cultural fantasies of Black sexual availability into real repetitious violations. While Mammy and Jezebel lack real substance, their mythos are implicated in the structural opacity of the very real and rampant sexual violations these tropes engender.

Under the subscripts of this relation, the Black female is produced as an oppositional sexual object, as the negation of her sexual freedom. To this point, Roberts argues, "There is a significant difference between the dichotomies of Mammy/Jezebel and Madonna/Whore, the latter helping to police white women's sexual behavior. Black sexuality is defined as *inherently* and *essentially* immoral; the Black female body represents promiscuity."[101] Roberts is working against the belief that Mammy/Jezebel is produced as a response to the performance of gender like the Madonna/Whore functions for white women. What is privileged here is that the dichotomy of Black female sexuality is not moralism of Christian ethics but is a delineation of racial sexuation that suspends Blackness into a permanent state of pure negation. Additionally, it is the negation of Black womanhood that gives coherence to white womanhood, where Madonna/Whore can serve to restrict the sexual freedom of white women without racially disempowering them.

The reason why thinking about negation is important for the argument here is to refigure and refashion the kind of Black womanhood being marked as either a problem or as liberatory. The mammy is a particularly reproductive category, in her theoretical contexts as well as at the level of the body. Reproductive, in each sense, by way of her captive maternal capacities, both her womb/belly and her care. To pivot towards maternity, or what Jackson terms the Black mater(nal), we want to think about Spillers's concept of being touched by the mother, and how this concept is often construed as a reductive inscription of a sort of cis-binarism of Black men being touched by an essential quality of Black womanhood.[102] Both of these categories can be taken up uncontested (as to reify their naturalness) to conflate and flatten experience across difference and across particularity and scale. In this respect, I want to think about the Black woman and the Black man in their cis-gender instantiations as signs like Aunt Jemima. Signs in the sense that they are functionally irrelevant without pointing to a signifier and the signified to make sense of the referent at the heart of their constitution and manifestations. What is concerning is the reliance on these gender categories as revealing a particular truth about the captive nature of slavery. Holding these categories as essential constitutions or as commonsense frames produces less an analysis of gender, and more an emphasis on gender that talks about the Black gender subject—cis, trans, and non-binary—as a conceptual subject like Aunt Jemima that is real and realized through identity. Rather, a critical analysis of gender would question the production of these types through the reproduction of the peculiarities of Black gender captivity.

The mammy is helpful for animating an analysis of gender, because she is held captive as a breeder and as a caregiver for the maintenance and production of white material and psychic comforts. Contextualizing the mammy as a breeder, we can find her alternative story to the trope of sexual nonexistence or negation. The mammy is sexuated into a world that foreclosed her sexual possibility, such that she may be read, as Ianna Hawkins Owens has argued, as asexual. Reading Saar's "Liberation of Aunt Jemima,"

Hawkins Owens emphasizes that "the mirrors that make up the interior walls of the box are most suggestive of 'recontextualisation' – replicating the juxtapositions of the figure backwards and forward in time, reaching towards us no matter how far into the future we become."[103] The mammy's womb/belly and care, revolutionary or not, comes to figure an interestingly contentious point. In the words of Christian, "as much as the mammy was seen as strong and powerful" in fantasy, she was also simultaneously completely disempowered and arbitrary. The implications of this also signal back to the womb/belly, that while being touched by the female slave brought forth captivity, by way of *partus sequitur ventrem*, that also touched by the female slave could render one void without signification with respect to their status in the world. Which is another way of saying that, the ~~mother~~ law of slavery is as important as it is inessential as the force of antiblackness.

Maternal Absence and Negative Pregnant Paternity

The 1806 case *Hudgins v. Wrights* offers a profound commentary on the antiblackness of maternal absence and its visual contours. In this case, a female slave, Hannah, and her unnamed daughter petitioned the Virginia courts for their freedom by arguing that they were not descendants of a female slave but instead a free native woman, Butterwood Nan.[104] On these grounds they argued that *partus sequitur ventrem* does not apply to them and as such they should be freed. The court framed the burden of proof as follows:

> Where persons or native American Indians or their descendants in the maternal line are claimed as slaves, the *onus probandi* lies on the claimant: but it is otherwise with respect to native Africans and their descendants, who have been and are now held as slaves.[105]

The onus probandi, or burden of proof, was placed on Hannah and her daughter to establish that they were not African and instead Native. Nan never appears before the court to substantiate the legitimacy of the claim of her nativeness. Instead, the court produced three witnesses who each bring Nan into existence by describing her and situating her in the trial as an imaginary visual referent of maternal relation through the appearance of Hannah. Two witnesses describe Nan as "an old Indian" and assert that as a result of her descent from Nan, Hannah "had long black hair, was the right Indian copper color, and was generally called Indian by the neighbors."[106] The sole named witness was a white man who spoke on behalf of the respondent who claimed ownership of Hannah and her daughter. His testimony was recorded and summarized as stating "the father of Butterwood Nan was said to have been an Indian, but he is silent as to her mother."[107]

For centuries, the law has occupied a peculiar force in mediating the reproductive bondage of Blackness. The law, as a technology of racial and gender subjectification, maintains, rather than establishes, the parameters of what cannot belong to Blackness. Maternal and paternal lineage are mediated in *Hudgins* as demarcating the lines of captivity and sovereignty that are construed as natal markers anchored to the body. As *Hudgins* establishes, there is an ontological order of freedom that the African is excluded from that drives the content of the ruling. Additionally, nativeness is perniciously oriented by the courts as a site of freedom, while binding its constitution to blood, which is a racializing project rooted in conquest and white settler desire for land theft and genocide. To this point Audra Simpson argues,

> An Indian woman's body in settler regimes such as the U.S. and Canada is loaded with meaning—signifying land itself, the dangerous possibility of reproducing Indian life, and most dangerously, other political orders . . . Indian women . . . transmit the clan, and with that: family, responsibility, and relatedness to territory.[108]

Nan, as a signifying figure, underwrites freedom from the bondage of Blackness while establishing a context of native maternal right that is operative as a visual order of distinction where what it means to be Native can be underwritten by a colonial determination of blood as the site of relation. "Indian blood," as Kim Tallbear explains, is an unstable category as "it could be diluted over generations through interbreeding with Euro-American populations . . . blood could also be overcome via mandatory boarding-school education, bans on religious practices, and the destruction of communal living and property arrangements."[109] These ideas of blood dilution were premised upon the perception that, unlike Africans, native people have the capacity for cultural evolution and Human advancement.[110]

The appellate court remarked upon the prior court's racial interpretation of Hannah's daughter by extending the following mediation:

> On the hearing, the late chancellor perceiving from his own view, that the youngest of the appellees was perfectly white, and that there were gradual shades of difference in color between the grandmother, mother, and grand-daughter, (all of whom were before the court;) and considering the evidence in the cause, determined that the appellees were entitled to their freedom; and, moreover, on the ground that freedom is the birth right of every human being, which sentiment is strongly inculcated by the first article of our "political catechism," the bill of rights,-- he laid it down as a general position that whenever one person claims to hold another in slavery, the onus probandi lies on the claimant.[111]

This remark, interestingly, asserts that Nan did appear before the lower court. However, she is only present as a reference as the appeals courts decided the fates of Hannah and her daughter. Legal scholar Adrienne Davis infers that, in all likelihood, at the time of the appeal, Nan "was deceased or had been sold out of the area and away from her family."[112] Hannah's daughter is described as "perfectly white," while there is a notable lightening of complexions across generations, such that Hannah's copper tone fades to white in her daughter. Apparent in the gradations of their skin is interracial sex, by which the case of female slaves or Native women whitening reflects upon the racializing projects of the New World. White men reproduce slaves and adulterate nativeness. Each condition extends the ontology of sexual violence wherein Blackness and nativeness are confounded by pervasive white sexual impropriety that exists under epistemological erasure. The visual scrutiny placed upon these three women exposes the racial appeal as preconditioned by Blackness or nativeness as perceivably biological yet deceptive and needing to be legally proven. The adjudication of the degrees of possible truth or deception in the claim of natural freedom in *Hudgins* is underwritten by a concern with what relation of racial sexuation Nan was construed by. The overarching question grappled with by the court pertained specifically to whether the maternal and paternal relations that produced Hannah and her daughter did so in relation to Humans or slaves.

While the sexual violence at the heart of the New World project employed theft of land and theft of bodies as a means of absolving white culpability as the preconditions for generativity and world-making, relations of sexuation are key to the status of slaves as unequivocally non-Human. The native, however, was not excluded from being Human but was mediated as perpetually ontologically bound by a whitening project of territorial expansion and genocidal erasure. As the court maintained in *Hudgins*, freedom was the natural birthright of Humans and, as such, freedom for the slave was an illegitimate claim. The slave was vacant of the capacity to wager a *postulatus* (claim). "Onus probandi lies on the claimant" to prove that a slave was one's property is not simply a burden placed upon the master. It also contends that the slave as a non-Human had no legal standing or right to proclaim the ontology of freedom. Connoting Hannah's daughter as "perfectly white" was not a declaration of her Europeanness but a proclamation that she was not Black. Indeed, the attorney for the appellees underscored that Hannah and her daughter's pursuit of freedom was not a Black desire. As he stated, "This is not a common case of mere blacks suing for their freedom; but of persons perfectly white."[113] He relists the visual descriptions of Hannah's hair and skin, noting that she was called Indian by the master's family and often seen in the company of Indians. He asks, "What more than strong characteristic features would be required to prove a person white?" He then calls upon the courts to uphold that the burden of proof to disprove these claims lie with the person claiming them as slaves and not with them as "persons perfectly white," emphasizing that despite a few incidents of war or other periodized exceptions "*all* Indians are free."[114] The respondent argued that Hannah and her daughter were native by paternal lineage. However, given that their owner could not produce proof of Nan as maternally Black, Hannah and her daughter were determined to be free on the grounds that they must have been Native by maternal lineage.

Upon rendering the final ruling in the case, the court established that the testimony of the white male witness, called upon for the respondent, was irrelevant. The judges argued, "As the rule of *partus sequitur ventrem* obtains in this country, the deposition of Robert Temple as to who was reputed to the father of Butterwood Nan, without noticing her mother is totally irrelevant to the cause."[115] By failing to remark on the status of the mother in a case pertaining to slaves, the judges maintained this testimony was "intended as a sort of negative pregnant."[116] A legal term, negative pregnant refers to a denied allegation where a person partially denies a claim while leaving a portion of the claim open with unresolved possibilities. Temple's silence about the maternal factor in the case left it open for any interpretation where the mother could have been Black, native, or potentially white. However, I also want to consider the negative pregnant as a silent commentary on the status of paternity, where paternal lineage from male slaves produces a condition of negative possibility in the case of the offspring. The appeal of Hannah and her daughter was premised upon a desire to escape *partus sequitur ventrem*, which legally entrenched them as breeders who cannot reproduce Human freedom.

In theory, slave breeding was a negative pregnant condition given that claims about the maternal allow for innumerable possibilities regarding the paternal. When a mother could not be produced in a case, as with Nan, contrary to the *Hudgins* ruling, the paternal figure does matter in determining the potential freedom or captivity of the offspring. To state the obvious tension here, patriarchal right was the central denominator for conferring status to all non-slaves in the common law kinship practices imported into colonial America and the nation's founding. However, the capacity for the conference of patriarchal right reflected the same Human slave distinction that arose in *Hudgins*, where the slave is absent of freedom as a birthright. In this respect, paternity was not a voided concern when determining the status of slaves. It bears asking, in the absence of the slave mother as material or psychic referent, what were the negative pregnant possibilities when the status of the offspring was wagered in relation to Black paternity?

Heritability and Antiblack Gender Worlding

The Virginia Act XII of 1662, which conferred maternal heredity for slaves into law, serves as a critical primer for understanding the gendering of modern racial slavery. Following the 1656 Virginia case of Elizabeth Key, who successfully sued for her freedom from slavery, there was question of the applicability and role of English common law in legislating and conferring freedom and rights for Black people.[117] A daughter of a white Englishman and a female slave, Key was granted freedom based on the English common law statute that held that a child follows the status of the father. The 1662 Virginia act racialized and gendered colonial law by establishing that maternal bondage would determine the heredity of slaves.[118] The act reads, in part,

Whereas some doubts have arisen whether children got by any Englishman upon a negro woman shall be slave or free, Be it therefore enacted and declared by this present grand assembly, that all children borne in this country shall be held bond or free only according to the condition of the mother—*Partus Sequitur Ventrem*.[119]

The case of Key, and any subsequent cases or discussions on Black freedom, cast the shadow of doubt that this law relegates as insignificant and invalid concerns. In this context, undoubtedly, the Black belly conferred the condition of bondage. Naming the female as the primary condition for consideration was a new and nuanced legal engagement when considering the status of offspring. Rather than employing the law to consider and confer rights, privileges, and potential advantages, Blackness, and particularly slave femaleness here, comes to represent an absolute form of disempowered bondage. The act further states, "And that if any Christian shall commit fornication with a negro man or woman, hee or shee soe [sic] offending shall pay double the fines imposed by the former act."[120] This renders whites (identified as Christians) as financially culpable for sexual acts with slaves. Though the fines and penalties for such acts were almost exclusively extended to white women.[121] Thus, the legislating of "mama's baby, papa's maybe" solidified in American law and broader culture that the sexual violation of female slaves, by white men and others, was necessary and essential for the production of a slave economy. Furthermore, the Virginia act demonstrates how law remarks upon and solidifies into materiality the psychic dimensions of Black ontological resistance as a conceptual impossibility.

Though crucial to the unfolding of slavery in seventeenth-century colonial America and thereafter, the Virginia act is but one legal iteration marking slaveness as the permanent status of Blackness. Contrarily, two years following the enactment of the Virginian law, Maryland refigured English common law under radically different terms. Unlike Virginia, Maryland maintained that slave status would continue as a form of paternal heredity similar to English common law. However, the racial status of the father determined the life conditions of the child. The Maryland law of 1664 was laid out in four provisions. The first stated, "All 'Negroes or other slaves,' whether already in the Province, or to be imported [sic] later, were to serve 'Durante Vita.'" Unlike Virginia where, "the transition to slavery was slow, and free black men and women gained some autonomy and maneuverability over the course of the first fifty years of colonial settlement," Maryland instituted a stark refusal to classify a distinction between slave and free Black.[122] Thus all Black people within its jurisdictional borders were deemed slaves without question. Maryland became a settler colony in 1634 and within a decade, this law was established. The second clause highlights an almost contradictory position from Virginia, stating, "All children born of any black or other slave were to be 'Slaves as their Fathers.'" The remaining clauses legislated the consequences for white women, who "'forgettfull [sic] of their free Condicion [sic] and to the disgrace of our Nation', married slaves," and further legislates the conditions of slavery for Black children born of free white mothers and slave fathers. The Maryland law of 1664 was, effectively, the first anti-miscegenation law.

Given the proximity of Maryland to Virginia, small geographic distinctions could tremendously shift how the auspices of slavery were carried out. While Virginia and its laws played a prevalent and prominent role in the establishment of larger United States legal, political, and social culture, it is not insignificant that its northern neighbor, Maryland, was practicing slavery using very different means. Compared to Virginia, Maryland was a much smaller colony and there were far fewer slaves in the province. Thus, Maryland relied on stricter laws to maintain the power of its slave economy. Maryland's refusal to adjudicate Black freedom and bondage, as being Black was the sole precondition of a slave, represents a much more draconian and pushed to the absolute law of slavery. However, these absolutes tell us something that I argue needs to be held onto. Furthermore, the Virginian act can be understood as legislating white male sexual freedom through its authoring of the sexual dispossession of female slaves. The female slave had no political right over *her* body, and as such possessed no legitimate claim against her permanent sexual dispossession, or the status of her children. Additionally, Maryland restricted white women's sexual freedom to maintain white womanhood as constricted but nevertheless embodying a capacity for racial and sexual volitional subjectivity, which was completely denied to the male slaves who were imagined as potential sexual partners. The male slave served as a conduit for the realization of white gender power by transposing the language of manhood onto *him* as a constitution of his being, while simultaneously obscuring his sexual vulnerability and powerless objecthood. In conversation, Virginia and Maryland mark whiteness as encompassing multiple vectors of racial and gendered freedoms. Though white women were not fully absolved, like white men, from facing repercussions for interracial sex, or the perception of the desire for such in the legal imaginary, white womanhood possessed the capacity for consent, will, freedom, and thus the standing to be violated—all forms of liberal Humanism that were completely foreclosed for slaves of all genders. For the slave, gender connotes a form of capture that is heritable and unbending. In denying the sexual subjectivity of both the female and male slave, to prop up sexual and gender political subjectivity of whites, the purported gender of the slave is of secondary concern in relation to their slaveness. Slave femaleness and maleness serve as two crucial technologies in solidifying the force of slavery at the expense of any semblances of ontological resistance for the slave.

The purpose of bringing these two laws in conversation is not about suggesting the law of Maryland refutes or changes the power of *partus sequitur ventrem*, which dictated "offspring follows the belly" as the wielding force of slavery. Instead, reading these competing legal frameworks together challenges the totality—though not the centrality—of maternal lineage and slave female sexual violability in determining the *durante vita* of the slave, or the life condition of the slave. Female slaves bearing the offspring of white men was far more common than male slaves or free Black men producing offspring with white women. As such, the desire to legislate the sexual couplings of white women and male slaves/Black men performed a deep psychic labor given that these couplings were rare, though not absent. It is worth noting that like the female slave, sexual violations for the male slave occurred without attention, discussion, or consequence. Thomas A. Foster argues,

> The shards of evidence we have about white women' sexual actions toward enslaved men would indicate that the occurrences were produced by the very conditions of slavery that also fostered sexual contact between white men and enslaved women—the sexual availability of enslaved people and the use of sexual contact to maintain hierarchies conducive to the slave system.[123]

Like the law, historical accounts of the sexual violations of male slaves have often characterized these encounters using the discourse of love and consent. Viewing the male slave as a consensual actor under the confines of slavery does more to graft the benefits of manhood as carried by white men onto a historical condition where such is unimaginable. The psychic labors of the law and its relationship to legislating the intimacies between white women and male slaves/Black men fine-tuned the capacities and limitation of power for white women. The slave served as a prop, or an object, in the mediations of white women's power.

Establishing a framework that acknowledges the sexual vulnerability of male slaves and the structural power of white women contributes to a shift in thinking as it pertains to gender. Pointing to such continues to demonstrate how white feminist engagements with patriarchy as power that binds the male over female in all instances, thus a supposed antagonism, is paradigmatically unsubstantiated. Gender is preconditioned by structural positionality. The power of white womanhood does not need to be theoretically imposed into thought but is revealed through material and psychic appearances of white women in the archive. What the Maryland law of 1664 brings into view is the fact that the law was invested in the property stakes of white womanhood relationally to white manhood, and also on its own terms. Those property stakes, while often discussed as economically interested, were unwittingly invested in the sexual economy of slavery and power. The law reads, "any free woman so marrying after the act's passage was to serve her husband's master during her husband's lifetime."[124] The interpretation of this clause could certainly lend to supporting the claims of feminist philosophy and feminist legal theory that law tells a patriarchal story. This taken at face value mandates that the white woman serve a sentence of servitude, for her union with a male slave/Black man, under the control of a white man, the master. However, the perception of a marriage between a slave and a free white woman skews the focus on power. Slaves could not legally marry, although, under many alternative arrangements, they did wed one another, though these unions were not legally recognized. Furthermore, in seventeenth-century Maryland, marriage was employed by white women to leverage their freedoms from indentured servitude and to climb social classes. As such, "The woman who immigrated to Maryland, survived seasoning and service, and gained her freedom became a planter's wife."[125] Additionally, it has been argued,

> She had considerable liberty in making her choice. There were men aplenty, and no fathers or brothers were hovering to monitor her behavior or disapprove her preference ... There is some evidence that the absence of kin and the

pressures of the sex ratio created conditions of sexual freedom in courtship that were not customary in England.[126]

By removing love as a buffer, marriage for white women in colonial Maryland served as a critical tool for economic mobility and power. The classification of these types of coupling as marriages serves to obscure the recognition of power and willful action. As such, "Characterizations of the men in sexual relationships with white women as 'lovers' and 'husbands' capture the general view of the relations as consensual."[127] But, consensual for whom? Given that male slaves are read through a lens of masculinity and not primarily as a slave, for whom gender does little to free them from bondage, we would assume consent is what only the white woman gives. Indeed, even in critiques of the myth of the Black male rapist, which would widely circulate post-emancipation, it is the white woman being proven to have consensually engaged in interracial sex that exposes the lie of the myth. These interpretations of consent, where consent is for the white woman to give, hinge on the representation of male slaves as legal subjects and bestows Black men with a derivational form of manhood, asserting that he was an empowered rights-bearing legal subjectivity of white men. For the slave, manhood served to distort his disempowered status and the absolute vulnerability he inhabited. This point will be discussed more in depth in Chapter 5.

The whites responsible for the settlement and development of the small colony of Maryland were guided by the imaginative potentials and psychic pleasures of white power.[128] White women were integral in the illegitimate conquest, claiming, and settling of the lands of first nation peoples and the proliferation of the enslavement of Africans. Arrival in the newly formed colonies serves as a dream space. "Until the 1660s, and to a lesser degree the 1680s, the expanding economy of Maryland and Virginia offered opportunities well beyond those available in England to men without capital and to the women who became their wives."[129] I assert that, in the context of seventeenth-century Maryland, white women possessed no vested interests in marrying slaves. Instead, they leveraged their sexuality to marry slave owners and other free propertied white men to ascend social and economic class and to position their claims for the psychic promises of a white republic.

More to the point, I choose not to evoke love as an alternative reading here, because totalizing power differentials makes interracial love impossible under these conditions. Also, love is often taken up as an evasive gesture to rewrite the relationship between power and desire with regard to freedom. If one can shore up a few examples of white women who perhaps demonstrated love interest in male slaves/free Black men, in seventeenth-century Maryland, they were the exception, not the rule. Rather, white women possessed their womanhood as a function to maintain sexual power, over their gendered bodies *and* over slaves. This was a new form of sexuality and gender being produced precisely through and by the paradigm that authorized the violent creation of the New World. Slavery and conquest fashioned the white woman and white womanhood anew, as relationally bound to white male power but also free from the same conscripts.

Unspoken in the Maryland law of 1664, because at the time of its production such may not have been the case, is that white women too owned slaves.[130] Under these advanced conditions of slavery, the servitude legally mandated as a punishment for sexual arrangements between white women and slaves becomes functionally void. Or the clause further serves to suture and bolster white women as a master class in the economy of slavery because, as the master, the white woman had no master to serve for her sexual encounters with male slaves.

The presumed permanent vulnerability of white women to the patriarchal rule of white men is critically destabilized when the slave is brought into view. Psychic actualizations of power and sexual and gendered being appear through the space of legislated victimhood and absolute power. The lexicon of whiteness is not gender exclusive but gender inclusive. What white gendering means for the slave, both legally and socially, sutured the slave as the position of the unthought. Under the purview of the law, in Maryland and Virginia, the violation of gender for the slave, as it was grafted from written text, signals a denial of white gendered capacity. The law unwrites the possibility for motherhood and fatherhood for the slave as it is imaginatively scripted for whiteness and its psychic possibilities, in its revisions of English common law as the standard as well as in its dream making of gender, sex, and race in the New World. The law did not chart and unwrite the particularities of an African prehistory to slavery that denies the particular relational, birthing, and childrearing customs of the many differing peoples who were slaves. Instead it conscripted Blackness, as devoid of prior constitution outside of slave-making, and holds the slave as an object in a captive relation with the maintenance and realization of white gender and sexual becoming, *durante vita*.

Although law is but a conduit of the paradigm of racial fantasies and violence, concern with the gender and sexual relation among slaves was omitted from the legal context, and was instead situated within the private sphere under the control of legitimate political subjects. While the political sphere, like the law, may have commented on or made reference to the slave as a gendered and sexual object, the processes of this (un)making were controlled exclusively by the slave estate as a violent psychic and material space where gendered and sexual beings were formed and slaves were decayed. To say this otherwise, gender and sexuality for the white, or Human, as a possessed state of being, willed its becoming through the dispossessed gender and sexuality of the slave. Slave law served as a gendering meeting ground.

As Hartman argues, when thinking through the violence of *partus sequitur ventrem*, "Gestational language has been key to describing the world-making and world-breaking capacities of racial slavery."[131] Hartman is remarking on how the violation of the Black belly makes the modern world possible. From the slave ship, to the plantation, and the afterlife of slavery, the "theft, regulation and destruction of black women's sexual and reproductive capacities" has been a crucial form of violence for the emergence and possibility of the onto-epistemological ways of knowing and existing that suture modernity.[132] The critical importance of this intervention privileges that the Virginia act, and similar legally and socially upheld practices, were the predominant material conditions of slavery, which imposed physical and psychically violent consequences on female slaves and the functions of their bodies.

If we are to expand our understandings of the reproductive language of slavery, what does the language of sexual fecundity, in reference to the male slave, bring to the fore? What does this do materially and psychically for the world? It is critically important to think about the particularities of the pained constitution of the male slave. However, I would caution against understanding that pained constitution as conditioned by denied forms of manhood or a reduced capacity to claim the benefits and rewards of patriarchy. Instead, it is essential to consider how gender for the slave, not specific to a gender, produced the confounded conditions from which Human capacity shrouds the ability to sit with the pained constitution of the slave's gendered and sexual (un)making. Rather than establishing that theory should contend with the paternal equivalent of the "offspring follows belly" by transmuting it into the "offspring follows loins," this argument seeks to diagnose the challenges that arise when the gender of the slave is foregrounded as the explanatory frame to ascertain an accountable logic for their reproductive foreclosures. Which is to say, this position is interested in thinking about racial sexuation and slavery, through the violence of slaveness as what makes gender and sexuality possible in the New World. This argument focuses on how slavery as a condition of accumulation and fungibility makes the reproductive capacities of flesh essential yet arbitrary in determining the gendering of slaves, highlighting that this condition is undergirded by a form of ontological absence, which gender brings into stark view. It is worth noting that neither a female or male slave could bear a free Black child under these constraints. To get at the centrality of this concern, the assumed explanatory power of femaleness and maleness at the site of the body must be called into question. The value of doing so is not to dispossess the slave of gender through analysis. Rather, it asks, how is gender weighed upon to provide explanatory power to violence? Furthermore, how do we diagnose a condition of gender and sexual captivity that does not rely on authorizing the sexed body in thought as a prescriptive site of gender? What does ontological absence mean, when it is multilaterally conferred, and not solely a maternal transfer? How do we displace the reliance on thinking bodily reproductive capacities as central to slave-making or the conferring of slave status?

Four

On Historicizing Sex and Sexual Sense Making

The primary concern of *Engendering Blackness* is extending the thesis that the slave is violated by a structure of violence that is external to but upholds the logics of gender. This interrogation also lends itself to considering how queer theory understands the sexual violation of the slave. In recent years, queer theory has had a direct confrontation with theories of Blackness as a structural positionality.[1] In the process, queer theory has shifted its focus to consider questions about slavery. Queer theorists, like Judith Butler, Lee Edelman, Jack Halberstam, Amber Musser, and others, have gestured toward contending with what slavery reveals about the sexual question.[2] At the same time, queer theory and its understandings of sexual difference and sexuality are construed by insistences that disavow the central claims of the Black studies interventions it purports sympathetic alignment with. Afro-pessimism, Black studies, and Black feminism (which all overlap in ways that may not be distinct) illumine how Blackness throws the investments of queer theory into crisis.

The insistence of maintaining queerness as universally explanatory glosses over the sexual content of slavery. Queer theorists, specifically those who confront slavery, are hobbled by their insistence on maintaining slavery as a Black specific question rooted in slave experience, historical situatedness, and plantation quandaries. This allows a strange form of allyship with Black studies predicated upon sophisticated obfuscation. Specifically, in current iterations of this gesture, afro-pessimism is perceived as a helpful thought exercise worth a momentary pause, but not an essential theoretic about the sexual life of the Human that annuls or reorients what queerness is perceived as extending or clarifying about the paradigm of sex and sexuality. The Black in queer theory is, ultimately, rendered an accumulated and fungible launching point to strengthen claims about the queer or queerness as the fundamental structural negation that gives credence and intelligibility to the sexual crises of the Human. Given this curious alignment, one must ask, is the privileging of queerness antiblack? Sidelined engagements with Blackness are the disavowal of this question in motion. Critiquing the assumptive logic of queerness does not make this argument invested in the re-enchantment of normative sexuality or sexual beingness. Contrarily, this position upholds a deep skepticism about queerness as a universally explanatory analytic to grasp hold of all forms of perceived sexual otherness, deviance, or non-normativity. Which is to say, Blackness is not an addendum to queerness. Instead, the absolute saturation of the slave by sex as violence and violence as sex fundamentally retools what is understood about the sexual and its violating qualities.

Blackness as Queer Theory's Rupture

Lee Edelman, in *Bad Education: Why Queer Theory Teaches Us Nothing*, contends that queerness imparts upon us a bad education, which "offers nothing by way of repair," and rests resolutely within jouissance.[3] This argument is structured by a recuperation and deployment of the Lacanian concept ab-sens, which is external to concerns of what it means "to be or not to be," indexing instead a fundamental structural absence upon which logic and speech cohere. Edelman writes,

> As the absenting of meaning from being, as the insistence of what can never be counted as part of any world, ab-sens has no place in the order of sense that assumes "the background of a totality" wherein being and meaning both depend on each other and prop each other up.[4]

As argued by Edelman, woman, Black, queer, and at time trans* each clarify the ab-sens as they "stand for a violent break with the governing constructs of a world, a break with its (onto)logics."[5] For Edelman, these categories "threaten to derealize a given order by exposing it as not-all" because they produce momentary lapses in structural logic by imposing glimpses at the Real, disallowing the subject to understand the world as complete or any being as a situated form of oneness. What is at the heart of this exposure is "the site where sex coincides with the primal subtraction of ab-sens."[6] Sex in this sense is not a component of how the world structures meaning but its fundamental orbit.

Lacan arrives at the ab-sens and its relation to sex through a reading of Sigmund Freud, which Edelman cites in support of the development of his argument. Lacan explains (as translated by Edelman), "Freud puts us on the path of that which ab-sens designates as sex; it's through the swelling up of this sens-absexe that a topology spreads out where the word is determining."[7] Sens-absexe operates by "putting *sex* in the place of subtraction . . . sex as the pure negativity that enables meaning but has none."[8] Sex, then, functions as a double negative that, when exposed by thought, is shrouded by an unthinkability that emerges precisely through an attempt to unearth its component features.

In this respect, woman, Blackness, and queerness orient forms of nothing that are repeatedly "cast out and rendered unthinkable by the world of sens-absexe."[9] To illustrate this argument, Edelman contends with feminist rethinking of philosophy, afro-pessimism, and his own theorizations of queerness. The latter is where the arguments of *Bad Education* are primarily rooted. For the sake of the argument presented here, I will focus most centrally on the reading of afro-pessimism Edelman extends in which the woman and the queer are offered as proximate understandings of Blackness and the Black.

To illustrate the ab-sens in relation to Blackness, Edelman draws on the work of Ronald Judy in *(Dis)Forming the American Canon: African-Arabic Slave Narratives and the Vernacular*. In these particular examples, Judy grapples with the significance of *The Interesting Narrative of the Life of Olaudah Equiano, or Gustavus Vassa, the African* by Olaudah Equiano as he describes the metaphysical transfer between the African and the Negro. Edelman cites Judy as describing how the slave narrative, via Equiano, serves as a conversion of the African as incomprehensible object to the negro as intelligible subject. Edelman contends that this shift homes in on the split or subtraction when the Real is made perceivable to thought. Furthermore, the negro as representational form "requires negating the negativity of Blackness."[10] As Judy contends "The muted African body is overwritten by the Negro, and the Negro that emerges in the ink flow of Equiano's pen is that which has overwritten itself and so becomes the representation of the very body it sits on."[11] The African, Edelman posits, "succumbs to ontological annihilation" and is recast into comprehensible terms "to affirm identity through an attachment to intelligibility."[12] This relational logic occurs without questioning if the African is the effect of some type of true materiality that is repressed or is it also, like the negro, a stand-in for a general fantasy of a type of existence that cannot be because it never was "one." To this point, Robert Reid-Pharr argues that the transition Equiano undergoes illustrates a performance of "dynamic modes of living that *he* believes typifies modern society" rather than his narrative exemplifying a collective structural adjustment.[13] Nonetheless, Edelman holds onto the African-to-negro as an essential declination of the real, which brings the ab-sens closer into view. This refusal to engage the African as a violent overwriting of forms that cannot be contained within the oneness it perceives allows Edelman to extend a thesis around afro-pessimism that tries to hold it accountable to a certain understanding of object to subject slippage.

It is from this vantage point that the work of Frank B. Wilderson III in *Red, White, and Black: Cinema and the Structure of U.S. Antagonisms* enters the conversation, as Edelman seeks to contend with the damning assessment of how Judy reads the accounts from Equiano extended by Wilderson. Wilderson does not rest on the slave narrative in *(Dis)Forming the Cannon* as a true leap from object to subject. Rather, he describes that Judy makes clear the impossibility of such a maneuver given that the negro has no referent. Wilderson pushes the argument further, dislodging its implications as a historical quandary by advancing the position that the Black scholar is emblematic of the paradigmatic capture of Black speech that Judy points to in *Equiano*. Wilderson writes that

> it is precisely to this illusive symbolic resistance (an aspiration to "productive subjectivity"), as opposed to the Negro's "abject muteness," and certainly not to the Slave's gratuitous violence, that many Black scholars in general . . . aspire when interpreting their cultural objects.[14]

How Edelman deals with the question of slavery and queerness, which is a point I will return to later, illustrates what Wilderson argues here. Edelman reads the work of Black scholars as misunderstanding the transcendent nature of symbolic resistance against negativity towards a clarified subjectivity. Thus, Edelman argues that the slave narrative, the constraints placed on the Black scholar (as described by Wilderson), and the understanding of "woman" extended by Catherine Malabou all figure a certain type of negation. He writes, "The unbearable Real of ontological negation, the ab-sens that undoes the oneness, the comprehensible *identity*, of the world, compels us to seek to preserve that world by affirming our oneness within it."[15] Edelman argues there is a discord between Wilderson's descriptions of the constitutive qualities of Blackness and the Black. As such Edelman argues that the Black is where a oneness seeps into afro-pessimism, demonstrating that the Black lacks the qualities of unique symbolic exclusion that Wilderson describes.

To this point, Edelman writes that "Wilderson . . . *does* attach a property to Blackness, one that particularizes the Black" and furthermore "coincides with Malabou's analysis of woman."[16] The superpositioning of the Black as the essential truth of the world, Edelman argues, is not a unique theoretical move but one also carried out by feminist philosophers. Edelman is pushing back against Wilderson's insistence that the Black is excluded from the symbolic order by way of social death. To do so, Edelman takes up Judy as a rejoinder to Wilderson. By connecting the Black to his reading of Judy's formulation of the negro, Edelman again emphases the African as a totalized exclusion. Yet he maintains that the negro, like the Black, is included, but as a negativity *within* the symbolic order. This allows the Black to reenter the symbolic fold, in which, he argues "Like woman, that is, the Black is a subject whose status *as a subject* is subject to doubt by virtue of figuring *within* the Symbolic the ab-sens excluded *from* it."[17] From here Edelman makes several pronouncements that are directed at the central tenets of afro-pessimism, without explicitly framing them as such. He contends that Wilderson rightfully calls for the end of the world, not because of the essential plight of the slave, but because antiblackness is "nothing other than logic itself as the syntactic imperative of making-sense." Or, to put it another way, antiblackness is but one vector that can dislodge the capture of the *ab-sens*.[18] Furthermore, he attempts his largest blow against afro-pessimism by delegitimizing its unflinching analysis of slavery. He contends that "despite the history that places them [Black persons] inextricably in relation to slavery" Blackness, the Black, or Black persons, "are not, in any given world, the singular or exclusive embodiment of ontological exclusion."[19] In this move, Edelman disavows the afro-pessimist insistence that slavery as a paradigm of structural positionality shapes the essential violence of the modern world.[20]

What, then, are we to make of slavery? According to Edelman, woman, Blackness, queerness, and trans* (as well as countless other names):

> all spring from the inextricability of ab-sens and sens-absexe and thus from the insistence of the not-all that makes the sexual relation impossible. All are rooted in the ontological antagonism that structures the logic of sense by which we are divided into being: divided between the subject of desire and of the subject of the drive, where the former consigns the latter to the status of what is not.[21]

Whether or not slavery situates a primacy for Blackness or theories of violence more generally, the way the Black bleeds through woman, queerness, trans* and other terms it is situated alongside demands a further investigation. For example, if we are to take for certain that the deployment of property by Wilderson and Malabou presents a structural congruency between Blackness and woman, where can we evidence this claim? For me, the problem is not rhetorical. Instead, it is a matter of whether theory can scale down to account for the structural predicaments that make theory thinkable. Which is to say, although woman, Black, and queer as conceptual framings exceed, escape, and fail to apprehend the subjects who are construed by these categories, can this abstracted queer theory dislodged from the material provide the universal theoretic of mundane and quotidian violence it presupposes? Some may argue this question fails simply through enunciation given that this investigation is not about the empirical, but instead tethered to questions of ontological ordering or situatedness. To which I respond by staking a position. Black people (queer, trans, cis-) have a higher relationality to deathly disregard than any other personhood who inhabits these unqualified categories. Whether slavery is essential to this ongoing arithmetic is perhaps a moot point. Yet, paramount to the evasive gesture that avoids direct confrontation with the structural predicament of Black suffering is also *the ways that slavery and the slave are shored up* in theory to vouch for general theorems that continue failing to adequately address antiblackness. What is the emancipatory value of situating woman along Blackness, or holding Blackness accountable to a general theorem of queerness? Can theory hold the material as well as psychic continuums of sex difference and sexuality that suspend Blackness as a curious and permanent violable other?

In gender and queer theories, there is a persistent usurping of Blackness or the slave as an inessential factor when assessing how violence meets the subject. Blackness is used as a qualifying term of the racial extension of conditioning yet is refused primacy in thought. However, many of these theories struggle to provide evidence in support of the notion that slaveness can be inhabited by any subject in a manner that would suture the non-Black as construed by the gratuitous violence that meets Blackness. Yet we are to believe that general violability presupposes structural alignment with Blackness rather than differing relations of structural positionality, as afro-pessimists have argued. As I will argue later in this chapter, the hobble is not only the aligning of queerness and Blackness as essential relationality, but also coupling the plights of woman and Blackness highlights a deep feminist philosophical insistence on de-blackening the slave to evade the antiblack violence of the woman(hood) at the center of inquiry.

To be clear, afro-pessimism does not argue that the slave is the only violated category of modern violence. Instead, afro-pessimism asks, what does the violation of the slave make possible? The response to this is the full coherence of the world as we know it, while, at the same time, slave suffering is muted. Which is to say, the violation of the slave serves to clarify the meaning and violation of other conditions of suffering in ways other conditions cannot make sense of the violability of the slave. This does not suggest that violation is the sole possession of Blackness or that violation does not overdetermine the relations of Human subjects. Rather, it clarifies why, in the discursive fields of the studies of race, gender, and sexuality, Blackness appears as a fungible object taken up to provide evidence of general conditions or as that which must be disavowed to usher in nuanced ways of attuning to the problem. Why does the Black, Blackness, and slavery repeatedly appear allegorically or analogously in literature on violence? I contend that these appearances are symptoms of structural predicaments that are reductively couched as disciplinary investments or squabbles among theorists.

Edelman is not immune to what I am identifying. He recognizes the force of the questions posed by Black studies. They cannot be ignored. Rather than avoiding the conversation, *Bad Education* sets out to refashion those questions as less specific and more refracted than afro-pessimists might argue.

He places primary focus on Blackness, like woman and queerness, as figuring a negativity within the ab-sens. However, the Black or the negro is not solely nor necessarily negativity. To draw from Fanon, what we are dealing with here is less what the negro is but what the negro is not (n'est pas). The desire to hold onto the symbolic as capacious enough to possess vast presentations of negativity is an inadequate framework to contend with the obliteration of Blackness.

This is not simply a problem of legibility that disallows theory to apprehend what exists prior to the emergence of the Black. Violence has shattered any understanding of a Black beingness or even personhood, such that when one speaks of Blackness as existence or Black person as a thing, what is referenced are phantasms of how speech has necessitated Black (dis)appearance for the task of rendering other forms of being legible or coherent. Although this structural condition may appear or even be theorized as negativity, it cannot firmly situate itself there. The absenting of Blackness from ontology, which is fundamentally a sexual arrangement, morphs the Black through, against, and outside of what appears as firm binary oppositions. Which is to say, the structural predicament of Blackness could also be filtered through a framework of positivity, as well as it can be completely external to the negativity or positivity of world-making logic.

On this note, let us return to slavery. By decentering slavery as foundational in order to align woman and Blackness through property, Edelman then shifts focus to consider the relationship between Blackness and queerness. Edelman eschews the position taken by Amber Musser that sexuality produces an aphasia for race, arguing instead, "the point is neither to silence nor to absolutize such identities but to assume them instead *as displacements*, as figural (mis)namings of ab-sens."[22] In this respect, woman, Blackness, and queerness function as covers or sutures for what is absented "in the reality of sens-absexe."[23] However, it is when engaging the work of Calvin Warren that Edelman dismisses a deep engagement with the violence that distinguishes slaves from non-slaves. Warren writes,

> A person understood as "queer" could purchase a black-object from the auction block like his/her heteronormative counterpart. In those rare in-stances where the black-as-object was able to participate in this economy and purchase a black-object as well, the black purchaser could, at any moment, become

another commodity—if found without freedom papers or validation from a white guardian—the system of fungible blackness made any black interchangeable and substitutional. This movement between object and subject is not a problem for queerness, but is an unresolvable problem for blackness. This is the important difference between the two.[24]

Edelman pushes back against the stark divide Warren maintains between Blackness and queerness. Edelman dismisses this provocation reducing the implications of slavery to "epistemic consequences of centuries in which legal and political institutions have reduced Black persons to the status of an object." How Blackness, in Warren's assessment, becomes "Black persons" here is a curious move that demands pause. It reduces concerns about ontological exclusion to empirical questions about racial treatment. Is "Black persons" a material and social identity that was subjected to and by slavery? Or is what we know as "Black persons" a phantasm only made perceivable because what existed prior was metaphysically expelled by the intractable violence of the Middle Passage? What does Black persons mean here in the context of an argument about sex, Blackness, and queerness?

Edelman contends that "we can trace the logic that enables that reduction" of Black persons "to the status of objects?"[25] But can we? And if so, how? The institutional logic Edelman applies here, as to maintain slavery as a traceable momentary movement of Blackness between subject and object, is a conceptual leap. This, for me, is where his arguments against afro-pessimism erode. He demonstrates a theoretical refusal to contend with slavery as structural positionality or (non)relationality rather than as a historical event or moment. Situating this obscure constellation of "Black persons" as the place where Warren (and Wilderson) assumedly slips or evades the similar situatedness of Blackness and queerness is a metaphysical impasse embedded in the critique Edelman attempts to stir. Warren's holding the queer subject accountable to the violent relations of slavery as imposing a historically fixed division between Blackness and queerness is met with Edelman's attempts to redirect the conversation towards the situational and empirical and away from the paradigmatic. Edelman contends that slavery is just something that happened to "Black persons," but many things have happened to some peoples. He argues, "Neither would 'have' a history but both, instead engender histories through the contingent destination of certain persons or groups."[26]

What is most apropos in this disagreement is to consider what histories Blackness and queerness engender, specifically pertaining to sex and sexuality. If the confounding of sens-absexe typifies what the ab-sens cannot emerge, what are the intractable sexual divergences that divide and differentiate what makes Blackness and queerness uncontainable? As Warren further cautions, queerness may be tethered to presumptions about deviance, but "Blackness is much more than deviance; it is the object that allows the distinction between deviance and normativity to have any meaning at all."[27] This point is expressively critical.

Where this conflation becomes salient is in recent readings of the pervasive and rampant discourses on deviant/divergent sexualities and Blackness in nineteenth-century sexology. Despite the hyper-prevalent concerns about what is queer and what is Black appearing in sexological inquiries, Warren rightfully asks that we hold these instances as separate. He reminds us that "we can only speak in *distorting similes*—the rhetorical practice of likening one thing to another."[28] Axelle Karera similarly warns of the seductive lures of relationality, where she argues, "blackness ruptures the 'spaces of ethics' and throws its most revered concepts—like relationality—into crisis."[29] She asks that we ponder "what would an ethics based on the radically non-relational look like?"[30] This question is staged in pursuit of continuing to maintain steadfast attention to the ongoing deathly disregard that constitutes Black suffering.

By historicizing the nineteenth century as the moment when queerness sediments as a thing that could be subjected to theorization, this argument holds that queerness and Blackness orient fundamentally distinct, though at times overlapping, logics of pathology and deviance. Nineteenth-century sexologists, naturalists, zoologists, and other scientists all repulse Black sex as its own stimulus to anxiety. While queerness becomes delinked from religious understandings of inherent deviance, it emerges in sexology discourses as an abnormal yet natural deviation in Human sexual instincts. Simultaneously Blackness, the African, and the Negro maintain clear distinctions in theory as a predation that erodes the development of Human sexuality, both heterosexual and queer. Black sex is regarded as a mindless drive that is guided by unrestrained impulsivity, that is inconclusively separate from what drives animal instinct.

One might argue that theory is not bound by the antiblack and queer pronouncements of nineteenth-century sexology as uncontested proof of an ontological divide that cannot otherwise be bridged. However, attempts to embrace deviance and negativity as shared relationality between Blackness and queerness demonstrate how Blackness struggles to embrace pejorative classifications as forms of flight. Blackness contains no fixed referent to sustain an alternative entry into contesting its condition that does not redouble and engulf it in violence. Edelman argues that his focus on the "indeterminacy of reference" for queerness "might slow, if not prevent" the slippage between ontological concerns and "fixed social identities." Yet the stakes of the argument are revealed by this deputizing of queerness over Blackness as an analytical framework that can contend with or dislodge Blackness from its place of no referent by relationally binding it to queerness. Because of its situatedness within the context of Human suffering, queerness possesses indeterminacy. It is tethered to the movement between subjectivity and objectification.

Embedded in Edelman's argument around "fixed social identities"—which have only been referenced when thinking Blackness and queerness through sweeping dismissals of slave suffering (in Warren's example of the purchased vs. purchasers)—is the Black studies insistence on holding theory accountable to material violence. For Edelman, this insistence is a misstep or a scaling down of theoretical focus. Edelman wants to avoid reducing queerness to examinations of sexuality as identity or acts while containing slavery as an analytic within general claims about acts and institutional impact on Black persons. However, Blackness does not have fixed social identities that emerge haphazardly in theory, nor is the idea of Black persons a situatedness. The social clarifies rather than mystifies Blackness as non-ontological. The Black continues to index subjectivity under erasure, not personhood, as Edelman contends. Rather than supplanting queer indeterminacy over and beyond the Black no referent as an assumed essential relationality (which reads much like a gesture of saving Blackness from itself), the stakes of such a project must expressively clarify why Blackness is required to reveal the resolute potential of queerness. Furthermore, it must make clear how this arrangement is not another iteration of slavery that binds Blackness to another master.

Is there another way to consider queerness and Blackness relationally without subtending one to the other? Halberstam argues that thinking through wildness "offers an alternative history of sexuality within which the so-called natural world is neither the backdrop for human romance nor the guarantor of normativity. Wildness indeed seeks the unmaking of that world and represents its undoing."[31] Thinking with Wilderson and Fanon, for which the end of the world necessitates a complete tabula rasa, Halberstam argues "the order of things as it emerges through a mania for classification and identification recognizes the wildness proper to racial otherness and is part of the structural machinery designed to render racial antagonism unthinkable."[32] Halberstam acknowledges that wildness is fundamental to the sexual captivity of the negro that extends into the twentieth century, where cases like the Central Park Five "shows how the intuitive connection between wildness and Black criminality had become by the end of the past century."[33] Wildness exposes the structural alignment of Blackness with notions of criminality and animality, such that Halberstam offers an additional vector to untether these intrinsic relational tropes. Positing that "we could look to the zombie" as an analytic tool is the presumed way out. Yet it is unclear how this thesis delinks Blackness from its own history of sexuality that is bound by perceptions of wildness that bars the Black from the ontological claim on sexual beingness.

The deeply entrenched violence of Black wildness as the ontological erasure of Black sexual beingness cannot be disappeared by deploying categories differently. By ontological erasure of Black sexual beingness, I mean the capacity of Blackness to unfold sexual subjectivities that clarify its essential operationalization by a binary sexual order as an innate form of otherness underwritten by assumptions of Black sex as predation and openness. Rather, in theory, Blackness gets folded into sexual logics incapable of grappling with how antiblack violent intrusion cannot be contained by a singular analytic that places Blackness in analogous relation to categories that emerge precisely through its violation. Halberstam betrays the insistence that only a complete obliteration of knowledge making can unhinge how antiblackness as a structural antagonism becomes unthinkable. At the heart of this problem is both an underscoring of the significance of

Blackness in the ontologizing of Human sexual beingness and the pervasive capture sexual violence commands over the depths with which theory can even begin to grasp Black sexual capture as that which makes all antiblack violence possible.

Wildness as a thesis sits at the heart of racial science of the nineteenth century that set out to prove that the African/negro is external to binary meaning making systems—hetero/homo, man/woman, masculine/feminine, human/animal. Almost in contradistinction, the African/negro was the essential factor in helping to cohere the distinction between these binary vectors because of its inability to be fully captured within the framing logics of any of these distinctions. The African/negro was always other because it was not completely nor primarily man, woman, hetero, homo, masculine, feminine, human or animal, etc. Blackness indexes its own sexual fractioning maintained by a totalizing saturation of speculation and proclamation about its grotesque stratification of difference.

Blackening the Phantasia of Sexuality

In the *History of Sexuality, Vol. I*, Michel Foucault argues that the prevailing story of the seventeenth century is that the period ushered in a radically different structural logic around sex. What was once open, discussed, and understood about sex and sexual acts takes on a repressive quality during the Victorian era. The depths of the repression of sexual expression and speech were tethered to broad censorship and control overwriting speech and acts with a profound level of prudishness. However, for Foucault, multiple sexual truths can exist at once. A reflection back on the "past three centuries" may emerge divergent yet co-constitutive engagements with sex. As such, while "there was a policing of statements" about when and how to speak about sex, "there was a steady proliferation of discourses concerning sex."[34] He contends that "utter silence, at least of tact and discretion," situated the relations of many imbalanced intimate power relations from "parent and child" to "masters and domestic servants."[35] Moreover, beginning in the eighteenth century, in the face of repressive dictates, there "was the multiplication of discourses concerning sex in the field of exercise of power itself: an institution incitement to speak about it ... and to cause *it* to speak through explicit articulation and endlessly accumulated detail."[36] While Foucault does not explicitly engage the New World plantation, the sexual status of the slave pushes back against the universalist understanding that masters and domestic servants were coded by a decorum of sexual silence. Blackness not only contests this point but radically complicates the question of silence. "Institutional incitement" around the sexual otherness of the Black slave imposed amplification and multiplication of explicit slave uses that were not repressed by speech but absent from the logic of language all together.

In the Foucauldian genealogy of sexuality, the nineteenth century plays a pivotal role in the reconstitution of the sexual act into forms of sexual being. Critical to this estimation was the conversion of once deemed aberrant sexual acts into codified forms. Foucault argues,

> Homosexuality appeared as one of the forms of sexuality when it was transposed from the practice of sodomy onto a kind of interior androgyny, a hermaphroditism of the soul. The sodomite had been a temporary aberration; the homosexual was now a species.[37]

Prior to what became the homosexual was once refracted acts and desires that were classified as variant and disparate at best. The medicalization, or perhaps more aptly the psychologization, of sex structured subjects through the emergence of species that encapsulated a "thousand aberrant sexualities" into a "one."[38] To this point Benjamin Kahan effectively synthesizes Foucault by stating, "these thousand aberrant sexualities . . . constitute a speciation akin to that of the homosexual and embody the proliferation of discourse about sexuality."[39]

During the span of the nineteenth century, sex became medicalized, where "the flesh was brought down to the level of the organism."[40] This scientific reorientation prescribed the sexual body as a glandular and organ structure contained by fundamental natural instincts. Foucault notes the 1846 work *Psychopathia Sexualis* by Heinrich Kaan as emblematic of nineteenth-century emergent theories on sexuality. For Foucault, the significance of *Psychopathia Sexualis* was that it demonstrated how sexuality was natural and innate, not excessive or perverse as Western Christianity had maintained for centuries. However, Foucault clarifies that, for Kaan, "it is not enough to determine completely, or rather, canalize completely the force of dynamism of this instinct."[41] He explains that in children, where sexual instincts are underdeveloped, there still lies a division of the sexes in childhood play that supports the eventual development of a fully formed sexual nisus, or sexual instinct.

But what about aberrations from this developmental structure? By studying the sexual proclivities of people who have intercourse with statues, Kaan determines that *"phantasia*, imagination, prepares the way for all the sexual aberrations" derived from "those who used a sexually polarized imagination in onanism and masturbation" during childhood."[42] For Foucault, this is a pivotal finding which "may seem a bit crude," but figures "that it is natural for the instinct to be abnormal," just as it may be natural for children to stratify themselves by gender in preparation for eventual heterosexual intercourse. The perceivability of instinct and (ab)normality are rooted in childhood. Lastly, Foucault considers "the privileged link that exists between the sexual instinct and *phantasia* or imagination" as the birth "of sexuality and sexual aberrations in the psychiatric field."[43]

While the Foucauldian project sought to prescribe a general genealogical thesis on discourses of sexuality, investigating the racial signifiers that emerge in the work of Kaan, as well as other sexologists and scientists of the nineteenth century, is essential. Kaan guides Foucault to consider the deployment of sexuality where "the nineteenth-century homosexual became a personage, a past, a case history, and a childhood."[44] However, during this same era the general scientific imagination is occupied with questions about Black sex. E. Frances White charts how, in *The Descent of Man and Selection in Relation to Sex*, Charles Darwin explores his monogenesis thesis through a focus on what he terms "fusion," basically miscegenation or racial-mixture. Fusion is a litmus test for the likelihood of interracial sex, where it is noted that, "the races of man are not sufficiently distinct to inhabit the same country without fusion."[45] Darwin turns to the United States as a case example for his thesis on fusion, a term White demystifies by emphatically expressing, "we know that a simpler term is more precise: rape."[46]

In determining the sexual compatibility and likeness of *Homo sapiens* as a species, White argues that Darwin understands the reproductive rates of "mulatto" people in the United States to be low because of "their absorption into the Black race."[47] For Darwin, Africa produces distinct and heightened visual sexual differences through the body as the premiere site/sight of sexual otherness. He writes, "Hottentot women offer certain peculiarities, more strongly marked than those occurring in any other race."[48] This scientific viewpoint was much like those of French naturalist and zoologist Georges Cuvier, who performed visual inspections of the body of Saartjie Baartman, the "Hottentot Venus," where he remarked that beyond her broad hips, extend buttocks, long breast, and African facial features, "she had no other deformities."[49]

For Darwin, the Hottentot and the negro are separate categories. The Hottentot represents an African racial type, specifically of the Khoikhoi of Southern Africa as he defines the category. The negro, on the other hand, is a figure of a global but particularly New World racial order, where race stands for new and forming ideas of species as well as social interrelation. Darwin writes, "The American aborigines, Negroes, and Europeans, differ as much from each other in mind as any three races that can be named."[50] The significance of this statement goes back to the work of sexologists like Kaan. If the imagination was determined as what weds the mind to the instincts of the body, situating the mind of races as fundamentally distinct—even if the body may carry similarities—matters. The distinction Darwin draws here has implications for the articulation of the psyche that was at the forefront of concern for fellow scientific travelers. Specifically, the question of what do the mind and body say about the sexual instincts of impulses of not *Homo sapiens* as a general type, but for the races as sexually distinct in both body and mind.

On this note, it should come as no surprise that to solidify his point about the vast distinctions between Natives, negroes, and Europeans, Darwin expresses that he in fact had sex with a "full-blooded negro." Noting his time on the HMS *Beagle* surveying the Brazilian coast, Darwin asserts the following,

> yet I was incessantly struck, while living with the Fuegians on board the "Beagle," with the many little traits of character, showing how similar their minds were to ours; and so it was with a full-blooded negro with whom I happened once to be intimate.[51]

Darwin implants his own body into the arithmetic of discerning racial difference at the level of the mind, asserting that his observations of the Fuegians emerge from social contact and his understanding of the negro from sexual contact. In short, sex with a "full-blooded negro" confirms and alibis Darwin's scientific observations of the racial organization of the New World.

Noting the absence of racial mixture in this sexual equation, it is with certainty that he asserts that the negro could not be more distinct in mind from the "our" that couples Europeans and Fuegians in likeness. Sex confirms for Darwin the capacity of the mind.

We have no way of tracing the relative freedom or captivity of the person, the "full-blooded negro," who is but a fleeting reference.[52] However, given his description of "fusion" in the United States as unremarkable given the loud silence about the force of the slave condition, it is hard to disprove or say with certainty under what context Darwin himself participated in interracial intimacy. Rather than speculating on the unknown, the observations of slave ship surgeon Alexander Falconbridge tell us something about the conditions of maritime interracial sexual encounters. Falconbridge writes,

> On board some ships, the common sailors are allowed to have intercourse with such the black women whose consent they can procure. And some of them have been known to take the inconstancy of their paramours so much to heart, as to leap overboard and drown themselves.[53]

Under these constraints consent may have likely always existed under coercion and the consequences of force propelled some to the choice of death.

What place does the mind figure in the sexological dealings with Blackness? Returning to Kaan, *Psychopathia Sexualis* notes sexual impulses along an axis of intensities that are bracketed by a set of racialized subscripts. In his estimation, "the sexual drive (pleasure, if it is satisfied; a punishment, if it is rejected) admits innumerable variations, if you consider the greater or lesser satisfaction of this desire."[54] In describing "the amplified or diminished nature of the sexual drive," Kaan asserts the heightened qualities as more profound in women, cannibals, hot regions, "most in Ethiopians, less in the Mongoloid, and least in the Caucasian," as well as more in laborers.[55] He argues that "among the various types of copulations, neither pantogamy nor polygamy are suitable for humankind—these types occur in the animal kingdom and exist among the primitive people of Africa and Asia."[56] Kaan asserts that by nature, "the structure of the human body is such that polygamy and pantogamy are harmful types of copulation."[57] If these types of copulation are reserved for the races of Africa and Asia and seemingly damage the human body by nature, Kaan is demarcating African and Asian people as non-Human. However, most significantly African and Asian people are ontologically distinctive from the Human subjects at the center of the psychiatric study he conducts on normal and aberrant sexual behaviors, mostly circulating around masturbation and onanism.

In what is heralded as the first study of homosexuality and bisexuality, Africans occupy an external space that is codified by intensified sexual drives rooted in desire and punishment. This suggests that the African, and the Asian to a lesser extent, as Kaan qualifies, function without dreams. Blackness figures the quintessence of impulsivity. Merging Blackness and animality asserts that both are "defined by instinct rather than cognition, while the animal enacts responsivity to external stimuli, there is no gap between an animal's activities and itself, only immediacy."[58] Divorcing Black sex from a cognitive enterprise concludes that it is exterior to the matters of sexological scientific inquiry. Additionally, primal instinct in the case of the Black and the animal should not be confused with the instinct Kaan articulates in his study. While animal instinct acts out primal sensibilities, for Kaan in Humans, physio-physiological development enacts a maturation of instinct from childhood to puberty that gives rise to the sexual instinct that is carried out by adult sexuality. Kaan sees this as distinct from animal instinct insofar as it is an excitement of sexual instinct in puberty that cannot be similarly found in animals.

While the animal throughout the texts plays a pivotal counterpoint to the sexual development of heterosexuality that Kaan spells out, the truth of *Psychopathia Sexualis* is a fear of blackening, not homosexual or bisexual divergence. He writes, "Psychopathia sexualis penetrates into the temperament in a horrendous way: it robs a young man endowed with a sanguine temperament, as they say, of all hope and taints his senses and thoughts with a black color."[59] This "suffering of the soul" is a disease that imparts a fundamental shift in the temperament of the subject, where a series of physical and emotional regressions overtake the body and mind. As Kaan argues, the excitement of the sexual drive has a more rapid onset for "the black race of mankind," thus deforming the natural progression of sexual excitement in Humans, which can be hetero, homo, and bi.[60]

Kaan does not connect "the black race" to "a black color" that washes over the subject when it is penetrated by psychopathia sexualis. However, I am extending the argument that Kaan makes when describing his sexual theorem of psychopathia sexualis, as a Blackening subtended by antiblackness.

How the subject is overtaken by psychopathia sexualis, I contend, cannot be separated from what Kaan understands as Africa, the Ethiopian (as a Black figure), people of the hottest climates, and women. Rather than sidestepping these assertions as racist examples of the nineteenth century, if, as Foucault asserts, sex is contained in the phantasia or imagination, then what is the phantasia of sexology? More specifically, if the emergent nineteenth-century shift in psychiatry can provide various case examples of same-sex Human desire but disavows and contains Africa as exponentialized sexual dereliction that is external to Human sexuality, then what is the relation between the imagination of homosexual personage and Blackened sexual decay?

Bringing this question back to slavery, in another volume of the same name, *Psychopathia Sexualis: eine Klinisch-Forensische Studie*, Austrian psychiatrist Richard von Krafft-Ebing offers a theory of sexual instinct as well as various case studies involving different forms of sexual pathologies. First published in 1886 and subsequently expanded into multiple editions and translations, these case studies are sub-headed by type of psychopathology, then listed by case number. While Kaan offers the first dedicated study on sexual psychopathologies, Krafft-Ebing's *Psychopathia Sexualis* is the first study on sadism and masochism.[61] In addition to exploring sadism and masochism through a series of case examples, "the object of this treatise is merely to record the various psychopathological manifestations of sexual life in man and to reduce them to their lawful conditions."[62]

Krafft-Ebing establishes the grounds for his study on a few prescripts about Humanity, race, and gender. For him, sexual desire is tethered to procreation. Sexual pleasure derived from sexual acts, or thoughts not rooted in the drive to reproduce, present a series of psychic, cerebral, and physical anomalies. Much like Kaan and Darwin, Krafft-Ebing weds the development of sexual impulses to climatology, where people of the North are figured as civilized and normative subjects. People of the south, specifically of Australia, Polynesia, and the Philippines, are cast as "savage races," with early onsets of puberty and sexual desire, which, he argues, can emerge in girls as young as eight. He describes women in these cultures as "'chattel,' an article of commerce, exchange or gift, a vessel for sensual gratification, and implement for toil."[63] This is evidenced for Krafft-Ebing by their nakedness and lack of reserve around public sex. What sets northern civilization apart from the inhabitants of the Pacific is the "refined sexual life" of the white woman who is freed from chattel as "she becomes an individual being, and, although socially still far below man, she gradually acquires rights, independence of action, and the privilege to bestow her favors where she inclines."[64] In this estimation, courtship stimulated by "mental and physical merits" leads Northern (read European) races to orient their normative sexual desire, like the Egyptians, Greeks, Romans, and Teutonic races, in a "high appreciation of virginity, chastity, modesty and sexual fidelity."[65]

For Krafft-Ebing, homosexuality is *antipathic sexuality* and characterized as "the total absence of sexual feelings toward the opposite sex."[66] Same-sex desire is "purely a psychical anomaly" that arises "in spite of the normally developed and active sexual glands." He attributes homosexuality to various grades of development that are "cerebral anomalies" rather than species or ontological differentiations. Sadism and masochism are cataloged as sub-divisions of paresthesia. Sadism couples "lust and cruelty," while masochism "springs from the impulse to create a situation by means of external physical force."[67] Krafft-Ebing is confounded by masochism because he cannot apprehend why men would want to subject themselves to the powerlessness that constitutes women.

His study also documents the fantasies of women. However, as Musser describes, "female masochists became legible to Krafft-Ebing only through a masculinization of their desires."[68] In either case, Krafft-Ebing's insistence on holding masochism accountable to the power of men subverted by male and female fantasy becomes less confounding when deciphered through an analysis of antiblackness. By considering the slave as an irrefutably Black substance carried by white fantasy and desires, masochism demonstrates a less vexing case study when its obscure deployment is delinked from gendered questions and refocused on racial ontological distinction.

Notably absent from Krafft-Ebing's dichotomy of civilized and savage races as well as normal and anomalous sexual development is an engagement with the African/negro. Rather than emerging in theories of civilized and developing races, Blackness starkly appears in *Psychopathia Sexualis* locked in the fantasies of the masochistic desires that are documented and analyzed. Writing "that masochism is a perversion of uncommonly frequent occurrence," he references the work of French writer Léo Taxil on "masochism scenes in Parisian brothels," demonstrating that men "affected with this perversion is also called 'slave.'"[69] As White appropriately situates Darwin's theory of fusion as produced by the sexual violence of modern racial slavery, the slave in masochism cannot escape its plantation mythos. The desire for slavery, contained by the yearning to feel the force of mastery, cannot be delinked from the global economy of modern slavery. The terms of the slave-master relation are inextricably construed by Blackness. Antiblack violence excites the power already contained by the speaking non-Black subject. The connection between arousal and gratification is much less a satisfaction as it is a drive that deepens and expands the violent capture of Blackness within the making of the subject and its desire to feel distinctive from antiblack dereliction.

The masochist in *Psychopathia Sexualis* Case 57 references his faculties as mentally and physically normal. Despite this, he expresses that since childhood, he can remember "the thought of slavery had something exciting in it for me, alike whether from the standpoint of master or servant."[70] The neutrality of the slave slips into Blackness as the violence of the scenario deepens. He continues, "that one man could possess, sell or whip another, cause me intense excitement; and in reading 'Uncle Tom's Cabin' (which I read at about the beginning of puberty) I had erections."[71] This case elucidates the interconnectedness between fantasies of Blackness, queerness, and the development of sexual subjectivity. In the masochist sexual fantasy, the American plantation emerges as the locus of puberty or the sexual development of the subject himself. To be brutalized as a slave, as a means to feel the absolute power of mastery, is not separate from the subject's understanding of his own sexual making, which is not bound to a materialized Black object. Instead, his sexual ideal is wedded to a belief about a violent relation that is specific to Blackness, and a structured arrangement of violence, i.e., slavery, and that is separate from his experience of self. His racially construed psychosexual development of pain, excitation, and release are attached fundamentally to the fantasy of the degradation of the Black male slave. Which, notably, is also a homoerotic fantasy about the unbridled and unrestrained wielding of white power. Queerness becomes the means toward embodying the affect of the absoluteness of antiblack force.

What conditions the context of the fantasy? Is it the content of some factual arrangements or the projection of white imagination and desire? Can fact and white imagination be distinguished? Published in two volumes in 1852, *Uncle Tom's Cabin*, a novel by white abolitionist Harriett Beecher

Stowe, animates a story about slavery rooted in docility that breeds general dishonor, gratuitous violence, natal alienation, and sexual violence. In the novel, Uncle Tom is beaten to death for refusing to share the whereabouts of runaway slaves. His beating was commanded by his master, Simon Legree, but carried out by two other slaves, Quimbo and Sambo. Additionally, Legree keeps Cassy, a slave, as a concubine and purchases fifteen-year-old Emmeline as a potential replacement. There are of course many other physical and sexual brutalities contained in the novel. Thus, it is impossible to precisely identify the descriptions that excited Case 57. It is critical that the appearance of this novel in the sexual imaginary of an Austrian man many miles away from the American plantation is not perceived as an apparition. Importantly, the same year of its publication *Uncle Tom's Cabin* was translated into German.[72] Case 57 demonstrates the global traffic of literature on slavery as well as the psychic significance of the Black slave in the sexual development of racial subjects the world over.

Case 84 of *Psychopathia Sexualis* brings together female masochism, the slave, and same-sex desire. The subject of this case, Miss X., is twenty-one years old and described as kin to several family members with psychological conditions, including a mother who "was a morphia maniac and died . . . from nervous disorders."[73] Miss X. was rarely ill and "considered herself to be physically sound, but periodically insane, viz., when she was haunted by the fancies which she thus described."[74] Like Case 57, her fantasy of being whipped began in early childhood. At five years old her father playfully placed her over his knee and whipped her. This developed a longing "of being caned, but to her great regret her wish was never realised."[75] Krafft-Ebing describes that from this experience and subsequent desire, "she wished to be the slave of a man who she loves; she would kiss his feet if he would only whip her."[76] Miss X. describes her fantasy by expressing,

> I reel in the idea of being whipped by him; but this changes often, and I fancy quite different scenes in which he beats me. At times I take the blows as so many tokens of love—he is at first extremely kind and tender, and then, in excess of his love, he beats me. I fancy that to beat me for love's sake gives him the highest pleasure. Often I have dreamed that I was his slave—but, mind you, not his female slave! For instance, I have imagined that he was Robinson and I the savage that served him. I often look at the picture in which Robinson puts his foot on the neck of the savage. I now find an explanation of these

strange fancies: I look upon woman in general as low, far below man; but I am otherwise extremely proud and quite indomitable, whence it arises that I think as a man (who is by nature proud and superior). This renders my humiliation before the man I love more intense. I have also fancied myself to be his female slave; but this does not suffice, for after all woman can be slave of her husband.[77]

Is this an interracial rape fantasy in the sense that Fanon queries, "Just as there are faces that ask to be slapped, can one not speak of women who ask to be raped?"[78] Or is it a fantasy of inhibition where the male slave serves as a conduit to circumvent or subvert the repressive speech acts placed upon nineteenth-century white same-sex desire? How does the slave displace the qualifiers of speech by turning the dream first and primarily towards the titillation of unbridled pleasure? She fantasized about the male slave over the female slave, not because the slave is a man, but she is able to sublimate her desire to embody manhood onto the slave. Her contestations with womanhood are a form of self-obliteration oriented by perceptions of lack that are directed at the female slave as epitomizing an irrelevant factor. The *Robinson Crusoe* fantasy allows Miss X. to assume an immutable Black sexual positioning without the constraints of white feminine expectation, which, as she notes quite similarly to Krafft-Ebing, is always a subordinate factor to manhood. Essentially nothing she emotes about the gender of slaves is about slaves but about her imagination of what total submission under a homosexual Human relation could feel like. The slave allows for the release of inhibitions where pleasure is fully imagined without the constraints of social determinacy placed on the proper behaviors of men. The male slave thus serves as a conduit to embrace the possibility of queer desire by using an absolutely derelict figure as the means to contest and subvert sexual expectation. Sexuality for the slave is submerged by a discursive field of sexual desire and subjective potential that can only imagine pleasure for the slave as pain and deformation. Desire in this case study does not speak forth from the slave, but imports the slave to bolster Human sexuality.

Is the gender ascribed to the fantasy the possession of male or female slave? In the truest sense, the fantasy is the possession of the masochist. Thus, what gender means in this scenario is a function of a symbolic ordering of presumed female insufficiency, where "not his female slave!" superimposes the structural lack Miss X. expresses about her own gender disempowerment as also the ontological predicament of the female slave. Similarly, the power Miss X. feels through the idea of manhood is redoubled back onto the male slave as his potential that is divorced from his body through physical and sexual torture. Foucault contends that a cost and benefit principle "makes it good to dream of sexual intercourse with slaves: one profits from one's possessions; that which one had purchased for the benefit of labor yields that benefit of pleasure besides."[79] For Miss X., transposing herself as the male slave allows her to mime the gratification of absolute submission to the power of white manhood. Dreaming of the forced submission of the male slave to the master extends the fantasy beyond a question of same-sex desire. Unlike the white woman or the white man, Blackness allows the fantasy to edge towards a paradigmatic distinction where queerness here is subsidiary to a totemic racial ordering.

Unlike deviating from the heteronormative expectation of sex, interracial sexual violence enacted upon the slave harkens on the truth of the paradigm. While sex is oriented on various scales of sexual development and desire for Human subjects (that can be and is violated in various ways), Black sex always exists under complete external possession. Unlike sexually deviant or violated Human subjects that maintain symbolic integrity outside of their sexual making, Blackness possesses no sexual quality that cannot be usurped by fusion and fantasy. Black sex is unmade by the force of mythos that produces a submission to power so immutable that it orients pubescent racial sexual development on a global scale. This psychic capture shortens the distance between the New World plantation and the psychiatric case studies collected by Krafft-Ebing.

Yet one could not say that the conjuring of slavery is produced by the individual. In either fantasy, Case 57 and Miss X. are remarking on and ideating towards a condition where historicity breaks in on the subject. There are material conditions that offer credence to their desires, yet at the same time we cannot say that the psyche is not inured by the very nature of the condition it conjures for pleasure. The psyche, like the plantation, is arranged by antiblackness. Under these conditions, the Black slave is submerged and possessed by the imposition of expectation placed upon it such that the weight of its myth is repeatedly confounded as to overdetermine its substance. The slave serves as a stand-in for what the masochist wants. We are not seeing the interior arrangements of the slave, but the essential role Blackness plays in animating how the subject comes into being through violent relations. These masochists expose the centrality of violence in sexuating the emergence of the slave as a conceivable sexual object. The absolute submission of the slave to all things, including most namely the fantasy of it, requires that the slave assume no definitive quality or response that cannot morph and hold the slave accountable to endless perceptions of its sexual quality.

The nineteenth-century psychiatry that develops from racial science offers the preconditions for the twentieth-century birth of psychoanalysis. The development of the study of the unconscious is undergirded by a merger of sexology and eugenics that sees the Black as primarily external to the development of a physic structure of sex even as it incorporates homosexuality as a natural abnormal development. Contrarily, Blackness does not evolve. It is external and antagonistic to Human development, thus ontologically foreclosed. As Kaan has shown, it erodes the Human, decaying the mind and organs. However, queerness sits squarely within the internal deviations of the Human. The queer is kin to an internal family quarrel primarily produced from concerns for and about the development of the Human as species, while the Black is unassimilable, occupying a completely other sexual concern that cannot be bracketed by questions of abnormality or negation. I contend, like Fanon, that the negro is not a negation but the pinnacle of dereliction. In the formation of thought itself, the Black does not simply figure a negation of the real. More damningly, the Black is vacant of sexual subjectivity that is infinitely bloated by projection and figuration of its form and inescapable violation. The Black is captured by the very gesture of thinking sex and sexuality because the very act of thought proceeds without recourse to an object construed by force and force alone.

As with Miss X., the assumptive logics of White queer and gender theory are themselves forms of masochism, where pleasure is derived from imagining the arbitrariness of the slave as a conduit toward announcements of the ontological significance of queerness and womanhood. Queer and gender theory operate on a phantasia of slavery that avoids close readings of the slave's ontological predicament in favor of projecting the slave and slavery as pure phantasm. These fields derive their theoretical oeuvre from using slavery as an empty example to strengthen claims for the ongoing significance of deblackened and general theorems of queerness or womanhood as the essence of suffering. This prevails despite how Black studies, by way of afro-pessimist interventions, continues to reveal the absolute saturation of the slave by sex as violence but also violence as sex. This position cancels any claims of sexual difference or sexuality as adjusting Blackness in order to incorporate a commentary on sex that Blackness does not already reveal or erode. While the first part of this chapter has dealt with queer theory in this respect, the chapter will conclude by examining White gender theory through similar vectors of argumentation.

Racial Fantasy and Rape Theory

Blackness and slavery occupy a curious position in feminist philosophies of rape. While Blackness is singled out as a repeated racialized rape example, very little is done to interrogate what about Blackness produces this unavoidable tension. While drawing on these vexed histories of racial sex, violence, and power to demonstrate the peculiarity of the Black example, some theorists fundamentally refuse to take these relations serious as substances that radically shift how race and sexual violence are theorized in their studies. At the same time, there is a forceful push to rethink sex/gender to avoid easy slippages that assume women as victims of their own ontology. Yet race becomes reduced to simple adherences where Black men are rethought as victimizers of women, although these readings are mildly sympathetic and not critical enough to arrive at any nuanced understandings of Black men. Additionally, Black women are subsumed under the veil of womanhood where their overrepresentation in the history of rape become evidence to the cause of universalized rape and gender arguments rather than critically centered to account for this particularity.

To grapple with the vexed fixedness of understandings of rape, this chapter engages the idiosyncratic nature of rape and also ravishment, which is a more expansive category of injury or offense. "In nineteenth century common law," rape "was defined as the forcible carnal knowledge of a female against her will and without her consent."[80] Ravishment predates the term rape, and is a medieval descriptor used to connote an array of violations involving the plight of women and children.[81] To ravish includes rape, as well as coerced marriage and child abduction, and is a general offense of force.[82] Given its more capacious definition, it might seem useful to situate ravishment as the real or true injury of the slave. Yet ravishment, as a way to conceptualize violence, is, like rape, an oxymoronic association for the slave, because force of any nature is not a transgression carried out against the slave but is foundational to its ontological unmaking. The intent of discussing ravishment in addition to rape is to highlight how the plight of the female slave exceeds the act of forced copulation and includes more expansive practices that are often conflated with rape or addressed in conjunction with it. Additionally, the coupling of these terms will illustrate the complexities of unnaming involved in subjugating female slaves as void of injury.

In *Rethinking Rape*, Ann J. Cahill offers a critical primer on divergences in feminist philosophical and legal interruptions on this matter, while foregrounding a rejoinder that exposes the problems of how rape is understood in some of the most radical feminist iterations. To stage a nuanced intervention, she interrogates two heralded perspectives on rape. The first is the refusal to address rape as a form of sex, or sexuality, instead foregrounding it as predicated purely on violence. This position, established by the work of sexual wave feminists, and particularly Susan Brownmiller, "provided a means by which the violence and cruelty of rape could be articulated without reference to the victim's sexuality, a reference that had only served to obscure the reality of women's experience of rape."[83] However, as Cahill points out, Brownmiller employs womanhood as natural and innately structurally vulnerable in a manner that relies, without explication, on biology as the justification for rape. Thus, Cahill argues that there are other ways to understand the male and female body, beyond the penetrator and the penetrable. Furthermore, if rape is political and not sexual, this argument "seems to forget that the rapist usually also achieves a sexual climax."[84] As such, Cahill maintains, at the very least rape needs to be understood at the intersections of power and sexuality. The harm in not attuning focus to such offers gender- or sex-neutral prescriptions for the problem of rape. Additionally, it fails to understand "the violence and power present in an act of rape are particularly sexualized; they gain, at least in part and perhaps entirely their meaning from a particular sexual hierarchy," which silences women and would amass "similar results" if gender neutral solutions were heralded.[85]

Cahill offers her second rejoinder to rape theory through an interrogation of the work of Catharine A. MacKinnon, and other radical feminist responses to second wave engagements with rape. She argues that their focus on the normalization of heterosexuality as what wills the rape of women is crucial but "overestimates the influence and coherence of the patriarchal construction of heterosexuality such that it identifies that construction with the impossibility of feminine agency."[86] Unlike Brownmiller, MacKinnon understands rape as force *and* as a crime connoted by the lack of consent for sex. However, because force is normalized in consensual heterosexual sex, this makes the capacity for the law and its practitioners to perceive the consensual distinction between rape and "normal" sex indecipherable. In this sense, heterosexuality is made socially compulsory by force, thus in all heterosexual engagements "there is no moment of 'true choice.'"[87]

Moreover, MacKinnon contends feminine sexuality is not the property of women, and is socially transfigured in a manner so pervasive as to structure *her* sex as inherently submissive and open for domination. Cahill contends that in this analysis, "The law's confusion in determining the difference between rape and consensual sex is due to its masculinist assumption that sex is, by definition, consensual, and that most women, most of the time freely consent to heterosexual intercourse."[88] Under these conditions, the law will forever be unable to distinguish any true distinction between sex and rape. Cahill disagrees that all heterosexual engagements are misogynistic because this viewpoint disempowers feminine agency. Instead, Cahill privileges the embodied experience of sex over perceiving the structure of sex as immutable. Simply, she argues that not all women experience their heterosexual sex as domination, despite the structural hetero-normalization of sex as predicated on privileging and preserving masculine domination.

In this respect, where do the choices of women factor into the framework? Cahill's theoretical departure occurs by way of recentering the feminine body as demanding further investigation and definition to rethink rape. She declares,

> The body is notoriously difficult to theorize, and the dangers of assuming it to be natural or clearly determined are well documented. Yet the politics of the body and the politics of gender are deeply intertwined, and rape, as a crime against specifically female bodies, takes place at the intersection of the two.[89]

In this way, the body helps to bring the sexuality and violence of rape into closer view. For Cahill, previous theories fall short of addressing the body, which is neither unique to Brownmiller or MacKinnon, but a broadly constituted feminist "stumbling block."

Beyond the dichotomous thinking that pervades most Western thought, and consequently feminism, Cahill argues that the body can "elucidate the meanings of the phenomenon of rape as an embodied experience, not to produce some generally applicable definition," but to ground "the specificity of female bodies and feminine experiences, an assumption that will attempt to correct the masculine bias inherent in previous definitions and analyses," to consider "rape as an embodied experience of women."[90] From here the arguments proceeds by detailing different and similar experiences of rape and their articulations by women. Cahill understands that embodiment means different things for different women and pushes against collapsing *the woman* into a universally derived biological category. Given that embodiment is culturally constructed, like rape culture for Cahill, it is impacted by a number of factors that challenge the singularity of the feminine body and the experience of rape. Thus, she argues, every rape is different; there is no one single definition or experience. Rethinking rape as multiply configured, she argues, does not reduce the impact of theorizing it but strengthens understandings as to open the possibility for effective resistance.

Cahill contends that Blackness, or rather the history of African Americans and rape, serves as a fundamental example of how the consideration of difference broadens perceptions of embodiment. Discussing the myth of the Black male rapist to think about how to approach the embodied experience of a white woman accusing a Black man of rape, the following argument is offered:

> The racial politics of rape is an example of the co-constitution of race and gender, in the production of a particular type of (white) femininity depended heavily on the racist stereotype of black masculinity. This complex co-constitution allows for no easy solution to any particular case of disputed interracial rape; it is impossible to argue for the position of either the accused or the accuser on its basis alone.[91]

In this regard, there is no right way to approach the issue. Feminism has taught us to protect the accuser at all cost. However, history makes it painfully clear that "this sexual myth—the quest for white flesh—perpetrated by alienated psyches, must no longer be allowed to impede active understanding."[92] As such, there is a way out of the problem. However, the question of embodiment privileged by Cahill fails to guide thought in the direction of contending with the antiblack psyche. Simply put, the imposition of Blackness challenges Cahill's analysis of rape. Despite its departure from previous feminist philosophical and legal thought, *Rethinking Rape* shares some of the limits of its predecessors. In its attempt to provide space for *all* forms of rape, *Rethinking Rape* is still fundamentally silent about the depths of interracial rape or, more to the point here, the antiblackness of rape theory. As is the case with suffering and freedom, holding space for *all* erodes focus on the particularities of Blackness. What occurs in the interracial forced sexual encounter is less a conversation about diversity, or how individuals experience their rapes differently. Rather, the touch point here is, what is interracial rape and how is it structured?

Race, or Blackness more specifically, is Cahill's "stumbling block." Though she attempts to account for race, like other feminists who maintain that race is a supplementary discussion to gender, Cahill still arrives belatedly to the conversation of antiblackness and sexual violence. As a framework, embodiment assumes the body as not only a possibility but also a given. In the case of Blackness, a body is a contested, if not impossible cartography. It cannot be proven that the body exists or is possessed by the Black. Thus, here is the tension. Cahill reads Black men and white women as constituted by different types of bodies. However, the fantasy of the white feminine body emerging precisely through the point of the false accusation is a psychic and material transfer of value produced by violence. Though it is not a stereotype (as Cahill noted), as in a false association, it is a truth of white–Black ontological distinction. The value of white feminine sanctity is produced and wagered against the fact that the Black man possesses no ontological resistance in the face of her claim. He, the Black man, has no value that can match or diminish her, the white woman's, truth. The truthfulness of the statement is irrelevant under these conditions, given that the accused and the accuser do not emerge from the same structural positioning of violence and sex. Furthermore, the constitution of this relation offsets the agentic feminine body as the pivotal focal point in the quest to understand what drives rape and what might dismantle its origins.

In Cahill's discussion of interracial rape, the structural distinction between white and Black are shored up to integrate antiblack sexual violence into a logic that racializes reconsiderations of perpetrators of rape but nevertheless fails to rethink the constitution of victimhood more broadly. This argument is emblematic of intellectual labors that remark upon the curious relationship between Blackness or Black history and sexual violation but do so within a framework that privileges the supremacy of universalized gendering to make sense of the racialization of sex. By evading concentrated focus on the racial history of gender, the reader is positioned to assume that the degradation of the Black agentic feminine body is the primary violation that undergirds antiblack sexual force, which is the assumptive logic that guides *Rethinking Rape*. Like death, sexual violation is the conditional possibility of all sentient beings. However, the metaphysical presuppositions of sexual violence do not constitute all beings as equivalently rapeable or sutured and arranged by the perceived submissive nature of femininity. Rather, the peculiarities of Black history that Cahill gestures towards, which in the above argument begins in a post-emancipation genealogy surrounding rape fantasies and lynching, is undergirded in the first instance by the force of slavery. Despite this fact, the analysis stops short of contending with slavery and its relationship to the feminine, for reasons I cannot wager. Most theories of rape operate on an assertion of how a feminine relationship to injury confers onto the violated body but are less equipped to consider forced copulation as a normative structural component of the Blackening of the slave. Engaging slavery turns this manner of perceiving rape upside down because it unveils a structure of violence predicated on a matrix of racial sexuation where equivalency across racial lines is an imposed cultural fantasy of ontological innocence that shrouds and obscures the role of womanhood and femininity in the structural operationalization of slave sexual violability.

Unlike Cahill, Brownmiller and MacKinnon find the locus of rape in structures of gender, the body, patriarchy, or the arrangements of the political and social. Yet an introspection into slavery erodes the structures they emphasize as appropriately explanatory to contend with dynamism of Black sexual violability. While these feminist theorists and others have been vastly influential in naming the problem of rape, the assumptive logics with which they operate are impoverished when considering the sexual status of the slave. As Saidiya Hartman has noted,

> It is not simply a matter of a woman's "no" not being taken seriously or of unveiling the crime when "it looks like sex." What is at issue here is the denial and restricted recognition of will or submission because of the legal construction of black subjectivity and the utter negation of the crime.[93]

What Hartman uncovers is how the question of Blackness radically destabilizes the assumptive logics of victimhood, consent, suffering, and culpability. This brings into sharp focus a contradictory assertion by Cahill that "few people (even among philosophers) would claim that rape does not, in virtually all conceivable contexts, constitute a serious moral wrong."[94] In the case of the sexual violation of the slave, there was no discernible crime or injury. Sexually violating a slave was not conceived as a moral wrong, but as an unremarkable structural position. As such, the stakes here are imbued by the capacity to see "the ways in which the captive is made responsible for her undoing and the black body is made the original locus of its violation."[95] This demonstrates that the marking of the slave as the sexually violable object of modernity reciprocally maintains the Black, or Blackness more specifically, as solely culpable for the sexual violability that produces and reproduces Black social death. There is no white aggressor, or culpable agent, that can be held accountable in a manner that would offset or underwrite this unethical arrangement.

Slavery circulates in rape theory as the recurrent example.[96] The sexual experiences of slaves are deployed as examples of the historical, racial, and terrifying grasp of rape within systems of domination, where the very act of forced copulation fails to register as rape given the status of the violated. However, it is often without contextualization that these examples appear. Slavery then operates as one of many examples of rape where the reader is asked to attend to rape as multiply inflective, where "we might remember rape as a way to make slaves, rape as a way to make workers, rape as a way to grab land."[97] While these excitations of the many contexts of rape are not untrue, as rape does figure the structural and lived experiences of so many categories of existence, the question here is what role does the slave occupy in invoking its sexual violation in relation to other forms of sexual injury? Secondly, considering the infinite ways that rape appears in the cultural histories of modernity, why is the slave an anticipated and permanent example to these claims when other examples fall in and out of view, or may never appear in rape theory at all?

The sexual status of the female slave is one of the most vexed yet widely discussed forms of violence during racial slavery.[98] American Studies scholar Andrea Smith argues that the female slave was rendered "inherently rapeable"; however, their rapes were seen as negligible given their property status.

She juxtaposes this argument against that of rape and Native genocide by stating, "Yet where colonizers used sexual violence to eliminate Native populations, slave owners used rape to reproduce an exploited labor force."[99] This passage goes on to cite *partus sequitur ventrem* as evidence of rape as a tool for the reproduction of labor. Indeed, two things can be true. Yes, slaves were sexually violated and bred and the offspring of this violence also assumed the position as slaves. Additionally, despite this reality, forced copulation was not solely predicated upon the reproduction of the plantation economy. Without presenting evidence, Smith espouses a commonly held position, which is that sexual violence served one predominating role in the lives of female slaves, which is to hold their reproduction capacities in perpetual captivity. Though, arguably this is a surface-level assertion.

Yet, if the arithmetic of the plantation was this logical, why the reappearance and incessant pause on the example of the female slave and her sexual violation? Is it because of the gravity and scale of slavery? Or could it be that the figure of the female slave is a porous example that can occupy many positions for argumentation's sake? Which to say, the female slave is a phantasmagoric figure where her sexual condition, both on the plantation and beyond, serves to buttress fantasies of suffering that bring recognition to the subjects that are called upon in relation to her status. This superpositioning does not illuminate her condition but rather submerges the particularity of her violable status in a web of relational associations that allow her to be everything yet nothing at the same time.

To transmute the suffering of forced copulation and other forms of reproductive violence into the conceptual frameworks and discursive schemas of rape and ravishment, the female slave must be transfigured as a gendered integrity that can be degraded by violation as an event rather than occupy violation as a permanent immutable status. Womanhood, for the female slave, I argue, is where the slave as pure violation is fantasied as a subject of gender as theory of contract and injury. The ontological absence of the male slave is deputized to wager claims about his freedom from sexual injury as a means to substantiate the female slave as the highest form of "signifying property *plus*," where female and male "as personal pronouns are offered in service of a collective function."[100]

The predicament of the female slave is bound by confining social logics that continue to replicate the clause that "male dominance is perhaps the most pervasive and tenacious system of power in history" and "it is metaphysically nearly perfect."[101] While female slaves were sexually violated by White men and male slaves alike, as well as by White women and possibly other female slaves, the question still remains: what constitutes the ontological arrangements that situate all slaves as captive to this structural predicament? Furthermore, why is the female slave repeatedly privileged as revealing a truth about sexual difference and slavery that is presumed an impossible exposure when looking at the predicaments of male slaves?

Contracting Womanhood

Following the abolition of slavery, much concern was placed on the ability of former slaves to enter into and manage contracts specifically pertaining to labor. Contracts were perceived to afford Black people with the capacity to opt into the labor market, which slavery stripped from them through the imposition of force. Abolitionist and social reformer William Lloyd Garrison was a strong proponent of the freedom of contracts for newly freed slaves. He proclaimed, "From the auction-block, to be sold to the highest bidder, to the ballot box, to vote and to be voted for . . . Freedman at work as independent laborers by voluntary contract!"[102] Contractual capacity was viewed as essential to undoing slavery and other forms of involuntary servitude. The impetus for this focus was based on testimony from slaves and former slaves about what was needed to establish themselves post-emancipation, as well as white abolitionist political mediations of Black desires.[103] While abolitionists were not all in agreement about how, and to what extent, the government should regulate contracts for the newly freed; nevertheless, they focused on this relation as pivotal for distinguishing slavery from freedom.[104] Despite these political imaginings, voluntary contracts did not impart a full capacity for self-determination or sovereignty for the newly freed Black population.

The conscription of former slaves as free from bondage obscured the ongoing structural forces of antiblackness that prevailed beyond abolition. Furthermore, the terms of freedom grafted onto former slaves also served as new mediating lenses for thinking and theorizing what constituted the wrongs of slavery. In this sense, the terms of emancipation reinscribed a logic onto the structure of slavery that presupposed the social relations of emancipation as the repressive drives that contributed to the rise and fall of the plantation. Contracts, or the lack thereof, became one of the central points of analyses. The inability of slaves to enter into voluntary social contracts cast a perception that slavery as an institution severed contractual capacitation as the divine right of all sentient beings. This framework of analysis does not extend far enough to grasp hold of the ontological relations of antiblackness as metaphysical impositions that underwrite structures of identification. Moreover, contracts were not suspended during slavery, such that the implications of their usages were delayed for slaves. Instead, slavery imposed an antiblack value on the contract as a form of valued self-possession because of its racially exclusionary function.[105] Instituting former slaves into the legal and social customs of contracts as voluntary arrangements required a shift in perspective about the capacity of slaves to engage in labor relations under different terms. However, this did not concretize a full-scale shift in the way antiblack carceral logics overdetermined what contracted labor could mean for the newly freed. Convict leasing and debt peonage nullified the incorporation of Black workers into civil society by refiguring the state or white employers as masters by different names.

Under these systems of reorganized captivity, sexual violence continued to overwhelmingly conscript the lives of former slaves. Black feminist historian Sarah Haley provides a critical perspective on the interrelation between post-slavery antiblack labor controls and sexual violation. She argues,

> The debt peonage and convict labor regimes created new, modern systems of captive labor and black women's roles as the reproducers of women and men who existed merely to work for the profit of white agricultural and industrial interests made the politics of their bodies and subject positions vitally important for the maintenance of Jim Crow/white supremacy. Black women's rape, the violation of the geopolitical space between their legs, made possible other spaces of exploitation and violence by reinforcing the black female subject's position as dispossessed of rights, of economic entitlements, of bodily integrity, safety, and mobility.[106]

The continued rampant exposure of Black women to sexual violence was evidenced by the number of births that occurred while they were under the control of the state in camps and prisons. Haley notes that childbirth records in Georgia camps indicated that while only one woman entered the camp pregnant, more than one woman birthed a child during her time under convict-lease.[107] While childbirth served as the material content to prove that Black women were being raped, even as they were socially understood as incapable of such, it is also worth noting that Black men under the control of debt peonage or convict leasing were also being subjected to rape and other forms of sexual mutilation. However, there were no similar structures of evidence like birth records to prove or substantiate this additional claim of Black men's rampant susceptibility to sexual harm. Nonetheless, under conditions of absolute power imbalances, between the confined and their confiners, sexual violation and assaults were fundamental to these captive arrangements, adding to the absolute terror of confinement.[108]

Labor contracts were but one component of how former slaves were presumed to be incorporated into preexisting Humanist ideals of social relations. Gender as a theory of contract additionally served as a container for mediating former slaves. Contractual relations of gender in the private sphere also entered the frame as something newly afforded to former slaves that was previously controlled by the master. Emancipation offered among many things the contractual promise of civilly recognized marriage, a contract underwritten by certain prescripts about gender relationality. Political economic participation, as well as the right to marry, not only embedded Blackness with a new boundedness to volition and civic and private relations, but it recast narratives about what slavery denied the slave with respect to economic and sexual choice.[109]

The promise of Black kinship relations situated an analytic focus on gender under slavery, with predominating theoretical assumptions maintaining that the inherent nature of patriarchal rule in governing gender imbalances dispossessed slaves of certain gendered potentials. Loss and perceptions of degraded gender are rooted in the steadfast belief of gender as an innate inscription of the body or that its capacitation is based on the natural right of Human life and existence. The sexual contract, where men are empowered over women in political and social life, is redoubled onto readings of plantation arrangements between slaves as well as between slaves and masters. The scope of investigation overdetermines manhood and womanhood as preceding and anticipating Blackness. Under this purview, uncovering the racial particularities of patriarchy functions to reveal the unique plight of the female slave as inured by a dual infliction of the sexual contract. Which is to say, this approach is invested in exposing the relations of the slave as construed by denied gender capacity that is racially conferred. Maintaining Black gender as repressed potential—whether in terms of labor or gender—attempts to humanize the slave under auspices that applying Human identificatory structures to the slave can repair its debilitated status. This commonly held myopic understanding, which appears in very rigorous assessments of the plantation, takes binary gender as a given social arrangement with private and public implications. However, slavery exposes how the cartography of gender is parasitic on Black incapacitation to clarify and strengthen its ontological reinvention. Investigations into the status of the female slave reveal a structural refusal to confront the incipient role of theorizing womanhood as progressive self-possession—a resistant claim against the sexual contract of patriarchy—in subordinating a focus on antiblack paradigmatic violence as that which disarrays the explanatory power of the gender binary.

There are many instances where the female slave occupies theory as an empty object used in service of deracialized arguments about gender. I will not spend time with these examples as they present too easy of an argument of the author's blind acceptances of racist maneuverings of history. However, these examples are not the only instances of undertheorizing regarding how slavery structures the conceptual coherence of gender and its capacities by naming the female slave as a theoretical appendage. In some of the most rigorous feminist arguments—some that, in fact, may mirror the most rigorous theories of racial slavery to date—the refusal to dissect the category of woman leaves these theories bare to refusals to engage the mistress as violent benefactor and agent of the plantation as a necessary gender structure to engage in relation to consider the violation of the female slave.

In *The Sexual Contract*, Carole Pateman offers a judicious reading—departing from the common sense of political philosophy—of the nonrelation between racial slavery and contract theory. While published over three decades ago, the book still maintains an important intervention into feminist and political theories of gender, sex, and contractual relations. *The Sexual Contract* argues that "the 'individual' is a patriarchal category," and as such the capacity of the individual to preserve itself under contractual relations is a fallacy for women and nonwhites made possible by institutions that veil subjugation as forms of freedom.[110] Departing from the centering of the contract as the root of societal ills, Pateman declares that "contract and slavery must be mutually exclusive," because the slave is not a laborer but instead, "becomes a thing, a *res*, a commodity that can be bought and sold like any other piece of property."[111] This position challenges the status quo of much political theory, which often contends that slavery is a derivative of capital, thus positing the slave as a degraded worker.

Writing against the "fanciful air" of "civil slavery" or "slave contracts," Pateman maintains a position against the deceptive lure of equating the slave to workers but also other forms of servants.[112] The point is not to suggest that the weak are not exploited and alienated by social contracts, which is "why socialists and feminist have focused on the conditions of entry into the employment contract and the marriage contract."[113] The imbalance of power that exists between unequal parties in a contract does not nullify the individual free will of the less powerful party. Although the individual free will and right of the weaker subject may be difficult to discern or exercise, it does not mean it is unimaginable. For instance, at the level of theory, it is conceivable how one might escape the unequal power placed upon them by the contract. The worker quits the job, the wife leaves the marriage. Or, on a grander scale, the worker permanently halts the mode of production and the wife smashes the patriarchy. The freedom for the individual to move against and despite its condition is sutured by political and social subjectivity.

However, the slave has lost the recognition of personhood, violently restructured as flesh. How does the slave, then, restore the cartography of a body? Drawing on the work of Orlando Patterson, Pateman identifies the slave as socially dead, "'dishonored in a generalized way' because his social existence and worth was entirely reflected through the master," which for her extends beyond simply turning human into property.[114] The free individual and the slave are disimbricated in form and matter given that "a person does not become a dishonoured, socially dead piece of property by entering a contract."[115] Contracts do not make a person a slave.

Up until this point, there are points of convergence between Pateman's observations and a founding point of departure for afro-pessimism, as theorized by Wilderson, where he and others discuss the distinction between the worker and the slave at great lengths. Wilderson addresses the slave–worker distinction with much force and vigor, arguing,

This structurally impossible position is a paradox because the black subject, the slave, is vital to civil society's political economy: s/he kick-starts capital at its genesis and rescues it from its over-accumulation crisis at its end—black death is its condition of possibility.[116]

Yet, Pateman, by not extending her argument to state the obvious tension here, does not grapple with what afro-pessimism eventually helps us take up. *The Sexual Contract* is unclear about what slavery and social death mean for the central thesis on sex, gender, and violation. It is an argument that is abandoned in favor of carrying gender forward as uninhibited by social death, when the slave is introduced to the argument as an example. Rather than racializing the slave and complicating gender further, the argument is staved off in favor of the feminist tendency to deviate toward woman as the first and primary slave.

To contend that the slave and the gendered subjects of contracts must be mutually exclusive, in the manner that Pateman emphatically states about the slave and the worker, would foreclose the general premise of the project. Setting up an antagonism between slavery and the explanatory power of the gender binary is antithetical to the desire to announce a theory of the fundamental social and political distinctions between how the world contractually conditions all women and men. For Pateman, the ontological presuppositions about womanhood or manhood are not up for question. The text imposes the task of rectifying how the terms of man and woman condition the subject, rather than calling into question the efficacy of the terms themselves as explanatory of all structures of violence. Gender difference is maintained in the text as an assumption about binary sex-gender divisions conditioned by biological life processes. Race is ushered in as corollary to gender.

In this calculus, slaves, when gendered, are repositioned outside of racial terms and privileged as a condition opened to womanhood. The slave basically functions as a metaphor for woman. In this vein, Pateman asserts without hesitation that, "the first slaves were *women*," citing Gerda Lerner's *The Creation of Patriarchy* to make her point.[117] From here, rape and ravishment are privileged as proof of this assertion, stating "women could be put to more uses than men slaves. Women can be used sexually by men in addition to being used as a labour force, and, through sexual use, the slave labour force can reproduce."[118] However, a general theorem of woman as slave is not supported by concerted modern evidence of all women occupying a structural position as slaves. Rather, it is a fantasy authorized by a symbolics of dispossession that suggests that to be exterior to manhood or subordinated within patriarchy is tantamount to being a slave. The text deviates between examples, which are largely drawn from the history of modern racial slavery and political philosophical generalizations of the slave as a general category in relation to Man. Gender and interrogations of sexual violence under the context of modern racial slavery are altogether abandoned towards investigating the patriarchal logics of the genealogy of the slave in political thought.

Pateman gestures toward the plantation mistress as a unique structural positioning, but marks her primary distinction as counterposed to other white wives rather than from the Black female slave.[119] Class sutures this divide and the racial congruence between wives regardless of economic or social standing is gravely unattended. This difference is charted for Pateman because although "American slave owners sold their slave, not their wives," white plantation mistresses had to suffer through their husbands maintaining white and Black "families."[120] While she notes the use of family in this context is "beautifully ambiguous," she nonetheless goes on to cite historian Eugene Genovese in saying that slave owners often protected their female slaves from male slave physical violence, even as they themselves showed no mercy when beating female slaves.[121] This entanglement of examples harkens upon the highlighting of the female slave as conditionally cared for and abused by slave owners, and this ambiguity serves not to elaborate her condition but to shift a sympathetic lens back on white women. From these examples, Pateman gestures to suggest that womanhood as a condition for Black and white women involved scales of care and violation, such that "a wife is like a civil slave," and given her absent wage, "she is more like a servant, who also is a domestic labourer."[122] What is gravely absent in this assessment of the wife as a racial social category is an analysis of political ontology, which would expose the unspeakable symbiosis of the plantation wife as the progenitor of the domestication of racial sexual violence. Her quality as such is not solely by way of her actions, although those are critically important, but through her structural positioning in plantation sexual and domestic arrangements.

In this respect, *The Sexual Contract* considers the Black slave insofar as its suffering can be deputized for the benefit of protecting the category of universally applied womanhood. This is a common and unsurprising gesture taken up as truth by many, like the feminist foreperson Mary Wollstonecraft, who writes,

> I shall not go back to the remote annals of antiquity to trace the history of woman; it is sufficient to allow that she has always been either a slave, or a despot, and to remark, that each of these situations equally retards the progress of reason.[123]

This is only one of several references to women as slaves and slavery throughout Wollstonecraft's *A Vindication of the Rights of Woman*, a text that continues to catalyze many into feminism.

German scholar Sabine Broeck takes on slavery in the white feminist imaginary in *Gender and the Abjection of Blackness*, in which she argues,

> In contrast to those competitive and successful white female negotiations of the human, which centralized the recognition of gender difference as a motor of humanism, "slave" was a term that enabled a different series of significations, allowing, as the necessary negative foil, feminism to think "freedom" (and "gender"), because "unfreedom" and "thingness" was perpetually fixed on the site of abjected Black being.[124]

Slavery, however defined, is usurped from Blackness and is deputized as a claim of the longue durée of the suffering of white women, which assumedly predates and exceeds the context of New World slavery.

Under this arrangement of thought, as articulated by Pateman, "The original contract is a sexual-social pact, but the story of the sexual contract has been repressed."[125] Pateman goes on to say,

> The original contract constitutes both freedom and domination. Men's freedom and women's subjection are created through the original contract—and the character of civil freedom cannot be understood without the missing half of the story that reveals how men's patriarchal right over women is established through contract.[126]

The other half of the story for Pateman, as referenced in this quote, is that modern patriarchy is built upon the same principles of the original contract, "the genesis of political right," which grants men the right to exercise power over women.[127] However, what is foundationally missing from the larger argument on slavery presented throughout the book is commentary on how gender as force is vested over the Black slave in a manner that differs from a question of political right. Instead, gender as white ontological distinction is based on an arithmetic of kinship, social, public, and private obligations that are mobilized by antiblack violence. To investigate this precise point, the historical realities of the violence and power of white women in the plantation South must be taken seriously as ontological questions rather than one of personal choice or individual malice.

While Pateman demonstrates an undeniably white feminist argument that refuses to waver on universal womanhood as the essential suffering subject position of the modern world, what may seem obvious about its assumptions are not as clear. Pateman is as hobbled by whiteness, which is readily apparent, but she also deputizes biocentrism, which is the buried anchor for her theory of the sexual. This latter point is where the assumptive logics of *The Sexual Contract* clarify a problem with gender analyses that extend beyond whiteness and into investigations of Black womanhood. Investigating womanhood—however racially configured—as a biological given allows for certain slippages to emerge with respect to violence. Contending that the wife is subordinated to the husband and the female slave is raped and beaten by the slave master as dual evidence of the violable status of womanhood prioritizes sociology over ontology, mathematically tallying violence to collect evidence of harm as opposed to interrogating violence as relation.

To clarify this point, the wife is in a contractual relation with the husband, no matter how socially and civilly constricted. The female slave, however, is a captive in a forced relation to the master *and* the mistress. Approaching suffering from the vantage point that womanhood is the essence of the real of gender violence deputizes a logic of contract, which assumes that the problem with gender is locating an equitable coexistence within the binary. At the same time, the female slave exposes that the gender binary as a contractual relation is sutured by a structure of identification and feeling that requires a permanent externalized Black object that is fictively incorporated as part and parcel to its affective scaffolding. Additionally, the violation of this objectified figure strengthens the perception that gender is genitally construed, given the sexed similarity between it and the representational racial pairing it is forced into community with. At the same time, the violence that is wagered against the Black object, which is sexually configured, is redoubled as evidence of its denied capacity for the same structure of racially sexuated gendering that creates the filial and affilial relations of whiteness or non-Blackness. The master and the mistress overcome their filial contractual conflicts, through their racial capacity to wield violence over and against Black slaves, which cannot be reciprocated, as a structural component of each of their gendering.

Another complication is the assumption that the condition of slaves, or the status of Black gender, mimes the sexual contract that exists between masters and mistresses. For example, there is a theoretical assumption that violability of female slaves can only be expressed in relational tension to the status of the male slave, under a presumed sexual contract between captives. We can see this dubious conclusion appear when it is expressed that the female slave suffers sexually, therefore the male slave is cast as a lesser vector of sexual violability. The overdetermination and hyper reliance on the gender binary in explaining sexual violence for the captive redoubles the fantasy of the female slave as mimed womanhood, as the status that can and should reshape plantation sexual arrangements by emerging as a contractual subject of grievance. Theorizing the structural predicament of the female slave bases her suffering in a biocentric understanding of gender and womanhood that is located at the level of the body, rather than within political ontology and violence. This framework deputizes the Black woman, or the enslaved Black woman, as the category from which redress for the female slave is staked and claimed. The pitfalls and troubles of this position, which, to be clear, grafts the sex-gender binary onto slaves as a form of natural relation, right, and intelligibility, relies on a contractual logic of suffering and reclamation out of which can only emerge a desired schema of gender potentiality through the paradigmatic obfuscation of the violence of the plantation mistress.

Great contention has been taken with the fields of feminist historiography, legal theory, and philosophy for their usages of the plight of the female slave. These usages include making claims of universal womanhood or to perversely argue that female slaves possessed agency in sexual dynamics with white men that made them structurally adjacent to or, in some sense, more powerful than the white mistresses of plantation homes. Countering feminist historiography that refuses to acknowledge the unfettered power of the white women on plantations, Thavolia Glymph makes it clear that "plantation mistresses were slaveholders," despite their vexed relationship to property rights and legal ownership of slaves.[128] Furthermore, white womanhood structurally occupied a capacity for violence in relation to the slave that is often veiled by gendered analyses that seek to privilege patriarchy and paternalism as the primary concerns of slavery.[129] Glymph exposes the fissures in these arguments by shifting focus to the raw brutality and violence enacted by plantation mistresses onto slaves. Highlighting how white women's violence is not accidental, but part of the structural architecture of slavery, where "she [the mistress] lives in a world that did not construe her actions as damaging to her reputation as *compos mentis*."[130] The adjustment Glymph makes between gender as sentiment, or allegiance to gender as violence, is profound. This allows one to broaden the frame beyond the individual or collective actions of womanhood during the antebellum period into thinking about womanhood as a conceptual framework that is violent on its own terms. Womanhood as a category makes violence possible for mistresses at the same time it serves to normalize and veil this violence by subordinating it as proxy to patriarchal desires, which lessens the scale of how its capacities are accounted for and understood. Citing the voices of former slaves, Glymph highlights how "slaves drew no such contrast between cruel masters and mistresses."[131] This equivalency demands pause. More, it reveals the terms of the gendered categorization of the mistress and how this framework remains operable. Is womanhood arbitrary insofar as it resonates new meanings or relations to violence when redeployed outside of the direct context of slavery? Or do gender concepts themselves, and, in this case, womanhood, persist in pulling a veil over violence, such that the ravishment carried out by the category itself is repeatedly left unscathed by an insistence that its relationship to violence is random, to cite Glymph again, and not structurally bound?

The deployment of Lerner by Pateman, to argue that the woman is the essential slave, is distinct from the assertion by Black feminist and cultural theorist Hortense J. Spillers that "the quintessential 'slave' is *not* a male, but a female."[132] Spillers structures this argument based on the premise that the African female "performed tasks of hard physical labor," coupled with evidence that the extent of the sexual violations against female slaves and "their own express rage against their oppressors" are concealed by the historical record.[133] This argument is not dissimilar on the surface from the one presented in the social contract, where sexual violence plus labor essentialize the woman slave over the man. However, what Spillers contends with, that Lerner and Pateman do not, is that "feminization" is a veil placed upon the female slave that superimposes a status that "enslavement kept at bay" and that is constituent of womanhood, a white/Human gender category.[134]

The slave elicits a crisis in the sex/gender divide by exposing womanhood as an ontological category to which the Black slave is exterior. Rather than holding onto slavery in the white feminist tradition as a relation between man and woman, Spillers's argument delineates differing modes of gendering and unnaming that are premised upon metaphysical violence, which racially sub-categorizes slaves as external to the kinship structures that reproduce womanhood and manhood. Under this paradigmatic structure, woman cannot, ontologically, be a slave. However, woman can mime the slave for the purposes of elaborating claims of suffering while masking the violence that womanhood, as a racial category, is structurally preconditioned by. This is not an equivalent statement as to assert that historically Black slaves were not at times referred to under such terms. They were. Contrarily, slavery for the slave constitutes "the displacement of the genitalia," as well as "the female's and male's desire that engender future," where the categories woman and man are empty signifiers that obscure the slave's violated status, not clarify it.[135] Gender is an ontological status of being and becoming. The slave concretizes a captive form of referentiality where suffering is only representable under the terms that presuppose the presence of sex/gender potential and the futurity of slave sexual desire that is distinct and counter to the desire of the gendered status of the master class, mistresses and white children included.

However, Spillers animates the argument about the status of the female slave on her own slippage; a reimposition of the female–male slave divide in a manner that mirrors the presuppositions that undergird the domination thesis of the sexual contract. In this respect, a value judgment is placed upon the "labors" of female and male slaves, where the reproductive function of the female slave is upheld as proof of exponentialized suffering and ravishment. The Middle Passage serves as evidence to the point that we have "no idea of the fate of the pregnant female captive and the unborn," thus making her status more precarious than that of the male slave.[136] Though Spillers, in her most cited clause, states earlier in this same essay the slave's

New-World, diasporic plight marked a *theft of the body*—a willful and violent (and unimaginable from this distance) severing of the captive body from its motive will, its active desire. Under these conditions we lose at least gender difference *in the outcome*, and the female body and the male body become territory of cultural and political maneuver, not at all gender-related gender specific.[137]

If, under the transmutation of the Middle Passage and the conditions of captivity, we lose gender difference and gender specificity, what then does gestation mean for the slave? I do not ask this as a means of being rhetorically obtuse. Rather, what do pregnancy and reproductive capacity mean without gender specification? How can the captive female be read outside of the logics of womanhood and "the benefits of a *patriarchilized* female gender?"[138] Is there a natural quality to the experience of femaleness that is distinctive from the sexual-social pact or contract of patriarchy that Pateman argues is foundational to understandings of freedom and domination?

The sexual function of the female slave is often described through "the productivity of the capitalized womb, a term . . . to refer to the ways enslaved women's bodies functioned as the essential production engine of the slave breeding economy."[139] This conceptual framework highlights the gratuity of the sexual violation of the slave as well as its metaphysical dilemma. Insofar as we can say the slave economy thrived on the rampant and incessant impregnation of slaves, we cannot say that those pregnancies were possessed by wombs of slaves as women, if we understand gender and slavery as co-constitutive. Simply, to be a slave and to be gendered were mutually exclusive. The theft of the African body results in the loss of "gender difference in the outcome," *and* (re)produces the conscious and unconscious parameters of gendered fantasies of possession and embodiment.[140] The fantasy of the slave's sexual injury, which is not to say the fact of such injury, provides cogency to the many meanings of gender. Referring back to the "capitalized womb," the uterus in this context is representative of organs without gender, in the sense that Gilles Deleuze and Félix Guattari write of the body without organs, where the "phenomena of individualization and sexualization are produced."[141] However, contrary to Deleuze and Guattari, who assert that "the first things to be distributed on the body without organs are races, cultures, and their gods," the sexual (re)productive function of slave organs are not individuated as constitutive markings of crystalized difference. The uterus, as well as all other physical and psychic dimensions of the slave, are sexually operationalized toward endless unbound and unrestrained violation. The nature of the violation is repeatedly undertheorized in support of extending the slave a semblance of assumed denied gendered recognition. How, then, can theory sit with the drives and fantasies that undergird the violation itself, while not escaping to assumptions about the qualification or quantification of injury and its implications or aftereffects? What is sexual violability for the female slave if it is not taken up as an assault on gendered or sexual capacity?

What occurs in the instance of subordinating the male slave to the female slave's reproduction function is a metastasizing the womb as the quintessential organ of slavery. Slaveness, then, necessitates providing evidence of endured brute force to grant primacy to one form of slave over another as exemplar of the peculiar institution's desire for sexual domination and conquest. The barometer of proof needed to prove the illegitimacy of slavery and its appetite for sexual violation is placed on the female slave. Can the female slave prove her suffering? The structural violence of the institution is obscured in favor of a slave tete-a-tete. Thus, the female slave is privileged as *the* sexually violable slave through the denial or refusal to understand the male slave as also, albeit differently, sexuated. Rape compounded with evidence of ravishment becomes the essential precursor for claiming gender suffering that can only move directionally towards womanhood or the logics of non-slave gender injury as the future redress and rightful position of the female slave. This projection relies on the dismissal or disavowal of the male slave as a sexualized category. However, as I will argue in following chapter, the male slave is mired with its own forms of disavowed sexualization.

There are moments when Spillers writes against the slippages that assert the slave female and male as antagonistic dualities. The writing highlights the complexities at the heart of describing refracted violation in relation to logics pertaining to (un)gender. Remarking on works produced in the 1980s, including Spillers's "Mama's Baby, Papa's Maybe: An American Grammar Book," Brittney Cooper asks "whether Black feminism needs its own metaphysics," stating further that Black feminists "must clear our throats of a metaphysics that is alien to how the vast majority of Black women ... are structurally positioned."[142] The assumptive logic that sustains this question and assertion suggests that desire and motive will constitute the inauguration of a metaphysics. Though Spillers argues that the (un)gendering of the captive condition severs the slave from any possessed motive, will, and desire that is distinctive, legible, and "liberated" from the violent acts that repetitiously constituted it as the zero degree of Human conceptualization. The indecipherability of gender that emerges in this context is least concerned with the question of slave subjectification as it is with the violence of racial sexuation. What is sexually violent becomes indistinguishable at the level of gender, as subjectivity and differentiation are marked as the terrains of the Human. What raises acts asserted against the slave to the level of violence that confers a type of legibility, logic, or recognizable form? What makes violence as a metaphysics discernable for the slave? Can the sexually violent acts and fantasies that "underwrite the modern world's capacity to think, act, and exist spatially and temporally" constitute a slave metaphysics?[143]

Instead, Spillers critically engages the "oceanic," a Freudian term designating undifferentiated identity, scaling focus down to the abstracted terrain of the flesh straddling the murky and unsettled economy left in the wake of the Middle Passage.[144] This argument focuses on a space where no traces of implied Humanity for the captive are found, where the atomizing of the body makes "personality and anatomical features," "one human personality from another," and "human personality and cultural institutions" indistinguishable.[145] Kinship has been stripped through the process of naming property. Negro functions synonymously with slave, female gender and male gender perform one another in drag, and the only legible relatedness existing between captives functions horizontally, being "invaded at any given and arbitrary moment by the property relations."[146] The saliency of this critique is in its critical attention to Black violability across registers. However, it is also striking for its capacity to render slavery as simultaneously fixed and pliably violent. In a sense it suggests that what is violent is banal and nuanced, decoded and encrypted, gendered and agender, spectacular and quotidian, and intimate and perverse. Thus, in navigating the both/and/neither/nor of these polarities, thought must grapple with a complex interplay of (anti)black (a)gendered(less) terms, a re-engagement with history as such, and a reconceptualization of slave sexual functionality on these grounds.

Following slavery as social death—without abandoning this relation as performed by the analysis of gender and slavery offered by Pateman—highlights the impossibility of womanhood as a stable claim from which to announce injury or freedom from suffering for the female slave. Contrary to the claim by Katherine McKittrick that "once the racial sexual body is territorialized, it is marked as decipherable and knowable—as subordinate, inhuman, rapeable, deviant, procreative, placeless," social death holds that territorialization is an incomplete and perhaps impossible project.[147] The terror of slavery is facing sexual force and phantasm as an unrepresentable paradigmatic imposition that is required for continued forms of gendered and sexual legibility. Yet those forms of legibility cannot render the slave and its violating quality representable because it is held captive by a structural logic of sexual difference and violation that continues to draw the slave into subject categories it was inextricably excluded from, to make sense of violence.

Five
Manning Black Gender

Courttia Newland writes with a meditative pause as he prepares for a confession. He is a writer and a Black man. Of these, he is sure. However, he is not quite confident about what or if there is a grammar to account for his continued experiences of sexual objectification and subsequent punishment. He proceeds anyway. Newland lost his job after refusing the unwanted sexual advances of his white woman superior. He was fired for failing to meet his boss at her house. She accosted him on several occasions, once glaring into his eyes while working, letting him know that "she had black friends . . . who would 'love'" him.[1] He never asks, love me how? He knows these are sexual overtures. When he received the call informing him that he was fired, he knew that what was required of him was sex and he was fired for not giving it. However, he never states this explicitly. Yet his angst makes clear that he understands there is a sexual requirement of him, one that he does not desire, that exceeds the singular or the particularities of his individual experiences.

Newland offers his story, entitled "And Me . . ." as an addendum to the growing fervor around the #MeToo movement.[2] His story is one in a collection of stories by Black British men who narrate the complexities of their daily realities in the edited volume *Safe: 20 Ways to be a Black Man in Britain Today*. In 2017, the #MeToo movement grew in popularity as a critical commentary on the sexually abusive culture of Hollywood after the hashtag was used by actress Alyssa Milano to shed light on the abuse of women in the entertainment business. However, MeToo was founded by Tarana Burke, a Black woman and sexual trauma survivor, over a decade prior in 2006, to bring attention to the unique silences surrounding the sexual abuse and violations of Black girls and women.³ Burke wanted to provide space for Black girls and women to share their stories and to find support, while also being critical of the racism and misogynoir that pervades discourses on sexual victimhood.⁴ Newland thus extends his own meditation on expanded discourses about sexual violation, wondering how, and if, Black men fit the frame. Unlike responses to #MeToo that minimize the significance of its aims by universalizing, Newland is interested in something quite different. He is thinking critically and pensively about how histories of racial violence and violation may trouble narratives about the genders of those who perpetrate harm and those who are its victims. At the same time, he is careful to not delegitimize the feminist narratives that make thinking sexual violence possible. He also does not want to privilege his singular experience as definitive evidence of some other veiled truth. In this respect, his story is just that, his story. Nevertheless, woven into his narrative are questions about history that open his individual experiences to structural implications.

He writes, "It's clear to me that this incident is an example of white female privilege being used to dominate a young black man."⁵ Newland understands this "privilege" as rooted in racial violence, yet he apologizes for his pronouncement, stating "it's obvious that none of my personal experiences come anywhere close to the heinous crimes of rape and enforced sexual harassment committed globally by men."⁶ In spite of, or more accurately so, *because of* the texture of patriarchal violence, he asserts, "I had to submit to being exoticised in accordance with the hypersexual stereotype that black men are often framed by."⁷ He offers more apologies as if he perceives his audience will assume he is being ungenerous to white women. "Of course, I'm not writing to generalise a whole race and gender."⁸ Perhaps this anxiety is elicited by what he has previously made the reader aware of: "When I refused to reciprocate, I was punished."⁹ His speech is congested by white women and their animus towards violence. He is a writer. The job he lost was as a writer. His white superior was an editor. He has lost at least two jobs because of his refusal to act in accordance with his sexualization. He remembers, "After that second incident, I was left in freefall, jobless, with a child to raise and a mortgage to pay."¹⁰ For his survival, he confesses to the public. Also, for his survival he tries to dial back the implications of the confession. Not all white people, he says. He confesses some more. Then he proceeds to weave a web of relation, where this predicament is not his alone.

Newland questions if the conversation is possible, if "the role white women play in the continual oppression of black men" can be discussed while "tracing the direct line from enslavement and colonisation."[11] Can we be honest about white women, he asks. However, before posing his question he again offers a general sympathy, stating they "obviously face a cis, white patriarchal system of oppression."[12] The central concern is whether there is an honest space to contend with how white women use the same white patriarchal system that violates them "to oppress those perceived as lower on the racial and social hierarchy?"[13] To this Newland offers a reply: "I believe we must."[14]

Why the caveats? Is there a theory that can account for the violation Newland has faced *and* the silencing he attempts to speak against, all while his tongue is gripped by the weight of his confession? It seems that Newland is aware of the answer to his question can we be honest? His writing, however, is belabored by the fact that Black speech exists under coercion or is captive before it emotes.[15] In his repeated pauses and apologetic prose is a clarity about his position as a Black man. His confession: as a Black man he is figured by an erotics that perverts the assumption of his patriarchal right, thus exposing him to the helm of white women and their fantasies and desires for his body as a sexual object of their taking. From this he proceeds without breath to enunciate a violating quality of Black male sexual objectification where he emphatically asserts,

> Still, the fact remains that black men's relationship with white women is fraught with complexity and rarely addressed, except, sometimes, as an examination into the lengths some men go to mine sexual otherness, or exoticism: black men's appreciation sex clubs almost exclusively visited by white women, mock plantation orgies, "beach boy" holidays in Africa and the Caribbean. These examinations are usually from a feminine perspective. What's missing is any deep analysis of black male psychology. The mental displacement needed to attend those parties and become a "bull" for the night, or be paraded on the arm of a white woman in Hastings, Barbados. Is sex work less morally demeaning if a man is the sex worker and a woman the client? Why is this seen as less mentally destructive, or nuanced?[16]

These questions are as material as they are psychic. They run deeper than the Du Boisian provocation "how does it feel to be a problem?"[17] They touch upon a particular form of speechlessness that is crowded out by a grammar of gender and its suffering that make Newland's feelings questionable and question themselves. Are Black men violated by a structure of sex that is perceived as the occupied space of women? And, as Newland asks, what does this have to do with slavery and colonialism?

A burgeoning branch of Black male studies, a field once oriented by queer theory and psychoanalysis, purports to have an answer to Newland's provocations. What is distinct in the new iteration of this field is its theoretical insistence on reading antiblack misandry, an inverse to misogyny or misogynoir, onto Black male sexual vulnerability. In this respect, the violations Newland experiences or perceives are marked as correlative to his Black manhood, with emphasis on the curiousness of manhood as open to an uncharted terrain of gender violence. Unlike studies on Black men, like David Marriott's groundbreaking text of the same name, where the psychosexual life of Blackness is taken up in examination of the mutilating and deadly sexual violations that tether cultural fantasies and experiences of Black men, the new focus displaces a concentrated examination on the question of Blackness for conjectures about the unseen vulnerability of manhood negated.

An emblematic text of this turn is *The Man-Not: Race, Class, Genre, and the Dilemmas of Black Manhood*. The book's author, Tommy J. Curry, argues, "Whereas Black male vulnerability expresses the actual disadvantage and violence Black males suffer as both Black and male, racist misandry expresses the vulnerability Black men and boys have to the obsessive hatred society directs toward them."[18] Curry deliberates on the question of Black male suffering to bring manhood, maleness, and masculinity into discussions about gender violence in hopes of removing these categories from the position as always already situated as the violator. To do so, he repositions them in their own relation to violated subjectivity.[19] From this vantage point, the response this iteration of Black male studies offers Newland is that what he has experienced is not singularly racial but also a structural degradation of his manhood.

The Man-Not, however, suffers from the symptoms of its own pronouncements. Curry takes issue with manhood as "rooted in the colonial formulation of sex designation, not gender," and presents various instable and shifting presumptions about manhood. Yet the concept of "the Man-Not" fails to establish what manhood, maleness, or masculinity are outside of cis-genderism and thus sex designation.[20] While Curry determines sex designation as a "white reality," the evaluation of the denied and violated manhood of Black men and boys is consistent with a white framing of gender as cis and undeniably heterosexual. Given the failure to think critically with queer and trans theory as well as with previous studies on Black men, like the aforementioned book by Marriott, "the Man-Not" is a heteronormative framework.[21]

The negative tropes ascribed to Black manhood elaborated by Curry, and the incessant desire to overcome those same tropes, are anchored by the white racial violence—or more aptly, antiblackness—of trans, queer, and misogynistic antagonisms. This is evident in the recapitulation of gender as genitalia, despite asserting this as the problem of dominant "hegemony" and social scientific discourses. In this respect, the text replicates the pathos of its diatribes. One cannot argue for an expansive understanding of Black male vulnerability rooted in the concept of manhood construed by biological assumptions without submitting to the foil of cis-gender supremacy or central importance.

This polemic on manhood suffers from an immutable horror, which is it cannot undo that for the Black, you are what they say you are. For the Black there is no distinction between the real and racist cultural fantasies.[22] Curry is never able to state what Black manhood, masculinity, or maleness are and suffers from a repeated conflation of these terms as he attempts to distinguish a culture of racist fantasies from the lived experiences of Black men and boys. He attempts to fight antiblack ontology with sociology. While stating Black men and boys are more than their grandiose fictionalizations as indolent and violable, *The Man-Not* similarly only engages them as such.

This however is not a personal flaw. Rather, Curry inadvertently demonstrates that "the n'est pas is not a choice, it is a humiliation that one submits to, it is the poison that exposes spirit to letter, error, misery, death and sin."[23] *The Man-Not* falls into the humiliation of its impossible exposure through its inability to describe a texture of Black manhood that is anything other than a desire for lactification. Blackness cannot announce itself through manhood because Black manhood is a category of dispossession. Lactification is present in the desire to produce Black manhood as a positive quality of self and a reigned dominion over others; in the case of Curry, the other is Black feminism. Through an elaboration of symptoms of accusation and exhaustion, Black manhood is levied as the antithesis to the most central issue the text announces, which is not with the whiteness of gender theory, but the structural logics developed by decades of Black feminist critical engagements and arguments.

The perception that one can escape the horror of Black male sexual violation, mutilation, and death to see their manhood differently is anchored by the dizzying effect of the entrapment that is Black manhood. As Marriott persuasively argues about the brute-like and inept figurations of Black men, "the disfiguring impact of those imagoes—internalized, they will haunt black men for the rest of their lives—and their effects on our unconscious beliefs and desires."[24] While the concern here is not with adjudicating these claims for Black men writ large, I am concerned with how this haunting appears in examinations of the relationship between sexual violence and Black men. Black male studies, or examinations of Black men and sexual violence—which take experience as proof that manhood can be violated on the basis of gender—cannot think the loss inherent in violated manhood as distinct from claims to patriarchal right and power. Why is the Black man violated in his manhood, maleness, or masculinity? In these accounts, the response continues circling back to understandings of the man-not, to use Curry's language, as a man with denied access to the visibility of gender violability by nature of his very existence.

In continuing to think with the questions posed by Newland, I want to consider how slavery is imagined by Curry in his explanations of the historical anchors that produce Black male sexual vulnerabilities. I will cite *The Man-Not* at length because it is a critical example of how conceptions of Black manhood can cathect to animus for Black feminist projects by deputizing manhood as a form of victimization erased by Black feminist theory. My purpose is not about rescuing Black feminism, which, as the previous chapters of this book make clear, deserves critical engagement for how it attends to sexual violation as part of the political ontology of Blackness. Rather, I attend to *The Man-Not* because its arguments rely on faulty evidence of what constitutes manhood to establish a framework of victimization based on a myriad of misplaced modifiers. While Curry seeks to qualify manhood, which differs from many Black feminist projects that challenge patriarchy and heteronormativity, his work shares some of the limitations of the Black feminist theorizing he seeks to repudiate in that Blackness is abandoned as the psychosexual condition that qualifies the experiences outlined throughout the book. I want to toil with his perceptions of Black feminism as a theoretical genealogy, which, in his calculation, not only fails Black men but also produces its own structure of misandry and antiblack male violence. Additionally, I consider how the texts he offers as a rejoinder to Black feminist analyses on gender and slavery suffer from the same analytical impediments as *The Man-Not*.

In examining Black feminist readings of sexual violence and slavery, Curry turns to *Scenes of Subjection: Terror and Self-Making in Nineteenth Century America* by Saidiya V. Hartman as a representative text of the field of Black feminist theory and historiography. For Curry, *Scenes of Subjection* exemplifies the elision of the male slave in analyses of rape. He argues, "Hartman's text, like the other Black feminist historiographies, continues to advance an understanding of rape during slavery as a kind of sexual violence specific to the Black female body."[25] What is curious about this assessment is how the female slave as a subject of concern becomes interpreted in this argument as the subject of truth. Hartman begins an examination on the legal occlusion of slave rape by stating,

> In nineteenth-century common law, rape was defined as the forcible carnal knowledge of a female against her will and without her consent. Yet the actual or attempted rape of an enslaved woman was an offence neither recognized nor punished by law.[26]

Contrary to the assertion by Curry that Harman makes rape "specific to the Black female body," the project Hartman advances is concerned with how the slave estate operates so as to refuse the inclusion of the female slave within the definition and recognition of female sexual injury as described by the law. Tracking the racial distinctions inherent in legal description and refusals, Hartman engages the partiality of the law with respect to its own terms. In doing so, Hartman elucidates how slavery unearths foundational contradictions in the law, its understandings, and usefulness as a barometer of injury. Furthermore, this critique calls to task feminist responses to the law that privilege will and consent as analytics for thinking rape and its justifications. Highlighting the female slave as an object devoid of the capacity for consent or willful subjectivity does less to suggest the male slave is not a subject of sexual violation than it does to provide a concentrated interrogation into feminist philosophical and legal understandings of the reach and concern of law over the agency of female subjects.

Beyond the premise of this interrogation, Hartman makes it clear that there are legal cases involving sexual violation of male slaves. These instances do not fall under the purview of the common law concern being advanced by her argument. However, the analysis is not naïve in its understanding of the breadth of sexual violence and slavery. In this respect, Hartman argues,

> The disavowal of sexual violence is specific not only to engendering "woman" in this particular instance but also to the condition of enslavement in general. In cases like *Humphrey v. Utz* and *Werley v. State*, essentially what was being decided was whether acts of genital mutilation and castration (legally defined as acts of mayhem) were crimes when perpetuated against the enslaved or acts of just and reasonable violence.[27]

At the heart of these two cases were sexual violations involving male slaves. Offering these examples is not just a sympathetic gesture. Instead, it illustrates how thinking the relationship of the female slave as certain foreclosed is not a proprietary claim of sexual suffering. Rather than asking why males are not present in nineteenth-century legal concerns about forcible copulation or carnal knowledge, Curry places the onus on Hartman and the argument she advances rather than attuning to the law and/or the social and political structures of gender.

While the chapter "Seduction and the Ruses of Power" provides a concentrated reading of rape and slavery, it is also, and perhaps most importantly, a critical interrogation of the category of womanhood itself. Not only is the argument aware of the relationship of female and male slaves to denied claims over sexual injury, it also uses legal examples of racial sexual violence to question the efficacy of gendered terms as a sole analytic. For Hartman, woman connotes "a particular racial economy of property that intensified its control over the object of property through the deployment of sexuality."[28] The nineteenth-century discourse on rape was as much a commentary on race as it was on gender. If rape was an impossibility for the slave, both female and male, because of their Blackness, gender also operated to obscure the "obtuseness of pain and injury."[29] This is a point Hartman and Curry agree on.[30] To rely on womanhood as explanatory of how the slave suffers reduces, rather than expands, our understanding given the constraints womanhood places on the intelligibility of harm. Womanhood is constrained by the racial injury and valuations placed on the fantasy and realities of gender made possible by antiblackness, or the violent racial divisions made possible by slavery. What is negated manhood to this history? And how might the use of the term obscure the impetus of sexual violation experienced by male slaves?

There are ample archival insistences to the effect of providing evidence of the pervasiveness of sexual harms perpetuated against male slaves. The first full length historical study of this sort is *Rethinking Rufus: Sexual Violations of Enslaved Men* by Thomas A. Foster. An extended examination of what Foster first presented in an article, "The Sexual Abuse of Black Men under American Slavery," *Rethinking Rufus* illustrates how sexual injury for male slaves was often ignored as sexual harm or attributed to other harms entirely.[31] For Curry, Foster's scholarship, and by extension, *Rethinking Rufus*, "explodes the intuitive deployment of gender as synonymous with female that Hartman makes use of in *Scenes of Subjection*."[32] Foster's book is a critical rejoinder to the infamous story of Rose, a female slave who fights off the sexual advances of Rufus, who is forcefully paired with her by their master. As a part of the Works Progress Administration slave narrative project, Rose shares her experiences with Rufus, whom she describes as "a bully" who tries to sexually assault her one night.[33] She successfully fights him off in several ways but most famously by hitting him in the head until he retreats from her cabin. Upon learning that their Master Hawkins sent Rufus to her cabin to "bring forth portly chillen," she complies.[34] Her compliance is under fear that she will be sold away and possibly beaten. Foster argues that Rufus has long been vilified in historical accounts as a sexual predator but instead should be understood as a victim of sexual violence like Rose. The reimagining Foster extends first offers credence to Rose's personal narrative of Rufus as a hostile figure in her life. The fact that they parted ways post-emancipation signals to Foster the "long-term resentment" that existed between them because of their forced coupling and breeding.[35] Acknowledging Rufus as a likely aggressor, however, does not limit the potential of imagining his joint victimization, which may explain but not excuse his treatment of Rose. Foster imagines what thoughts and feelings Rufus may have had about his forced pairing with Rose based on a series of historical incidents where male slaves provided narrative accounts of their experiences. Rufus is given voice through theory, as his story was never recorded, and his theoretical voice is bolstered to offer manhood as the descriptive anchor for the implications of slave male sexual violability. Revising the story of Rufus, Foster argues that sexual torture is veiled as pleasure given the assumption that male slaves enjoyed their sexual experiences on the plantation. Foster maintains that this premise is flawed and asserts that instances like Rufus's demand further investigation as an elaborate array of sexual violations particular to male slaves.

Using the story of Rufus as an anchor to ground the arguments of each chapter, Foster first documents multiple instances of explicit and implicit sexual abuse of male slaves. He looks to instances that involved forced coupling, white fantasy about the Black male form, white women as perpetrators of sexual violence, forms of mutilation and torture, as well as same-sex sexual violations. Foster is methodologically a historian and a cultural theorist. In this sense, *Rethinking Rufus* is a historical excavation that compiles archival evidence of multiple iterations of sexual violence, and it is also an expanded political commentary. The presentation of a history involves a metacommentary on the meaning and significance of what is revealed. Meditations on what is lost by Black male slaves given their sexualization is where the political anchor of the text emerges. Loss presupposes that something exists prior to violation. For Foster, the loss is inherent to an ontological claim on manhood, termed as "manly autonomy."[36]

The physical torture, which was in part sexual, rendered male slaves, Foster contends, as "less physically able to enact manly norms of capability" by "violating private dignity and emasculating men through public exposure."[37] Foster argues that in the face of sexual violation the male slave established and exercised "inherited traditions of West African manhood that emphasized roles of father, husband, and warrior."[38] Manhood in these terms lacks definition but is presented as a premodern (read: pre-slavery) constitution that is perfected in sexual relationships with women and the desire to have and maintain nuclear kinship structures. Foster does not offer an elaborate rejoinder to this form of manhood as distinct from white patriarchy, opting, instead, for conjecture. He implies that "these aspects of manhood were widely shared in white nineteenth-century culture as well, but for enslaved men they took on special meaning, given that masters so regularly denied enslaved men autonomy in these decisions."[39] What is particularly special or distinct about this form of manhood harkens upon ideas of strength and honor that are tied to heterosexual kinship and patriarchal control. Yet the quality of difference is only maintained through its performance by male slaves.

Foster positions Rufus as powerless and essentially operating as an extension of the master's prerogative and domestic authority. Under these conditions, the meaning of setting up a household Foster maintains was likely complicated for Rufus as it was for other male slaves. The focus on the household as the space where manhood is worked out and subsequently diminished as "masters denied them privacy and full autonomy by monitoring their intimate relationships with women," makes it unclear where the master's prerogative exits and male slave desire enters. By scaling down analysis to the operations of the household as an autonomous space, there is silence about what makes the nuclear household possible and psychically desirable as a fantasy space of untapped manhood. While feminists have argued that the home is a microcosm of state power, the slave quarter is both an enactment and extension of the master's ontology, where kinship is mapped out through gendered and domestic relations that mark sexual division in racial terms. Foster argues that manhood for male slaves is performed through the desire to command, protect, and maintain autonomous intimacy with female slaves and to protect and rear slave children. On these terms, manhood, or the lack thereof, Foster argues, is not only worked out through the fiction of household relation, but is most viscerally felt for male slaves when these bonds are upheld, refused, or deracinated.

Foster's consideration of sexual violation reproduces the trope that the premiere assault on slave manhood is the male slaves' inability to protect female slaves from sexual abuse and slave children from being sold on the auction block. Also emerging in this articulation is the fixation of sex and sexualization to a heterosexual dyad. By reinserting the female slave as central to how slave manhood was negotiated and experienced, there is a perceivable refusal to conceive of manhood at the level of the male body or the fleshly encounters of slave sexuation. Although same gender sexual encounters are discussed by Foster, they are not considered as the place where manhood is mediated by male slaves themselves, but how manhood is imposed from without by violent forces. His argument is premised on the claim that manhood for male slaves is prefigured and remains uncontested when men intimated sex and its violations against other men. Theorizing manhood as reproduced through desire and sexual relation, as in the case of heterosexual couplings, is evacuated in the elaboration of same-sex intimacy. Furthermore, interracial same-sex fetish and violation against male slaves is concluded to be that which "undercuts the subject's manhood," rather than as an ontological mediating ground for manhood's psychic structure (how it is perceived) and affect (how it is felt).[40]

For Curry, Foster provides a more honest account of historical injury by refocusing on the immense terror of sexual harm for male slaves *and* the invisibility of this terror inured by Black feminist analyses. Foster's account is treated as a true history that dislodges the hold Black feminism places on theories of antiblack sexual and gender violence, in which Black men can only be perceived as perpetrators of sexual harm, rather than its victims. What unwrites this assessment is that Curry and Foster, albeit differently so, are hobbled by an investment in manhood. While making legible the sexual violation of male slaves, Foster's imposition of manhood in his theorizing sequesters the implications of this recognition to questions of kinship, right, property, and manly autonomy. Additionally, even in examinations of same-sex sexual violations, manhood continues to carry the same tenor as previous discussions, where manhood serves as a constant that is not retooled by the question of differing modes of desire. In Curry's case, slavery is but one example of this matrix of refused recognition of injury and serves as material evidence of historical harm. Curry contends that Black feminism is largely responsible for this history being obscured, as it outright refuses to discuss or take seriously the sexual harms experienced by Black males. Curry writes,

> In alerting us to our *inability to speak or think about* the sexual coercion of Black men (making an enslaved man have sex), our tacit dismissal of the claim and its significance depends on the racist assumptions about predatory Black men who desire to rape or the sexual insatiability of the Black male who always craves sex.[41]

What Curry is calling aphasia or dysrationalia is an attempt at inciting discord in Black theory according to presumed gender divisions. Yet the erasure that he identifies is not an erasure at all. The projection of sexual desire as a justification for and nullification of claims to harm is present in nineteenth-century conversations around sexual violence and Black men. Focusing specifically on post-emancipation lynching, which is a form of sexualized mutilation, Ida B. Wells-Barnett instrumentalized exposing the Southern lie about Black men as rapists, illustrating the centrality of white racial fantasy and desires for domination at the heart of the lynching spectacle. Furthermore, Wells-Barnett argued,

> Hundreds of such cases might be cited, but enough have been given to prove the assertion that there are white women in the South who love the Afro-American's company even as there are white men notorious for their preference for Afro-American women.
>
> There is hardly a town in the South which has not an instance of the kind which is well known, and hence the assertion is reiterated that 'nobody in the South believes the old thread bare lie that negro men rape white women.'[42]

Writing in 1892, Wells-Barnett is well aware that white women have a sexual appetite and fantasy for Black men that is projected as the rape fantasy of the Black men they possess racial sexual power over. Wells-Barnett connects her arguments and findings to the long traditions of the South that are rooted in slavery. Though Wells-Barnett is but one example, her work has vast reach and has influenced the premise of many arguments around sexual violence and Black violation and mutilation for well over a century. Indeed, an interrogation of the myth of the Black male rapist is common to many Black feminist critiques of sexual violence.

Given that Curry continually bolsters arguments by claiming erasure when such can be proven otherwise, the question becomes what, then, can be imagined or understood as the contention at the heart of his concerns? I argue that what Curry is fighting against is not erasure but more so *how* Black males appear as sexually violable. The historic record, as well as Black feminist engagements, do not produce evidence of Black manhood deracinated by sexual harm. Instead, what emerges is Black male violated flesh that is dissected into erogenous zones, such as the Black penis, the Black hole, and lacerated broken apart Black flesh. *The Man-Not* refuses to take seriously the fragments that dissect and objectify, and, frankly, have a much more expansive understanding of how truly vulnerable Black men are to sexual violation. Instead, Curry opts for an alternative perception of cohesive manhood as a bioessentialist ontic that proceeds violation, and that scholarly recognition of this violation is meant to repair.

What is most outrightly omitted in this excavation of truth and blame is the question of desire as it relates to sex and violence. Removing the accusation of harm perpetuation from Black men as the throughway to reveal true victimization stops short of grappling with the psychic dimensions of projected Black male power and objectification. Lindon Barrett argues that the relationship between the Black male as perceived hypersexual rapist and the economy of homosexual desire are inverses of two competing and contradictory engagements with desire. Barrett argues,

> Race—and rape as a paradigmatic signifier of race—forecloses the question of desire. Rather than merely marking a criminal encounter involving two individuals, the paradigmatic signifier of a black man raping a white woman remains a part of the symbolic mechanisms aimed at disciplining every member of the population. The image forwards the assurance that its aberrant sexual congress is not desired, but violent and coerced. Conversely, homosexuality is aberrant precisely because it is so *plainly* about desire, to the point of displacing reproduction although and thus, to the point of placing desire dangerously out of control. In these and other cases the purity and perpetuation of the race—the production and reproduction of a particular "strain" of the human species (most especially, dominant racial whiteness)—are jeopardized.[43]

In responding to the accusation of Black men as rapists, desire is completely voided by Curry and supplanted with an overdetermined conversation of power as physical force and access. Thinking about the psychosexual dimensions of the accusation where whoever says rape, says negro, as Frantz Fanon has shown us, cannot be displaced by shifting focus from Black men to white men or white women as the true assailants of harm.[44] While history is clear that the structure of white violence far superseded Black aggression and was often projected onto Black people as their own making, the economy of this reversal is one less marred in truth. Rather, there is a desire economy surrounding the very concept of Black manhood that is relational to fantasies about his sexual propensities and proclivities that are not erased by shifting focus to a new assailant. Desire must be addressed *plainly* to unravel manhood as a truth of sex difference, exposing it instead as a sedimentation of sex and violence.

A question from this position: what if the perceivability of Black manhood is reproduced by its sexual violability rather than impaled by it? Curry is emphatic that revealing the pervasiveness of white women's role in the sexual violation of Black men complicates homoeroticism and "reconfigures the heteronormative myths" that he believes makes seeing white women as rapist impossible. It is curious why white women's sexual power rewrites the script on homoeroticism or makes the history appear differently. Rather than contending with white feminist historiography that imagines white women as passive actors of patriarchal power or of plantation economies, Curry turns to intersectionality, a Black feminist theory, as the site that makes Black men and boys invisible in analyses of sexual and gender violence. For him, intersectionality, a theory of interlocking identities, overdetermines the femaleness of suffering, thus making Black men and boys invisible. If the concern is white women and their role in violence, why place emphasis on Black feminist theory in lieu of white feminist historiography? Have Black feminists been lenient on white women's violence or the violence of white womanhood? Or do analyses that are honest about the fact that non-men are violated because of their genders and cis-men are not violated on the basis of gender produce a fundamental injury to Black men and boys?

My contention is that the problem is not with Black feminism making white women's violence invisible; rather, it is, as my book stresses, what types of violence Black feminism assists in clarifying. Purporting to revise history by centering white women's violence as the unseen and unsaid is not only a shallow reading of Black feminism, given that this violence is widely spoken of, but rather is a veiled attempt to reinscribe sex, even in its violating quality, in heteronormative terms.[45] It is a proverbial attempt at putting the penis back in the vagina. Curry avoids a serious engagement with Black queer theory entirely, in a gesture that is symptomatic of the architecture of the arguments of the text, where it claims the absence of discussions that have existed for decades (if not centuries). Black queer theory has engaged at length Black male sexualization dating from slavery to the present, as well as interrogated the complex relationship between Blackness and manhood.[46]

The position taken by Curry is not a failure of rigor or research, as in a misstep of action, but a deep antagonistic anxiety about same-sex desire and queerness assumedly veiled by staging a critique of Black feminism. Black queer theory brings the erogenous zones of Black male flesh closer into view, exposing the Fanonian insistence that "for the negro is only biological," wherein the negro is affected and made affectable by impulses, urges, feelings, and sensations, which are fleeting and challenging to grasp.[47] Curry resists considering the psychic life of the Black male as sexual object and, instead, turns toward history as a philosophy of immutable fact rather than as a space of obscured desire and fantasy that continues to pervade the present.

The tension between the psychic and the material is most present in *The Man-Not* when Curry engages a discussion of homoerotic desire by drawing on James Baldwin's short story "Going to Meet the Man" to illustrate white male sexual fantasies of Black men. In this story, Baldwin presents a white cop, Jesse, who is unable to sexually perform with his wife and thus fantasizes about his experiences with raping, beating, and lynching Black people to reignite his libido. The raw material for Jesse's fantasies are Black people; however, for Curry, the Black man is the essential component of his sexually violent climax. Curry writes, "The white man learns of himself through the death of the Nigger."[48] In this reference, "the Nigger" is gendered as the Black man. The reading Curry offers pushes back against a possible Black feminist reading of the text that might argue that the rape of Black women, which appears at the offset of Baldwin's story, may be the connective tissue that binds every fantasy that arrives thereafter. Yet Curry argues that the ending, where the climax is obtained following Jesse's violent memories of castration and lynching, is where the truth of his libidinal appetites is revealed. However, it is curious if either Black men or Black women are the essence of Jesse's violent desire. How are we to separate Baldwin's imagination from Jesse's fantasy? "Going to Meet the Man" presents a plausible fictional account of white male blood and sexual thirst that places various emphases throughout on homoeroticism and interracial sexual aggression. But is the genital fantasy at play a Black male specific erotic?

Baldwin masterfully illustrates how genital pleasure for Jesse is not particular to a singular Black sexualized figure. Rather, it is sutured by a death drive that is interconnected and inseverable from the sexuating forces of the racial order and racial cultural fantasies. For example, in expressing his inability to feel the "ugliness" of Black women again through his sexual conquests, Jesse thinks "never hear those moans again or what that blood run down or the fat lops slops or the sealed eyes struggle to open." Jesse's vivid imagery and sonic pleasures are interwoven with his violent fantasies, which need sexual force as much as they need physical acts of mutilation and/or aggression for sensation.[49] Baldwin pushes this further, beyond the heterosexual interracial rape schema, where fantasy and the real are interwoven, and brings in an additional erotic scene that complicates whether sex with Black women is the truth of Jesse's violent neurosis. While lying in bed with his wife, Jesse recalls an incident where he beats a Black Civil Rights protester until he is nearly unconscious. The protester speaks as blood spews from his mouth and reminds Jesse that this Black man is the grandchild of "Old Julia," a woman Jesse assumedly abused financially and sexually. As he shouts at the prisoner/protester exclaiming that he should feel lucky that white men "pump some white blood" into Black women, his body retreats and he is unable to perform.[50] Again, Jesse is confronted with sexual/white impotence at the level of his fantasy, which aligns with reality in that he is still unable to perform with this wife. Thus, he continues to transverse his fantasies until he can (re)claim his sexuality. He moves through Negro spirituals as a transfer point that leads him to his memory of attending a lynching at the age of eight. It was at the commencing of the lynching spectacle, where a Black man was castrated, dismembered, and burned, that he comes to embody a love for his father—"more than he had ever loved him"—where he felt his father revealed for him the "key to life forever."[51]

Curry reads this final scene as the moment of transference for Jesse, where he argues,

> He is able to fuck his wife; he is a man, because his whiteness (civilized, reason, order) can temper the Nigger's (savage) sexual potency. His manhood is thereby defined in overcoming the bestiality he imagines to be symbolized by the Black phallus.[52]

Curry's analysis begs the question, is the infinite quest for the death and mutilation of Black men what makes the ontology of white manhood perceivable? Arguably what is severed in this scene is not a Black phallus, but a Black penis, which lacks the symbolic power of the ontological presence of the phallus. The metaphysics of the phallus are at play in Jesse's relation to his father, where the Black penis operates as an object that aids the search for a reclamation of the violence of white being. The phallus in the scene is the white father, the symbolic signifier that made and continues to animate the infinite potential of white male sexual power and violence. This is what allows the white man to possess the world. It is through narcissistic identification with the white male ego ideal that Jesse is able to finally perform with his wife. Just as Jesse's fantasies of Black men are not tethered to his fantasies of Black women, "white masculinity as dependent on the castration and death of Black men and boys" is also not a fixed relational constant.[53] While it is plausible, it is not the truth as there is no true violence of antiblackness.

In the end, Baldwin suggests a drive that is contrary to the insistence by Curry that the "Black phallus" is the pinnacle of white male sexual desire. Instead, Baldwin homes in on the violent narcissistic identifications and impulse of white life. The white male ego ideal passes through, rather than permanently affixes to, any particular antiblack violation to fortify life. Arguably what Baldwin reveals is that the life instincts of whiteness are subtended by cultural fantasies of myriad unbound and unending Black violations. Black people, dismembered and mutilated, are the objects of his story, while the subjects are white men and their kin. Jesse's climax is not akin to the insistence that "[t]he death of Black men arrests the yearning white men have for their flesh and phallus."[54]

Curry argues that castration is an act of dominance where the Black man is rendered a lifeless corpse, noting that white masculinity is dependent on this relation because of an incessant need to take what the Black man has and bask in his death. Contrarily, inorganic matter—castrated, dismembered, unalive Black flesh—is not dispossessed of the phallus by repetitious death. It is "only insofar as we are bodies can we become subjects, and conversely, only insofar as we are subjects do we acquire a sexed body."[55] The penis alone is not a sexed body but a symbol of the sexual capacity or incapacitation of its racial epidermal schema. In the case of lynching and castration, the Black penis heightens the specter of Black male immobilization by the scene of violence and the structural paradigm that authorizes the possession of Black sexual organs. Reading the Black penis qua Black phallus is a statement that the Black man possesses a power that the white man exists in an obsessional relation to and thus makes his own through castration. This is a fictive arithmetic because the sexed body or the phallocentric subject cannot be undone by castration. The claim to Black manhood and its unraveling by castrated death is simply that, a claim.

Antiblack castration as death is a metaphysical terror of non-arrival at the point of phallocentric articulation. Which is to say, the climax that Jesse emotes as imparted upon him by his father is the feeling of the sexed body's claim on manhood. The phallogocentrism of this claim stays intact even with the penis in absentia. Though his father has died, he still owns it, which is the realization Jesse arrives at when he releases and relaxes. What makes his white manhood possible cannot be dispossessed through an act of castration nor through impotence because of his ontological claim on violence. What Jesse's father demonstrates to him is that he can do to Black men something that Black men could never do to him. This is supremely gratifying. It is also a metacommentary on manhood, where the possibility of such is a racial claim on the capacity to make violent fantasies real.

The lynched, dismembered and scorched Black body is where violent fantasy and sadism converge, exposing the scales of violence upon which manhood stands. The deceased is exterior to the subjectivity that emerges from this scene. Though the affectedness of the body is on central display, it is impossible to perceive that the consciousness of those structurally positioned alongside the lynching victim is left undisturbed. A masochistic desire emerges here too, where the attribution of manhood, the phallus, becomes the foil imagined to rid the Black male of the death currents of sexual violability. Thus, when Jesse emotes to his wife, "I'm going to do you like a nigger," this expression is interpreted by Curry as "the Black phallus" being taken by this sexual arrangement. But what is at play is the belief that the Black penis is possessed prior to the sexual encounter, and prior to castration, which is what drives the passion of the engagement by the biological bespoke of sensations that the Negro is. Jesse and his wife are not basking in stolen Black phallic power as the particularity of Black manhood but the *fungibility* of Black sexual status. Simply, there is nothing uniquely heterosexual about this encounter as the Black penis can be devoured by a broad arrangement of sexual displays and acts.

What is owed to Black men in the analysis of sexual violence offered throughout *The Man-Not* is manhood, a conclusion derived by avoiding how relations of slavery make Black manhood oxymoronic, even as Curry momentarily makes this same claim.[56] Furthermore, transmuting the desire of white men to castrate Black men through the figure of the white wife is a refusal to engage same-sex desire and violability. As Marlon B. Ross argues, "rape powerfully communicates that black men are in constant jeopardy of having their manhood plundered by more powerful men," and "the notion of castration as emasculation . . . utterly fails to capture the steps intervening between the impact of physical assault and the ongoing impact reverberating from a psychological injury of incalculable portions."[57] Castration as physical vulnerability that imparts psychic potentials onto white men is an emasculation thesis that transmutes power onto Black men and recuperates a desire for access to heteropatriarchy, without contending with the actual lived realities of the power of white men. It goes without saying that Black men are not structurally more powerful than white men. Asserting that the *true* power of manhood is the Black man and his faculties, which feed the power possessed by white men, is a ruse about the totalities of deracinating violence faced by the racial sexual question. Also, the psychic implications of castration and rape for Black men are not effectively remediated by the emasculation thesis or the propriety of Black manhood. Instead, they are almost entirely concealed.

Altogether, what was homoerotic about slavery is abandoned by Curry in favor of analyzing the lynching scene, a post-slavery phenomenon. Though there is not a stark distinction between the structural relations that exist during slavery and the prominent era of lynching, it seems Curry calls on the post-emancipation moment to avoid a direct confrontation with slavery as an erosive condition that makes sexual and gender power imperceivable as an autonomous Black claim. In his reading of "Going to Meet the Man," heterosexual sex and desire are privileged through repeated emphases on Jesse "fucking his wife" as the central focal point of analysis. Black men are deployed in this sense as proxy and excess in the white heterosexual drive while Blackness is divorced from a permanent structural relation to Jesse and his wife. From this vantage point, Black men are not possessed by white fantasy but deployed by it to make white hetero sex real. In analyzing sex and slavery, disconnecting Black presence from ownership as a totalizing delegitimization of being would be an impossible argument to carry, given the real property status of being a slave. Black captivity as partiality or contingency roots Curry's argument. The Black penis, then, becomes a conditionally captive site, marking it as separate from the question of possessed Black being. Black manhood is destabilized through the homoerotic act of castration that, for Curry, lends its true power to the white man who then possesses Black phallic potential as their own. The transmutation of the castrated Black penis into the stolen Black phallus amounts to nothing more than an assertion that "constructs race as masculine on the premise that only men can be emasculated—that is, only men can be cut off from the social power owed them."[58] I would also add that this position holds that only Black cis-men with penises can be emasculated, which profoundly excludes and refuses to think against the arrangements of force that situate Black trans men and trans masculine people within the complications of Black manhood and masculinity. Additionally, as Jared Sexton critically reminds us, "it is important to recall that women can be castrated too."[59]

Ultimately, theories of Black cis-manhood orbit around the materiality, threat, and fear of castration. In *Sex and Racism in America*, Calvin Hernton contends that the Negro male "must act like a eunuch," which reproduces an overwhelming sense of "dread and self-mutilation."[60] Someone who is a eunuch has been castrated or, perhaps more profoundly, "psychologically he experiences himself as castrated," which delegitimizes his sense of sexual resistance or capacity.[61] In *Soul on Ice*, imprisoned intellectual and early Black Panther Party leader Eldridge Cleaver similarly upholds the Black eunuch as a signifier of sexual disempowerment and racial angst. Identifying himself as "the Black Eunuch, divested of my Balls," Cleaver describes being driven by a racially displaced vengeance that "would kill a black man or woman quicker than I'd smash a fly, while for the white man I would pick a thousand pounds of cotton a day."[62] The suggestion here is that political resistance is gendered as masculine and castration leaves him blind to his true oppressor and enemy.

Cleaver's suggestion is telling, as it places hyperfocus on castration as the defining racial sexual injury to the Black male, while demonstrating, as Sexton poignantly observes, that castration "serves as an all-purpose term to designate the loss of the so-called administrative function in the black man, a function that includes the ability to think for oneself as well as the crucial rite/right of male sexual sovereignty."[63] By propelling the black penis to the stature of a phallus dispossessed in a war of positions between white and Black men, same-sex sexual violation is recast under the logic of war and holds that assumptive framing to a racial heteropatriarchal schema. The castrated penis as a symbolic signifier of dispossessed sexual-gendered right maintains castration as the most destabilizing sexual violation of Black men, which, ultimately, is claimed to be the cause of Black women's vulnerability to sexual violence from whites. The oft repeated narrative of Black castration presupposes that by castrating the Black man, the white man leaves the Black man disempowered and unable to protect the Black woman from interracial rape. The Black Eunuch, as theorized by Cleaver, stands in the way of undoing the sexual traumas of slavery and unseating the power of white men.

Beyond castration, the eunuch also beckons an entirely different meaning. The term directly translates as a bedroom guard. The fixation on castration creates a double-blind effect, reducing sexual injury to binary terms. From this vantage point, the Black Eunuch emerges as a bedroom guard of what unthought violence buttresses heteronormativity and, by extension, white male or female aggressivity as the dominant thesis of racial sexual violence. Sexton argues that Cleaver inevitably overprescribes "sexual violence historically committed against the black man strictly as castration, whereas the black woman is exclusively ravaged by rape." The castration thesis (castration as permanent Black male sexual dispossession) disintegrates when rape is decoupled primarily from Black women and is also interrogated as an anxiety of the Black male sexual predicament. Sexton clarifies that "the fear of rape and the fear of penetration must be carefully distinguished."[64] Sexual violability or capacity is not wedded to the penetrative act, nor is it an act of conquest. "This conceptual internment," as Sexton contends, positions thought away from perceiving Black male sexual vulnerability as an expansive, rather than a singular, racial entanglement.[65] The embrace and repulsion of castration demonstrate how conceptions of negated Black manhood mistook the body as the map of racial sexual antagonisms.[66] Which is to say, investigations of penetration and/or castration should lead inquiry away from the act as the locus and explanation of the condition.

In discussing rape and slavery using the analytic of the Black (power) bottom—a sexual position where the penetrated carries the sexual act through endurance and heightened capacity to handle repeated plundering—Darieck Scott argues,

> The ability to take pleasure in abjection, or in racialization through sexual humiliation (which, to be clear, is not the same thing as experiencing pleasure only because of such humiliation, or experiencing that humiliation as fully or immanently pleasurable), may well make use of this presumably universal

psychic past, in the form of a skill set, as it were, that becomes readily available in the form and perhaps the misleading guise of a *racial* past."[67]

The quest for a just and true history of slavery is an incurable neurosis. While it can be argued that a theoretic that centers the slave is a more apt way of contending with violence, settling the inconsistencies of the archive and how those caesuras may appear in contemporary theory are impossible feats. Fantasy and desire are centrally at play as what makes separating the past from the present so difficult to discern. The pleasure in abjection, as Scott contends, can be a power position, where the myth of a racial past is redoubled through a reclamation of sexual humiliation. For Curry, the pleasure in abjection arrives from correlating sex/gender as cohesively mappable onto Blackness. However, unlike the power bottom that can make the act of sex their own, sex/gender is a fictive power move insofar as antiblackness is the ground upon which sex as gender is reified. Black manhood as an analytic of self-possession or collective harm is not a reclaiming or an undoing of the humiliation of sex and slavery, but an attempt at subverting structural relations. Which is to say, the search for slave men is insolvable insofar as what it means to be a man is predicated on the bracketing of sex/gender in the terms of perceivability and coherence made possible by slavery. As Scott argues,

> there is value to the identification with being violated: if there is a value to *being* violated, it evades us—because the "I" necessary to assessment of a notion of value we can assimilate to our ego-structured world is difficult to locate under those circumstances.[68]

As the slave was violated it is impossible to apprehend if the experience of cleaved manhood was felt in the moment of or through the violation. Scott contends that violation can be experienced as both pain and pleasure. In the case of Rufus, the violating context of his sexual captivity may in fact have been pleasurable, which, as Foster illustrates, does not make it less violating. The sensorial experiences of pain and pleasure experienced by male slaves through a series of violating sexual acts and conditions may culminate on the question of manhood or on differing analytics altogether. If manhood is the quality imparted upon the meaning of these violations by Curry and others, then manhood demands a more substantive evaluation that exceeds the ego or self-descriptive. What is the material and psychic quality of manhood? Is

Black manhood perceivable simply through and by way of violation, where without it, manhood is impossible to discern given how slavery racially sexuated genitalia?

Humphrey v. Utz and Archival Omissions: The Castration and Genital Mutilation of "the Boy Bob" or Ginger Pop, a Slave

I want to turn to *Humphreys v. Utz* (*Utz*), one of the cases referenced by Hartman as involving the sexual violation of male slaves, which was legally classified as mayhem. The complexities of this case—which Hartman notes is an historical legal example of genital mutilation and castration—interrogate if negated manhood is an adequate analytic to evaluate the web of contradictions and terrors that arose from the sexual violence against a male slave. *Utz* is a case that is defined in the legal record as mediating particular concerns about libel and employment discrimination. However, the transcript reveals a twisted and prolonged scene of antiblack sexual torture and escape, and the silences that pervade the coming together of these terms.

Utz is a unique case given that it was never entered into legal indexes, meaning it could not serve as precedent in other cases because the record was, in essence, lost. Legal scholar Judith Schafer discovered the handwritten transcripts of the case "in one of several boxes that had been left in the vault of the supreme court when the court's antebellum records were transferred" to the University of New Orleans.[69] Though *Utz* was lost in the material legal record, the violence that emerges during the testimony for this trial is not anomalous and illustrates the quotidian encounter slaves had with extreme forms of sexual mutilation and torture. Schafer describes the case as "provid[ing] compelling proof that the Supreme Court of Louisiana had an unspoken policy of under reporting or omitting entirely from its reported cases involving cruelty of a sexual nature to slaves."[70] While it may be that the state of Louisiana intentionally omitted such cases, Schafer's claim seems far exaggerated considering most, if not all instances of slavery involved some form of sexual offense. Perhaps this fact is not as evident in the historical proceedings that are found in the state legal indexes, as sexual violence emerged both pervasively and silently in utterances perceived to be of different matters entirely, just as *Utz* was documented as a case regarding wrongful termination and libel.

The assumptive tone Schafer provides in her introductory notes to the revived transcript of the *Utz* case suggests that something has gone awry because the case has seemingly vanished in the legal record until she finds and republishes it. Schafer states, "*Utz* provides rare documentary evidence, evidence considered too horrible to be published, of the savagery that could result when the law allowed some members of society to treat other human beings as property."[71] What this analysis misinterprets is the manner in which *Utz* has been forgotten and also not forgotten. The assumption Schafer makes in prefacing the case before presenting it does not take seriously the paradigm the case is located within. As the transcript states,

> Witness has often seen deft whip the Boy Bob or Ginger Pop, he died about three o'clock in the evening and he was buried at seven next morning, there were no other white persons on the place except deft and witness.[72]

The concern by Schafer is also present in the law itself, which suggests that witnessing and remembering only happens by way of the official record or the white defendant and witness. The law has no obligation to the slave to remember or acknowledge its centrality within its paradigm of violent erasure. There are of course "unofficial" witnesses, the slaves who were forced to see this torture and to also exist within the torment of knowing the same fate may await them.

In the final pages of the *Utz* legal transcript, the following equation is found:

```
1 January 10 19 Aug (incl.) 7 mon. & 19 days
12/$800.00 - per annum
      66.66 - per month
         x7
      466.62
       33.33
        6.66
        2.22
        ——
```

$508.83 — wages to 19th Aug inclusive
$388.86 — verdict of the jury [in] favor [of] deft
$120. — amt. deducted from wages by the jury

These figures represent the amount the court determined Henry Utz, an overseer and the defendant in the case, was entitled to receive from his former employers, brothers John C. Humphreys and George W. Humphreys, for working on their plantation and carrying out the duties of his job. Utz killed Ginger Pop, a slave, also known as Bob, who continued to run away from the Humphreys' plantation. The court determined Ginger Pop simply died and there was no evidence of murder. Ginger Pop was repeatedly sexually mutilated by Utz until his death, yet such details were deemed insignificant by the court. The petition of the plaintiffs, the Humphreys brothers, also held that "Utz inflicted a similar outrage upon a certain negroe boy named Dave or David also the property of your petitioners and under the control or management of said Utz as overseer on the Buckland Plantation."[73] Beyond this statement, nothing further is mentioned of the slave identified as Dave or David. Having previously been acquitted of any criminal wrongdoing, Utz appealed in prayer to the high court of the State of Louisiana to uphold the lower court's decision and find that he, in fact, did not cause any monetary loss to the Humphreys. Utz maintained that he carried out the stipulations of his employment dutifully. He rested on faith that the court would act upon this as a divine truth. The courts heeded his prayer, finding that his termination was wrongful and awarded him the above sum of back wages with interest, minus a slight jury deduction.

Utz is a heinous case; there is no other way to describe it. The appellant's brief provides a terse and grueling summary to the several pages of witness statements, and judicial comments, highlighting gratuitous pronouncements of sexual violence and torture inflicted upon Ginger Pop. A section of the brief reads,

> That one of said slaves, whose name was "Ginger Pop," died from the effect of cruelties inflicted upon him by the defendant, in nailing the privates of said negro to the bedstead, and then inflicting blows upon him until said negro pulled loose from the post to which he had been pinned, by driving an iron tack or nail through his penis or privates.[74]

The case is representative of how the violent acts that sexuate Blackness appear in the political arena at the behest of the desire and motive will of others. The status of Blackness becomes consumed into an array of legal contestations, i.e., was Utz wrongfully or legitimately terminated, was his reputation unjustifiably sullied by the Humphreys brothers, or who can serve as witness to an alleged crime when only slaves are present. The sexual relation between Utz and Ginger Pop is unmediated except in moral pleas by the appellant attorney. The appellant's brief conceded that Utz "had literally *worn out* a poor, helpless negro; he had robbed of life, by his merciless cruelties," citing that "a prejudiced jury failed" to uphold the tenets of the law and find Utz at fault for the death of Ginger Pop.[75] The attorney decries that slaves are made in the image of god yet dogs are treated better by their master than slaves, who are denied the protection of being a human being. The courts fundamentally disagreed that this was a case of moral reprehensibility and decided instead that the matter at hand was solely about termination, compensation, and reputation.

The judgment rendered by Judge Alonzo Snyder of the Tenth Judicial District Court of Louisiana states,

> By reason of the law and the evidence in this case being in favor of the defendant and by further reason of the verdict of the jury it is ordered that the defendant have judgment against the plaintiff in Solido in the same Three Hundred and Eighty Eight dollars and Eight Six cents, and that the said plaintiff pay the cost of this suit.[76]

This judgment sidestepped testimony about the physical torture inflicted upon Ginger Pop. The details of sexual cruelty were passed over and seen as circumstantial, unproven, and unwitnessed. The ruling is symbolic of the violent preservation of white social life. It maintains Utz as ontologically free from the *accusation*. It stops short of adjudicating the legitimacy of acts of sexual mutilation and torture. Judge Snyder determines that there is nothing to see or say about the actions of Utz because the accusation of wrongdoing misaligned his white racial claim to ontological innocence in terms of all manners and acts involving slaves.

The court designating Utz as innocent is not solely or primarily about his material life as a worker. It reflects more broadly on the status of his sexual subjectivity wagered against the objectified sexual status of Ginger Pop. Every action performed by Utz was determined as justified by the courts, making Ginger Pop the culpable agent of his own sexual depravity. It is crucial to restate that Ginger Pop did not simply die, but that his manner of death was by the repeated infliction of sexual injuries, which was Utz's preferred method for controlling slaves. As an overseer, Utz used sexualized violence as his means of commanding, breaking, and killing slaves. Each time Ginger Pop ran away, Utz intensified his sexual force until the point where the pain Ginger Pop endured from taking "two or three licks" resulted in a jolt of resistance so intense in his body that it severed his penis that was nailed down to a bedstead and ultimately killed him.[77] Ginger Pop's castration was, in the immediate sense, due to his reaction to the pain being inflicted upon his body, and how his penis had been positioned to receive that pain.

To Riemer, a fellow white resident of, and worker on, Burkland Plantation, Utz described the death of Ginger Pop as the consequence of "'Infective' chills."[78] A confidant to Utz, Riemer expressed first-hand knowledge of the many times Utz tortured Ginger Pop. Just eight weeks before his death, Riemer narrates in grotesque detail how Utz drove a ten penny nail into Ginger Pop's ear by several means, first by trying to whip the nail in, secondly, using a hand vice, and lastly, by screwing it in several times, making his ear bleed profusely. Utz's gruesome fantasies were not his alone. Riemer demonstrates the white collective mediation of these violent fantasies into real acts, as he served in a vestibular function for Utz, listening to his ideas and confirming that they were sound and just ways to contain a slave suffering from drapetomania, a mental illness classified by Samuel A. Cartwright as the cause of slaves escaping.[79] In assessing the significance of this "choice" of method, using sexual pain to rear and punish—how does one separate personal enjoyment and pleasure from work, or from the daily liberties of white life? Or is such a distinction even necessary to engage the racial sexual fantasies that pervaded plantation social life and death?

The sexual torture Ginger Pop endured lent to the intelligibility of Utz as a racial, legal, political, and social subject. The sexuality of Utz was also on display through his actions, social engagements with Riemer, and the responses of the courts. In action, Utz mapped out the violent extremities of unimaginable and incurable sexual obsessions that were deputized in service of him being a laborer, one tasked with containing the mobility of slaves, both sexually and physically. By sexually mutilating Ginger Pop, Utz intimated the conditions of racial sexual difference by reducing Ginger Pop's attempts to be free back down to the biological function of his sexual capacities and bodily faculties. Ginger Pop ran, Utz returned him to his place in the sexual order—pinned down, flayed, possessed. Yet, at the same time, Utz was also construed within the domain of sexuality, which allowed him to use sex freely and frequently as his preferred method, while simultaneously being able to escape sexual definition and containment. Utz is emblematic of a paradigm where white men can use sex as a means of engagement in excessive and grotesque ways, all while escaping, to use the words of Linda Brent, being understood as "the strangest freaks of despotism."[80] Instead, he is construed by the court, which is representative of a paradigm of relation, as simply doing his job, all while dreaming about and enacting a web of genital fantasies.

Contrary to Curry's reading of Jesse, the white cop in "Going to Meet the Man," Utz did not use castration to take Ginger Pop's "Black phallus" as a transference of power from dismembered Black flesh to his white manhood.[81] While Utz had a fantasy of using the penis to destabilize Ginger Pop's claim to motive will and movement, he also employs a flippant disregard of his Black penis as possessing any value or meaningful attribution. Utz responds to his penis like it is waste. This is not to suggest that waste, rather than power, is the true function of the Black penis in the white male psyche. Rather, it is to argue that Blackness does not possess a singular sexual function in the desire field of antiblackness. As Marriott argues, "Blackness persists as the always already retrievable (bucketed) figure of human being emptied of its Humanness: and this evacuation is itself the separation of human being from a black phenomenal matter that is shitty and abject."[82] That Ginger Pop was severed from his organ, disemboweling his compatibility with life, indexes a coeval between the endless consumption of Blackness as empty and itemizable, where an individual body can be broken down into fleshly parts and offered up as meaning and matter for the sustenance of Human capacity and intelligibility. The act of antiblack castration, then, reifies, extends, and strengthens the claims of Utz as a white worker by solidifying antiblack dismembering violence as essential and unremarkable. Though the claims possessed by Utz, or fictive Jesse, are infinite and unable to be articulated as something that can be contained and fundamentally recognized. Nonetheless, the claim is rooted in a relation to violence and the capacity for its wielding that is ontologically conferred.

The appeals court in the *Utz* case served as the mechanism that brought ontology back into stark relief, illustrating how moral claims are vacant when thinking about the unflinching violence that is carried out against

Blackness. Curry's argument pertaining to Black manhood and castration is inadequate in this context because it attempts to particularize and name the motive(s) behind a repeated violent act that oscillates through empty Black signification to concertize Human possibility. *Utz* details sexual violation that is less about the qualification of manhood for Ginger Pop and more so a glimpse into a world of fantasies where genitals are expansive beyond gender claims as their essential psychic and material operation. In this respect, manhood, or the denial of such, arrives late to the ontological predicaments laid forth by violence as that which destabilizes Blackness by reproducing its sexual thingification through fungible disorder.

Mediating Manhood

In three separate texts, Frederick Douglass details his violent encounters with Edward Covey, a slave breaking overseer enlisted by Douglass's master, Thomas Auld, to tame him.[83] The accounts Douglass provides of his encounters with Covey are strikingly similar to the pretext for the *Utz* case. Much like Utz, Covey, a poor white overseer, has a reputation of using unrelenting violence to command and break slaves of the will to resist the confines of their conditions. Unlike Ginger Pop, Douglass survives the brutal beatings inflicted by Covey. Douglass describes,

> I was whipped, either with sticks or cowskins, every week. Aching bones and sore back were my constant companions. Frequently as the lash was used, Mr. Covey thought less of it as a means of breaking down my spirit than that of hard and continued labor.[84]

After months of intensified physical and mental cruelty, he asserts, "Mr. Covey succeeded in breaking me. I was broken in body, soul and spirit . . . the dark night of slavery closed in upon me; and behold a man transformed into a brute."[85] Manhood is emblematic here as a form of integrity that is broken and rearranged into animality. For Douglass, being a man and a slave are not mutually exclusive, wherein susceptibility to violence severs the two. As he qualifies the manhood that was broken from him by Covey, his adjectives describe it as untamed, full of body, mind, and spirit, naturally elastic, intellectual, and curious. The bruteness that slavery forced upon him by lash and torture was dark and transformative.

On one occasion Douglass walks seven miles to his master's home to detail what he had endured at the hands of Covey, only to be returned by his master, who failed to heed him any sympathy while doubling down on the necessity of his treatment. He writes,

> My master, who I did not venture to hope would protect me as *a man*, had even now refused to protect me as *his property*; and had cast me back, covered with reproaches and bruises, into the hands of a stranger.[86]

Again, his narrative draws upon manhood to elicit an understanding of respectable Humanity, which his condition personified as lack, as he is denied what he perceives as the rightful protection of property.

For Douglass, manhood is a recurring theme of fashioned existence across his published works, as well as his famed speeches. In *The Narrative of the Life of Frederick Douglass*, he writes of manhood as something that can be lost and restored. He notes how his experiences with Covey, which led to a final battle, "rekindled the few expiring embers of freedom, and revived within me a sense of my own manhood."[87] He qualifies manhood by affording it the attributions of self-confidence and a "determination to be free," which cannot be disturbed by "death itself."[88] Deborah E. McDowell argues that,

> In choosing autobiography as a form, Douglass committed himself to what many feminists consider an androcentric genre. In its focus on the public story of a public life, which signifies the achievement of adult male status in Western culture, autobiography reflects and constructs that culture's definitions of masculinity. Douglass's *Narrative* not only partakes of these definitions of masculinity, but is also plotted according to the myth of the self-made man to which these definitions correspond.[89]

Douglass draws on the slave as a universal signifier of political reason, where the context of American slavery is in many respects absent from his broad elaborations of the dualities between man and slave or slavery and freedom. By dichotomizing gender against the slave, or subtending the slave as a topological ascription of manhood, Douglass isolates the male slave as a category to evacuate on the quest for self-determination or self-making. This teleological approach to slave manhood as a stage of gender infancy that can and must be broken, and furthermore cannot be returned to even in death, is individuated. Triumph is a masculine trope of progression and power that is disingenuous about the plight of the everyday Black male slave. However, the quality of slave gender that Douglass seeks and claims, the achievement of escaping, is also revealed through the juxtaposing language of what the free man is, and the male slave is not.

After being turned away by Auld, Douglass headed back out to the woods, hiding along his pursuit as he has stolen away in an act of defiance, only to be confronted by Covey, who, lurking in the dark, was intent on tying him up and beating him once he reached the property line. Douglass escapes Covey by running back into the woods to stave off his brutality. After a night confiding in a wise slave named Sandy and Sandy's wife, who he encountered in the woods, Douglass was determined by Sandy's encouragement to arm himself with a root of an herb that could afford him protection. This would make it "impossible for Covey to strike me a blow; that with this root about my person, no white man could whip me."[90] Skeptical about the power of this root but desperate for relief, Douglass adorned the root and followed the advice of Sandy to set out for Covey's home as if nothing had happened, to test the power of nature.

Just as Douglass entered the property, he encountered Covey and his wife on their way to church. To his surprise, Covey assumed an almost angelic like quality such that Douglass began to question if "Sandy's herb had more virtue in it than I, in my pride, had been willing to allow."[91] Despite doubting his own courage, Douglass was not swayed by Covey's demeanor, noting that "his religion hindered him from breaking the Sabbath, but not from breaking my skin."[92] This was a correct assumption given that by Monday morning, Covey resumed his role as a slave breaker where he again slyly accosted Douglass in a horse stable with the intent of beating him. Douglass responded with a new sense of self-vigor stating, "I now forgot my *roots*, and remembered by pledge to stand up in my own defense."[93] An infamous battle between the two then ensued.

Douglass postures that *"I was resolved to fight"* where "fighting madness" took over him to the point where he describes, "I found my strong fingers firmly attached to the throat of my cowardly tormentor."[94] To him, Covey was a coward because he was like a serpent who repeatedly appeared unbeknownst to Douglass rather than facing him head on in a battle of men.

Douglass took on a defensive posture against Covey, dodging his attacks while gripping him "firmly to the throat, that his blood followed me nails."[95] In this moment where brute force met brute force, with a mark of clarity Douglass describes that "He held me, and I held him."[96]

Douglass contends that "this battle with Mr. Covey was the turning-point in my career as a slave."[97] Describing the enlightenment he experienced following his fight with Covey, he writes,

> I felt as I never felt before. It was a glorious resurrection from the tomb of slavery, to the heaven of freedom. My long-crusted spirit rose, cowardice departed, bold defiance took its place; and I now resolved that, however long I might remain a slave in form, the day had passed forever when I could be a slave in fact.[98]

After fighting Covey in a grand act of self-defense, Douglass notes that Covey never beats him again. Although he expected that Covey would have him sent to the whipping-post for daring to raise his hand to a white man, he contends Covey chose not to do so in order to spare his reputation by not inflicting such brutality on a sixteen-year-old boy. This is purely the speculation of Douglass but not a fact he knew for sure, especially given that slavery did not extend the protections of childhood to slaves.[99] Nonetheless, Douglass was sure that the fight and subsequent relaxation of Covey's violence transformed him, such that "I was nothing before; I was a man now."[100]

Remarking on Douglass and Covey, Paul Gilroy argues, "Douglass can be read as if he is systematically reworking the encounter between master and slave in a striking manner which inverts Hegel's own allegorical scheme."[101] The Hegelian master–slave (lord–bondsman) dialectic is a commentary on recognition where out of a life or death struggle the self-consciousness of the master emerges as the victor as the slave is subsumed in the master's image of self as the progenitor of all things. Gilroy argues that in the context of American slavery, Douglass provides evidence of a reversed arrangement of power where the slave emerges as the true site of consciousness. In a similar vein, but in an argument that predates the one offered by Gilroy, Angela Davis argues Douglass and Covey illustrate an interdependence, where the master's existence is wholly reliant on the slave. Davis writes,

Only, the slave is the buffer-zone, and in this sense, the slave is somewhat of a master—it is the slave who possesses the power over the life of the master: if he does not work, when he ceases to follow orders, the master's means of sustaining himself has disappeared.[102]

Davis contends that Douglass clarifies that the slave is to true site of slavery's power, revealing that the master is buttressed by the slave and is empty without Black beings in bondage. The fight, but mostly the consciousness Douglass enters after the fight, exposes a deep philosophical myth for Davis, where "we have to uncover in order to reach the real substance behind it."[103] While Davis exposes the brute force behind the labor relation of slavery, the Hegelian dialectic is a commentary on recognition and reciprocity. It is difficult to conclude that after the battle between Covey and Douglass, Covey is forced to understand himself as codependent upon Douglass's image as a slave or at a paradigmatic level that the slave emerges as the true site of empowerment.

My concern with this evacuation of the violence of the master in favor of the slave as the true source of power is that it orients slavery through a hegemonic relation where truth about existence can be exposed. Yet the slave possesses no truth. Instead, the slave embodies repeated subsumption. The grand milieu of slavery illustrates a different orientation of life and mythos that the death of Ginger Pop clarifies in contradistinction to what Davis proposes. Utz and Covey were not wealthy masters who relied on "the very institution of slavery, which provided his wealth."[104] Each man was a poor white overseer whose vested interest in slavery was not the security of riches. For Utz, his fantasies of destabilizing the slave through sexual mutilation and torture were not the desires of the Humphreys, but his actions were authorized by them up until Ginger Pop was murdered, which they argued before the courts was an unwanted capital loss. In this sense, while his violence against Ginger Pop was permitted by the Humphreys, it put Utz at risk of having class conflict with them in terms of his employment and their loss of property. This suggests Utz privileged the opportunity to mutilate slaves over his own economic concerns.

For Covey, his violence encapsulated the will of Auld; however, the technologies of violence he deployed and the excitement of its execution were his possessive investment in the enterprise of conditioning slaves. The role of the overseer clarifies that the slave does not serve a single master (or that the only master is the one who owns slaves), for which a dialectical relationship emerges, revealing a truth about the chattel arrangement. The overseer epitomizes that the slave functions in service of multiple masters where there is no static truth about what binds the slave to whomever wills the command of violence over their existence.

The philosophical engagements with recognition and Blackness offered by Fanon help to clarify the hypervisibility, erasure, and unthinkable redress of the violent obliteration of the slave. What is revealed through his interrogation of the Hegelian dialectic is that the Black is trapped in a condition that tethers recognition to the objectification that produces the recidivistic necessity for recognition. There is no way out of the problem. The Black is unable to articulate a self-subject that is not a priori and a fortiori violated and violable. The violence of slavery cannot move beyond the spectacle and shock of the encounter, to produce a definitive description of what occurred, apprehend its cause(s), and ascertain any imaginable forceful imperatives for redress that meet the magnitude of the innumerable presentations. The fight between Douglass and Covey, catalyzed by ruthless beatings, cannot be untethered from the recognition of manhood Douglass seeks and the way that manhood is subsequently framed and understood. What recognition, as theorized by Fanon, makes clear about the predicament Douglass faced under the care of Covey is that the problem is not one of untapped thought or political potential, but recognition itself is indicative of the problem. At stake in what Fanon puts forth is the necessity of slave violation, which is not historically bound, and is progressively disappeared by manhood. The slave as the penetrable object of the modern world is continually reproduced to fortify the subjective understanding that to not be a slave is to be something. Douglass typifies this assertion in his hyper emphasis on man as beyond the boundaries of the slave, which, to him, is beyond the true site of nothingness; as he asserts, "I was nothing before; I was a man now."[105]

In breaking with the assumed reciprocity of the Hegelian master–slave dialectic, Fanon imposes the negro condition as a counterpoint. With the Hegelian assumption, Fanon asserts, "there is an absolute reciprocity which must be emphasized. It is in the degree to which I go beyond my own immediate being that I apprehend the existence of the other as a natural and more than natural reality."[106] As such, Fanon interrogates the perception that whiteness and Blackness are represented by a binary opposition that has the potential to recognize and incorporate the negro as Human. Instead, he argues,

> Man is human only to the extent to which he tries to impose his existence on another man in order to be recognized by him. As long as he has not been effectively recognized by the other, that other will remain the theme of his actions. It is on that other being, on recognition by that other being, that his own human worth and reality depend. It is that other being in whom the meaning of his life is condensed.
>
> There is not an open conflict between white and black. One day the White Master, *without conflict*, recognized the Negro slave.
>
> But the former slave wants to *make himself recognized* . . .
>
> If I close the circuit, if I prevent the accomplishment of movement in two directions, I keep the other within himself. Ultimately, I deprive him even of this being-for-itself.[107]

In this context, Man enters the frame of Humanness through recognition from another being already constituted as Human.[108] It is not a self-deputized ascription. Value and matter are wagered against the prior constituted Human, and how that position, or multiple positions, reify and affirm the replication and expansion of their form. As Sylvia Wynter has argued, the Human is not stagnated into a single form but strengthens its hold on the perceivability of Humanness by the expansion of its genres.[109] What Fanon is marking here is a paradigmatic foreclosure of Blackness as a genre of the Human. The circuit is closed for the Black through its designation as the anti-human, or that which is the antithesis of Human subjective capacity.[110] This distinction is registered at the level of violence. The brutality of Covey and Utz could not be the proprietary engine of racial civil citizenship for Douglass and Ginger Pop. Although his fight with Covey led Douglass to abandon his pacifist views in favor of slave self-defense and violent resistance, this is purely an ideological abolitionist stance for him that is not taken up in direct action.[111]

Furthermore, it is crucial to attune to Fanon stating that the white master recognizes without conflict the negro slave. This is referential to Covey's retreat from brutalizing Douglass. Notably, Fanon argues that this recognition is of the negro slave, not the negro as Man. How is the negro slave recognized beyond self-designation? What is recognition under captivity? Recognition is stifled in each case by the imposition of the permanent collapse, Negro (read slave), slave (read Negro). The progression of time does not relieve this imposition; however, time is precisely the arithmetic Douglass employs to theorize man beyond the slave.

Gilroy contextualizes Douglass's viewpoint in gendered terms, arguing that his "tale can be used to reveal a great deal about the difference between the male slave's and the master's views of modern civilization."[112] He also argues that Douglass's turn towards death "as a release from terror and bondage . . . accords perfectly with Orlando Patterson's celebrated notion of slavery as social death."[113] What is curious here, and in the estimations offered by Davis, is how slave consciousness is privileged as purely distinct from the master, and how it is heralded as the untapped tipping point of upending being a slave. Social death is not inhibited by a lack of slave agreement or acquiescence to its terms and obligations. It is a metaphysical predicament reproduced and maintained by force. The declaration by Douglass that "I am a man" is a violently imposed identification that arises out of necessity. To be a man, as Douglass describes, is a progression away from or beyond slaveness, an exit from nothingness into subjectivity.

Contending that Douglass offers a "distinctly masculinist resolution of slavery's inner oppositions," Gilroy also expresses concern with masculinity being read as men against women.[114] Given that Douglass narrates manhood as a becoming, from nothing to man, from slave to man, Gilroy understands his argument as "masculinity is largely defined against the experience of infantilism on which the institutions of plantation slavery rely rather than against women."[115] However, in the midst of a seemingly absent examination of manhood in relation to female slaves or white women, these gendered positions still wager solely upon what man is and its meaning for the male slave.[116] In the backdrop of assessments of the value of manhood are racial assessments of the value of womanhood and the incapacitation of the female slave.

Although this chapter has dealt primarily with the predicament of manhood, it is vital to consider Black (en)gendering as multi-inflected relations. Manhood reflects and refracts across racial boundaries. Nevertheless, how men enact and are recipients of the violence of men or manhood "is preoccupied by the homosocial relation while disavowing black men's relation to Black women and the abjection of black womanhood and their contiguity to the existential predicament of the problem space."[117] On this note, I will end this chapter by underscoring that Black manhood here is not exceptional but constitutive of the concerns outlined throughout this book about how subtending slave sexual violability to gender difference is a failed explanatory model.

Returning to the concern Newland expressed about the role of history in his racial sexual predicament, what, then, is the place of history when deciphering the constraints of Black gender? As Marriott argues, with respect to the work of Fanon,

> If history thus names a disciplinary organization of meaning and power that is total but not total because it is not totalizable, then what is most radically the matter with history is not that there may be no way out of *their* referential reality ... but more aporetically, that the binarisms of us and them, white and black become meaningless and the ideological effects they ground impossible as history.[118]

The historical impossibility of totalizing binarisms as referential truth emanates from the present, the place where the desire for meaning is grounded. History is a culmination of acts and events that are imported into an analytical structure to shape coherence. The annunciation of what history means undoubtedly shifts, augments, and morphs with the movement of contemporary technologies of meaning and knowledge production. However, the violence of history, which is bloody and abused, does not change, though our relationship to such may. The *return* to the archive or history is not a return as much as it is a staked position on the mattering of what was done for the present-future.

This final point brings us back to the insidious misogyny embedded in the logic of the iteration of Black male studies that was interrogated throughout this chapter. The expectation that Black feminism owes Black male studies an operable logic that represents Black manhood as purely affectable is a harbinger of cis-heterosexism and trans antagonism. The perception that theories like intersectionality are inherently antiblack male or that Black feminism was historically deputized by white women and white feminist social issues disguised as Black concerns is reductive and assumes that the material and psychic structures of the world can be pinpointed to specific people, places, or things. While it is undoubtedly true that some theories, thinkers, events, or institutions permeate thinking in ways that must be interrogated and traced, it is another point entirely to refuse to consider how structural positionality and relationality breed certain understandings that can be arrived at regardless of if a field of thought has engaged a certain thinker. This is all to say, if Black feminism does in fact pose a problem for thought with respect to Black men, the way to arrive at such a conclusion about the historic and pervasive nature of a problem is not to rest on a narrative of victimization that presumes a total absence of discussion or thought. Rather, the starting point is to contend with how studies of Black men, particularly Black queer and trans theories, have employed Black feminist analyses of gender to trouble and problematize the type of manhood that the present Black male studies levies as an inalienable truth.

Six
Toils of Flesh

My final chapter interrogates how the aestheticization of slavery, through cinematic portrayals of the exceptional individual, obscures the relationship between Black gender and sexual force. Specifically, this chapter draws into question the cinematic and narrative thrusts of two major motion pictures, the independent British film *Belle* and the biographical drama *12 Years a Slave*, both released in 2013. Both *Belle* and *12 Years a Slave* are directed by Black people, Amma Asante and Steve McQueen, respectively, and produced by Fox Searchlight Pictures. *Belle*, a costume drama about a Georgian-era Black woman living in a British estate, employs the concepts of care and moral innocence to render the protagonist Dido Elizabeth Belle (Gugu Mbatha-Raw) a rare image of Black wealth and sexual freedom. *12 Years a Slave* visualizes the autobiographical narrative of Solomon Northup by using brutally violent imagery to animate the terror of his time on the Epps plantation in Louisiana. This chapter looks specifically at how, in *12 Years a Slave*, the sexual and physical violation of Patsey (Lupita Nyong'o), a female slave, is deployed to make slavery appear real in cinematic form.

Given that the cinema is where the everyday person is confronted with the visuality and intensity of fantasy, rather than the truth, of slave suffering, it is critical to engage with the slave film genre to contend with how the physical and sexual brutalization of the slave demonstrates the impossibility of representing slavery as historically fixed. The replication of this genre is rooted in present desires to consume and spectate Black suffering. Film clarifies how the status of the slave cannot be represented as a truthful representation of any historicity of Blackness because the visual scope of truth is dependent upon present demands that Black flesh presented on film is brutalized, lacerated, and disregarded as historical content. The slave film serves as the mediating grounds for perceptions and beliefs about the real content and texture of the peculiar institution, particularly sexual violence.

In *Belle* and *12 Years a Slave*, notions of universal human community and transcendence are deployed as buffers to refuse a direct confrontation with violence. Instead, the productions attempt to undo the violence of slavery by suggesting the promises and possibility of freedom for each film's protagonist, Dido and Solomon. Amplifying the protagonists as natural free Black persons is reliant on depicting the sexual captivity of female slaves. This juxtaposition projects and sustains the visual and narrative scope of the heightened stakes of Black freedom. While the films end with Dido and Solomon free from physical chains, the sexual bondage of the female slaves, which gives the films their conceptual scandals, is not relieved, but is disregarded as the necessary content for the possibility of love. The sexually violated slave is treated as mere historical reflection, and a rhetorical device in a storyline of from bondage to freedom.

Thus, the sexual terror of slavery is psychically relieved for the viewer by the cultural consensus that emancipation restored subjective capacity for the Black. There is a belief that the arrangements of the plantation are no longer totalizing or terrifying because Humanness and self-possession are now possible for Black people. What I am naming as cultural consensus here, film scholar Kara Keeling has referred to as common sense, which, she writes,

> is the general form of a collective historical endeavor or, to speak of its mental aspects, of a set of collective historical endeavors that is necessarily "disjointed and episodic" because it consist of several sediments of past images that themselves provide a record of the success of past philosophies and situations.[1]

What constitutes the cultural consensus—or common sense—that meets the image in slave films is the incapacitation of the slave by violence. The narrative tells a story of strife and overcoming, the image crystallizes on raw violence, piecing together, as Keeling describes, fragments or discontinuities of psychic and philosophical distillations of the Black slave as purely violated matter. The narrative and the image are meant to ameliorate contradictions for the viewers, not the slave. The scale and stakes of antiblack violence contradict the possibility of film to represent Blackness through individual sovereignty and differentiation. Yet the viewer is appeased by the assumption of the film as historically situated, which is buttressed by the narrative arc that offers up individual freedom as redress for structural violence. This assists in assuaging the liberal viewer's potential psychic crisis, as the desire to witness in the carnal drive to beat and rape Black people for enjoyment may betray the assumption that we live in the time of emancipation.

While the script or narrative traffics through the potential downfalls and triumphs of shared Human community, the aesthetic frame relies exclusively on the physical mutilation of the Black actor as the fleshly content of examination to determine if the imagery is a just depiction of history. While it may be argued that the intent of dramatizing slavery is to ensure that no such atrocity ever occurs again, the question remains: can representation capture slavery? Furthermore, if the scale of its violence always escapes representation, and I argue here it does, what are we to make of the replication of violent images that attempt to perceive violation for the slave? As film scholar Marco Abel contends, "the violence of a literary or cinematic event... fails at accomplishing its goal of lessening violence precisely because it itself *adds* (however unintentionally) more violence to the specific environment within which it operates."[2] From this vantage point, the slave film does not represent history through a sequence of prior events. Rather, film is generative; it produces and commands an entirely new semantic field of slavery as visuality. In other words, the film makes slavery real and extends the scope of its violence. The moving image stages the precipice of freedom by titillating the viewer with limitless presentations of the extremities of deracinating Black flesh.[3]

The psychosexual status of the slave serves as the quintessential reference point for how care and love are mediated through the staging of slave films. How is slavery counterposed to one's love, as evidence of its divine right and freedom from force? How does gazing upon an object so dispossessed as to lack any capacity for sexual consent fortify the value of consent but also the desire to be Human, and not a slave? The availability of reflecting on the sexualized slave, to mark an ontological distinction from its state of being an object to the whims of a sexual paradigm that dispossesses consent before speech, is structurally demarcated. The Black is deputized by force to (re)produce the pleasure of Human value, though it is barred from metaphysically distinguishing itself from its own deracination. As such, the cinematic portrayal of the sexual violation of the slave is not a commentary on history. Instead, it functions to secure antiblack psychic security, through the ability to mark a distance between subjects with cartographies of suffering and Blackness, which is engulfed paradigmatically by incomprehensible levels of violence that are repetitiously summoned.

There is no representational dearth when it comes to the slave's sexual suffering. Yet, the recovery project is unending. Scaling the discussion of sexual violence and slavery up to the level of theory opens the possibility of exploring how the incessant calling upon the sexually abused slave/Black is integral to the structure. The act and the replication of the act are sutured by the same matrixes of force. This becomes apparent when it is seriously considered that there are no adequate arguments about how and why the sexually violable slave matters and means with respect to the current state of the world. Nevertheless, the image and narrative of the sexually injured slave continue to be called upon. Furthermore, the sexual violation of the slave maintains a belated position in discussions about the problems inherent to slavery and being a slave. I maintain sexual violence gives slavery its orbit. Thus, what does it mean to represent Black sexual violability? Is representation of it possible? Is sexual violability redressable as the primary concern of the slave? How does fact-telling serve to reify the necessity of violence? What does it mean to (re)produce the sexual violable Black thing?

Belle's Haunting

A 1779 David Martin portrait[4] hanging in the Scone Palace in Scotland prompted Misan Sagay to imagine the story of the Black woman captured in this history.[5] For Sagay, the image, depicting two Georgian-era women, one Black and one white, situated side-by-side, was striking. Unlike other visual imagery of Black people during this time, this painting did not depict servitude or show the Black woman groveling as less than her white counterpart. Instead, the women pose equally dignified, equally situated in time. The Black woman captured in this painting is Dido Elizabeth Belle, an heiress and daughter of a female slave, Maria Belle. Her father was Sir John Lindsay, a white man born of wealth and a British Naval captain, who captured Maria on a Spanish slave ship off the coast of the West Indies. Dido spent her life living in England at the estate of her uncle, William Murray, Lord Chief

Figure 5. Portrait of Dido Elizabeth Belle Lindsay (1761–1804) and her cousin Lady Elizabeth Murray (1760–1825) by David Martin. Source: From the Earl of Mansfield's Collection, Scone Palace, Perth, Scotland. Reprinted with Permission.

Justice Mansfield. From there, the movie *Belle* emerges, as Sagay labored to bring the story of the Black woman figure in the painting to life. However, Sagay's vision for *Belle* was contested and rewritten by Amma Asante, the film's director. According to Asante, "The original script was 'history-lite' and not a weighty piece of work" and was thus rewritten from a more realistic and convincing perspective.[6] While aspects of the story are historically accurate, the majority of the film is a fictionalized interpretation. Black history, and specifically the history of slavery becomes the contested terrain that simultaneously grants and denies the ability to write a Black female protagonist into a broader narrative of individual existence and gendered exceptionalism.

A 2014 *Guardian* review describes *Belle* as "a ripe costume drama with teeth" in which "Amma Asante delivers some sharp lessons on slavery" and

"Dido must find her own space in a world in which her colour marks her as unique among her peers."[7] The film is described as a variation of a woman's empowerment story, involving "a nuanced performance that perfectly embodies the increasingly independent spirit who refuses to accept that—in issues of both race and gender—'we are but their property.'"[8] A superficial account, indeed. Yet the final phrase, drawn directly from the film, gestures at the power dynamics and begs the question, what type of property? As British Black studies scholar Kehinde Andrews argues, the protagonist "equates the bondage of gender to that of slavery."[9]

Despite the *Guardian* review's single-axis dissection of race and gender as separate but similar impediments to personal growth and transcendence, the review highlights a primary issue with the writing of Black gender, namely Black womanhood, into a period piece about slavery that is categorized in the romance genre. The film is gratifying without critical thought because of its unspoken refusal to mediate Black gender in relation to social death and sexual violation. Dido is assumed to transcend slave status through familial relation and personal desires, whence her acquiescence to a script of gender that attempts to erase Blackness from its understanding. In this respect she is propped up as a post-slavery Black subject, embodying gender and sexual subjectivity in a manner unavailable to her mother. However, Dido is an aberration of the lives of Humans. Her animation is based upon what Jared Sexton has termed "borrowed institutionality."[10] The feel-good nature of the film employs Black womanhood as a conduit towards a desire for forms of Human gendered integrity that are sutured by what Joy James conceptualizes as the Black captive maternal—a Black person who is captive, conflicted, and used for other's actualization and survival—and most specifically to the point here by sexual violence.[11]

The politics of care play a central role in buttressing the film's narrative arc. The viewer must believe the following in order for the cinematic plot to hold: Sir Lindsay rescued Dido because he cared for her, and he chose the child because he cared for her mother. What undergirds this rubric is a conceptual scandal; as a slave, Dido's mother is not a subject of consent but rather an object produced by force. She is speechless, in the film and structurally. Her desire carries no symbolic integrity against the will of the master. Sir Lindsay is not her lover but her captor. Can sex between slaves and masters, or slaves and Humans, ever be ethical? This is all to say, the slave that birthed Dido was not a sexual subject because of her status as a slave. She is unable to give consent to any sexual encounter or to decide on the future of the child. Dido is structured by natal alienation borne of the paradigmatic relations of slavery, which are not conditional on her being a slave in chains but based on the stain of Blackness.

As Saidiya V. Hartman poignantly argues, "by emphasizing complementarity, reciprocity, and shared values, this hegemonic or consensual model of slave relations neutralized the dilemma of the object status and pained subject constitution of the enslaved and obscured the violence of slavery."[12] Notions of "mutuality" and "the recognition of the captive's humanity" are gestures that "protect" the master, not the slave.[13] Given that Sir Lindsay (Matthew Goode) presents as kind with a concerned demeanor, Dido's mother is held captive to his performances of care. Leaving Dido in the care of Lord and Lady Mansfield (Tom Wilkinson and Emily Watson), Sir Lindsay remarks, "sweet child, a ship is no place for one so precious as you."[14] The viewer is left to imagine this imposition of care under the stewardship of white aristocrats is what her mother desired. However, she may have desired Margaret Garner's imperative, to kill the child rather than see her transferred into another form of captivity, which "was the right thing to do," as Toni Morrison concludes, even if "she had no right to do it."[15]

To reimagine the life of Dido, the film *Belle* fictionalizes the story of *Gregson v. Gilbert*, an insurance case that documents the murderous atrocities that happened aboard the *Zong*, an eighteenth-century British slave ship, from which 132 slaves were mercilessly thrown overboard.[16] The *Zorgue*, a Dutch ship, later recast as the *Zong* after its capture by the British, set sail from São Tomé, an island off the coast of Gabon. With 442 enslaved Africans onboard, the ship was brutally overcrowded. The Africans had been captured and loaded at various points along the west coast of Africa, where *Zong* made stops at the Cape Coast, Accra, and, finally, São Tomé so that, prior to the voyage across the Atlantic, "some captives might as well have already been imprisoned on the ship for a year."[17] One-third of the captive Africans were murdered, thrown overboard across the Atlantic and the Caribbean in three separate murderous events. Others were noted as having thrown themselves to their deaths or having died from sickness. The *Zong* was a nightmare upon any account, although the information of what transpired and why is murky and vague. What records tell us is that the slave ship arrived in Black River, Jamaica, with only 208 slaves on board.

Zorgue or *Zong*, meaning "care" in Dutch on face value, lacks the personification of feminized gender often given to slave ships to mark their beauty and abundant glory.[18] Yet, the designation of care connotes a form of feminized labor and a peculiar relationship between those marked as cargo and the enslavers who are marked as Humans. The context of care on the *Zong* made the choppy treacherous waters of the Atlantic and the Caribbean Sea the mass grave of 234 lives, who prior to their deaths were already cast into a state of nonexistence, awaiting fates in lands unknown.

The *Zong* case catalyzes Dido into a politically imbued form of womanhood, which contests and resists the Mansfield family belief of her proper place in society. Furthermore, it is through the *Zong* case that Dido establishes and maintains a connection with her white love interest, John Davinier, or Mr. Davinier (Sam Reid), as he is referred to throughout the film. Dido falls for a man who, like her father, is propelled to right the wrongs of slavery by assisting Lord Mansfield with the evidentiary phase of *Gregson v. Gilbert*, the *Zong* case. When Mr. Davinier gives up on the case, it is Dido's insistence on moral truth and justice that persuades him to continue to fight and bar the enslavers from making capital gains from the murder of slaves.

The interweaving of Blackness, gender, the life of Dido, and the *Zong* merges together a peculiar relation, one predicated on subtending slavery as a question of morality rather than as a terrain that marks Black and Human difference at the level of violence. Sylvia Wynter argues, "given the 'visual and oneiric power' of the film's image to shape and control human perception and, therefore, our behavioral responses; we can no longer afford . . . innocence' with respect to the phenomenon of the aesthetic."[19] *Belle* is a white redemption story, masquerading as a radically different script of Black female empowerment.[20] However, when the veneer of innocence is removed from the film, the impossibility of writing Black cis-womanhood as a natural right, unmediated by the violence of Human, is exposed.

Though the film intends to write Dido as a gendered subject of consent, who fights for love and acceptance as a lady of the mind, not the body, the mise-en-scene sutures this transformation to the sexualization and assault of Dido's flesh. She is sexually assaulted by James Ashford (Tom Felton), the brother of a potential suitor, and, I argue, by Mr. Davinier, her love interest.

Figure 6. Close-up shot of Dido and James Ashford as he assaults her behind the brush in *Belle* (2013). Source: Searchlight Pictures (formerly Fox Searchlight Pictures). Reproduced under Fair Use.

Although the film does not portray this latter point as such, the incident with James clarifies the sexual nature of a prior encounter Dido has with Mr. Davinier.

Earlier in the film, James says to his brother, who is interested in marrying Dido, "One does not make a wife of the rare and exotic, Oliver. One samples it on the cotton fields of the Indies." At a picnic of multiple British high society families, James confronts Dido on these terms, accosting her while she is standing alone behind the brush. He insults her, insisting she is desperate to find a husband. She returns an insult about his family and their dwindling wealth. He then grabs her and shoves her. She walks back towards him. He briefly lustfully caresses her face. His affect immediately shifts to rage. He violently grabs her again and shoves his hand up her dress. The camera pans closely into their faces to capture her horrified reaction and his disdain. Her face is taken over by shock, anger, sadness, and confusion, making it clear that he is sexually fondling her with his hand (see Figure 6). Dido cries out, "That is painful, sir." James replies, "have you never been manhandled?" Dido screams, "how dare you? how dare you?" to which James taunts, "with ease." The camera pans back showing that others are in the distance, yet no one notices what happens to Dido.

In the following scene, there is a short pause that suggests Dido is reflecting on what happened to her body. She stands in the frame of a window, appearing only as a shadow in the distance (see Figure 7). There is no dialogue directly after to meditate on this sexual assault, just a solo reflection. Though she later

Figure 7. Wide shot of Dido's darkened silhouette gazing out the window.
Source: Searchlight Pictures (formerly Fox Searchlight Pictures).
Reproduced under Fair Use.

attempts to share this with her white cousin and lifelong companion, Lady Elizabeth (Sarah Gordon), her ill feelings about James are met with a reassertion from Lady Elizabeth that Dido is Black, thus implying her perspectives lack importance. As the window scene fades, Dido is next to Mr. Davinier, discussing his aunt and her desire for him to marry. They share laughs and the scenes continue to progress day-by-day showing their growing personal relationship. In the sequence of events, Dido and Mr. Davinier develop a strengthened companionship not in spite of what occurred with James, but because of it. Mr. Davinier is the character positioned as the man who respects her mind and does not covet her body. Together they discuss the *Zong* in secrecy, after Lord Mansfield fires Mr. Davinier as his legal apprentice. The details of the *Zong* continue bringing them back together as they work to decode the case and unlock the riddles of the events and decisions that occurred onboard.

After Mr. Davinier departs from his post, Dido feverishly wants to see him to get him to continue investigating the *Zong* case. When Dido sees Mr. Davinier in a crowd of people at the Ashford estate during a social gathering, she is determined to speak with him about the *Zong*. As she and Mr. Davinier sneak away to speak without being seen, a group of guests pass, potentially exposing their presence behind a hedge. Mr. Davinier pulls Dido close, attempting to protect her from being seen in the private company of a man who is not her suitor. As he shoves her body into his, the camera quickly pans to her breast, accentuated by a single lock of curled hair and a

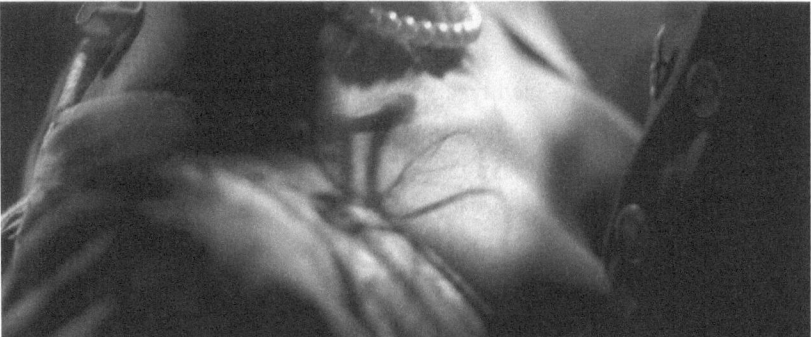

Figure 8. Light casts onto Dido's breasts as she is embraced by John Davinier to protect her from being seen by other partygoers. Source: Searchlight Pictures (formerly Fox Searchlight Pictures). Reproduced under Fair Use.

Figure 9. Close-up shot of Dido's lips as she is held close by John Davinier. Source: Searchlight Pictures (formerly Fox Searchlight Pictures). Reproduced under Fair Use.

string of pearls (see Figure 8). The image immediately shifts to Dido's lips closely positioned as to occasion or invite a kiss, a shadow cast onto her face (see Figure 9). The scene ends with Mr. Davinier gazing into her eyes. The scene almost mirrors the scene between Dido and James but with an inverse affect.

This moment in the film, which is used to announce Mr. Davinier's affection for Dido, performs an insidious labor. Depicted as being protected, in the moment, by Mr. Davinier, the handling of Dido's body and the focus on her breast illuminate Blackness in a manner the film labors to contest.

It makes her a focal point of sex and sensuality because of her Blackness, not by choice of her mind. Contrary to Mr. Davinier referring to Dido as "Lady," this hypersexualized treatment in the film bastardizes the meaning of this designation. The effort of the film to assert affection through the thrusting of her body against a man elides the periodization of the film. If the intentions were to present Dido as equally capable of love as her white female counterparts, specifically Lady Elizabeth, why is Dido the only body that is groped in a sexual manner multiple times on screen? What is equally striking is that Mr. Davinier never apologizes for his forceful gripping of her body, which is an encounter that disrespects the gender formalities of this era.[21] What the scene reveals is that Dido is situated in the film by a sexual script that disrupts the intent of the film to orbit around universal gender concerns.

The situation of Dido, though framed as a concern with associative categories, denies mediation on what structures the usage of her body as a vessel for the appearance of others. The triangulation between Mr. Davinier and his growing love for Dido, and James Ashford and his sexually aggressive behaviors, use each scenario as a counterpoint of expression. Dido makes the choice not to marry Oliver Ashford (James Norton), professing, "My greatest misfortune would be to marry into a family who will carry me as their shame—as I have been required to carry my own mother." The dual implications of this statement liken the Ashford family and her experiences at the Mansfield estate as symbolic of a refusal to engage her Blackness. This is true. Without saying explicitly but through action, Mr. Davinier is credited with offering Dido the possibility of an unrestrained existence in the world. He, unlike anyone else, asks of her mother, to which she replies, "I know very little of her other than the color she has given me." Mr. Davinier's question opens up a dialogue that was vacant in her previous relationships, a question of where her Blackness emerges from. Such scenes suggest that Mr. Davinier respects Dido's mind and filial quandary. Yet all the while the film uses the body of Dido to broach the symbolic coming together of the two. Through her self-assertions and developing political consciousness, Dido is positioned as maintaining an ultimate control over her life, yet no attention is given to her inability to determine her own body autonomy irrespective of her speech.

To assert Dido as neither Black nor slave, the film moves through her sexual assault by inserting her courtship with Mr. Davinier as evidence that she is gendered by her capacity to consent to love, which can be violated at any moment but is not an ontological determination or exclusion, such as for slaves. However, the ease with which the film displays this violation, while refusing to reflect upon what occurred, illustrates the argument by Hortense Spillers, that

> in the *stillness* of time and space eventuated by the "mulatto/a"—its apparent sameness of fictional, historical, and auto/biographical content—we gain insight into the *theft* of the dynamic principle of the living that distinguishes the subject from [their] objectification.[22]

If *Belle* is about the transcendence of race and gender, as asserted by the *Guardian* review, why are Dido and her mother the only gendered figures that bear the sexual markings of violation? If, according to the *Guardian*, the borrowed phrase "we are but their property" is supposed to connote race and gender, why must Dido be represented as sexually violable in order to prove her Black subjectivity? Why are the cultural objects of Whiteness—dresses, carriages, and mansions—the only substantive renderings of Dido's gender otherwise? If cis-gender is continuity of the organisms of mere life, why is the writing of Black cis-womanhood in *Belle* repeatedly oscillated through Black sexual and gendered captivity and white gendered potential to cohere her transcendence? Why is her Black cis-womanhood incoherent without sexual violence? Can she actually transcend?

If we read the film through the valence that *Belle* obscures, a sequence of varying forms of capture, then we come to realize the entire film happens aboard a slave ship, in the hold of its conceptual frameworks of gendering, violence, and the deathliness of capture. Hartman explains that, "orthography provides the illusion of direct testimony, immediacy, and authenticity, which only serves to (re)produce the master's text, even if donning the rags of the slave."[23] In the case of *Belle*, the illusive orthography is adorned with Elizabethan dress, the corridors of the Mansfield mansion, the auspices of high society life, the privilege of inheritance, the emotion of courtships, and the affect that arises from the capacity for political will and choice. Dido is cloaked by subjectivity that is contingent on the status of the Human. Care becomes the psycho-affective mode that destabilizes viewers' capacity to understand that Elizabethan garb and a costume drama do not make one less a slave.

My contention with *Belle* is how its discursive field belabors the sexual and gendered terror of slavery as something to overcome by the acquiescence of forms of cis-gendered personhood, as natural and divine right or inscription. However, the obscuring of sexual force makes this film possible. Force, rather than love, enables one to think critically about the ciphering of Black cis-womanhood through championed and revered individualism. Furthermore, the opacity of Black sexual vulnerability is necessary to produce the psycho-affective registers that perceive the sexual order of slavery as a conditional, rather than a structural, predicament. Wynter argues, "'Human Life' is *not*, as it is believed to be in our present system of knowledge, that of a natural organism which exists in a relation of pure continuity with organic modes of life."[24] In this respect, gender as an extension of Human Life is not a continuous formation of "organic modes of life."[25] What is gender without slavery? How can one know the limits of their gender violation without juxtaposing it against the limitlessness of the slave's sexualized gender?

Andrews describes *Belle* as a film that contributes to and is made possible by what he terms the psychosis of whiteness. He argues that this allows racism, or antiblackness, to be erased from the film's imaginative portrayals. "Class is key to the psychosis because the idea that poor Whites suffer equally or worse than Black communities allows issues of racism to be obfuscated. Belle consistently reinforces this discourse throughout the film."[26] Depictions of class struggle in the film are animated through scripts of love and moral devotion, with Dido conscripted into a narrative of womanhood that is fighting for the recognition of her capacity for consent and choice, like her white women counterparts. Attributions of love, care, and morality carry the narrative arc and cinematic affect of the film, all the while there is a glaring silence about slavery. As Andrews observes, Dido is written as naïve about the violence of slavery, and Britain is heralded as an abolitionist space that is distinct and unsullied by its enslaving empire.[27] These fantasies rely on the consent of the viewer to ignore that Dido is Black. By suspending her Blackness into a desire to believe that perhaps one Black woman, in the time of slavery, may have lived freely by the same terms deployed for the people who kept the woman who birthed her and countless other Black people as slaves, the film is rendered pleasurable and rewarding.

The role Lord Mansfield plays in rendering the legal decision in *Gregson v. Gilbert*, the *Zong* case, is the moment the film relies on to liberate Dido from the position of a partial subject. Dido is unsure how Lord Mansfield will rule in the case, so she, adorning a dark cloak, sneaks into the court full of white men, some assumedly enslavers or politically pro-slavery. She listens intently, and, to her shock, realizes Lord Mansfield rules as she hoped, in favor of the insurers. However, his ruling in the film is less about fraudulent insurance claims and more an outcry about the moral wrongs of slavery. The film implies he has had a change of heart because of his relationship to Dido.

Following the decision, Dido removes her cloak and emerges in a public space where she meets Mr. Davinier. They rejoice and embrace with a kiss. She is no longer fearful that her dark skin will cast her aside or render her captive. Her capacity to maneuver in the world by way of choice, in this case, through her ability to choose a spouse publicly, is the film's emancipatory release. This scene perceivably frees Dido from the uncertainty of being neither slave nor Human but of both worlds and no longer conditionally free. In this respect, she is freed from the confines of constricted sexual consent but not from sexual force. While Human gender concerns of liminal consent, will, and desire are released at the end of the film, "how does one grapple with issues of consent and will when the negation or restricted recognition of these terms determines the meaning of enslavement?"[28]

To animate the psycho-affective field of transcendence, *Belle* rewrites the *Zong* ruling to cast Lord Mansfield as caring and benevolent. As James Walvin argues, "the Lord Chief Justice [Mansfield] and the Solicitor General agreed with the slave traders that the killing of 132 Africans was *not* a matter of murder," demonstrating the actual ruling was contrary to the film's depiction.[29] This brings us back to the point by Asante about the film paying respect to history. If historical accuracy was the concern of the film, why was the ruling on the *Zong* massacre falsified? What kind of imaginative possibility is denied for the film if it contrarily narrates the actual relationship of Lord Mansfield to the *Gregson v. Gilbert* decision? What history is *Belle* redeeming?

Freedom, here, is not wagered for the unthought sexual positionality of Dido's mother or by questioning if a legal ruling offsets the paradigm of violence that produced the conditions of possibility for the *Zong* massacre. M. NourbeSe Philip argues in "Notunda," a prologue to the poetry collection *Zong!*, "the *ratio* at the heart of *Zong!*, however, is simply the story of being which cannot, but must, be told."[30] The story of the *Zong* repeats itself as a ship equipped for less captive bodies than it carried and loaded with a particular capacity of water, food, and supplies, conditions in which some slaves succumbed to illness and malnutrition and others were murdered by being deliberating chained together and tossed overboard. This is not the story, and its repetition is elusive as it reduces structural violence to tractable terms of a singular set of events. The journeys of the unnamed and unknown, violently produced as cargo, are stories written into permanent obsolescence. Philip suggests, "not-telling" to expose "where the law attempts to extinguish being, as happened for 400 years as part of the European project, being trumps the law every time."[31] What Philip offers is a way to antagonize the terms of engagement by refusing to graft stories of Human morality or injury as accident onto Black incapacitation. Not-telling is a Black imposition that acknowledges the mere existence of the Human continues to expand the incompleteness of abolition beyond the scope of emancipation.

Belle breathes life into a painting, a still image where desires are imported into the frame rather than contained by any truthful substance represented by its rendering. Contrary to the film, little is known about Dido outside of her time living with Lord Mansfield. The biography *Belle: The Slave Daughter and the Lord Chief Justice* says very little about the life of Dido and, in fact, is more a history book about Lord Mansfield, so much so that the title shares his name.[32] Furthermore, her reference as a slave daughter is no off-hand coincidence but speaks to her position in relation to the Mansfield family and her striking invisibility in history given her familial ties. As one online commenter writes in a review of this book,

> This ends up being, more than anything else, a short biography of William Murray, Lord Mansfield . . . As Dido's biography, this book is certainly

frustrating, because we simply can't know her intimately, and it almost feels unnecessary (not because her story doesn't need to be told, on the contrary, we need way more narratives about [people of color] in Europe . . .[33]

The history of Dido labors as a history of Lord Mansfield that marks him a dutiful white who granted residence to a Black child during the time frame he adjudicates two of the most charged cases on slavery in British history, *Somerset v. Stewart* and *Gregson v. Gilbert*.[34]

While some might desire that the presence of Dido at Kenwood House mattered for British legal history, this assumption must discount how the proximity to Black people—as slaves, servants, free peoples, and children of interracial sex—factors in the global history of slavery.[35] Intimacy is not the balm of Black accumulation and fungibility but its intensifying factor. The film solidifies Dido, like other Black people, as bound and construed by a racial arithmetic that binds the assumption of her capacity to the subjectification of those who control her movement toward or away from freedom. For the central love story, Dido becomes a conduit for Mr. Davinier as he emerges as morally outraged by slavery. His opposition is strengthened by his willingness to accept a Black woman as a counterpart. Where his subject develops through his care and love for a Black woman, she is rendered naïve to the condition of other Black people given her physical location in the Mansfield estate. The scope of her character is not broadened by her love interest. Mr. Davinier serves as the true hero of the film, facilitating Dido's empowerment by guiding and granting her access to information about Black people beyond the confines of her gilded slave quarters.

Furthermore, the history of Lord Mansfield is vast and well circulated, yet there is very little known about the Black female who resided in his home.[36] This erasure is not accidental but underscores how Blackness sutures her historical and discursive insignificance in a story about the actions of a powerful white man. The film labors to obscure that Dido is not free. One crucial fact that is known about her existence is when Lord Mansfield died, he manumitted Dido in his will.[37] Despite the film's attempt to unwrite that the Mansfield family understood Dido as a slave, casting her instead as kin, the film script and visual field cohere precisely because Dido is tethered to their family name and social class, a captive at their estate. Dido is an object of Lord Mansfield's subjectivity, where she is historically absent in his continued historical presence. Contrarily, Lady Elizabeth Murray does appear in biographies about Lord Mansfield. Despite the film framing Dido as more advantaged than Lady Murray, who was supposedly nearly impossible to pair with a suitor because she lacked a dowry and was not an heiress like Dido, Blackness, not class, was their true dividing factor. History has more to say about Lady Elizabeth than Dido, simply because she was white.

"Remembering is otherwise" and recasting the sexual vicissitudes of slavery "disappear again as though nobody ever walked there."[38] *Belle* cannot reconcile the slave status of Maria Belle, so it disappeared her into a story of distant plantation love with a Royal Navy captain that recapitulated the tragic mulatta trope for Dido. Although not an actual slave ship captain, Dido's father commanded a ship for the militaristic wing of a slavocracy. Which is to say, the navy ship and the slave ship are two vessels of the same guard, although only one was fit for slave cargo. The cargo cannot consent to sex with the captain. Furthermore, the progeny born of their sexual coupling cannot be free from the violence that produced the conditions of possibility for the forceful encounter. There is no love under these structurally incongruent arrangements. As Morrison wrote in the context of slavery, "Not the breath of the disremembered and unaccounted for, but wind in the eaves, or spring ice thawing too quickly. Just weather. Certainly no clamor for a kiss."[39] The (slave) ship, the capture of the Africans on board, and its wake, sans the implantation of romanticism, is the genesis of Black engendering. Black gender struggles to find its grammar and ghosts at the nexus of the feminization of slave ships as the frontier of domesticity and interracial intimate relation, where white sexual fantasy and Black sexual violability collide.[40]

Still a Slave

The physical site of the plantation is a crucial element of the brutal animation of slavery in cinema. *Belle*, a slave film without the plantation in the backdrop, weighed upon this visual absence to obscure the contexts of captivity for Dido. By replacing the plantation with a wealthy estate, *Belle* relied on aesthetics of wealth to stage a claim of Dido's exceptional freedom. However, to stage the difference of her Black gender, the film relied upon vulgar and casual groping scenes to mark her racial sexual distinction. Coupled with the allures of high society life, these sexually violent scenes were privileged as inessential to the truth of Dido and her story. In films where the plantation is the primary mise-en-scene, the visualization of violence is scaled up to convey the toils of the flesh. Thus, violence occupies the central scope of engagement to capture the essence of what it means to be a slave.

In the 2013 cinematic portrayal of 12 Years a Slave, the 1853 autobiography of Solomon Northup, the sexual(ized) brutalization of Patsey, a female slave, figures a peculiar crux. Solomon (Chiwetel Ejiofor), a free-born Black man who was sold into slavery and renamed Platt, spends his time on the Epps plantation in Louisiana, wallowing in his angst to reclaim his freedom. His "illegitimate" captivity and enduring quest for freedom are juxtaposed and heightened against the life of Patsey, who suffers endlessly.[41] Born into slavery, she is the quintessential slave. What distinguishes her from Solomon is her inescapable sexual captivity. After being kidnapped and sold down South into slavery, his struggle to get free from the plantation and return to his family up North provides a peculiar contradistinction to the cinematic portrayal of Patsey. She is a "rightful" slave, whereas Solomon is a "wrongfully enslaved" Black man.

The scene that reveals Patsey as the object of sexual violation and violence is particularly brutal. After a day toiling under the intense Louisiana sun, the slaves are commanded from their sleep to entertain the plantation master and mistress in the big house. Dressed in their bedclothes, the slaves dance the waltz, as their limbs drape heavily towards the floor with exhaustion and anguish. Solomon does not dance; he plays the violin, which he learned during his time living free in New York. Master Epps (Michael Fassbender) cheers and claps with a gallivanting sadistic affect, jousting the slaves to uplift their mood with his bifurcated look of pleasure and violence. Recessed in the backdrop, Mistress Epps (Sarah Paulson) also fixates a lustful glare onto Patsey. She then glimpses at her husband who, in a mesmerizing trance, has placed his focus on dancing Patsey. Without pause, Mistress Epps turns to her liquor cart, grabs a crystal liquor bottle, takes a few steps forward, and launches it, striking Patsey's face (see Figures 10 and 11). Patsey howls out in sheer terrified pain as she falls to the floor clutching her wound. The camera immediately cuts to Solomon, capturing his shock. The Epps then proceed to engage in a verbal exchange. No one attends to Patsey, though the slaves stare down at her on the floor. Minutes later, when Master

Figure 10. Close-up shot of Mistress Epps grabbing a crystal decanter to throw at Patsey in 12 *Years a Slave* (2013). Source: Searchlight Pictures (formerly Fox Searchlight Pictures). Reproduced under Fair Use.

Figure 11. Mistress Epps throws a crystal decanter at Patsey's face while other slaves avert their gazes at the floor. Source: Searchlight Pictures (formerly Fox Searchlight Pictures). Reproduced under Fair Use.

and Mistress Epps finish their exchange, an unseen being drags Patsey while she still lays on her side. As she disappears, the slaves return to dancing, and Solomon continues playing the violin.

12 *Years a Slave* relies on sexual captivity to amplify the violence of the slave estate in a manner that demands critical attention. Director Steve McQueen employs the autobiography of Northup, which is riddled with violence in its own right, and imagines a different tale.[42] Remarking on his role as director, McQueen states, "Everybody in the audience is Solomon Northup. What he goes through you go through."[43] From this vantage point it may

seem that McQueen willfully dispossesses Solomon of subjectivity and individual integrity to tell a universal story of suffering and triumph that is broader than the original autobiography. However, Solomon is so effortlessly evacuated of a sense of interiority because he is socially dead. He is a transubstantiation of the modern demand for the slave, the political ontological divisions of slavery, and the reification of the metaphysical freedom extended ab initio to non-Black subjects. Which is to say, slavery produces Solomon and Patsey, as well as the other slaves in the film, as ontologically absent, which is deputized by the film to present an "unflinching account of slavery."[44] This signifies that there are limited constraints on how slavery is imagined. The differences between the autobiography and film have not substantially impacted the circulation of the latter. Beyond purported historical fact or fiction, there are two consistent expectations placed upon engagements with slavery, that there is ample antiblack physical and sexual violence, enough to convince the witnessing subject that the representation is just and true.

The scene that epitomizes the brutality of the Epps plantation is the infamous beating of Patsey, first by Master Epps, who then commands Platt (Solomon) to continue the beating on his behalf. Patsey sneaks off to the Shaw residence to retrieve a bar of soap, to cleanse herself from being forcefully disallowed to bathe by Mistress Epps. She returns to the Epps plantation walking with the speed of desperation, when Master Epps charges at her, violently grasping her neck and demanding to know where she has been. His commanding tone suggests he perceives that she was returning from having sex. Solomon intervenes with his body as to protect Patsey, but Master Epps strikes him across the face and he falls gripping his injury. His wounded face, like Patsey's in the earlier dance scene, marks a psychosexual realization. In an attempt to protect Solomon, Patsey reveals the soap in her hand, yelling with her mouth gaped open as to hold back tears, "five hundred pounds of cotton, day in and day out," conveying just how much she reeks of the utter stench of unceasing severe labor. Unconvinced by her pleas, Master Epps instructs an overseer to prepare her to be whipped. Patsey is drug to a tree, her pink dress ripped open exposing her bare breast, and her hands tied. Master Epps whispers, "you have done this to yourself." He turns to whip her, and Mistress Epps commands him to "do it," out of spite for her husband sexually abusing Patsey, which she perceives as a form of sexual competition. He hesitates and thus reclaims his power against *and*

Figure 12. Mistress Epps stands in the backdrop as Master Epps commands Platt (Solomon) to whip Patsey. Source: Searchlight Pictures (formerly Fox Searchlight Pictures). Reproduced under Fair Use.

with her directive by turning to Platt (Solomon) and commanding that he beat her instead (see Figure 12).

Master Epps performs an allegiance to the idea of Patsey's exceptionalism by refusing to whip her to torment his wife and transmutes his desire for the pleasure of sadism through Solomon as a further extension of the thrust of his power. He wants to own without contestation his right to enter the slave cabins in the dark of night with a kerosene lantern in tow to sexually violate Patsey. He wants her, "queen of the fields," as he refers to her, as the property of his fully realized power. Unwilling to risk his own beating or death by refusing, Platt submits to the pleasure of Master and Mistress Epps. The latter stands in close view to witness and enjoy Patsey cry in agony as her back tears open. When Master Epps orders Platt to whip Patsey, the perception of him as conditionally captive is undone. It is in this exchange that he is revealed as equivalently sexually violable, and thus a slave. Solomon is sexually mediated through this relation where he is not external to the sexual violation of Patsey by Master Epps or the violence of Mistress Epps but he is an implement of sexual malice and a constituent component of the sadism of white sexual pleasure and gratification.

I draw on this film not to profess it as an exceptional rendering of the promises and failure of narrating slavery but because of its banality. It illustrates a commonplace understanding of slavery: that amplified physical brutality makes slavery real, and that sexual violence is the silent, yet omnipotent scandal of the conditions of sentient chattel property. What unfolds in the above scene is grotesque. Through Solomon and Patsey, *12 Years a Slave* demonstrates that the relational interplay of physical violence and sexual violence for the slave is preconditioned by the openness of their captive status. If we displace slavery as history and consider it a relation, then captivity, the laceration of Black flesh, and sexual force all situate a paradigmatic demand placed upon the slave as a productive focal point for recognition. The beating of Patsey by Platt situates the meeting grounds of force and pleasure that undergird antiblackness. The scene augments the visual scope by positioning Blackness as culpable for its own violation. In fact, if one were to turn on the film at this precise moment, the only thing visible is Blackness. Platt is whipping Patsey alone in the frame (see Figure 13).

The pleasure of witnessing, like Mistress Epps standing in the backdrop, enlivens the insistence that engaging the injury of the slave from a distance is simply an innocent amusement. Arguably, the sexual and physical brutalization of Patsey serves as the content to express the horror of slavery and why individual freedom is necessary for Solomon. However, *12 Years a Slave* does not, perhaps because it cannot, offer a commentary for Patsey, even if fiction, about what freedom from her condition could be expressed or lived as. This film, like other popular and theoretical renderings of slavery, demonstrates that the psychosexual confines of the plantation transcend temporality.

Commenting on her role as Mistress Epps in the film, actress Sarah Paulson explains that she had no qualms about playing the role and that

Figure 13. Close-up shot of Patsey's pained face as she is whipped by Solomon, who stands blurred in the backdrop. Source: Searchlight Pictures (formerly Fox Searchlight Pictures). Reproduced under Fair Use.

her sympathies lay with Mistress Epps, who "feels like she's being usurped by another woman in her home."[45] Here, Paulson asserts Patsey as structurally equivalent to Mistress Epps and also a willing participant in her own sexual degradation. However, this is not an affect of the past, but an aftershock of the relations of slavery that transmute the slave into categories and actionable circumstances that they were structurally barred from accessing. In the end, the violence of Patsey's condition is made void in service of granting sympathy to her violent abuser, her mistress. The inability of the slave to possess its being as free from the imposed will and desire of others continues to (pre)condition Blackness. Non-slaves, like Mistress Epps, are conferred by varying degrees of, and access to, power, yet are not barred from the classification as Human, and thus not a Black slave. In response to Paulson, actress Vera Farmiga exclaims that she wanted the role as Mistress Epps, demonstrating the lure of genuflecting the master's power and prerogative as white feminine desire.

The conversation between Paulson and Farmiga is sutured by an assumptive logic that is premised upon deploying history to obscure the ongoing lust for participation in Black abjection. The liberated spirit of white women vying for the role of plantation mistress does not and cannot extend to the Black actors who worked on this film. What exists between the divide of the white and Black actors are the structural antagonisms of antiblackness, where white pleasure is parasitic upon repeated Black suffering. On screen, the violated is not the historical slave but the Black flesh that is slave to the violating demands of the film script and scopophilic lens, the Black actors themselves. The actresses discussing Patsey as a sexual competitor to Mistress Epps and themselves as rivals vying for the opportunity to portray a trope of white womanhood scorned is a commentary on their relationality to Nyong'o, not the fictional Patsey. If we still inhabit a world where two white women can discuss the violation of a female slave as a love triangle rather than absolute powerlessness, and seek to play the role to convey to the audience the mistress as a woman scorned rather than understanding Patsey as her property—of whom Mistress Epps is complicit in her sexual brutalization—then we do not simply have a problem of discourse.

The film and the fanfare of its marketing expose the structural cataclysms that emerge in each instance slavery is narrated as an event of the past. Paulson and Farmiga show that there is not a consensus on what slavery did to

Black people and what role whites occupied in relation to that violence. As such, the Black temptress that Paulson and Farmiga see in Patsey is directly relational to their, and most importantly the world's, containment of Black women's sexuality as deceitful and lascivious. Nyong'o is not portraying this assumption in Patsey. Rather, her capacity to play Patsey, and to be understood as a just and true representation of her, means that these same metaphysical impositions about female slave sex are placed upon her as the locus of her making. She is not simply playing a role but her incapacity to play the role in a manner that shifts the narrative of the slave she embodies to illustrate her absolute inability to resist sexual and physical brutality is a structural predicament, not one of actor training. The on-screen role by Nyong'o is not mediated through history or her acting persuasiveness, but through the force of Black dispossession that usurps the possibility of narrating a slave film completely and wholly as white violence in every utterance. This is the force of slavery, where the seduction of locating subjectivity for the slave obscures the absolute violability and subsumption of its status.

Discussing the discomfort she felt about the abject cruelty experienced by Patsey, Nyong'o recounts McQueen as directing her to understand Patsey as "effortlessly sensual." McQueen wants Nyong'o to *feel* slave sexual violability as sexual capacity and consent. To channel this emotion of the slave as a seductress, Nyong'o found a quote on the sensual or sensuality from James Baldwin to be instructive. Baldwin writes, "To be sensual, I think, is to rejoice in the force of life itself and to be present in everything one does from the effort of loving to the breaking of bread."[46] The interpretation of this quote by Nyong'o to channel the embodiment required of her role is quite telling. She states, "And so Patsey was present, and that's what made her so sensual." Patsey is vacant of sensuality at the level of action. Nyong'o seems aware of this, so she transposes sensuality into the crudest of terms and exposes both the absurdity of the directive from McQueen and the essence of existence for Patsey. What Nyong'o clarifies in this quote is that as a slave, Patsey is sex personified in her bruised, battered, lacerated, filthy, and sexually violated state of (non)existence. Presence for her, and thus sensuality, is wanton sex that is limitless and unbound.

Despite seeking to channel Patsey as a sensual being, Nyong'o was still haunted by what it meant to embody her. When asked how she got into character, she explains, "It's all about the crack of the whip. You hear it. And you feel it."⁴⁷ Her expressions about the role are cast as feelings or forms of affect that escape the capture of complete definition. She recalls being unable to sleep when wearing her makeup scars from the whipping scene home overnight to lessen her time in the makeup chair the following day. She weeps through the night. Noting that this particular night was especially restless, she was unable to sleep well over the course of time shooting the entire film. She states, "I recognized that my discomfort was temporary and the woman who I was playing was permanent. It still brings me to tears."⁴⁸ The temporality she ascribes here to distinguish herself from Patsey is vexed.

While Nyong'o is not Patsey and lives a categorically distinct life as a Hollywood actress from a Kenyan diplomatic family, there are connective tissues that bind their flesh together.⁴⁹ Visualizing the sexually abused and tortured female slave in a twenty-first-century film produces the same antebellum subjective understanding of her as a lusty wench from the director, actors, and spectators. McQueen narrates her sexual status as a love story, demonstrating the perversity of the redeployment of the sexual violation of slaves and its ubiquitous assumption as the content of conflictual interracial sexual triads. While Nyong'o is sorrowful about the life of Patsey, she does not contest her classification as a sensual being. She embraces it. Nowhere in any of these accounts is a tarrying with objecthood, except perhaps the assertion by Nyong'o that what Patsey endured was permanent. The permanence of this condition is not a matter of the past; it expands beyond the temporal markers of the physical life and indexes the hold of antiblackness on the capacity to conceptualize and carry a story about slavery that does not slip into the desire to flee from the unbearable confines of a life strictly marked by its relation to unmediated violation.

12 Years a Slave attempts to write against the irreconcilable antagonisms of antiblackness as the anchor and repeated lure of the slave film. It presents Solomon on an individual quest for the restoration of stolen freedom. His exceptionalism is cast in contradistinction to the plantation slave. For example, in an exchange with a female slave Eliza (Adepero Oduye), who sobs and moans loudly daily for her children who were sold away, Solomon questions and challenges her unending mourning, stating that she "will drown in it." Unmoved by his contempt for her style of grief, Eliza asks if he has stopped mourning his own children. Solomon cries out that "They are my flesh," yet he maintains faith that he, unlike Eliza, will be reunited with his children.

He carries this surety by holding out hope for a benevolent white to believe that he is a free Black. In this respect, the slaves Solomon encounters on his journey are props to animate the complexity of his predicament as a Black man who was "wrongfully enslaved." Slaves like Eliza, whose suffering is uncharted, are circumstantially divorced from his plight, which is a movement towards transcendence and familial reconciliation.

Additionally, the figure of the female slave repeatedly catalyzes the angst for his freedom. Redress from their sexual and reproductive plights is not as easily reduced to the ability to leave the plantation, as it is for Solomon. Furthermore, the static condition of the female slave antagonizes the faith Solomon has in the moral compass of some whites. Eliza and Patsey are burdened by a condition that cannot be dislodged by the desire to perceive slavery as controlled by *some* immoral whites. Their suffering cannot be disarticulated from the white desire and pleasures that are rooted in the ontologizing of whiteness as a Humanistic drive. It is important to note that Solomon is also constricted by the same predicament; however, the insistence on granting him a superposition as an illegitimate slave assuages the feeling of this antagonism for viewers. In the film, being free and unfree are highlighted as the scandal Solomon is suspended within. However, the film struggles to distinguish how, for him, Blackness differs on and off the plantation because both statuses are construed and controlled by whites.

After Solomon receives a violin from Master Ford (Benedict Cumberbatch), he exclaims to Eliza that "Master Ford is a decent man!" Without hesitation, Eliza responds, "He is a slaver." Solomon doubles down, contending that Master Ford is one of "circumstances." Eliza is unmoved, and retorts, "under the circumstances he is a slaver." This dialogue hinges upon an antagonism of positions. Eliza offers a steadfast interrogation of the political ontological arrangements of slavery as simply white over Black.[50] Contrarily, the impending and eventual manumission of Solomon allows for individual white benevolence to seductively relieve the viewer of understanding all whites as beneficiaries of the violence of slavery. Although this relief is the intent of the cinematic arc, manumission for Solomon does not erode the structure of antiblackness that authorized his capture and deputized whites as the ontological authority of the terms of freedom. Why is the viewer relaxed by knowing that white people can free a Black man who cannot free himself? Frank Wilderson describes the narrative arc as consisting of three meta-episodes, equilibrium, disequilibrium, and equilibrium-restored, in which equilibrium is the meta-moment prior to social death (disequilibrium), then . . . the snarl that manumission presents to the narrative arc is an aporetic irruption between disequilibrium, and equilibrium- restored.[51]

Under this premise, social death only constitutes the time Solomon spent on the plantation, twelve years of his life, which is seemingly undone through a reclamation of freedom when he is manumitted from slavery. However, his eventual freedom from the plantation is upheld and maintained by white mutual agreement rather than by him entering into being, what Wilderson terms a subject of conveyance. Wilderson contends that Solomon "is merely an object of transaction."[52] Simply, Solomon does not reclaim his freedom as much as he is transferred from one white to another.

Bass (Brad Pitt), the carpenter who delivers a message for Solomon to his white friend up North, and Mr. Parker (Ron Steinberg), the man who travels from up North to retrieve Solomon from the Epps plantation, are ontologized to possess the capacity to operationalize benevolence as another claim over Blackness. Bass and Mr. Parker are cinematically mediated through friendship and care as to obscure the incongruence between their structural position and Solomon. Conversely, Solomon cannot use benevolence or morality to free himself or the other slaves on the Epps plantation. Despite the import of kindness, Bass relays to Mr. Parker, who contracts with Mr. Epps to manumit Solomon in a sequence of transactions. Manumission here is different, by degrees of violence, but structurally equivalent to the market, where the constituent elements of Human political and social relations wager claims over the appropriate levels of freedom or constriction for Blackness, which can be usurped and reconstituted by white fantasy and desire at any time.

In this respect, Solomon leaves the Epps plantation but is still a slave. Yet for over a century and half after the publication of his autobiography, he enfleshes the fantasy that his suffering and freedom are universal. Though it is a ruse, it has import. However, Patsey demands that sexual(ized) violability not be similarly folded into a universal theory of the slave, that pauses on, then evacuates without explicating how sexual violence dynamizes slavery as a relation. Although Solomon's freedom is phantasmagoric, the anticipation of it that overshadows and underscores his violent captivity cannot be similarly afforded to Patsey. It is painfully unclear how she will ever be free because the brutality of her condition is profoundly sexual and thus permeated by desires and drives for Black flesh that are not fixed nor erased. Which means this condition is produced at a psychic level that does not require chains to be terrifying and totalizing. The sexually violated female slave on screen is not a mere historical reflection that is derived from the transference of the Middle Passage, held captive by the slave estate, and set free by the great emancipation. Rather, the reanimation of the slave as gratuitously sexually available is predicated on the continuous nature of the empty signification of that very category.

To assume the sexually violated slave as a linear substance that has reached its limits in terms of both representation and desire is a misappropriated understanding. The sexually violated slave is not imparted with definitive meanings, qualities, or reasons of suffering that are solidified by the past and simply re-presented for historical knowing in the present. The sexual violation of the slave is a contested terrain that resists static form and meaning. As this chapter has argued, sexual violence and slavery are as a porous of a substance in the historical archive as they are in present attempts at re-presenting what constitutes the violating quality of sexual openness and injury. Additionally, the origination of this substance is not historically contingent on what texture was given to the sexually violated slave by the plantation economy, but is lodged in a fantasy that is reliant upon the deployment of nuanced figurations of what it means to occupy the space and assumed time of racially Black sexual openness.

Conclusion
After/Wards: Notes on Representing Slavery and the Ontology of Sexual Violence

In a 2005 interview, installation artist Mildred Howard described her work *Crossings* as "mirroring Africans locked in the Middle Passage."[1] Showcased to celebrate the thirty-fifth anniversary of the Berkeley Arts Center, *Crossings* features 4,000 white ceramic eggs cascading in what appears as an endless sequential pattern illuminated by indigo and red hues. The eggs were used to "make a parallelogram in an octagonal shaped room." Then "a large gilded Mayback mirror was placed on the wall, so that if you stand in certain positions, you are amongst the eggs."[2] Howard was clear about her intention with the work, which is to offers a metacommentary on positionality. The spectator gazes upon a representational scene of carnal violence. The piece begs the question, *how has slavery made you?*

The placement of the mirror was an artistic foresight into knowing that the mere utterance of such would lead to the desire for flight. Those wanting to escape are non-Black and Black alike, although the capacity to attend to this question is not structurally equivalent across the divide. Nonetheless, the rallying call of the transcendental Humanist imperative has always been, and continues to be, "I am not a slave." Irrespective of one's positionality with respect to the peculiar institution, refusal and absolve, shrouded in the arrogance of knowing, texture views of slavery, thus occluding deep thought and inquiry into its inner contours. Yet, if disavowal and retreat proceed, how can one understand the structural dynamics of slavery and what constitutes the slave? Howard's mirror anticipates the commonsense reflex, forcing the spectator back in despite assumptions about personal will or desire.

After/Wards: Notes on Representing Slavery and the Ontology of Sexual Violence 263

Figure 14. Mildred Howard, *Crossings*, 1997 mixed media installation, dimensions variable. Source: Lewis Watts©. Reprinted with Permission.

Crossings challenges the belief in the "I," and refashions it among and in (non)relation to the eggs, the yet to become.

Installation has the ability to transport the viewer into the theoretical design of the art. As a proceeding medium to the contemporary use of virtual reality and artificial intelligence, installations and sculptural elements augment assumptions of reality, place, and form by recasting narratives into visual displays.[3] The power of the art is not left to the artist alone; the audience occupies a role in its making and interpretation. Howard explains,

> I try to bring to my work an experience or something that helps people think about how they see the world differently, and how the world is portrayed differently. More importantly is how they view the work, because when I'm making the work that's one thing, but then once it's done, I become a viewer and spectator of the work.[4]

What Howard describes is a process by which, after she completes her work, she ceases to be its sole proprietor and enters the role of spectator in the unfolding of what was once her creation. From this vantage point, there is no singular way to see or exist in relation to the work. In this respect, *Crossings* pushes one to consider how we see or know what we see, or do we see anything at all when it comes to slavery?

As a Black artist making Black art, Howard points out that intention cannot control the work nor the understandings that proliferate once the work is deployed. Nevertheless, *Crossings* is not an abstracted interpretation of existence, but a rendering of a very visceral occurrence—the transatlantic slave trade. How slavery is seen has profound implications that exceed the purview of the art space. Reflecting on Crossings in a 2021 interview with the Berkeley Arts Center, Howard reiterates her inspiration, stating, "I was also thinking about the Middle Passage. When 15 million—15 *million*— Africans lost their lives. Some jumped overboard, others were killed. Others were . . ."[5] The ellipsis is intended to leave the impact open ended, encapsulating the endless known and unknown terrors experienced by the captives on board those ships. The ellipsis is not, Howard goes on to say, simply a historical marker or a representation of the past. "The Middle Passage started it, but it's continued. And until this country, and those countries that have been a part of colonization, come to terms with this and deal with it, it's going to continue."[6] The continued horror set in motion by the global investment in the kidnapping, traffic, and sale of Black flesh continues to reverberate onto Blackness in the present.

The ellipsis for *Engendering Blackness* rests firmly on and with the discomforts and contradictions of theorizing the ongoing conceptual and metaphysical implications that emerged from centuries of antiblack sexual violence under modern racial slavery. If the image, narrative, and theoretical replication of the sexually violated slave continues to (re)appear, it is because there is present saliency in its productivity. The reanimation of the slave's sexual violation is deployed to analogize and cohere meaning and matter as it relates to Blackness, sex, gender, violence, and/or transcendence. The embrace or repulsion of this condition sutures two divisive points: Fanon's Human recognition, or the non-conflictual recognition of the negro slave, with Blackness at the merger. Animating the sexual violability of the slave is bracketed by the duality of Fanonian recognition. The gesture serves to dismiss the antagonism born of sexual violability by applying reason to the condition to develop a narrative arc of Black transcendence and claim entrance into the Human field of recognition.

Such engagements are unidirectional as the antagonism is situated between the historical Black qua the present-future Black. For those seeking to Humanize Blackness, the Black is the primary object of concern, thus relieving pressure from the structure of violence. Or, more aptly, the sexually violable slave is redoubled to pressurize the antagonism that collapses raw sexual openness into Blackness. The trap that this position exposes is that *the* story cannot be told. It is too refracted beyond reason, conditioning violence out of thought. You can put a pulse on it. Allude to it. But you cannot name or say it. If the sexual violence of history is so gratuitous as to make and decay slaves, structurally position and divide beings, extend power and objectification by antiblack sexual(ized) means, and as a result is vast because it is so violent that it resists a cartographic schema, then what future have *we* inherited? What is the present world?

Most engagements with sexual violence and slavery do not sit with the anxieties that emerge from a condition wrought with antagonisms that cannot be reconciled. Instead, what is offered in the face of centuries of sexual torture, violation, domination, and terror is the Black's capacity to become a perfected integrated subject in the face of all that is uncovered. Black reason, post-enlightenment refined Black subjectivity is the only imaginable response. The story goes, now that the Black can think, act, and have sex as a willful and consenting subject, then the confines of sexual violence under slavery have disintegrated. The assumption that undergirds this proposition is the belief that the sexualized terror of slavery degraded the Black at the level of access to a system of gender and sexual identity. What is forgone is a critique of the structure of antiblackness, to ask if willful Black (liberal) personhood should be the solution or can be the solution to a world-building and consciousness-producing paradigm built on the sexual vulnerability of the Black slave. The pervasiveness of this structure I have argued is so impenetrable that it even pervades the contours of political and social imaginary.

Not only does liberalism fail to fully address the sexual vulnerability of slaves and the paradigm of slavery, so too do radical projects. Whereas liberalism depicts the Black as a rights-bearing individual, radical projects "Humanize" Black people by treating their insurgency, resistance, or violence as extreme measures that are nonetheless legible, and thus sympathetic, when filtered through the lenses of gender or class struggle. When wedded to a multiracial struggle, whether feminist, queer, or anti-capitalist, the suffering of Black people becomes urgent but relatable. We are to understand, for instance, that Margaret Garner's infanticide was the result of her behaving like a protective mother, not as a female slave.

What, then, does it mean to move forward?

Through Fanon, David Marriott offers a way, stating, "Fanon's future imperfect: a moment of inventiveness whose introduction necessarily never arrives and does not stop arriving, and whose destination cannot be foreseen, or anticipated, but only repeatedly traveled, and, therefore, not future at all."[7] In this respect, by taking up the sexually violable slave to offer no way out, no arrival, no future, no destination, this book has put into theory the proclamation by Fanon, "O my body, make of me always a man who questions!"[8] Theorizing from the position of the sexually violable slave questions political commitments and conclusions more than it offers any in return. Though it does put forth theory that challenges any articulation of freedom, that disregards the unreasoned hyper-prevalence of antiblack sexualization as what constitutes the suffering of the slave, and places unrelieved pressure on the assumed reconcilability of slavery using the available terms of the present world.

As movements arise that attest to carrying out a mission to right the failed promises of emancipation, the question still lingers: how is redress for the sexual violability of the slave accounted for in these political imaginings? This question haunts, most notably, the prison-industrial complex (PIC) abolitionist movement, which extends the visions of the abolition of slavery into the present by organizing to end the structural dependence on and investment in prisons and the intersecting institutions such as police and hegemonic modes of power and domination that feed on carcerality and carceral logics to extend the life of unfreedom, violence, and exponentialized suffering.

Mariame Kaba posits, "PIC abolition is a vision of restructured society in a world where we have everything we need: food, shelter, education, health, art, beauty, clean water, and more things that are foundational to our personal community safety."[9] These tenets of liberal Humanism are based in an unspoken belief that the basis of human life has the right to autonomous subjectivity where a morally constituted society removes the constraints to accessing an abstract constitution of liberty and justice. This arrangement of life, in its absolute realized form, is reciprocally afforded to and by all sentient beings. While Kaba stresses how antiblackness structures criminalization, it is unclear how slavery and its inherent sexual violence can be addressed through such a vision of abolition.[10]

The earliest articulations of the necessity of PIC abolition understood that the sexual terror of slavery is implicated in the structural proliferation of prisons, which took on new racial dimensions following emancipation. In one of the earliest published works on PIC abolition, *Are Prisons Obsolete?* Angela Y. Davis argues, "If we expand our definition of punishment under slavery, we can say that the coerced sexual relations between slave and master constituted a penalty exacted on women, if only for the sole reason that they were slaves."[11] Davis then likens this relation to the sexual abuse and rape of female prisoners by prison guards. The relational status between slave and prisoner is sutured here by their proximity to confinement. However, the congruency between or explanatory relation is muddled when the slave as structurally Black is placed in contradistinction to the prisoner, who is often overrepresented as Black, but can be of any race. The point here is to ask, when we move from slavery to post-emancipation, what happens to the centrality of Blackness in visions of abolition? Do the failed promises of emancipation cease to register as purely concerns of Blackness and its making and unmaking? Furthermore, if emancipation was a failed promise, who was unattended to in this dreamwork—the Human or the slave? Or is the Black free from slavery by means of physical distance from the master such that the fetters of the plantation now seep into a more generalized form of suffering subtended by the broader projects of racialization, patriarchy, and capitalism?

Ruth Wilson Gilmore contends that the linkage between slavery and mass incarceration is hyperbolically extended. Gilmore writes, "The problem with the 'new slavery' argument is that very few prisoners work for anybody while they're locked up. Recall, the generally accepted goal for prisoners has been *incapacitation*: a do-nothing theory if ever there was one."[12] More, Gilmore emphasizes,

> "mass incarceration" has, unfortunately, but for understandable reasons, come to stand in for "this is the terrible thing that happened to Black people in the United States." It *is* a terrible thing that happens to Black people in the United States! It happens also to brown people, red people . . . and a whole lot of white people. And insofar as ending mass incarceration becomes understood as something that only Black people must struggle for because it's something that only Black people experience, the necessary connection to be drawn from

mass incarceration to the entire organization of capitalist space today falls out of the picture.[13]

While Gilmore is correct in asserting the prison as part of the structure of capitalism and as a multiracial do-nothing space, for the slave, the plantation or slavery writ large was a Black *be*-nothing space. Wherein the plantation was a large-scale economic arrangement, the paradigmatic structural position of the slave was rooted in ontological incapacitation, not simply forced or stolen labor. The concern with slavery and its relationship to the ongoing nature of captivity is, in some ways, a question of *doing* but it should also be a meditation on *being*. What it means to be Black in prison time is fundamentally destabilized when it is considered that the Black has not entered prison time, insofar as slave time still haunts its presence. Which is a way to say, while non-Black people may be hobbled by the idleness of prison space and time, Blackness is incapacitated by the world such that entering the prison envelopes a clarification of Black suspension by the forces set in motion by slavery, rather than imparts a new denominator on its existence. In this respect, the prison renders the non-Black subject civically dead or idle, while the Black in prison and in the world is socially dead, marked by a paradigm of racial sexuation that awaits, anticipates, and requires antiblack capture, violability, and death.

Any person with a modicum of political consciousness cannot dispute the significance of demanding a world without prisons. However, for the slave, the demand is also and *primarily* a fight for the end of the world. As this book has maintained, the slave gestated Blackness through its sexual violability, which means that the violence of slavery (which is less about forced labor as it is about sheer openness and vulnerability) is inextricably bound to Blackness. Thus, if Blackness still exists in a world without prisons, it demands explication how its violability ceases to be coeval with the Human and its desired principles of capacitated liberties. Rather than trying to attend to Black suffering through extending the benevolence of Human being, which is the very logic of redress offered to the slave by the master (recognition by becoming the master form), perhaps definitive political imaginings should rest with the acceptance that what can be named as a perfectly imperfect future was made pleasurable, desirable, and namable by slavery. There is no outside of this arrangement. Rather than investing in naming the value of a future, abolitionism that holds true to emancipation as a failure then must consider the slave as the unthought form of nonexistence that tethers all forms of coherence and political struggle. Worlding is made possible by antiblack sexual force and is a predicament of racial sexuation, which reproduces the distinctions between the kin and the kinless, the living and the socially dead, the Human and the slave, the Black and the non-Black. If abolition is world-making, it is, in essence, a death drive for the slave. After the wards of the plantation spill into the post-emancipation world, the confined states of Black existence antagonize the assumptive logic of the universality of the social and political configurations of life and rebellion.

Throughout this book I have maintained the contention that the sexual terror of slavery is not adequately accounted for in any of the political languages presently available. Not the logics of abolition, Marxism, feminism, or progressive Black politics. Most of all, this is because there is a fundamental misunderstanding of the racial sexuation of the slave. In many ways, the sexual violation of the slave is subtended to the logics of other forms of violence, like capitalism and white heteropatriarchy. While both are important frameworks for understanding gender violence, the sexualized terror of the slave must be understood as both relational and on its own singular terms. Which is to say, if we are to comprehend at the most basic level the daily terror of Black life today, we must contend with the pervasiveness of how sexualized terror was woven into every making, unmaking, and remaking of the slave, such that it became no longer remarkable but understood as a necessity for the proliferation of world-making. That is, for slaves and non-slaves alike. The seduction of liberal Humanism, as well as its critics, the radicals, is produced by this relation, and its ideals are not the remedy, but the extension of the antiblack sexuation that thwarts the end of the world.

The arguments presented in this book have paused on sexual violence as a pervasive form of physical, material, psychic, and metaphysical capture. *Engendering Blackness* considers how to interrogate slavery's sexual violence beyond acts to think about its permissibility as a structural form of violability that captures and recaptures the slave, and what its suffering has the capacity to mean. Looking at history as a lens, the preceding chapters contend that the sexual violation of the slave serves as an ontological anchor through which subjectivity and the scales of Humanness are mediated. Which is to say, historical and contemporary engagements with the pervasiveness of slave sexual openness displace focus on the question of violence for the slave by projecting injury as the necessary content for making subjects anew. While subjectivity emerges through fracture, this book has refused subjectivity as a possibility for the slave by focusing on the gravity of unmaking, upon which sexual violation is sutured. Simply, sexual violence and resistance against it are not the necessary content to make slaves into Human. Rather, Human beings are oriented as distinct from slaves because the scale and types of sexual openness preserved for Blackness makes slaves categorically non-Human. These broader theoretical concerns were dissected to consider questions of temporality, gender, rape, sexuality, breeding, blood, death, mutilation, womanhood, manhood, the slave mother, representation, to name but a few concerns.

In the end, *Engendering Blackness* rest upon the belief that sexual violence and slavery are unable to be settled given the ongoing nature of its violent reverberations. It is critical that sexual violence under slavery not be subtended to other concerns but rather treated as the fundamental arrangement of captivity that incapacitates the slave by relationally binding its deracination to the ontological predicaments of the Human. To state that the condition is ongoing is not a linear nor teleological pronouncement, but a statement about structural positionality as a relation. Sexuality for the Human exists because the slave is void of the capacity to claim sexual injury or to possess sexual choice. And Blackness is not free from this paradigm as it continues to be restricted by the antagonisms reproduced by slavery, as a structure of violence made possible by the psychic and material operationalization of sexual force wagered against and upon the slave.

Notes

Introduction

1. Frantz Fanon, *Black Skin, White Masks*, trans. Charles Lam Markmann (New York: Grove Press, 1967), 159.

2. Prior to his murder in prison, Jackson and Davis corresponded regularly about Black politics and history. These letters appear in George Jackson, *Soledad Brother: The Prison Letters of George Jackson* (New York: Coward-McCann, 1970).

3. Angela Davis, "Reflections on the Black Woman's Role in the Community of Slaves," *Black Scholar* 12, no. 6 (November/December 1981): 3.

4. Davis, "Reflections," 5.

5. Davis, "Reflections," 13.

6. Davis, "Reflections," 7.

7. Davis, "Reflections," 7.

8. Hortense Spillers, "Mama's Baby, Papa's Maybe: An American Grammar Book," *Diacritics* 17, no. 2 (1987), 66.

9. Spillers, "Mama's Baby, Papa's Maybe" 80, emphasis in original.

10. Davis, "Reflections," 5.

11. The Combahee River Collective, "A Black Feminist Statement," in *The Second Wave: A Reader in Feminist Theory*, ed. Linda Nicholson (New York: Routledge, 1997), 64.

12. Davis, "Reflections," 8.

13. Evelyn Hammonds, "Black (W)holes and the Geometry of Black Female Sexuality," *Differences* 6, no. 2-3 (1994), 138.

14. Hammonds, "Black (W)holes," 138.

15. Thomas A. Foster, *Rethinking Rufus: Sexual Violations of Enslaved Men* (Georgia: University of Georgia Press, 2019), 3.

16. Foster, *Rethinking Rufus*, 3.

17. I would caution that a white imagination is not solely possessed by white people. Here a white imagination symbolizes a form of (un)reason that is produced by insurmountable levels of antiblack violence historically perpetrated by whites. However, this (un)reason is a structuring logic of modernity and thus is often carried as an unconscious modality that is called upon by all people, including some Black people, to justify and explain away the gratuitously violent nature of antiblackness.

18. For more on the racist tropes of the rape victim and perpetuator, see Daina Ramey Berry and Leslie M. Harris, *Sexuality and Slavery: Reclaiming Intimate Histories in the Americas* (Athens: University of Georgia Press, 2018); Angela Y. Davis, "Rape, Racism and the Capitalist Setting," *The Black Scholar* 12, no. 6 (April 1978): 24–30; Angela Y. Davis, *Women, Race & Class* (New York: Vintage Books, 1983); Fredrick Douglass, *Why Is the Negro Lynched* (Bridgewater, VA: J. Whitby and Sons, 1895); Jones-Rogers, *They Were Her Property*; Ida B. Wells, *Southern Horrors: Lynch Law in All Its Phases* (New York: New York Age Print, 1892).

19. See Davis, *Women Race and Class*. The original text states "were viewed as profitable labor units" as opposed to "socially dead." While I agree with the original framing, I want to extend the framework for thinking gender under slavery beyond questions of economic viability, capital, and physical labor. I contend with the position that capital is not fully explanatory of the suffering of slavery. Social death offers a framework to consider capital, *and* the psychic constitution of the slave as implicated within economic concerns but also exceeding that framework. *Engendering Blackness* extends an analysis that considers sexual violence through questions of structural positionality, political ontology, as well as Human ontology. Which is to say, the shifting of the language of this quote is a claim about what emphasis helps to clarify the gendered predicament of the slave, at the same time this book itself stages the ground of support to buttress this argument.

20. Michel Foucault, "Confinement, Psychiatry, Prison," in *Politics, Philosophy, Culture: Interviews and Other Writings 1977–1984*, ed. Lawrence D. Kritzman (New York: Routledge, 1988), 200.

21. Spillers, "Mama's Baby, Papa's Maybe," 64–81.

22. Frank B. Wilderson III, *Red, White, and Black: Cinema and the Structure of U.S. Antagonisms* (Durham: Duke University Press, 2010), 20–21.

23. *Fanon, Black Skin, White Masks*, 110.

24. Wilderson, *Red, White, and Black*, 44.

25. These constituent elements of slavery are drawn from Orlando R. Patterson, *Slavery and Social Death: A Comparative Study* (Cambridge, MA: Harvard University Press, 2018).

26. Jared C. Sexton, "Afro-Pessimism: The Unclear Word," *Rhizomes* 29 (2016): 18.

27. I employ the terms sexual violation, sexuation, and sexualization (and derivatives of each) interchangeably. Each term marks the various ways slaves were made vulnerable to sexual acts, and other acts which were not perceivably sexual but arguably were used to bar the slave from entrance into the Human sexual order. This condition was propagated by the imbued and/or degraded desire, agency, will, and consent of the captive.

28. Scholars such as Stephanie Camp, *Closer to Freedom* (Chapel Hill: University of North Carolina Press, 2004); Deborah Gray White, *Ar'n't I a Woman: Female Slaves in the Plantation South* (New York: Norton, 1985); Glymph, *Out of the House of Bondage*; Jessica Marie Johnson, *Wicked Flesh: Black Women, Intimacy, and Freedom in the Atlantic World* (Philadelphia: University of Pennsylvania Press, 2020); Marisa J. Fuentes, *Dispossessed Lives: Enslaved Women, Violence and the Archive* (Philadelphia: University of Pennsylvania Press, 2016); Jennifer L. Morgan, *Laboring Women: Reproduction and Gender in New World Slavery* (Philadelphia: University of Pennsylvania Press, 2004); Angela Davis, "Reflections on the Black Woman's Role in the Community of Slaves," *Black Scholar* 3 (December 1971): 2–15; Catherine Clinton et al., *Sexuality and Slavery: Reclaiming Intimate Histories in the Americas*, eds. Daina Ramey Berry

and Leslie M. Harris (Athens: University of Georgia Press, 2018); Marietta Morrisey, *Slave Women in the New World: Gender Stratification in the Caribbean* (Lawrence: University Press of Kansas, 1989); Barbara Bush, *Slave Women in Caribbean Society, 1650–1832* (Bloomington: Indiana University Press, 1990) have written extensively about the ways that female slaves resisted sexual subjection.

29. The reference to congealed blood is drawn from Audre Lorde, who writes, *"if we lose/ someday* women's blood *will congeal/upon a dead planet."* See Audre Lorde, "Age, Race, Class, and Sex: Women Redefining Difference," in *Sister Outsider: Essays and Speeches* (Berkeley: Crossing Press, 2007).

30. Spillers, "Mama's Baby, Papa's Maybe: An American Grammar Book," 67–68.

31. This question is a reference to arguments pertaining to violence extended in Walter Benjamin, "The Critique of Violence?" in *Walter Benjamin: Selected Writings 1: 1913–1926*, eds. Marcus Paul Bullock and Michael W. Jennings (Cambridge, MA: Belknap Press of Harvard University Press, 2004), 236–252.

Chapter 1

1. Gilberto Freyre, *The Masters and the Slaves: A Study in the Development of Brazilian Civilization*, trans. Samuel Putnam (Berkeley: University of California Press, 2022), 324.

2. W.E.B. Du Bois, *Black Reconstruction in America: 1860–1880* (New York: The Free Press, 1998), 3.

3. Du Bois, *Black Reconstruction in America*, 3.

4. Du Bois, *Black Reconstruction in America*, 4.

5. Du Bois, *Black Reconstruction in America*, 4.

6. Jennifer L. Morgan, "*Partus sequitur ventrem*: Law, Race, and Reproduction in Colonial Slavery," *Small Axe* 22, no. 1 (March 2018): 1.

7. "An Act Concerning Negroes & other Slaves," Md. Laws 533–534, September 1664. This law is discussed further in-depth in Chapter 3.

8. Michel Foucault, *The History of Sexuality Volume One: An Introduction*, trans. Robert Hurley (New York: Vintage Books, 1990), 157.

9. Jean-François Lyotard, "Emma: Between Philosophy and Psychoanalysis," in *Lyotard: Philosophy, Politics and the Sublime*, ed. Hugh J. Silverman (New York: Routledge, 2002), 32.

10. Lyotard, "Emma: Between Philosophy and Psychoanalysis," 42.

11. Theodore Dwight Weld, *American Slavery as It Is: Testimony of a Thousand Witnesses* (New York: American Slave Society, 1839), 45.

12. Weld, *American Slavery as It Is*, 46.

13. Weld, *American Slavery as It Is*, 46.

14. Weld, *American Slavery as It Is*, 46.

15. Weld, *American Slavery As It Is*, 54.

16. William Goodell, *The American Slave Code in Theory and Practice*, 3rd ed. (New York: American and Foreign Anti-Slavery Society, 1853), 212.

17. Goodell, *The American Slave Code*, 122.

18. For more on "fine looking man" as a reference to mark lighter-skinned Black men as sexually attractive and available, see Thomas A. Foster, *Rethinking Rufus: Sexual Violations of Enslaved Men* (Athens: University of Georgia Press, 2019).

19. Foster, *Rethinking Rufus*, 16.

20. Elaine Scarry, *The Body in Pain: The Making and Unmaking of the World* (New York: Oxford University Press, 1985), 35.

21. Scarry, *The Body in Pain*, 35.

22. Scarry, *The Body in Pain*, 35–36.

23. In the 1845 *Narrative of the Life of Frederick Douglass*, Douglass recounts seeing his Aunt Hester beaten by her master and listening to her tortured screams. Frederick Douglass, *Narrative of the Life of Frederick Douglass, an American Slave*, 1999 electronic ed. (Boston: Anti-Slavery Office, 1845), 6–8, https://docsouth.unc.edu/neh/douglass/douglass.html.

Douglass explains that this moment was his first confrontation with the brutal and bloody horrors of slavery. How Douglass narrated the context of Aunt Hester's scream has come to figure debates in Black studies about how to approach the spectacle and its redeployment. The most frequently recounted debate involves a response by Fred Moten to the reading Saidiya V. Hartman provides of the sound of Aunt Hester's beating. Hartman begins the introduction to *Scenes of Subjection: Terror, Slavery, and Self-Making in Nineteenth-Century America* with a refusal to animate Aunt Hester's scream. This serves as provocation about the casual nature Black pain and violation circulate without critical pause. Furthermore, she wants the reader to consider how the terrorizing spectacle shrouds and overshadows the mundane and quotidian ways that violence conditions what it means to be a slave. In the introduction to *In the Break: The Aesthetics of the Black Radical Tradition* Moten offers a rejoinder to this position, arguing that invoking the violence even without detailing it inevitably reproduces the violation it seeks to quiet, despite the intentions at the heart of the argument. He contends that the scream is repressed, first by Douglass, and then extended by Hartman. From here Moten wonders if there is a way to break from the totalizing violence such that the response is not destabilization but some other radical maneuver. Hartman, *Scenes of Subjection: Terror, Slavery, and Self-Making in Nineteenth-Century America* (New York: Oxford University Press, 1997), 3–4; Fred Moten, *In the Break: The Aesthetics of the Black Radical Tradition* (Minneapolis: University of Minnesota Press, 2003), 1–24. For further engagements with Hartman and Moten's differing strategies for confronting the violence of spectacle, see Parisa Vaziri, "Blackness and the Metaethics of the Object," *Rhizomes* 29 (2016); Tendayi Sithole, "Meditations on the Dehumanisation of the Slave," in *Decolonising the Human: Reflections from Africa on Difference and Oppression*, eds. Melissa Stevyn and William Mpofu (Johannesburg: Wits University Press, 2021), 130–42; Janet Neary, *Sight Unseen: Contemporary Visual Slave Narratives* (New York: Fordham University Press, 2017), 29–53.

24. Ariane Cruz, *The Color of Kink: Black Women, BDSM, and Pornography* (New York: NYU Press, 2016), 54.

25. See Thavolia Glymph, *Out of the House of Bondage: The Transformation of the Plantation Household* (New York: Cambridge University Press, 2003); Stephanie E. Jones-Rogers, *They Were Her Property: White Women as Slave Owners in the American South* (New Haven: Yale University Press, 2019); Sara-Maria Sorentino, "Mistresses as Masters?: The Textual Pleasures of the Plantation Present," *differences: A Journal of Feminist Cultural Studies* 32, no. 2 (September 2021).

26. Sigmund Freud, *A General Introduction to Psychoanalysis*, trans. G. Stanley Hall (New York: Boni & Liveright, 1920), 284.

Notes to Chapter 1   275

27. Michel Foucault, *Discipline and Punish: The Birth of the Prison*, trans. Alan Sheridan (New York: Vintage Books, 1995), 180.

28. See John G. Aikin, *A Digest of the Laws of the State of Alabama* (Philadelphia: Alexander Towar, 1833), 391.

29. Dred Scott v. Sandford, 60 U.S. 393, 407 (1856).

30. Saidiya Hartman, "Venus in Two Acts," *Small Axe* 12, no. 2 (2008): 2.

31. William J. Anderson, *Life and Narrative of William J. Anderson, Twenty-Four Years a Slave*, 2000 electronic ed. (Chicago: Daily Tribune Book and Job Printing Office, 1857), 19, https://docsouth.unc.edu/neh/andersonw/andersonw.html.

32. Anderson, *Twenty-Four Years a Slave*, 19.

33. Anderson, *Twenty-Four Years a Slave*, 19.

34. Anderson, *Twenty-Four Years a Slave*, 19.

35. Anderson, *Twenty-Four Years a Slave*, 19.

36. Anderson, *Twenty-Four Years a Slave*, 19.

37. Goodell, *The American Slave Code*, 86.

38. Jacques Lacan, "The Deconstruction of the Drive," in *The Four Fundamental Concepts of Psychoanalysis*, ed. Jacques-Alain Miller, trans. Alan Sheridan (New York: Norton, 1998), 167.

39. Anderson, *Twenty-Four Years a Slave*, 19.

40. Foucault, *History of Sexuality Volume One*, 141.

41. Foucault, *History of Sexuality Volume One*, 136.

42. Michel Foucault, *Society Must be Defended: Lectures at the Collège de France 1975–76*, trans. David Macey (New York: Picador, 2003), 245.

43. Foucault, *History of Sexuality Volume One*, 136.

44. Silvia Federici, *Caliban and the Witch* (Brooklyn, NY: Autonomedia, 2004), 144.

45. To understand this point further, consider how Slave Codes varied from state to state, practices varied by region, and there were inconsistent practices between plantations that all fell underneath the same regulatory codes. Thinking beyond the United States as example, New World slavery took on many forms that challenge the precept that consistency or predictable governance or structure can be assigned to the paradigmatic structure of the institutional practices. The only rule of slavery that was maintained was the slave possesses no rights that any sentient being was bound to respect.

46. Foucault, *History of Sexuality Volume One*, 140.

47. Foucault, *Discipline and Punish*, 146.

48. Calvin Warren, "Onticide: Afro-pessimism, Gay Nigger #1, and Surplus Violence," *GLQ: A Journal of Lesbian and Gay Studies* 23, no. 3 (June 2017): 394.

49. Foucault, *Discipline and Punish*, 7; Foucault, *History of Sexuality Volume One*, 148, italics in the original.

50. See Achille Mbembe, "Necropolitics," trans. Libby Meintjes, *Public Culture* 15, no. 1 (January 2003): 21. Mbembe goes on to write a full-length book on necropolitics, which illustrates the arguments initially proposed in the article with further depth. Most notably, in *Necropolitics* Mbembe expands his previous arguments about slavery where he argues that modern slavery is distinct from ancient forms by its ability to extract surplus capital. Additionally, he argues that the task of the twenty-first century is grappling with a predicament

involving slaves without masters. Arguing against theories of social death, Mbembe contends that African and African American history is less bound by death and desiccation and rather harkens upon the production and reproduction of "life flows" that exist in spite of captivity and destruction. At the root of this argument is a similar privileging of creative and cultural productions over a strident focus on death, which one might rightfully assume a theory of necropolitics is centrally concerned with. For more on the development of this theory see Achille Mbembe, *Necropolitics*, trans. Steve Corcoran (Durham: Duke University Press, 2019).

51. Mbembe, "Necropolitics," 39.
52. Mbembe, "Necropolitics," 21.
53. Mbembe, "Necropolitics," 21.
54. Mbembe, "Necropolitics," 22.
55. Mbembe, "Necropolitics," 22.
56. Jared Sexton, "People-Of-Color-Blindness: Notes on the Afterlife of Slavery," *Social Text* 28, no. 2 (Summer 2010): 35.
57. See Hartman, *Scenes of Subjection*, 42–47, 76.
58. Mbembe, "Necropolitics," 21.
59. Sexton, "People-Of-Color-Blindness: Notes on the Afterlife of Slavery," 39.
60. This argument is textured by multiple examples. *Scenes of Subjection* includes a chapter "Innocent Amusements: The Stage of Sufferance," which argues that slave performance does not possess an essential quality that protects it from the imposition of the master's prerogative and the violent strictures of their condition. Hartman argues, "The forms of redress enacted in performance are a necessarily incomplete working through of the event of breach because of the constancy of assault and the inability to transform social relations through such practices or generate an event that would result in the reversal of forces." Hartman, *Scenes of Subjection*, 76. Sexton engages this and other positions presented by Hartman in opposition to Mbembe's privileging of performance as a counter force to the cruelty of slavery. For Sexton the impossible possibility of the female slave's resistance to her sexual condition offers a counterargument against the saliency of slave performance that returns focus back to the deathliness of slavery and the suicidal imperative that is implicated in the slave's acting back against its violent condition.
61. For more on Celia's case see Hartman, *Scenes of Subjection*, 82–86; Melton A. McLaurin, *Celia, A Slave* (New York: Avon Books, 1993).
62. Sexton, "People-Of-Color-Blindness: Notes on the Afterlife of Slavery," 42.
63. Sexton, "People-Of-Color-Blindness: Notes on the Afterlife of Slavery," 42.
64. Douglass, *Narrative of the Life of Frederick Douglass*, 6.
65. Douglass, *Narrative of the Life of Frederick Douglass*, 7.
66. For more on resistance to sexual violence see Stephanie Camp, *Closer to Freedom: Enslaved Women & Everyday Resistance in the Plantation South* (Chapel Hill: University of North Carolina Press, 2004); Deborah Gray White, *Ar'n't I a Woman: Female Slaves in the Plantation South* (New York: Norton, 1985); Glymph, *Out of the House of Bondage*; Jessica Marie Johnson, *Wicked Flesh: Black Women, Intimacy, and Freedom in the Atlantic World* (Philadelphia: University of Pennsylvania Press, 2020); Marisa J. Fuentes, *Dispossessed Lives: Enslaved Women, Violence and the Archive* (Philadelphia: University of Pennsylvania Press,

2016); Jennifer Morgan, *Laboring Women: Reproduction and Gender in New World Slavery* (Philadelphia: University of Pennsylvania Press, 2004); Angela Davis, "Reflections on the Black Woman's Role in the Community of Slaves," *Black Scholar* 3 (December 1971): 2–15; Daina Ramey Berry and Leslie M. Harris, eds. *Sexuality and Slavery: Reclaiming Intimate Histories in the Americas* (Athens: University of Georgia Press, 2018); Marietta Morrisey, *Slave Women in the New World: Gender Stratification in the Caribbean* (Lawrence: University Press of Kansas, 1989); Barbara Bush, *Slave Women in Caribbean Society, 1650–1832* (Bloomington: Indiana University Press, 1990);

67. Hartman, *Scenes of Subjection*, 83.

68. *State of Missouri v. Celia*, Vol. 2 Index to Court Cases of Callaway County, File No. 4496 (1855).

69. McLaurin, *Celia, A Slave*.

70. Roberto Esposito, *Immunitas: The Protection and Negation of Life*, trans. Zakiya Hanafi (Malden, MA: Polity Press, 2011), 113.

71. Henry Bibb, *Narrative of the Life and Adventures of Henry Bibb, an American Slave*, 2000 electronic ed. (New York, 1849), 38, https://docsouth.unc.edu/neh/bibb/bibb.html.

72. Caroline Randall Williams, "You Want a Confederate Monument? My Body Is a Confederate Monument," *New York Times*, June 26, 2020, www.nytimes.com/2020/06/26/opinion/confederate-monuments-racism.html.

73. Williams, "You Want a Confederate Monument?"

74. Williams, "You Want a Confederate Monument?"

75. Williams, "You Want a Confederate Monument?"

76. Tiffany Lethabo King, *The Black Shoals: Offshore Formations of Black and Native Studies* (Durham: Duke University Press, 2019), 40.

77. "Meet Mata Little, UNC Student Whose Protest Ignited the Movement to Topple a Racist Confederate Statue," *Democracy Now!*, August 22, 2018, www.democracynow.org/2018/8/22/meet_maya_little_unc_student_whose; Virginia Bridges, "UNC Student Who Poured Blood and Ink on Silent Sam Confederate Statue Found Guilty, but Gets 'Prayer for Judgement,'" *Winston-Salem Journal*, October 15, 2018, https://journalnow.com/unc-student-who-poured-blood-and-ink-on-silent-sam-confederate-statue-found-guilty-but/article_956218e2-9520-5f1f-909f-368ba80a4dd4.html.

78. Williams, "You Want a Confederate Monument?"

79. Toni Morrison, "The Site of Memory," in *Inventing the Truth: The Art and Craft of Memoir*, ed. William Zinsser, 2nd ed. (Boston: Houghton Mifflin, 1995), 83–102.

80. Morrison, "The Site of Memory," 87 and 90.

81. Morrison, "The Site of Memory," 90.

82. Morrison, "The Site of Memory," 90–1.

83. Hartman, *Scenes of Subjection*, 3.

84. Harriett Jacobs, *Incidents in the Life of a Slave Girl*, ed. Lydia Maria Child (Boston: Published for the author, 1861), 55.

85. Lydia Maria Child, "Introduction by the Editor," in *Incidents in the Life of a Slave Girl*, ed. Lydia Maria Child (Boston: Published for the author, 1861), 8.

86. Hannah Natanson, "Two Centuries Ago, University of Virginia Students Beat and Raped Enslaved Servants, Historians Say," *Washington Post*, October 6, 2019,

www.washingtonpost.com/history/2019/10/06/two-centuries-ago-university-virginia-students-beat-raped-enslaved-servants-historians-say.

87. Natanson, "Two Centuries Ago."

88. Natanson, "Two Centuries Ago."

89. This quote is taken from remarks provided by Saidiya V. Hartman at "In the Wake: A Salon in Honor of Christina Sharpe," filmed February 2017 at Bernard Center for Research on Women, New York, NY, video, https://bcrw.barnard.edu/videos/in-the-wake-a-salon-in-honor-of-christina-sharpe/.

90. Natanson, "Two Centuries Ago."

91. Natanson, "Two Centuries Ago."

92. Natanson, "Two Centuries Ago."

93. Morrison, "The Site of Memory," 91.

94. Morrison, "The Site of Memory," 92.

95. Morrison, "The Site of Memory," 97.

96. Morrison, "The Site of Memory," 99.

Chapter 2

1. Carissa Harris, "A History of the Wench," Electric Literature, June 3, 2019, https://electricliterature.com/a-history-of-the-wench/.

2. Jared Sexton argues that there is no interracial sexual relationship. This position is an extension and departure from Jacque Lacan's formulae of sexuation. Sexton elaborates his argument through an interrogation of the interracial, the sexual, and relationship each on their own terms, as well as in conversation. For more on this argument see *Amalgamation Schemes: Antiblackness and the Critique of Multiculturalism* (Minneapolis: University of Minnesota Press, 2008).

3. For a discussion of the "lying slut" in rape discourse see Catharine A. MacKinnon, "#MeToo Has Done What the Law Could Not," *New York Times*, February 4, 2018, www.nytimes.com/2018/02/04/opinion/metoo-law-legal-system.html.

4. Abolitionist William Goodell asserts, "Rape committed on a female slave is an offence not recognized by law," in *The American Slave Code in Theory and Practice*, 3rd ed. (New York: American and Foreign Anti-Slavery Society, 1853), 71.

5. See Angela Davis, "Reflections on the Black Woman's Role in the Community of Slaves," *Black Scholar* 3 (December 1971): 2–15; Jennifer L. Morgan, *Reckoning with Slavery: Gender, Kinship, and Capitalism in the Early Black Atlantic* (Durham: Duke University Press, 2021); Daina Ramey Berry and Leslie M. Harris, eds., *Sexuality and Slavery: Reclaiming Intimate Histories in the Americas* (Athens: University of Georgia Press, 2018); *More Than Chattel: Black Women and Slavery in the Americas*, eds. David Barry Gaspar and Darlene Clark Hine (Bloomington: Indiana University Press, 1996).

6. Ann duCille, "The Occult of True Black Womanhood: Critical Demeanor and Black Feminist Studies," *Signs* 19, no. 3 (Spring 1994): 591–629.

7. bell hooks, *Black Looks: Race and Representation* (Boston: South End Press, 1992), 12.

8. See The Combahee River Collective, "A Black Feminist Statement," in *The Second Wave: A Reader in Feminist Theory*, ed. Linda Nicholson (New York: Routledge, 1997), 63–71; Cherríe L. Moraga and Gloria E. Anzaldúa, eds., *This Bridge Called My Back: Writings by*

Radical Women of Color (New York: Kitchen Table, Women of Color Press, 1983); Gloria Anzaldúa, *Borderlands: La Frontera*, 2nd ed. (San Francisco: Aunt Lute Books, 1999).

9. Oyèrónkẹ́ Oyěwùmí, *The Invention of Women: Making an African Sense of Western Gender Discourses* (Minneapolis: University of Minnesota Press, 1997), 9.

10. Orlando Patterson, *Slavery and Social Death: A Comparative Study* (Cambridge, MA: Harvard University Press, 1982), 21.

11. Sylvia Wynter, "Beyond Liberal and Marxist Leninist Feminisms: Towards an Autonomous Frame of Reference," *CLR James Journal* 24, no. 1–2 (Fall 2018): 36–7.

12. See Marisa J. Fuentes, *Dispossessed Lives: Enslaved Women, Violence, and the Archive* (Philadelphia: University of Pennsylvania Press, 2016); Habiba Ibrahim, *Black Age: Oceanic Lifespans and the Time of Black Life* (New York: New York University Press, 2021); Jessica Marie Johnson, *Wicked Flesh: Black Women, Intimacy and Freedom in the Atlantic World* (Philadelphia: University of Pennsylvania Press, 2020); C. Riley Snorton, *Black on Both Sides: A Racial History of Trans Identity* (Minneapolis: University of Minnesota Press, 2017).

13. Darlene Clark Hine, "Rape and the Inner Lives of Black Women in the Middle West," *Signs* 14, no. 4 (Summer 1989): 912.

14. Evelyn M. Hammonds, "Toward a Genealogy of Black Female Sexuality: The Problematic of Silence," in *Feminist Theory and the Body: A Reader*, eds. Janet Price and Margrit Shildrick (Edinburgh: Edinburgh University Press, 2022), 180.

15. Zakiyyah Iman Jackson, *Becoming Human: Matter and Meaning in an Antiblack World* (New York: New York University Press, 2020), 47.

16. Jessica Marie Johnson, *Wicked Flesh: Black Women, Intimacy and Freedom in the Atlantic World* (Philadelphia: University of Pennsylvania Press, 2020), 173.

17. Johnson, *Wicked Flesh*, 172–173.

18. Morgan, *Reckoning with Slavery*, 208.

19. Morgan, *Reckoning with Slavery*, 208.

20. Womanist, and by extension womanism, was introduced by Alice Walker in *In Search of Our Mothers' Gardens: Womanist Prose*, where she argues, "Womanist is to feminist, as purple is to lavender." Alice Walker, *In Search of Our Mothers' Gardens: Womanist Prose* (San Diego: Harcourt Brace Jovanovich, 1983), xii.

21. In "Occupying the Terrain: Reengaging 'Beyond Miranda's Meanings: Un/Silencing the 'Demonic Grounds of Caliban's Woman," Carole Boyce-Davies, co-editor of the *Out of Kumbla* collection clarifies aspects of Wynter's contribution to the edited volume. Boyce-Davies notes that what appears in "Beyond Miranda's Meanings" is a truncated version of the initial ninety-page manuscript Wynter submitted. The final piece includes the introduction and conclusion from the original submission, which Boyce-Davies and co-editor Elaine Savory Fido felt "had the most direct response to this first book of criticism on Caribbean women's writing." Carol Boyce-Davies, "Occupying the Terrain: Reengaging 'Beyond Miranda's Meanings: Un/Silencing the 'Demonic Grounds of Caliban's Woman," *American Quarterly* 70, no. 4 (December 2018), 839. Boyce-Davies states the arguments that were presented in the middle of the piece appear in other later published works by Wynter, one being "Beyond Liberal and Marxist-Leninist Feminisms: Towards an Autonomous Frame of Reference," where she maps a more elongated critique of various forms of feminisms and calls for an "autonomous feminism" that breaks with Western humanist investments in gender

as a genre of the Human. See Boyce-Davies, "Occupying the Terrain"; Wynter, "Beyond Liberal and Marxist Leninist Feminisms."

22. Sylvia Wynter, "Beyond Miranda's Meanings: Un/silencing the 'Demonic Ground' of Caliban's 'Woman'," in *Out of the Kumbla: Caribbean Women and Literature*, eds. Carole Boyce-Davies and Elaine Savory Fido (Trenton, NJ: Africa World Press, 1990), 358.

23. Wynter, "Beyond Miranda's Meanings," 360.

24. Wynter, "Beyond Miranda's Meanings," 360.

25. Wynter, "Beyond Miranda's Meanings," 362–3.

26. Friedrich Nietzsche, *The Genealogy of Morals*, trans. Horace B. Samuel (New York: Boni and Liveright Publishers, 1923), 177.

27. Wynter, "Beyond Miranda's Meanings," 366.

28. Wynter, "Beyond Miranda's Meanings," 366.

29. Cecilio M. Cooper, "Fallen: Generation, Postlapsarian Verticality + the Black Chthonic," *Rhizomes* 38 (2022).

30. David Marriott, "Inventions of Existence: Sylvia Wynter, Frantz Fanon, Sociogeny, and 'the Damned,'" *CR: The New Centennial Review* 11, no. 3 (Winter 2011): 49.

31. Katherine McKittrick, *Demonic Grounds: Black Women and the Cartographies of Struggles* (Minneapolis: University of Minnesota Press, 2006), 133.

32. McKittrick, *Demonic Grounds*, 133.

33. Wynter, "Beyond Miranda's Meanings," 361.

34. John Caspar Lavater, *Essays on Physiognomy*, ed. Thomas Holcroft (London: William Tegg and Co., 1878), 298.

35. Lavater, *Essays on Physiognomy*, 298.

36. Lavater, *Essays on Physiognomy*, 241.

37. Mary Olmsted Stanton, *A System of Practical and Scientific Physiognomy* (Philadelphia: F. A. Davis, 1890), 242.

38. Stanton, *A System of Practical and Scientific Physiognomy*, 355.

39. Stanton, *A System of Practical and Scientific Physiognomy*, 442.

40. Stanton, *A System of Practical and Scientific Physiognomy*, 442.

41. Siobhan B. Somerville, *Queering the Color Line: Race and the Invention of Homosexuality in American Culture* (Durham: Duke University Press, 2000), 3.

42. Somerville, *Queering the Color Line*, 3.

43. Wynter, "Beyond Miranda's Meanings," 360–1.

44. Wynter, "Beyond Miranda's Meanings," 365.

45. Hortense J. Spillers, "Mama's Baby, Papa's Maybe: An American Grammar Book," *Diacritics* 17, no. 2 (1987): 80.

46. Cooper, "Fallen."

47. Gayl Jones, *Corregidora* (Boston: Beacon Press, 1987), 125.

48. For an in-depth introspection into the libidinal economy, the affective formation of antiblackness, see Jared Sexton, *Amalgamation Schemes: Antiblackness and the Critique of Multiracialism* (Minneapolis: University of Minnesota Press, 2008).

49. Gayl Jones, *Corregidora*, 183–4.

50. Gayl Jones, *Corregidora*, 184.

51. Sexton, *Amalgamation Schemes*, 185.

52. Christina Sharpe, *Monstrous Intimacies: Making Post-Slavery Subjects* (Durham: Duke University Press, 2010), 65.

53. Anna Julia Cooper, *A Voice from the South*, 2000 online ed. (Xenia, OH: Aldine Printing House, 1892), 111, https://docsouth.unc.edu/church/cooper/cooper.html.

54. See Jennifer Nash, *Rethinking Black Feminism: After Intersectionality* (Durham: Duke University Press, 2019).

55. See C. Riley Snorton, *Black on Both Sides: A Racial History of Trans Identity* (Minneapolis: University of Minnesota Press, 2017).

Chapter 3

1. *Cincinnati Daily Gazette*, January 30, 1856.

2. The strikeout represents the idea of the slave mother as always existing under erasure, given that slavery made being a slave antithetical to the modern understanding of mothering, which is the capacity to govern and rear the life of the child, however exercised. Similarly, Frank B. Wilderson III and Calvin Warren have used the strikeout to illustrate subjectivity and being as forms of erasure or metaphysical nothing for the slave/Black. These in-text stylistic gestures attempt to bring a visual quality to a structure of deracination that is impossible to discuss without employing the same terms that were impossible qualifications for Black captives.

3. *Cincinnati Daily Gazette*, January 30, 1856.

4. Mark Reinhardt, *Who Speaks for Margaret Garner?* (Minneapolis: University of Minnesota Press, 2010), 39.

5. During the nineteenth century inquests played a pivotal role in the adjudication of infanticide. Felicity M. Turner argues that "Adjudication of infanticide cases depended on knowledge about women's bodies. In legal forums such as inquests and in day- to- day practice, those who laid claim to that knowledge often asserted a form of ownership or possession over what they knew. Those claims, in turn, had the effect of turning the knowledge into something akin to property. Indeed, knowledge of the human body could translate directly into claims to property rights, legitimating authority over physical bodies and control of people, themselves." Felicity M. Turner, *Proving Pregnancy: Gender, Law, and Medical Knowledge in Nineteenth-Century America* (Chapel Hill: University of North Carolina Press, 2022), 3. However, Turner argues that what differentiated inquests conducted in the first half of nineteenth century from those conducted near and around the abolition of slavery are the subjects who were considered knowledgeable about incidents of infanticide and the body. She argues that while "white women, free Blacks, and the enslaved, who lived in those bodies or who had extensive experience working with them," were once the primary experts in infanticide cases, near the mid-nineteenth century the experts in these cases became overwhelmingly white men. Turner, *Proving Pregnancy*, 3. This shift solidified legal as well as medical structural adjustments in who became institutionally construed as the subjects of knowledge over pregnancy, infanticide, and criminality as well as gendered and racial divisions.

6. Reinhardt, *Who Speaks for Margaret Garner?*, 111–12; Delores M. Walters, "Re(dis)covering and Recreating the Cultural Milieu of Margaret Garner," in *Gendered Resistance: Women, Slavery, and the Legacy of Margaret Garner*, eds. Mary E. Frederickson and Delores M. Walters (Urbana: University of Illinois Press, 2013), 5.

7. For more on Garner and the fugitive slave acts, see Mark Reinhardt, *Who Speaks for Margaret Garner?*; Stanley Harrold, *Border War: Fighting over Slavery before the Civil War* (Chapel Hill: University of North Carolina Press, 2010), 156–58.

8. Elizabeth Mehren, "A Haunting Death Inspires 'Beloved': Novelist Morrison Writes of Families, Freedom and Slavery," *Los Angeles Times*, October 14, 1987, www.latimes.com/archives/la-xpm-1987-10-14-vw-9326-story.html.

9. Mehren, "A Haunting Death Inspires 'Beloved'."

10. Walters, "Re(dis)covering and Recreating the Cultural Milieu of Margaret Garner," 5.

11. It is known that Garner was sold down south after the end of her trial in Ohio. Christina Sharpe notes that, "Remember that Margaret Garner is recaptured, and in her attempt to deny ownership to those who would claim her and her children as property, she succeeds in killing her daughter Mary. After which she is recaptured, held, tried, and put on the Henry Lewis, that ship that will return her slavery, this time to New Orleans, a place from which almost no enslaved people managed to escape." Christina Sharpe, *In the Wake: On Blackness and Being* (Durham: Duke University Press, 2016), 104.

12. In "Fixed Methodologies" Barbara Christian argues that within a few short years of *Beloved*'s publication there was an oversaturation of critical readings and responses to the text. She writes, "Toni Morrison's *Beloved* has, since its publication in 1987, received much acclaim from academic critics as well as more commercially inclined commentators . . . Yet I am perturbed by the attention, by the *kind* of critical attention *Beloved* has attended to receive, or to put it in our current literary critical language, by the critical discourses that I fear are beginning to appropriate this complex novel." "Fixed Methodologies: Beloved," *Cultural Critique* 24 (Spring 1993): 5. Evident in Christian's criticism is the intense fervor the text was met with from the time of its publication, as this essay was published a mere five years later. Since, the readings of *Beloved* have exponentialized. For a recent insightful engagement with the text see *Becoming Human: Matter and Meaning in an Antiblack World* by Zakiyyah Iman Jackson, where she approaches the text from the question of Manhood using the analytics of ontological plasticity and animality in relationship to Blackness. Zakiyyah Iman Jackson, *Becoming Human: Matter and Meaning in an Antiblack World* (New York: New York University Press, 2020), 45–83.

13. Garner provides a brief testimony on whether or not she had been to Ohio before the fateful escape. She notes that she was taken to Ohio at the age of seven to care for the young child of her mistress Mrs. Gaines. This testimony was objected to by the claimant James Marshall who states, "never knew one of that age employed to nurse a child even in the presence of her mistress; have no recollection of ever seeing a girl 7 years old take a child," 105. The issue before the court was whether or not Garner was free by her current or previous presence in the free state of Ohio. The facts of the death of the child were less disputed. Deciding her free or captive status would then determine who was the responsible party of the deceased child, Garner or her master Mr. Gaines. This decision served as the crux in settling upon what crime Garner would be charged with committing, murder if she were a free citizen of Ohio or theft of property if she and thus her children were deemed the property of Gaines. In the end the court decided that Garner and her children were the property of Gaines and not free at the time Mary was killed. For Garner's testimony and other responses, see Reinhardt, *Who Speaks for Margaret Garner?*

14. Sharon Patricia Holland, *Raising the Dead: Readings of Death and (Black) Subjectivity* (Durham: Duke University Press, 2000), 57.

15. For more on slave infanticide see Michael P. Johnson, "Smothered Slave Infants: Were Slave Mothers at Fault?" *Journal of Southern History* 47, no. 4 (Nov 1981): 493–520; Jeff Forret, "'The Prisoner . . . Thinks a Great Deal of Her Virtue': Enslaved Female Honor, Shame, and Infanticide in Antebellum Virginia," in *The Field of Honor: Essays on Southern Character and American Identity*, eds. Todd Hagstette and John Mayfield (Columbia: University of South Carolina Press, 2017), 217–30; Marcela Micucci, "'Another Instance of That Fearful Crime:' The Criminalization of Infanticide in Antebellum New York City," *New York History* 99, no. 1 (Winter 2018): 68–98; Sarah N. Roth, "'The Blade Was In My Own Breast': Slave Infanticide in 1850s Fiction," *American Nineteenth Century History* 8, no. 2 (2007): 169–85; Turner, *Proving Pregnancy*.

16. Brigitte Fielder, *Relative Races: Genealogies of Interracial Kinship in Nineteenth-Century America* (Durham: Duke University Press, 2020), 149.

17. Danille Taylor-Guthrie, ed., "A Conversation: Gloria Naylor and Toni Morrison," in *Conversations with Toni Morrison* (Jackson: University Press of Mississippi, 1994), 207.

18. In *Driven Toward Madness*, Nikki M. Taylor asserts that "Our contemporary sensibilities cannot fathom how a mother could kill her child to save it from anything. Moreover, most of us would never consent to proclaiming a child-killer a hero—even if she had killed for seemingly noble reasons." Nikki M. Taylor, *Driven to Madness: The Fugitive Slave Margaret Garner and Tragedy on the Ohio* (Athens: Ohio University Press, 2016), 119.

19. Saidiya V. Hartman, *Scenes of Subjection: Terror, Slavery, and Self-Making in Nineteenth-Century America* (New York: Oxford University Press, 1997), 79.

20. For more on Garner's expression of "joy" at hearing of the death of Cilla see Reinhardt, *Who Speaks for Margaret Garner*; Sharpe, *In the Wake*, 105.

21. Sharpe describes the death of Cilla by remarking, "As the Henry Lewis set out on its trip to Gaines' Landing in Arkansas, it collided with the boat the Edward Howard. Margaret and Cilla Garner were thrown or jumped overboard. Twenty-five people died in that accident, and the Garners' infant daughter Cilla was among them. Cilla was the nursing daughter whom Garner had tried unsuccessfully to kill in order to prevent her re-abduction into slavery." Sharpe, *In the Wake*, 104. In this respect the death of Cilla fulfilled, by will or accident, Margaret Garner's desire not to see the children returned to slavery.

22. See Taylor, *Driven Toward Madness*.

23. Alys Eve Weinbaum, *The Afterlife of Reproductive Slavery: Biocapitalism and Black Feminism's Philosophy of History* (Durham: Duke University Press, 2019), 64.

24. Sara Clarke Kaplan, *The Black Reproductive: Unfree Labor and Insurgent Motherhood* (Minneapolis: University of Minnesota Press, 2021), 99.

25. Kaplan, *The Black Reproductive*, 99.

26. Hortense J. Spillers, "Mama's Baby, Papa's Maybe: An American Grammar Book," *Diacritics* 17, no. 2 (1987): 80.

27. Kaplan, *The Black Reproductive*, 99.

28. Gwendolyn Brooks, "the mother," in *The Essential Gwendolyn Brooks*, ed. Elizabeth Alexander (New York: Library of America, 2005), 2–3.

29. Fielder, *Relative Races*, 121.

30. Fielder, *Relative Races*, 121.

31. Fielder similarly identifies killing the child as an act of desperation, noting, "Garner's act is one of desperation, in her view the best choice among a scope of limited and terrible options." Fielder, *Relative Races*, 152.

32. For more on the various contested understandings of afro-pessimism, see Jared Sexton, "Afro-Pessimism: The Unclear Word," *Rhizomes* 29 (2016).

33. Frank B. Wilderson, *Red, White, and Black: Cinema and the Structure of U.S. Antagonisms* (Durham: Duke University Press, 2009), 58.

34. For more on gender and afro-pessimism, see Wilderson's discussion of the films *Bush Mama* (1975), *Antione Fisher* (2003), and *Monster's Ball* (2001) as well as his discussion on white and Black feminisms in *Red, White, and Black*.

35. Wilderson, *Red, White, and Black*, 306.

36. The use of disabled here draws on disability studies and crip theory, which asserts that disability is not a state of immobility or lack but a reoriented relationship to existences of operability. This is not to suggest that white women as a structural positionality is disabled; rather it is to say that patriarchal violence does not thwart their relationship to enacting violence, it simply shifts their orientation to it.

37. Wilderson, *Red, White, and Black*, 306.

38. Wilderson, *Red, White, and Black*, 305.

39. Hortense J. Spillers, "Notes on an Alternative Model—Neither/Nor," in *Black, White, and In Color: Essays on American Literature and Culture* (Chicago: University of Chicago Press, 2003), 305.

40. C. Riley Snorton, *Black on Both Sides: A Racial History of Trans Identity* (Minneapolis: University of Minnesota Press, 2017), 83.

41. Snorton, *Black on Both Sides*, 83.

42. Snorton, *Black on Both Sides*, 107.

43. Snorton, *Black on Both Sides*, 107.

44. Snorton, *Black on Both Sides*, 135.

45. Snorton, *Black on Both Sides*, 135.

46. Hartman, *Lose Your Mother: A Journey Along the Atlantic Slave Route* (New York: Farrar, Straus, and Giroux, 2007), 85.

47. Hartman, *Lose Your Mother*, 6.

48. Spillers, "Mama's Baby, Papa's Maybe," 80.

49. Christian, "Fixed Methodologies," 7.

50. Hartman, *Lose Your Mother*, 6.

51. Hartman, *Lose Your Mother*, 6.

52. Alice Walker, *In Search of Our Mothers' Gardens: Womanist Prose* (San Diego: Harcourt Brace Jovanovich, 1983), 243.

53. Alice Walker, *In Search of Our Mothers' Gardens*, 243.

54. Spillers, "Mama's Baby, Papa's Maybe," 80.

55. Spillers, "Mama's Baby, Papa's Maybe," 70.

56. The strikeout here references that the body for the Black exists under erasure despite the assumption of its givenness in humanist discourse.

57. Zakiyyah Iman Jackson, "Suspended Munition: Mereology, Morphology, and the Mammary Biopolitics of Transmission in Simone Leigh's *Trophallaxis*," *Parse* 12 (2020).

58. Thinking about gender as a becoming without an identifiable locus or end, Judith Butler argues "A political genealogy of gender ontologies, if it is successful, will deconstruct the substantive appearance of gender into its constitutive acts and locate and account for those acts within the compulsory frame set by the various forces that police the social appearance of gender." *Gender Trouble: Feminism and the Subversion of Identity* (New York: Routledge, 2006), 45. Butler offers an astute framework for interrogating gender as it is performed through regulatory norms or practices. What separates what Butler presents from the question posed above is an assumption about compulsory acts that frame and reframe gender into a socially regulated type or intelligible presentations. The statement expressed about the real condition of Black womanhood harkens upon a different understanding entirely because of its concerns with Black gender or the blackening of gender. The Black woman is not represented by a set parameter of practices that serve to correct and modulate her appearances and presentations. Rather, the Black woman disappears as any intelligible substance the more gender tries to define her presence. Unlike Butler's position, which is extended through de Beauvoir, gender for the Black woman is not a becoming but a site of incapacitation and absenting. While similar to the position by Butler, the origin of the Black woman cannot be defined, although her constitution can be located in arrangements of violence that is situated from without. Which is to say, it is not compulsory acts of Black women that confound her but violent impositions that undo her possibility or potential for existence. See Simone de Beauvoir, *The Second Sex*, trans. H. M. Parshley (New York: Vintage Books, 1989)

59. "Voices of Slavery: 'They Were Saving Me For a Breeding Woman'," *This Cruel War*, accessed August 15, 2018, https://thiscruelwar.wordpress.com/2016/08/25/voices-of-slavery-they-were-saving-me-for-a-breeding-woman/.

60. "Voices of Slavery: 'They Were Saving Me For a Breeding Woman'"

61. Charles C. Sawyer, "When This Cruel War Is Over," 1863; Grant Taylor and Malinda Taylor, *This Cruel War: The Civil War Letters of Grant and Malinda Taylor*, eds. Ann Blomquist and Robert A. Taylor (Macon, GA: Mercer University Press, 2021); Chandra Manning, *What This Cruel War Was Over: Soldiers, Slavery, and the Civil War* (New York: Alfred A. Knopf, 2007).

62. This Cruel War, https://thiscruelwar.wordpress.com.

63. "Voices of Slavery: 'They Were Saving Me For a Breeding Woman'"

64. Susan J. Brison, *Aftermath: Violence and the Remaking of a Self* (Princeton: Princeton University Press, 2023), 5.

65. Brison, *Aftermath*, 4.

66. Ophelia Settle Egypt, Fisk University Social Science Institute, *Unwritten History of Slavery: Autobiographical Accounts of Negro Ex-slaves* (Washington: Microcard Editions, 1968), 1.

67. Egypt, *Unwritten History of Slavery*, 1.

68. Egypt, *Unwritten History of Slavery*, 1.

69. Egypt, *Unwritten History of Slavery*, 1.

70. Egypt, *Unwritten History of Slavery*, 2.

71. Egypt, *Unwritten History of Slavery*, 1.

72. Frantz Fanon, *Black Skin, White Masks*, trans. Charles Lam Markmann (New York: Grove Weidenfeld, 1967), 139.

73. Fanon, *Black Skin, White Masks*, 116.

74. Frank B. Wilderson III, "The Vengeance of Vertigo: Aphasia and Abjection in the Political Trials of Black Insurgents," *InTensions* 5 (2011): 3.

75. Donna Haraway proposes making kin as a radical act against the violent project of reproducing family or making babies. Haraway argues, "Making kin as oddkin rather than, or at least in addition to, godkin and genealogical and biogenetic family troubles important matter, like to whom one is actually responsible." *Staying with the Trouble: Making Kin in the Chthulucene* (Durham: Duke University Press, 2016), 2. The premise for *Staying with the Trouble* is based on an understanding of kin as a radicality that cannot be contained despite the continued attempts of domesticating it. However, this argument is underdeveloped when considering the way kin and making kin were violently weaponized against slaves as the racial project of whiteness or the whitening of populations, such as native peoples. For a more robust argument about the antiblack assumptions in Haraway's understanding of kin, see Sarah Haughn, "Life Expectancy: Antiblackness, Gestational Violence, and the Poiesis of Antagonism" (PhD Dissertation, University of California, Davis, 2022).

76. Lauren Berlant, *Cruel Optimism* (Durham: Duke University Press, 2011), 1.

77. Berlant, *Cruel Optimism*, 2–3.

78. Berlant, *Cruel Optimism*, 3.

79. Patricia Clough, "The Affective Turn: Political Economy, Biomedia and Bodies," *Theory Culture and Society* 25, no. 1 (2008): 1.

80. Tyrone S. Palmer, "Otherwise than Blackness: Feeling, World, Sublimation," *Qui Parle* 29, no. 2 (2020): 271.

81. Formation and deformation here think with work in Black disability studies that consider how Blackness is mediated through varying perceptions of ability and incapacitation. For a precise argument on the intersection between black studies and disability studies, see Moya Bailey and Izetta Autumn Mobley, "Work in the Intersections: A Black Feminist Disability Framework," *Gender and Society* 33, no. 1 (February 2019): 19–40.

82. John Murillo III, *Impossible Stories: On the Space and Time of Black Destructive Creation* (Columbus: Ohio State University Press, 2021), 60.

83. Hartman, *Scenes of Subjection*, 116.

84. Octavia E. Butler, *Kindred* (Boston: Beacon Press, 2003), 260.

85. Butler, *Kindred*, 260.

86. In reference to the imaging of Aunt Jemima and the legal battle over the possible estate of the Black women hired to play her for Quaker Oats in the 1930s, Sara Clarke Kaplan notes that, "In August 2014, D. W. Hunter and Larnell Evans filed a $3 billion class-action lawsuit against Quaker Oats and its parent company, PepsiCo, on behalf of all descendants of their great-grandmother, Anna Short Harrington. The daughter of sharecroppers from Wallace, South Carolina, Harrington was hired by Quaker Oats in 1935 to portray Aunt Jemima, the kerchief-wearing, griddle-toting brand icon for the company's boxed pancake mix . . . Hunter and Evans argued that they were owed not only back royalties

for the use of Harrington's image but also revenues for sixty-four original recipes that Quaker Oats had ostensibly stolen from Harrington and used to create foods marketed under the Aunt Jemima brand. The pancakes sold under the Aunt Jemima name, they alleged, were in fact based on Harrington's family recipe, stolen and marketed without permission or remuneration," *The Black Reproductive*, 29–30.

87. Omar Ricks, "Of Ambivalence: The Help, Obama, and the Ultimate Slave Remix," *The Feminist Wire*, February 27, 2021, https://thefeministwire.com/2012/02/of-ambivalence-the-help-obama-and-the-ultimate-slave-re-mix/.

88. Kaplan, *The Black Reproductive*, 29.

89. Kaplan, *The Black Reproductive*, 30.

90. Kaplan, *The Black Reproductive*, 32.

91. Kimberly Juanita Brown, *The Repeating Body: Slavery's Visual Resonance in the Contemporary* (Durham: Duke University Press, 2015), 112.

92. Following the 2020 uprisings in response to the murders of George Floyd, Breonna Taylor, Toni McDade, and Ahmaud Arbery and in the wake of COVID-19, the Aunt Jemima parent company Quaker Oats decided to concede to the century-long demand to remove the racist mammy figure as their logo, in an attempt to perform an anti-racist gesture. Though important, this maneuver served as one of many seemingly empty responses to demands to radically reorganize society. I see this gesture as purely symbolic and self-referential because the families of women who represented Aunt Jemima and/or had their family recipe used for the boxed pancake mix were not compensated. For more on the history of Pearl Milling Company, and the name change from the perspective of the brand, see https://www.pearlmillingcompany.com/our-history#:~:text=Pearl%20Milling%20Company%20was%20a,the%20breakfast%20table%20ever%20since (accessed May 21 2023)

93. Following the removal of the Aunt Jemima image, Saar was quoted as saying "Fifty years later she has finally been liberated herself. And, yet more work still needs to be done." Sarah Cascone, "Quaker Oats is Retiring the Aunt Jemima Brand, Whose Racist Origins Have Inspired Artists' Biting Interpretations for Decades," *Artnet News*, June 17, 2020, https://news.artnet.com/art-world/aunt-jemima-retired-brand-1887860.

94. "Liberation of Aunt Jemima," The Berkeley Revolution, http://revolution.berkeley.edu/liberation-aunt-jemima/.

95. Josephine Withers, "Betye Saar: Art," *Feminist Studies* 6, no. 2 (Summer 1980): 337.

96. In *Wayward Lives, Beautiful Experiments* (New York: Norton, 2019), Hartman describes the concept of the minor figure as "The minor figure yields to the chorus. All the hurt and the promise of the wayward are hers to bear." 17.

97. Interview with Barbara Christian from Marlon Riggs, *Ethnic Notions*, 1986.

98. Riggs, *Ethnic Notions*.

99. Dorothy Roberts, "The Paradox of Silence and Display: Sexual Violation of Enslaved Women and Contemporary Contradictions in Black Female Sexuality," in *Beyond Slavery: Overcoming Its Religious and Sexual Legacies*, ed. Bernadette J. Brooten (New York: Palgrave Macmillan, 2010), 46.

100. Roberts, "The Paradox of Silence and Display," 51.

101. Roberts, "The Paradox of Silence and Display," 51.

102. Spillers argues that "the African American male has been touched, therefore, by the *mother, handed* by her in ways that he cannot escape, and in ways that the white American male is allowed to temporize by a fatherly reprieve." Spillers, "Mama's Baby, Papa's Maybe," 80.

103. Ianna Hawkins Owens, "Still, Nothing: Mammy and Black Asexual Possibility," *Feminist Review* 120, no. 1 (2018): 75.

104. Butterwood Nan's name bears an uncanny similarity to the pancake syrup brand Mrs. Butterworth, which was created by Unilever in 1961 and at the time of the publication of this book is owned by Conagra Brands. The irony in the similarity to Butterwood Nan is that Mrs. Butterworth, unlike Aunt Jemima, is not explicitly racialized as Black. The questions about the race of Mrs. Butterworth have led to debates about whether or not she represents the racist iconography of the mammy or if she is possibly white, given that she was voiced by a white actress in early commercials for the brand. See Maria Cramer, "After Aunt Jemima, Reviews Underway for Uncle Ben, Mrs. Butterworth and Cream of Wheat," *New York Times*, June 17, 2020, www.nytimes.com/2020/06/17/business/aunt-jemima-mrs-butterworth-uncle-ben.html.

105. *Hudgins v. Wrights*, 11 Va. 134, 134 (1806).

106. *Hudgins v. Wrights*, 11 Va. 134, 134 (1806).

107. *Hudgins v. Wrights*, 11 Va. 134, 134 (1806).

108. Audra Simpson, "The State Is a Man: Theresa Spence, Loretta Saunders, and the Gender of Settler Sovereignty," *Theory and Event* 19, no. 4 (2016): 1-30, 15.

109. Kimberly Tallbear, *Native American DNA: Tribal Belonging and the False Promise of Genetic Science* (Minneapolis: University of Minnesota Press, 2013), 45-6.

110. Tallbear, *Native American DNA*, 45-6.

111. *Hudgins v. Wrights*, 11 Va. 134, 134 (1806).

112. Adrienne D. Davis, "'Don't Let Nobody Bother Yo' Principle': The Sexual Economy of American Slavery," in *Black Sexual Economies: Race and Sex in a Culture of Capital*, eds. Adrienne D. Davis and BSE Collective (Champaign: University of Illinois Press, 2019), 24.

113. *Hudgins v. Wrights*, 11 Va. 134, 135 (1806).

114. *Hudgins v. Wrights*, 11 Va. 134, 136 (1806).

115. *Hudgins v. Wrights*, 11 Va. 134, 137 (1806).

116. *Hudgins v. Wrights*, 11 Va. 134, 137 (1806).

117. For more on Elizabeth Key and her case, see "The Case of Elizabeth Key, 1655/6," in Billings, Old Dominion, 195-99; Warren M. Billings, "The Cases of Fernando and Elizabeth Key: A Note on the Status of Blacks in Seventeenth-Century Virginia," *William and Mary Quarterly* 30, no. 3 (July 1973): 467-474; Taunya Lovell Banks, "Dangerous Woman: Elizabeth Key's Freedom Suit—Subjecthood and Racialized Identity in Seventeenth Century Colonial Virginia," *Akron Law Review* 41 (2008): 799-837.

118. Jennifer L. Morgan argues, "With the passage of the 1662 Act, legislators made the connection between heredity and race explicit. But the ruling did more than simply inscribe notions of heritable descent into law; it actually subverted them," in *"Partus sequitur ventrem*: Law, Race, and Reproduction in Colonial Slavery," *Small Axe: A Journal of Criticism* 22, no. 1 (2018): 3.

119. Laws of Virginia, 1662 Act XII; Latin added by William Henig, *The Statutes at Large*, 1819.

120. Laws of Virginia, 1662 Act XII; Latin added by William Henig, *The Statutes at Large*, 1819.

121. Thomas A. Foster, *Rethinking Rufus: Sexual Violations of Enslaved Men* (Georgia: University of Georgia Press, 2019), 70–71.

122. Morgan, "*Partus sequitur ventrem*: Law, Race, and Reproduction in Colonial Slavery," 3.

123. Foster, *Rethinking Rufus*, 69.

124. "An Act Concerning Negroes & other Slaves" (September 1664). Maryland law of 1664, Md. Archives vol 1 533–534. GENERAL ASSEMBLY (Law Record) An Act Concerning Negroes and Other Slaves, 1, September 1664, 1 533–534 could also be: "Md. Laws 533–534."

125. Lois Green Carr and Lorena S. Walsh, "The Planter's Wife: The Experience of White Women in Seventeenth-Century Maryland," *William and Mary Quarterly* 34, no. 4 (1977): 550.

126. Carr and Walsh, "The Planter's Wife," 551.

127. Foster, *Rethinking Rufus*, 69.

128. Carr and Walsh write, "Maryland was settled in 1634, but in 1650 there were probably no more than six hundred persons and fewer than two hundred adult women in the province. After that time population growth was steady; in 1704 a census listed 30,437 white persons, of whom 7,163 were adult women," from "The Planter's Wife," 543.

129. Carr and Walsh, "The Planter's Wife," 546.

130. See Stephanie E. Jones-Rogers, *They Were Her Property: White Women as Slave Owners in the American South* (New Haven: Yale University Press, 2019).

131. Saidiya Hartman, "The Belly of the World: A Note on Black Women's Labor," *Souls* 18, no. 1 (2016):166.

132. Saidiya Hartman, "The Belly of the World," 166.

Chapter 4

1. My use of queer theory here is demarcating a subset of the field that is not expressively rooted in Black studies.

2. Lee Edelman, *Bad Education: Why Queer Theory Teaches Us Nothing* (Durham: Duke University Press, 2022); Lee Edelman, "Queerness, Afro-Pessimism, and the return of the Aesthetic," *REAL* 35, no. 1 (December 2019): 11–26; Jack Halberstam, *Wild Things: The Disorder of Desire* (Durham: Duke University Press, 2020); Amber Jamilla Musser, *Sensual Excess: Queer Femininity and Brown Jouissance* (New York: New York University Press, 2018); Amber Jamilla Musser, "The Queerness of Blackness in *The Cambridge History of Queer American Literature*, ed. Benjamin Kahan (Cambridge: Cambridge University Press, 2024); Judith Butler *Who's Afraid of Gender?* (Farrar, Straus, and Giroux, 2024).

3. Edelman, *Bad Education*, 43.

4. Edelman, *Bad Education*, 4.

5. Edelman, *Bad Education*, 5.

6. Edelman, *Bad Education*, 6.

7. Jacques Lacan, "L'Étourdit"; *The Letter: Irish Journal for Lacanian Psychoanalysis* 41 (Summer 2009): 31–77; *Bad Education*, 6.

8. Edelman, *Bad Education*, 6–7.

9. Edelman, *Bad Education*, 9.

10. Edelman, *Bad Education*, 16.

11. Ronald A. T. Judy, *(Dis)Forming the American Canon: African-Arabic Slave Narratives and the Vernacular* (Minneapolis: University of Minnesota Press, 1993), 89.

12. Edelman, *Bad Education*, 16.

13. Robert Reid-Pharr, introduction to *The Interesting Narrative of the Life of Olaudah Equiano, or Gustavus Vassa, The African* by Olaudah Equiano (New York: Random House, 2004), viii (my italics).

14. Frank B. Wilderson III, *Red, White, and Black: Cinema and the Structure of U.S. Antagonisms* (Durham: Duke University Press, 2010), 39.

15. Edelman, *Bad Education*, 16–7, emphasis in the original.

16. Edelman, *Bad Education*, 18.

17. Edelman, *Bad Education*, 18–9, emphasis in the original.

18. Edelman, *Bad Education*, 19.

19. Edelman, *Bad Education*, 19

20. There are contentions within Black studies about the applicability of Lacanian psychoanalysis for mediating issues pertaining to Blackness. In *Red, White and Black* Wilderson argues, "Whereas Lacan was aware of how language 'precedes and exceeds us,' he did not have Fanon's awareness of how violence also precedes and exceeds Blacks." 76. This position mirrors a similar contention by Spillers who expresses a pause with the seeming limits of Lacanian psychoanalysis to stage a confrontation "with the 'reality' that breaks in on the person,.." Hortense Spillers, "'All the Things You Could Be by Now If Sigmund Freud's Wife Was Your Mother': Psychoanalysis and Race," in *Black, White and in Color: Essays on American Literature and Culture* (Chicago: University of Chicago Press, 2003), 381. Reality here perhaps can be read as the violent intrusion Wilderson emphases. David S. Marriott however does not see Lacanian psychoanalysis as the racial foreclosure that Wilderson and Spillers argue. Marriott argues that Wilderson's conclusion "that Lacanian psychoanalysis is unable to account for a becoming that passes through not alienation but the absence of relationality . . . does not conceive Blackness as the *ab-sent* that has no being or *sens*, but arises as the topographical outside." David S. Marriott, *Lacan Noir: Lacan and Afro-pessimism* (New York: Palgrave McMillan, 2021), 137–8. This outside for Marriott, as for Edelman, produces an unprovable assumption of slavery as an essential outside, or essential violence, that is singular, transcendent, and unending. On this note, Marriott argues that afro-pessimism misunderstands Fanon on violence generally but also in response to the value of Lacan for the potential of the afro-pessimist project. He writes, "Afro-pessimism loses sight of why Fanon poses violence as a fact of structure, a structural operator (Φ) that is not so much circular, or a logic of repetition, but a tabula rasa (Φx) invoking a real that has yet to be written for it is always being written, but this is a writing which has no essence for no signifier can signify it as an exception without it already being misconstrued, ablated." Marriott, *Lacan Noir*, 135–6. In this respect, Marriott presents the Fanonian thesis on violence as not holding a single referent that is returned to, circulated, and recasts

irredeemability, like slavery. Instead, Marriott complicates and clarifies the tension between Lacan and Fanon that Wilderson alludes to. He argues, "Fanon's break with Lacan rests on one precise point; it is a matter of knowing whether non-being is that which veils division or that which dwells between nothingness and infinity." Marriott, *Lacan Noir*, 19–20.

21. Edelman, *Bad Education*, 19.
22. Edelman, *Bad Education*, 23.
23. Edelman, *Bad Education*, 23.
24. Calvin Warren, "Onticide: Afropessimism, Queer Theory, Ethics," Ill Will, November 18, 2014, https://illwill.com/onticide-afropessimism-queer-theory-and-ethics, 20.
25. Edelman, *Bad Education*, 25.
26. Edelman, *Bad Education*, 29.
27. Calvin Warren, "Onticide," 20.
28. Warren, "Onticide," 19.
29. Axelle Karera, "Blackness and the Pitfalls of Anthropocene Ethics," *Critical Philosophy of Race* 7, no. 1 (2019) 47.
30. Karera, "Blackness and the Pitfalls of Anthropocene Ethics," 47–8.
31. Halberstam, *Wild Things*, 29.
32. Halberstam, *Wild Things*, 26.
33. Halberstam, *Wild Things*, 27; the Central Park Five is an infamous 1989 case where five Black and brown teenagers were falsely accused of raping a white jogger in Central Park in New York City. Popular media sensationalized the case—which at the time was referred as the Central Park Jogger case—as evidence of Black and brown male propensity and heightened desire to rape white women. Media and other discourse surrounding the case advanced the false claim that the teens were participating in a larger group activity called "wilding" where they were seeking out a victim to rape. In reality these five teens as well as other New York City teens were spending a social night outside as was common for youth at this time. Decades after their convictions the youth were exonerated as overwhelming evidence proved their innocence. They are now referred to as the Exonerated Five, to highlight their innocence and the catastrophic injustice they endured at the hands of the New York City Police Department, criminal justice system, and racist sexist media and political spectacle that engulfed the case. For more on the Exonerated Five, see Joy James, "Searching for a Tradition: African-American Women Writers, Activists, and Interracial Rape Cases," in *Black Women in America*, ed. Kim Marie Vaz (Thousand Oaks, CA: Sage Publications, 1995), 131-158. See also Yusef Salaam, *Better, Not Bitter: Living on Purpose in the Pursuit of Racial Justice* (New York: Grand Central Publishing, 2021).
34. Michel Foucault, *The History of Sexuality Volume 1: An Introduction*, trans. Robert Hurley (New York: Pantheon Books, 1987), 18.
35. Foucault, *History of Sexuality, Vol. 1*, 18.
36. Foucault, *History of Sexuality, Vol. 1*, 18.
37. Foucault, *History of Sexuality, Vol. 1*, 43.
38. Foucault, *History of Sexuality, Vol. 1*, 44.
39. Benjamin Kahan, *The Book of Minor Perverts: Sexology, Etiology, & the Emergences of Sexuality* (Chicago: University of Chicago Press, 2019), 4.

40. Foucault, *History of Sexuality*, Vol. 1, 117.

41. Michel Foucault, *Abnormal: Lectures at the Collège de France 1974–1975*, trans. Graham Burchell (New York: Verso, 2003), 278.

42. Foucault, *Abnormal*, 280.

43. Foucault, *Abnormal*, 280, 282.

44. Foucault, *History of Sexuality*, Vol. 1, 43.

45. Charles Darwin, *The Descent of Man and Selection in Relation to Sex* (New York: D. Appleton and Company, 1871), 217.

46. E. Frances White, *Dark Continent of Our Bodies: Black Feminism and the Politics of Respectability* (Philadelphia: Temple University Press, 2001), 92.

47. White, *Dark Continent of Our Bodies*, 92.

48. Darwin, *The Descent of Man*, 217.

49. Georges Cuvier, *Discours sur les révolutions de la surface du globe: et sur les changements qu'elles ont produits dans le règne animal* (Paris, 1825), 214. Quoted in T. Denean Sharpley-Whiting, *Black Venus: Sexualized Savages, Primal Fears, and Primitive Narratives in French* (Durham: Duke University Press, 1999), 24.

50. Darwin, *The Descent of Man*, 223.

51. Darwin, *The Descent of Man*, 223.

52. Darwin returns from his voyage on the HMS *Beagle* with a staunchly anti-slavery stance. He notably writes, "On the 19th of August we finally left the shores of Brazil. I thank God, I shall never again visit a slave-country. To this day, if I hear a distant scream, it recalls with painful vividness my feelings, when passing a house near Pernambuco, I heard the most pitiable moans, and could not but suspect that some poor slave was being tortured, yet knew that I was as powerless as a child even to remonstrate." Charles Darwin, *The Voyage of the Beagle* (New York: P.F. Collier, 1909), 502. Despite his often lauded sympathy for slaves and disdain for slavery this does not absolve Darwin nor his theses on monogenesis from theorizing Black sexuality as a derelict presentation of Human sexuality. As White argues, Darwin's understandings of Africa and the slave were imbued with the anti-black sentimentality and assumptions about racial gendered difference and sexuality that were endemic to nineteenth-century scientific projects. White, *Dark Continent of Our Bodies*.

53. Alexander Falconbridge, *An Account of the Slave Trade on the Coast of Africa* (London: J. Phillips, 1780), 23–24.

54. Heinrich Kaan, *Psychopathia Sexualis*, ed. Benjamin Kahan, trans. Melissa Haynes (Ithaca: Cornell University Press, 2016), 76.

55. Kaan, *Psychopathia Sexualis*, 77.

56. Kaan, *Psychopathia Sexualis*, 75.

57. Kaan, *Psychopathia Sexualis*, 76.

58. Zakiyyah Iman Jackson, *Becoming Human: Matter and Meaning in an Antiblack World* (New York: New York University, 2020), 94.

59. Kaan, *Psychopathia Sexualis*, 141.

60. Kaan, *Psychopathia Sexualis*, 64.

61. Benjamin Kahan convincingly argues that despite Krafft-Ebing publishing a more widely read and distributed *Psychopathia Sexualis* he and other sexologists were influenced by Kaan's early work. He writes, "Although Kaan did not have many readers (because,

among other reasons, he wrote in Latin), his impact on sexology, and on Iwan Bloch, Havelock Ellis, Auguste Ambroise Tardieu, Benjamin Tarnowsky, and particularly on Krafft-Ebing, is of immense importance. Kaan not only creates the field of sexology but plays a critical role in the regimes of knowledge production and discipline about psychiatric and sexual subjects. Of course, Kaan did not conjure sexology out of thin air. As I will argue, the medical literatures on syphilis and anti-onanism and the discourse of popular botany provided important precedents. Without Kaan's outline of a sexual nosography and innovations in case history, however, Krafft-Ebing would have been unable to establish his extensive system of sexual taxonomy." Benjamin Kahan, editor's introduction to *Psychopathia Sexualis*, by Heinrich Kaan (Ithaca: Cornell University Press, 2016), 2.

62. R. von Krafft-Ebing, *Psychopathia Sexualis*, trans. F. J. Rebman (New York: Medical Arts Agency, 1922), vi, https://books.google.com/books/about/Psychopathia_Sexualis.html?id=ARsiScIQ8J4C&printsec=frontcover&source=kp_read_button&hl=en&newbks=1&newbks_redir=0#v=onepage&q&f=false.

63. Krafft-Ebing, *Psychopathia Sexualis*, 2.

64. Krafft-Ebing, *Psychopathia Sexualis*, 3.

65. Krafft-Ebing, *Psychopathia Sexualis*, 3.

66. Krafft-Ebing, *Psychopathia Sexualis*, 54.

67. Krafft-Ebing, *Psychopathia Sexualis*, 52–3.

68. Amber Jamilla Musser, *Sensational Flesh: Race, Power, and Masochism* (New York: New York University Press, 2014), 5.

69. Krafft-Ebing, *Psychopathia Sexualis*, 166.

70. Krafft-Ebing, *Psychopathia Sexualis*, 144.

71. Krafft-Ebing, *Psychopathia Sexualis*, 145.

72. For more on the historical and contemporary usages of *Uncle Tom's Cabin* in Germany, and other European countries, see Tracy C. Davis and Stefka Mihaylova editors, *Uncle Tom's Cabins: The Transnational History of America's Most Mutable Book* (University of Michigan Press, 2018); Erica Hellerstein, "Letter from Germany: A Strange and Enduring Love Affair with the Antebellum South" www.codastory.com/rewriting-history/uncle-toms-cabin-germany/; Denise Kohn, Sarah Meer, and Emily B. Todd, eds., *Transatlantic Stowe: Harriet Beecher Stowe and European Culture* (University of Iowa Press, 2006); Bettina Hofmann, "Uncle Tom's Cabin in Germany: A Children's Classic," *Zeitschrift für Anglistik und Amerikanistik* 53, no 4 (2014): 353–368.

73. Krafft-Ebing, *Psychopathia Sexualis*, 197.

74. Krafft-Ebing, *Psychopathia Sexualis*, 197.

75. Krafft-Ebing, *Psychopathia Sexualis*, 198.

76. Krafft-Ebing, *Psychopathia Sexualis*, 198.

77. Krafft-Ebing, *Psychopathia Sexualis*, 198–9.

78. Frantz Fanon, *Black Skin, White Masks*, trans. Charles Lam Markmann (New York: Grove Weidenfeld, 1967), 156.

79. Michel Foucault, *The History of Sexuality, Vol. 3: The Care of the Self*, trans. Robert Hurley (New York: Vintage, 1988), 32.

80. Saidiya V. Hartman, *Scenes of Subjection: Terror, Slavery, and Self-Making in Nineteenth-Century America* (New York: Oxford University Press, 1997), 79.

81. See Shannon McSheffrey and Julie Pope "Ravishment, Legal Narratives, and Chivalric Culture in Fifteenth-Century England," *Journal of British Studies* 48, no. 4 (Oct., 2009): 818.

82. McSheffrey and Pope, "Ravishment, Legal Narratives, and Chivalric Culture in Fifteenth-Century England."

83. Ann J. Cahill, *Rethinking Rape* (Ithaca: Cornell University Press, 2001), 20.

84. Cahill, *Rethinking Rape*, 28.

85. Cahill, *Rethinking Rape*, 36.

86. Cahill, *Rethinking Rape*, 37.

87. Cahill, *Rethinking Rape*, 38.

88. Cahill, *Rethinking Rape*, 40.

89. Cahill, *Rethinking Rape*, 48.

90. Cahill, *Rethinking Rape*, 109.

91. Cahill, *Rethinking Rape*, 116.

92. Fanon, *Black Skin, White Masks*, 81.

93. Hartman, *Scenes of Subjection*, 226, note 6.

94. Cahill, *Rethinking Rape*, 167.

95. Hartman, *Scenes of Subjection*, 227.

96. Cahill refers to the rape of the female slave in her discussion of the theories of rape produced by Brownmiller. She argues that the framework provided by Brownmiller "can account for the phenomenon of rape during slavery, where the forcible taking of slave women as sexual partners was an assertion of the slave owner's power as well as a demonstration of the powerlessness of the male slave. Under this rubric, the *male* slave is emasculated (and therefore dehumanized, rendered powerless) by being denied sole access to the slave woman." Cahill, *Rethinking Rape*, 18. This argument like the one Cahill makes about post-emancipation interracial rape places primary focus on the condition of the male slave without any elaboration of the consequences or strictures of what forced partnership does for the female slave. Instead, this argument assumes that the general theory of rape that is nonspecific to slavery incorporates a sufficient understanding of predicament of the female slave.

97. Rana Jaleel, *The Work of Rape* (Durham: Duke University Press, 2021), 7.

98. In *Scenes of Subjection*, Hartman dedicates a chapter to investigating of the legal omission of rape of the female slave. For more on her argument see "Seduction and the Ruses of Power," in *Scenes of Subjection*, 79–112.

99. Andrea Smith, *Conquest: Sexual Violence and American Indian Genocide* (Durham: Duke University Press, 2005), 16.

100. Hortense J. Spillers, "Mama's Baby, Papa's Maybe: An American Grammar Book," *Diacritics* 17, no. 2 (1987): 65.

101. Catharine A. MacKinnon, "Feminism, Marxism, Method, and the State: Toward Feminist Jurisprudence," *Signs* 8, no. 4 (Summer 1983): 638.

102. William Lloyd Garrison, "Is the Cause Onward?" *Independent*, January 14, 1869, https://archive.org/details/sim_independent_1869-01-14_21_1050.

103. Rebecca E. Zietlow, "Slavery, Liberty, and the Right to Contract," *Nevada Law Journal* 19, no. 2 (Winter 2018): 447–478.

104. Zietlow, "Slavery, Liberty, and the Right to Contract."

105. There were ways slaves contracted their labor for small monetary and other privileges; however, these instances did not grant slaves a collective right to control their labor power, nor did it afford them a wage that could emancipate their bondage.

106. Sarah Haley, *No Mercy Here: Gender, Punishment, and the Making of Jim Crow Modernity* (Chapel Hill: University of North Carolina Press, 2016), 110–11.

107. Haley, *No Mercy Here*, 108.

108. While there is a gap in research around sexual assault experienced by Black men during convict leasing, there are sources that speak to the racial, gender, and sexual power dynamics that exist under conditions of confinement. For contemporary sources on this topic please see Jasbir K. Puar, "Abu Ghraib and U.S. Sexual Exceptionalism," in *Terrorist Assemblages: Homonationalism in Queer Times*, 10th anniversary ed. (Durham: Duke University Press, 2017), 79–114; "Sexual Abuse of Men in Prisons," in *Sexual Assault: The Victims, the Perpetrators and the Criminal Justice System*, 2nd ed., eds. Frances P. Reddington and Betsy Wright Kreisel (Durham: Carolina Academic Press, 2009), 149–166; *No Escape: Male Rape in U.S. Prisons* (Human Rights Watch, 2001), www.hrw.org/reports/2001/prison/report.html.

109. See Amy Dru Stanley, *From Bondage to Contract: Wage Labor, Marriage, and the Market in the Age of Slave Emancipation* (Cambridge: Cambridge University Press, 1998).

110. Carole Pateman, *The Sexual Contract* (Stanford: Stanford University Press, 1988), 168.

111. Pateman, *The Sexual Contract*, 62–3.

112. Pateman, *The Sexual Contract*, 62.

113. Pateman, *The Sexual Contract*, 62.

114. Pateman, *The Sexual Contract*, 64.

115. Pateman, *The Sexual Contract*, 64.

116. Frank B. Wilderson III, "Gramsci's Black Marx: Whither the Slave in Civil Society?" *Social Identities* 9, no. 2 (June 2003): 225–240.

117. Pateman, *The Sexual Contract*, 65.

118. Pateman, *The Sexual Contract*, 65.

119. Pateman, *The Sexual Contract*, 122.

120. Pateman, *The Sexual Contract*, 122.

121. Pateman, *The Sexual Contract*, 122.

122. Pateman, *The Sexual Contract*, 124–5.

123. See Mary Wollstonecraft, "A Vindication of the Rights of Woman," 2nd ed. in *A Vindication of the Rights of Woman*, ed. Eileen Hunt Botting (New Haven: Yale University Press, 2014), 82.

124. Sabine Broeck, *Gender and the Abjection of Blackness* (Albany: State University of New York Press, 2018), 66–7.

125. Pateman, *The Sexual Contract*, 1.

126. Pateman, *The Sexual Contract*, 2.

127. Pateman, *The Sexual Contract*, 1.

128. Thavolia Glymph, *Out of the House of Bondage: The Transformation of the Plantation Household* (New York: Cambridge University Press, 2003), 227.

129. Glymph, *Out of the House of Bondage*, 4.

130. Glymph, *Out of the House of Bondage*, 30.

131. Glymph, *Out of the House of Bondage*, 39.

132. Spillers, "Mama's Baby, Papa's Maybe," 73.

133. Spillers, "Mama's Baby, Papa's Maybe," 72–3.

134. Spillers, "Mama's Baby, Papa's Maybe," 73.

135. Spillers, "Mama's Baby, Papa's Maybe," 73.

136. Spillers, "Mama's Baby, Papa's Maybe," 73.

137. Spillers, "Mama's Baby, Papa's Maybe," 67, emphasis in original.

138. Spillers, "Mama's Baby, Papa's Maybe," 73, emphasis in original.

139. Ned Sublette and Constance Sublette, *The American Slave Coast: A History of the Slave-Breeding Industry* (Chicago: Lawrence Hill Books, 2016), 24.

140. Spillers, "Mama's Baby, Papa's Maybe," 67.

141. Gilles Deleuze and Felix Guattari, *Anti-Oedipus: Capitalism and Schizophrenia*, trans. Robert Hurley, Mark Seem, and Helen R. Lane (Minneapolis: University of Minnesota Press, 1983), 85.

142. Brittney C. Cooper, "Love No Limit: Towards a Black Feminist Future (In Theory)," *Black Scholar* 45, no. 4 (Winter 2015): 12.

143. Wilderson, *Red, White, and Black*, 2.

144. Christina Sharpe describes the wake as a set of overlapping, converging, and distinct reverberations. She extends the thesis that she wants "to think 'the wake' as a problem of and for thought." Christina Sharpe, *In the Wake: On Blackness and Being* (Durham: Duke University Press, 2016), 5.

145. Spillers, "Mama's Baby, Papa's Maybe," 68.

146. Spillers, "Mama's Baby, Papa's Maybe," 74.

147. Katherine McKittrick, *Demonic Grounds: Black Women and the Cartographies of Struggle* (Minneapolis: University of Minnesota Press, 2006), 45.

Chapter 5

1. Courttia Newland, "And Me . . .," in *Safe: 20 Ways to be a Black Man in Britain Today*, ed. Derek Owusu (London: Trapeze, 2019), 62.

2. For more on the emergence of #MeToo see Tarana Burke, *Unbound: My Story of Liberation and the Birth of the Me Too Movement* (New York: Flatiron Books, 2021).

3. Burke, *Unbound*.

4. Burke, *Unbound*.

5. Newland, "And Me . . .," 62.

6. Newland, "And Me . . .," 63.

7. Newland, "And Me . . .," 62.

8. Newland, "And Me . . .," 64.

9. Newland, "And Me . . .," 62.

10. Newland, "And Me . . .," 69.

11. Newland, "And Me . . .," 63.

12. Newland, "And Me . . .," 63.

13. Newland, "And Me . . .," 63.

14. Newland, "And Me . . .," 63.

15. Frank B. Wilderson places Jacques Lacan and Frantz Fanon in conversation to illustrate how Black speech always exists under violent coercion. He notes that Lacan understands that language always anticipates and overdetermines the subject and Fanon clarifies how violence anticipates and exceeds the Black. Under these conditions Black speech is neurotic as it tries to evade or unravel its inevitable conscription by violence. For more on this argument see *Red, White, and Black: Cinema and the Structure of U.S. Antagonisms* (Durham: Duke University Press, 2009), 67–91.

16. Newland, "And Me . . .," 64.

17. W.E.B. Du Bois, *The Souls of Black Folk* (New York: Simon and Schuster, 2005), 7.

18. Tommy J. Curry, *The Man-Not: Race, Class, Genre, and the Dilemmas of Black Manhood* (Philadelphia: Temple University Press, 2017), 170.

19. I am engaging *The Man-Not* at length here because of the curious and intense traction it has garnered in the field of Black male studies. I am concerned with how the arguments of the text veil deep anxieties about Black feminism and Black queer theory that are both ungenerous to each field and also politically hostile to theories that challenge the givenness of binary gender and heterosexual significance for Black people.

20. Curry, *The Man-Not*, 7.

21. Curry does briefly cite Marriott. However, his engagement with Marriott serves as evidence to a point he makes about the writings of James Baldwin and is not a deep engagement of the terms and ideas presented in Marriott's articulations of Black men and manhood.

22. The connection between real and racist cultural fantasies is a reading of Fanon taken up by David S. Marriott in *On Black Men* (Edinburgh: Edinburgh University Press, 2000).

23. David S. Marriott, *Lacan Noir: Lacan and Afro-pessimism* (Cham: Springer International Publishing, 2021), 150.

24. Marriott, *On Black Men*, xiv.

25. Curry, *The Man-Not*, 157.

26. Saidiya V. Harman, *Scenes of Subjection: Terror, Slavery, and Self-Making in Nineteenth-Century America* (New York: Oxford University Press, 1997), 79.

27. Harman, *Scenes of Subjection*, 97.

28. Harman, *Scenes of Subjection*, 101.

29. Harman, *Scenes of Subjection*, 101.

30. To this point, Curry argues, "Enslaved Blacks were denied manhood and womanhood; they were defined as beasts of burden whose bodies were used at the discretion of whites. Violence against the enslaved took no gendered form. It was unbridled violence against Black bodies where rape was enacted against both sexes," *The Man-Not*, 158.

31. Thomas A. Foster, "The Sexual Abuse of Black Men under American Slavery," *Journal of the History of Sexuality* 20, no. 3 (September 2011): 445–464.

32. Curry, *The Man-Not*, 159.

33. Slavery in Texas Staff, "Rose Williams," *Slavery in Texas*, accessed February 11, 2023, http://slaveryintexas.org/items/show/53.

34. Slavery in Texas Staff, "Rose Williams."

35. Foster, *Rethinking Rufus*, 30.

36. Foster, *Rethinking Rufus*, 30–45.

37. Foster, *Rethinking Rufus*, 30, 32.

38. Foster, *Rethinking Rufus*, 30, 32.

39. Foster, *Rethinking Rufus*, 30, 32.

40. Foster, *Rethinking Rufus*, 95.

41. Curry, *The Man-Not*, 160.

42. Ida B. Wells, *Southern Horrors: Lynch Law in All Its Phases* (New York: New York Age Print, 1892), www.gutenberg.org/files/14975/14975-h/14975-h.htm.

43. Lindon Barrett, *Blackness and Value: Seeing Double* (New York: Cambridge University Press, 1999), 230.

44. See Frantz Fanon, *Black Skin, White Masks*, trans. Charles Lam Markmann (New York: Grove Weidenfeld, 1967), 166.

45. Thavolia Glymph, *Out of the House of Bondage: The Transformation of the Plantation Household* (New York: Cambridge University Press, 2003); Stephanie E. Jones-Rogers, *They Were Her Property: White Women as Slave Owners in the American South* (New Haven: Yale University Press, 2019); Norrece T. Jones, *Born a Child of Freedom, Yet a Slave* (Middletown, CT: Wesleyan University Press, 1990); Elizabeth Fox-Genovese, *Within the Plantation Household* (Chapel Hill: University of North Carolina Press, 1988); Christine Walker, *Jamaica Ladies: Female Slaveholders and the Creation of Britain's Atlantic Empire* (Williamsburg, VA: Omohundro Institute of Early American History and Culture, 2020).

46. Some pivotal Black queer texts on Black male sexualization, degradation, and manhood include *Black Queer Studies: A Critical Anthology*, eds. E. Patrick Johnson and Mae G. Henderson (Durham: Duke University Press, 2005); Darieck Scott, *Extravagant Abjection: Blackness, Power, and Sexuality in the African American Literary Imagination* (New York: NYU Press, 2010); Marlon B. Ross, *Manning the Race: Reforming Black Men in the Jim Crow Era* (New York: NYU Press, 2004); Marlon B. Ross, *Sissy Insurgencies: A Racial Anatomy of Unfit Manliness* (Durham: Duke University Press, 2022); Robert F. Reid-Pharr, *Black Gay Man: Essays* (New York: NYU Press, 2001).

47. Fanon, *Black Skin, White Masks*, 165, 167.

48. Curry, *The Man-Not*, 148.

49. James Baldwin, *Going to Meet the Man* (New York: Dell Pub. Co., 1966), 200.

50. Baldwin, *Going to Meet the Man*, 204.

51. Baldwin, *Going to Meet the Man*, 217.

52. Curry, *The Man-Not*, 149.

53. Curry, *The Man-Not*, 150.

54. Curry, *The Man-Not*, 150.

55. Teresa de Lauretis, "The Stubborn Drive," *Critical Inquiry* 24, no. 4 (Summer 1998): 863.

56. Curry, *The Man-Not*, 158.

57. de Lauretis, "The Stubborn Drive," 313.

58. Marlon B. Ross, "Race, Rape Castration: Feminist Theories of Sexual Violence and Masculine Strategies of Black Protest," in *Masculinity Studies and Feminist Theory: New Directions*, ed. Judith Kagan Gardiner (New York: Columbia University Press, 2002), 307.

59. Jared Sexton, "Race, Sexuality, and Political Struggle: Reading *Soul on Ice*," *Social Justice* 30, no. 2 (2003): 35.

60. Calvin Hernton, *Sex and Racism in America* (New York: Grove Press 1966), 59.
61. Hernton, *Sex and Racism in America*, 59.
62. Eldridge Cleaver, *Soul on Ice* (New York: Dell Pub. Co., 1968), 241.
63. Sexton, "Race, Sexuality, and Political Struggle," 35.
64. Sexton, "Race, Sexuality, and Political Struggle," 36.
65. Sexton, "Race, Sexuality, and Political Struggle," 35.
66. This sentence makes reference to the Sylvia Wynter essay, "On How We Mistook the Map for the Territory, and Re-Imprisoned Ourselves in Our Unbearable Wrongness of Being, of Désêtre: Black Studies Toward the Human Project," in *Not Only The Master's Tools: African-American Studies in Theory and Practice*, eds. Lewis R. Gordon and Jane Anna Gordon (Boulder: Paradigm Publishers, 2006), 107–169. In this essay, Wynter argues that the institutionalization of Black studies deradicalized its potentials by allowing major Black figures to define the course of the field and by wavering towards a multiculturalist agenda. Wynter argues that, "gender role allocations mapped onto the biologically determined anatomical differences between male and female have been an indispensable function of the instituting of our *genres* or sociogenic *kinds* of being human." Wynter, "On How We Mistook the Map for the Territory," 117. This point is critically helpful to the argument being extended in this chapter. With respect to theories of Black manhood or the negation of such, there is a strict adherence to the belief that violation also fits an anatomical bifurcation of male and female. Which is to say, what happens to the sexed anatomical body is considered distinctive and based solely on the distribution of acts onto organs. However, I contend these flat theorizations of sexual harm and gender need to think more critically about how the enunciation of gender as a claim to injury can redouble the very identificatory structure that reproduces the conditions of possibility for the aphasia that makes Black male sexual vulnerability a belated or omitted consideration for thought. With respect to Wynter, I say this to hold firm to the argument that there are more radical subversive and destabilizing ways to engage Black gender that do not fail into the binary as a fundamental or starkly held division; Or even worse, that do not produce a theory that serves up Black male sexual vulnerability as a gotcha moment in the face of decades of Black queer theorizing about that very structure.
67. Scott, *Extravagant Abjection*, 169.
68. Scott, *Extravagant Abjection*, 168.
69. Judith K. Schafer, "Sexual Cruelty to Slaves: The Unreported Case of *Humphreys v. Utz*," *Chicago-Kent Law Review* 68, no. 3 (1993): 1313.
70. Schafer, "Sexual Cruelty to Slaves," 1313.
71. Schafer, "Sexual Cruelty to Slaves," 1314.
72. Schafer, "Sexual Cruelty to Slaves," 1319.
73. Schafer, "Sexual Cruelty to Slaves," 1316.
74. Schafer, "Sexual Cruelty to Slaves," 1332.
75. Schafer, "Sexual Cruelty to Slaves," 1335.
76. Schafer, "Sexual Cruelty to Slaves," 1327.
77. Schafer, "Sexual Cruelty to Slaves," 1319.
78. Schafer, "Sexual Cruelty to Slaves," 1320.
79. Samuel A. Cartwright, "Report on the Diseases and Physical Peculiarities of the Negro Race," in *Health, Disease, and Illness: Concepts in Medicine*, eds. Arthur L. Caplan,

James J. McCartney, and Dominic A. Sisti (Washington: Georgetown University Press), 28–40.

80. Harriett Jacobs, *Incidents in the Life of a Slave Girl* (Boston, 1861), 289.

81. Curry, *The Man-Not*, 149.

82. Marriott, "On Decadence: Bling Bling," *E-Flux Journal* 79 (February 2017).

83. Descriptions of the fight between Douglass and Covey can be found in Fredrick Douglass, *Narrative of the Life of Frederick Douglass* (Boston: Anti-Slavery Office, 1845), https://docsouth.unc.edu/neh/douglass/douglass.html; Frederick Douglass, *My Bondage and My Freedom* (New York: Miller, Orton, and Mulligan, 1855); Frederick Douglass, *The Life and Times of Frederick Douglass* (Boston: De Wolfe and Fiske Co., 1893).

84. Douglass, *My Bondage and My Freedom*, 215.

85. Douglass, *My Bondage and My Freedom*, 170.

86. Douglass, *My Bondage and My Freedom*, 233.

87. Douglass, *Narrative*, 72.

88. Douglass, *Narrative*, 72–3.

89. Deborah E. McDowell, "In The First Place: Making Frederick Douglass and the Afro-American Narrative Tradition," in *African American Autobiography: A Collection of Critical Essays*, ed. William L. Andrews (Englewood Cliffs: Prentice Hall, 1993), 36–58.

90. Douglass, *My Bondage and My Freedom*, 238.

91. Douglass, *My Bondage and My Freedom*, 240.

92. Douglass, *My Bondage and My Freedom*, 240.

93. Douglass, *My Bondage and My Freedom*, 242, emphasis in the original.

94. Douglass, *My Bondage and My Freedom*, 242, emphasis in the original.

95. Douglass, *My Bondage and My Freedom*, 243.

96. Douglass, *My Bondage and My Freedom*, 243.

97. Douglass, *My Bondage and My Freedom*, 243.

98. Douglass, *Narrative*, 73.

99. For more on the nullification or impossibility of childhood, which absents manhood for the male slave, see Habiba Ibrahim, *Black Age: Oceanic Lifespans and the Time of Black Life* (New York: NYU Press, 2021).

100. Douglass, *My Bondage and My Freedom*, 190.

101. Paul Gilroy, *The Black Atlantic: Modernity and Double Consciousness* (New York: Verso, 1993), 60.

102. Angela Davis, *Lectures on Liberation* (1971), 22, https://archive.org/details/AngelaDavis-LecturesOnLiberation/mode/2up.

103. Davis, *Lectures on Liberation*, 21.

104. Davis, *Lectures on Liberation*, 21.

105. Douglass, *My Bondage and My Freedom*, 190.

106. Fanon, *Black Skin, White Masks*, 217.

107. Fanon, *Black Skin, White Masks*, 216–17, emphasis in the original.

108. I do not take man here as representing cis-gender. Instead, I read man as representative of the political philosophical constitution of subjectivity that can, and has, expanded to include multiple gendered forms.

109. See Sylvia Wynter, "Unsettling the Coloniality of Being/Power/Truth/Freedom," *CR: The New Centennial Review* 3, no. 3 (2003); Greg Thomas and Sylvia Wynter, "PROUD FLESH Inter/Views: Sylvia Wynter," *Proud Flesh*, no. 4 (2006).

110. Wilderson argues that the Black is structured as the anti-human, where he writes that, "If, as an ontological position, that is, as a grammar of suffering, the Slave is not a laborer but an anti-Human, a position against which Humanity establishes, maintains, and renews its coherence, its corporeal integrity; if the Slave is, to borrow from Patterson, generally dishonored, perpetually open to gratuitous violence, and void of kinship structure, that is, having no relations that need be recognized, a being outside of relationality, then our analysis cannot be approached through the rubric of gains or reversals in struggles with the state and civil society, not unless and until the interlocutor first explains how the Slave is of the world. The onus is not on one who posits the Master/Slave dichotomy but on the one who argues there is a distinction between Slaveness and Blackness. How, when, and where did such a split occur?" Wilderson, *Red, White, and Black*, 11.

111. For more on Douglass's embrace of self-defense following his fight with Covey, see Bernard R. Boxill, "The Fight with Covey," in *A Political Companion to Frederick Douglass*, ed. Neil Roberts (Lexington: University Press of Kentucky, 2018), 61–83.

112. Gilroy, *The Black Atlantic*, 63.

113. Gilroy, *The Black Atlantic*, 63.

114. Gilroy, *The Black Atlantic*, 64.

115. Gilroy, *The Black Atlantic*, 64.

116. Deborah McDowell comments that the sexual and physical brutality of female slaves is omitted from the understandings of freedom and personal advancement extended by Douglass. She argues that sexual bondage for female slaves is represented as a constant upon which freedom for male slaves is buttressed and clarified. Additionally, McDowell argues, "If, as Douglass observes, the slave master derives pleasure from the repeated act of whipping, could Douglass, as observer, derive a vicarious pleasure from the repeated narration of the act? I would say yes. Douglass's repetition of the sexualized scene of whipping projects him into a voyeuristic relation to the violence against slave women, which he watches, and thus he enters into a symbolic complicity with the sexual crime he witnesses." McDowell, "In the First Place," 50.

117. Zakiyyah Iman Jackson, *Becoming Human: Matter and Meaning in an Antiblack World* (New York: New York University Press, 2020), 84.

118. David S. Marriott, "Inventions of Existence: Sylvia Wynter, Frantz Fanon, Sociogeny, and 'the Damned,'" *CR: The New Centennial Review* 11, no. 3 (Winter 2011): 53.

Chapter 6

1. Kara Keeling, *The Witches Flight* (New York: Duke University Press, 2007), 42.

2. Marco Abel, *Violent Affect: Literature, Cinema, and Critique After Representation* (Lincoln: University of Nebraska Press, 2007), 218.

3. Jasmine Cobb argues that film is but one component of the long history of visual objectification of Blackness. She writes, "To circumscribe screen portrayals of slavery to questions of accuracy easily reproduces the cultural problems that haunted black life in the

nineteenth century, while leaving too few opportunities for imagination that might be useful to contemporary audiences. A cultural commitment to the objective/objectifying portrayal of black raciality haunts black life captured via camera—from slave master daguerreotypes to slavery-oriented feature films." "Directed by Himself: Steve McQueen 's 12 Years a Slave," *American Literary History* 26, no. 2 (Summer 2014): 343–344.

4. It was previously believed that this portrait was painted by Johann Zoffany; however, this was recently corrected to reflect the true artist.

5. Scott Myers, "Interview [Part 2]: Misan Sagay, Screenwriter, 'Belle,'" Medium, accessed January 21, 2016, https://gointothestory.blcklst.com/interview-part-2-misan-sagay-screenwriter-belle-7df4dd679a95.

6. Anita Singh, "Belle Authors in Bitter Feud over Writing Credit," *The Daily Telegraph*, August 3, 2014, accessed January 21, 2016, www.telegraph.co.uk/culture/film/11008121/Belle-authors-in-bitter-feud-over-writing-credit.html.

7. Mark Kermode, "Belle Review—A Ripe Costume Drama with Teeth," June 15, 2014, www.theguardian.com/film/2014/jun/15/belle-review-costume-drama-teeth-slavery.

8. Kermode, "Belle Review."

9. Kehinde Andrews, "Psychosis of Whiteness: The Celluloid Hallucinations of 'Amazing Grace' and 'Belle,'" *Journal of Black Studies* 47, no. 5 (July 2016): 450.

10. Jared C. Sexton is credited with the idea of borrowed institutionality, where he describes how Black people are made to slip on forms of subjectivity that are inherently antiblack and racially exclusive forms of being. For more on this point see Cecilio M. Cooper and Frank Wilderson III, "Interviews on Critical Race and Trans/Queer Approaches to Filmmaking: Incommensurabilities—The Limit of Redress, Intramural Indemnity, and Extramural Auditorship," *Performance Matters* 6, no. 1 (January 2020): 72–4.

11. See Joy James, "The Womb of Western Theory: Trauma, Time, Theft, and the Captive Maternal," *Carceral Notebooks* 12 (2016): 253–296.

12. Saidiya Hartman, *Scenes of Subjection: Terror, Slavery, and Self-Making in Nineteenth-Century America* (New York: Oxford University Press, 1997), 53.

13. Hartman, *Scenes of Subjection*, 53.

14. *Belle*, directed by Amma Asante (Fox Searchlight Pictures, 2013), 1:43:00.

15. Toni Morrison, interview by Bill Moyers, 1990, https://billmoyers.com/content/toni-morrison-part-1/.

16. James Walvin, *The Zong: A Massacre, The Law, and The End of Slavery* (New Haven: Yale University Press, 2011).

17. Walvin, *The Zong*, 74.

18. For more on the feminization of slave ship naming practices see Rachael Pasierowska, "All Aboard the *King George* and *Happy Captive*: European Shipnaming Practices in the Trans-Atlantic Slave Trade, 1750–1755," *International Journal of Maritime History* 34, no. 1 (February 2022): 183–195; Marian Vann, "Sirens of the Sea: Female Slave Ship Owners of the Atlantic World., 1750–1870," *Coriolis: Interdisciplinary Journal of Maritime Studies* 5, no. 1 (2015): 25.

19. Sylvia Wynter, "Rethinking 'Aesthetics': Notes Towards a Deciphering Practice," in *Ex-iles: Essays on Caribbean Cinema*, ed. Mbye Cham (Trenton, NJ: Africa World Press, 1992), 239.

20. The argument present in this sentence about the illusion *Belle* is operating upon is drawn from the final line of "Mama's Baby, Papa's Maybe: An American Grammar Book," where Hortense J. Spillers argues, "Actually claiming the monstrosity (of a female with the potential to 'name'), which her culture imposes in blindness, 'Sapphire' might rewrite after all a radically different text for a female empowerment." *Diacritics* 17, no. 2 (1987): 80.

21. For more on eighteenth-century courtship, see Margaret E. France, "Cutting Edge Courtship in Eighteenth-Century London," *ABO: Interactive Journal for Women in the Arts, 1640–1830* 10, no. 1 (2020), https://digitalcommons.usf.edu/abo/vol10/iss1/1; Wendy Moore, "Love and Marriage in 18th-Century Britain," *Historically Speaking* 10, no. 3 (June 2009): 8–10.

22. Hortense J. Spillers, "Notes on an Alternative Model—Neither/Nor," in *Black, White, and In Color: Essays on American Literature and Culture* (Chicago: University of Chicago Press, 2003), 302, emphasis in the original.

23. Hartman, *Scenes of Subjection*, 53.

24. Wynter, "Rethinking 'Aesthetics,'" 241.

25. Wynter, "Rethinking 'Aesthetics,'" 241.

26. Andrews, "Psychosis of Whiteness," 449.

27. Andrews, "Psychosis of Whiteness," 449.

28. Hartman, *Scenes of Subjection*, 81.

29. James Walvin, *The Zong*, 213.

30. M. NourbeSe Philip, *Zong!* (Toronto: The Mercury Press, 2008), 200.

31. Philip, *Zong!*

32. Paula Bryne, *Belle: The Slave Daughter and the Lord Chief Justice* (New York: Harper Perennial, 2014).

33. Claire, "Community Reviews on *Belle: The Slave Daughter and the Lord Chief Justice*," Goodreads, May 11, 2014, accessed February 1, 2016, www.goodreads.com/book/show/18038255-belle.

34. *Somerset v. Stewart* (1772) is a case often attributed as responsible for catalyzing the eventual end of slavery, at least in England. In this case, Lord Mansfield and Chief Justice of the Court of King's Beach ruled that the defendant Charles Stewart could not transport James Somerset, a slave he purchased in Virginia and brought to England, to Jamaica to sell into slavery. During his time enslaved by Steward, Somerset ran away and was recaptured by Stewart and held on a boat awaiting transport to Jamaica. This is when anti-slavery abolitionists brought Somerset's predicament before the court. This ruling was interpreted to mean that slavery was unlawful in England and served as justification for anti-slavery activists to abolish the institution on English soil. For more on *Somerset v. Stewart* and Lord Mansfield see Eliga Gould, "Zones of Law, Zones of Violence: The Legal Geography of the British Atlantic, circa 1772," *William and Mary Quarterly* 60, no. 3 (July 2003): 471–510; George Van Cleve, "Somerset's Case and Its Antecedents in Imperial Perspective," *Law and History Review* 24, no. 3 (Fall 2006): 601–646; Mark S. Weiner, "New Biographical Evidence on Somerset's Case," *Slavery and Abolition* 23, no. 1 (2002): 121–36; Edmund Heward, *Lord Mansfield* (Chichester; London: Barry Rose Publishers Ltd., 1979); C. H. S. Fifoot, *Lord Mansfield* (Oxford: Clarendon Press, 1936).

35. Henry Louis Gates Jr., "Who Was the Real Dido Elizabeth Belle?," *The Root*, August 26, 2014, accessed February 6, 2016, www.theroot.com/articles/history/2014/05/did_belle_really_help_end_slavery_in_england.html.

36. See note 34 for biographical references on the life and legacy of Lord Mansfield.

37. Henry Louis Gates Jr., "Who Was the Real Dido Elizabeth Belle?"

38. Toni Morrison, *Beloved* (New York: Vintage Books, 2004), 43.

39. Morrison, *Beloved*, 43.

40. See, Frank B. Wilderson III, "Grammar & Ghost: The Performative Limits of African Freedom," *Theatre Survey* 50, no. 1 (2009): 119–25.

41. The use of scare quotes here indexes the oxymoronic nature of being an illegitimate Black slave. Insofar as Black captivity or freedom, regardless of geographical locale in the United States, was determined by white authority and authorization, racial Blackness, not law, serves as the precondition for slaveness. As such freedom from slavery for Black people during the antebellum period existed in flux, with slavery serving as the status quo. For more on the vexed status of the free Black, see Patrice D. Douglass, "The Claim of Right to Property: Social Violence and Political Right," *Zeitschrift für Anglistik und Amerikanistik* 65, no. 2 (2017): 145–59; Calvin Warren, *Ontological Terror: Blackness, Nihilism, and Emancipation* (Durham: Duke University Press, 2018).

42. In "Social Death and Narrative Aporia in *12 Years a Slave*," Frank B. Wilderson III interrogates the differences and convergences that exist between the autobiography of Solomon Northup and the film. He argues that Northup narrates slavery as a concern of morals or morality, while McQueen visualizes slavery as the pleasure of slave-owning decadence. See Frank B. Wilderson, "Social Death and Narrative Aporia in *12 Years a Slave*," *Black Camera: Newsletter of the Black Film Center/Archives* 7, no. 1 (Fall 2015): 134–49.

43. Steve Ramos, "'Truth Is Truth': Steve McQueen On Making '12 Years A Slave,'" *Fast Company*, October 25, 2013, www.fastcompany.com/3020648/truth-is-truth-steve-mcqueen-on-making-12-years-a-slave (accessed August 5, 2020).

44. Ramos, "Truth Is Truth."

45. The Hollywood Reporter Staff, "Vera Farmiga to Sarah Paulson: I Wanted Your '12 Years a Slave' Role," *The Hollywood Reporter*, May 21, 2014, accessed February 28, 2022, www.hollywoodreporter.com/news/general-news/vera-farmiga-sarah-paulson-i-706160/.

46. James Baldwin, "A Letter From a Region of My Mind," *The New Yorker*, November 9, 1962, www.newyorker.com/magazine/1962/11/17/letter-from-a-region-in-my-mind.

47. Jada Yuan, "Lupita Nyong'o on *12 Years a Slave*, Getting Into Character and 'Imposter's Syndrome,'" *Vulture*, October 2, 2013, www.vulture.com/2013/10/lupita-nyongo-on-12-years-a-slave.html.

48. "Actress Lupita Nyong'o talks about her role in '12 Years a Slave,'" www.kpcc.org/show/take-two/2013-11-18/actress-lupita-nyongo-talks-about-her-role-in-12-years-a-slave.

49. Yuan, "Lupita Nyong'o on *12 Years a Slave*."

50. In "Perfecting Slavery" Anthony P. Farley uses white-over-black to illustrate how the racial rule of slavery is embedded in legal logic and implicated in the pleas for rights by the

slave and the free black. See Anthony Paul Farley, "Perfecting Slavery," *Loyola University of Chicago Law Journal* 36, no. 1 (2004).

51. Wilderson, "Social Death and Narrative Aporia," 138.

52. Wilderson, "Social Death and Narrative Aporia," 138.

Conclusion

1. Margaret Porter Troupe, "An Interview with Mildred Howard," *Black Renaissance/Renaissance Noire* 6, no. 3 (Spring 2006): 85.

2. Troupe, "An Interview with Mildred Howard," 85.

3. These forms of digital technologies, such as artificial intelligence and virtual reality, are progressive advancements for representing people and knowledges but are distinctively antiblack. These technologies, which are often purported to exceed the constraints of Human functionality, are made by humans using the logics of the present world, which was built by slavery. For more on the racial pitfalls of technology, see Ruha Benjamin *Race After Technology: Abolitionist Tools for the New Jim Code* (Medford, MA: Polity, 2019); Safiya Umoja Noble, *Algorithms of Oppression: How Search Engines Reinforce Racism* (New York: New York University Press, 2018); Virginia Eubanks, *Automating Inequality: How High-Tech Tools Profile, Police, and Punish the Poor* (New York: St. Martin's Press, 2018).

4. Troupe, "An Interview with Mildred Howard."

5. Yétúndé Olagbaju and Taylor Brandon, "Revisiting the Archive: Mildred Howard, 'Crossings' (1997)," *Berkeley Art Center*, June 2021, www.berkeleyartcenter.org/revisitng-the-archive-crossings.

6. Yétúndé Olagbaju and Taylor Brandon, "Revisiting the Archive: Mildred Howard."

7. David S. Marriott, "Inventions of Existence: Sylvia Wynter, Frantz Fanon, Sociogeny, and 'the Damned,'" *CR: Centennial Review* 11, no. 3 (Winter 2011): 53–54.

8. Frantz Fanon, *Black Skin, White Masks*, trans. Charles Lam Markmann (New York: Grove Weidenfeld, 1967), 232.

9. Mariame Kaba, *We Do This 'Til We Free Us: Abolitionist Organizing and Transforming Justice* (Chicago: Haymarket Books, 2021), 2.

10. Kaba, *We Do This 'Til We Free Us: Abolitionist Organizing and Transforming Justice* (Chicago: Haymarket Books, 2021); it is the chapter "A People's History" where she addresses this.

11. Angela Y. Davis, *Are Prisons Obsolete?* (New York: Seven Stories Press, 2003), 49.

12. Ruth Wilson Gilmore, *Golden Gulag: Prisons, Surplus, Crisis, and Opposition in Globalizing California* (Berkeley: University of California Press, 2007), 21.

13. Petitjean, Clément. "Prisons and Class Warfare: An Interview with Ruth Wilson Gilmore." *Verso*, August 2, 2018. www.versobooks.com/blogs/news/3954-prisons-and-class-warfare-an-interview-with-ruth-wilson-gilmore.

Bibliography

Abel, Marco. *Violent Affect: Literature, Cinema, and Critique After Representation*. Lincoln: University of Nebraska Press, 2007.
Aikin, John G. *A Digest of the Laws of the State of Alabama*. Philadelphia: Alexander Towar, 1833.
Anderson, William J. *Life and Narrative of William J. Anderson, Twenty-Four Years a Slave*. 2000 electronic edition. Chicago: Daily Tribune Book and Job Printing Office, 1857. https://docsouth.unc.edu/neh/andersonw/andersonw.html.
Andrews, Kehinde. "Psychosis of Whiteness: The Celluloid Hallucinations of 'Amazing Grace' and 'Belle.'" *Journal of Black Studies* 47, no. 5 (July 2016): 435–453.
Anzaldúa, Gloria. *Borderlands: La Frontera*. 2nd ed. San Francisco: Aunt Lute Books, 1999.
Asante, Amma, dir. *Belle*. 2013; Beverly Hills, CA: Fox Searchlight Pictures. DVD.
Bailey, Moya, and Mobley, Izetta Autumn. "Work in the Intersections: A Black Feminist Disability Framework." *Gender and Society* 33, no. 1 (February 2019): 19–40.
Baldwin, James. "A Letter From a Region of My Mind." *The New Yorker*, November 9, 1962. www.newyorker.com/magazine/1962/11/17/letter-from-a-region-in-my-mind.
Baldwin, James. *Going to Meet the Man*. New York: Dell Pub. Co., 1966.
Banks, Taunya Lovell. "Dangerous Woman: Elizabeth Key's Freedom Suit – Subjecthood and Racialized Identity in Seventeenth Century Colonial Virginia." *Akron Law Review* 41 (2008): 799–837.
Barnard Center for Research on Women. "In the Wake: A Salon in Honor of Christina Sharpe." Filmed February 2017 at Bernard Center for Research on Women. New York, NY, video.
Barrett, Lindon. *Blackness and Value: Seeing Double*. New York: Cambridge University Press, 1999.
Benjamin, Ruha. *Race After Technology: Abolitionist Tools for the New Jim Code*. Medford, MA: Polity, 2019.
Benjamin, Walter. "Critique of Violence." In *Walter Benjamin: Selected Writings Volume One, 1913–1926*, edited by Marcus Bullock and Michael W. Jennings, 236–252. Cambridge, MA: Belknap Press of Harvard University Press, 1996.
Berlant, Lauren. *Cruel Optimism*. Durham: Duke University Press, 2011.

Berry, Daina Ramey, and Harris, Leslie M., eds. *Sexuality and Slavery: Reclaiming Intimate Histories in the Americas*. Athens: University of Georgia Press, 2018.

Bibb, Henry. *Narrative of the Life and Adventures of Henry Bibb, an American Slave*. 2000 electronic edition. New York, 1849. https://docsouth.unc.edu/neh/bibb/bibb.html.

Billings, Warren M. "The Cases of Fernando and Elizabeth Key: A Note on the Status of Blacks in Seventeenth-Century Virginia." *William and Mary Quarterly* 30, no. 3 (July 1973): 467–474.

Boxill, Bernard R. "The Fight with Covey." In *A Political Companion to Frederick Douglass*, edited by Neil Roberts, 61–83. Lexington: University Press of Kentucky, 2018.

Boyce-Davies, Carol. "Occupying the Terrain: Reengaging 'Beyond Miranda's Meanings: Un/Silencing the 'Demonic Grounds of Caliban's Woman." *American Quarterly* 70, no. 4 (December 2018): 837–845.

Bridges, Virginia. "UNC Student Who Poured Blood and Ink on Silent Sam Confederate Statue Found Guilty, but Gets 'Prayer for Judgement.'" *Winston-Salem Journal*, October 15, 2018. https://journalnow.com/unc-student-who-poured-blood-and-ink-on-silent-sam-confederate-statue-found-guilty-but/article_956218e2-9520-5f1f-909f-368ba80a4dd4.html.

Brison, Susan J. *Aftermath: Violence and the Remaking of a Self*. Princeton: Princeton University Press, 2023.

Brooks, Gwendolyn. "the mother." In *The Essential Gwendolyn Brooks*, edited by Elizabeth Alexander, 2. New York: Library of America, 2005.

Brown, Kimberly Juanita. *The Repeating Body: Slavery's Visual Resonance in the Contemporary*. Durham: Duke University Press, 2015.

Bryne, Paula. *Belle: The Slave Daughter and the Lord Chief Justice*. New York: Harper Perennial, 2014.

Burke, Tarana. *Unbound: My Story of Liberation and the Birth of the Me Too Movement*. New York: Flatiron Books, 2021.

Bush, Barbara. *Slave Women in Caribbean Society, 1650–1832*. Bloomington, IN: Indiana University Press, 1990.

Butler, Judith. *Gender Trouble: Feminism and the Subversion of Identity*. New York: Routledge, 2006.

Butler, Judith. *Who's Afraid of Gender?* New York: Farrar, Straus, and Giroux, 2024.

Butler, Octavia E. *Kindred*. Boston: Beacon Press, 2003.

Cahill, Ann J. *Rethinking Rape*. Ithaca: Cornell University Press, 2001.

Camp, Stephanie. *Closer to Freedom: Enslaved Women & Everyday Resistance in the Plantation South*. Chapel Hill: University of North Carolina Press, 2004.

Carr, Lois Green, and Walsh, Lorena S. "The Planter's Wife: The Experience of White Women in Seventeenth-Century Maryland." *William and Mary Quarterly* 34, no. 4 (1977): 542–571.

Cartwright, Samuel A. "Report on the Diseases and Physical Peculiarities of the Negro Race." In *Health, Disease, and Illness: Concepts in Medicine*, edited by Arthur L. Caplan, James J. McCartney, and Dominic A. Sisti, 28–40. Washington: Georgetown University Press, 2004.

Cascone, Sarah. "Quaker Oats Is Retiring the Aunt Jemima Brand, Whose Racist Origins Have Inspired Artists' Biting Interpretations for Decades." *Artnet News*, June 17, 2020. https://news.artnet.com/art-world/aunt-jemima-retired-brand-1887860.

Child, Lydia Maria. "Introduction by the Editor." In *Incidents in the Life of a Slave Girl*, edited by Lydia Maria Child, 7–8. Boston: Published for the author, 1861.

Christian, Barbara. "Fixed Methodologies: Beloved." *Cultural Critique* 24 (Spring 1993): 5–15.

Cleaver, Eldridge. *Soul on Ice*. New York: Dell Pub. Co., 1968.

Clough, Patricia. "The Affective Turn: Political Economy, Biomedia and Bodies." *Theory Culture and Society* 25, no. 1 (2008): 1–22.

Cobb, Jasmine. "Directed by Himself: Steve McQueen's 12 Years a Slave." *American Literary History* 26, no. 2 (Summer 2014): 339–346.

The Combahee River Collective. "A Black Feminist Statement." In *The Second Wave: A Reader in Feminist Theory*, edited by Linda Nicholson, 63–70. New York: Routledge, 1997.

Cooper, Anna Julia. *A Voice from the South*. 2000 online edition. Xenia, OH: Aldine Printing House, 1892. https://docsouth.unc.edu/church/cooper/cooper.html.

Cooper, Brittney C. "Love No Limit: Towards a Black Feminist Future (In Theory)." *Black Scholar* 45, no. 4 (Winter 2015): 7–21.

Cooper, Cecilio M. "Fallen: Generation, Postlapsarian Verticality + the Black Chthonic." *Rhizomes* 38 (2022). https://doi.org/10.20415/rhiz/038.e01.

Cooper, Cecilio M., and Wilderson III, Frank. "Interviews on Critical Race and Trans/Queer Approaches to Filmmaking: Incommensurabilities—The Limit of Redress, Intramural Indemnity, and Extramural Auditorship." *Performance Matters* 6, no. 1 (January 2020): 68–85.

Cramer, Maria. "After Aunt Jemima, Reviews Underway for Uncle Ben, Mrs. Butterworth and Cream of Wheat." *New York Times*, June 17, 2020. www.nytimes.com/2020/06/17/business/aunt-jemima-mrs-butterworth-uncle-ben.html.

Cruz, Ariane. *The Color of Kink: Black Women, BDSM, and Pornography*. New York: NYU Press, 2016.

Curry, Tommy J. *The Man-Not: Race, Class, Genre, and the Dilemmas of Black Manhood*. Philadelphia: Temple University Press, 2017.

Cuvier, Georges. *Discours sur les révolutions de la surface du globe: et sur les changements qu'elles ont produits dans le règne animal*. Paris: Chez G. Dufour et Ed. d'Ocagne, 1825.

Darwin, Charles. *The Descent of Man and Selection in Relation to Sex*. New York: D. Appleton and Company, 1871.

Darwin, Charles. *The Voyage of the Beagle*. New York: P.F. Collier, 1909.

Davis, Adrienne D. "'Don't Let Nobody Bother Yo' Principle': The Sexual Economy of American Slavery." In *Black Sexual Economies: Race and Sex in a Culture of Capital*, edited by Adrienne D. Davis and BSE Collective, 15–38. Champaign: University of Illinois Press, 2019.

Davis, Angela Y. "Rape, Racism and the Capitalist Setting." *The Black Scholar* 12, no. 6 (April 1978): 24–30.

Davis, Angela Y. *Are Prisons Obsolete?* New York: Seven Stories Press, 2003.

Davis, Angela Y. *Women, Race and Class*. New York: Vintage Books, 1983.

Davis, Angela. "Reflections on the Black Woman's Role in the Community of Slaves." *Black Scholar* 3 (December 1971): 2–15.

Davis, Angela. *Lectures on Liberation*. 1971. https://archive.org/details/AngelaDavis-LecturesOnLiberation/mode/2up.

Davis, Tracy C., and Stefka Mihaylova, eds. *Uncle Tom's Cabins: The Transnational History of America's Most Mutable Book*. Ann Arbor: University of Michigan Press, 2018.

de Beauvoir, Simone. *The Second Sex*. Translated by H. M. Parshley. New York: Vintage Books, 1989.

de Lauretis, Teresa. "The Stubborn Drive." *Critical Inquiry* 24, no. 4 (Summer 1998): 851–877.

Deleuze, Gilles, and Guattari, Felix. *Anti-Oedipus: Capitalism and Schizophrenia*. Translated by Robert Hurley, Mark Seem, and Helen R. Lane. Minneapolis: University of Minnesota Press, 1983.

Democracy Now! "Meet Mata Little, UNC Student Whose Protest Ignited the Movement to Topple a Racist Confederate Statue." August 22, 2018. www.democracynow.org/2018/8/22/meet_maya_little_unc_student_whose.

Douglass, Frederick. *My Bondage and My Freedom*. New York: Miller, Orton, and Mulligan, 1855.

Douglass, Frederick. *Narrative of the Life of Frederick Douglass, an American Slave*. 1999 electronic edition. Boston: Anti-Slavery Office, 1845. https://docsouth.unc.edu/neh/douglass/douglass.html.

Douglass, Frederick. *The Life and Times of Frederick Douglass*. Boston: De Wolfe and Fiske Co., 1893.

Douglass, Fredrick. *Why is the Negro Lynched*. Bridgewater, VA: J. Whitby and Sons, 1895.

Douglass, Patrice D. "The Claim of Right to Property: Social Violence and Political Right." *Zeitschrift für Anglistik und Amerikanistik* 65, no. 2 (2017): 145–59.

Du Bois, W.E.B. *Black Reconstruction in America: 1860–1880*. New York: The Free Press, 1998.

Du Bois, W.E.B. *The Souls of Black Folk*. New York: Simon and Schuster, 2005.

duCille, Ann. "The Occult of True Black Womanhood: Critical Demeanor and Black Feminist Studies." *Signs* 19, no. 3 (Spring 1994): 591–629.

Edelman, Lee. *Bad Education: Why Queer Theory Teaches Us Nothing*. Durham: Duke University Press, 2022.

Edelman, Lee. "Queerness, Afro-Pessimism, and the return of the Aesthetic." *REAL* 35, no. 1 (December 2019): 11–26.

Esposito, Roberto. *Immunitas: The Protection and Negation of Life*. Translated by Zakiya Hanafi. Malden, MA: Polity Press, 2011.

Eubanks, Virginia. *Automating Inequality: How High-Tech Tools Profile, Police, and Punish the Poor*. New York: St. Martin's Press, 2018.

Falconbridge, Alexander. *An Account of the Slave Trade on the Coast of Africa*. London: J. Phillips, 1780.

Fanon, Frantz. *Black Skin, White Masks*. Translated by Charles Lam Markmann. New York: Grove Weidenfeld, 1967.

Farley, Anthony Paul. "Perfecting Slavery." *Loyola University of Chicago Law Journal* 36, no. 1 (2004).

Federici, Silvia. *Caliban and the Witch*. Brooklyn, NY: Autonomedia, 2004.

Fielder, Brigitte. *Relative Races: Genealogies of Interracial Kinship in Nineteenth-Century America*. Durham: Duke University Press, 2020.

Fifoot, C. H. S. *Lord Mansfield*. Oxford: Clarendon Press, 1936.

Fisk University Social Science Institute. *Unwritten History of Slavery: Autobiographical Accounts of Negro Ex-slaves*. Washington: Microcard Editions, 1968.

Forret, Jeff. "'The Prisoner . . . Thinks a Great Deal of Her Virtue': Enslaved Female Honor, Shame, and Infanticide in Antebellum Virginia." In *The Field of Honor: Essays on Southern Character and American Identity*, edited by Todd Hagstette and John Mayfield, 217–230. Columbia: University of South Carolina Press, 2017.

Foster, Thomas A. "The Sexual Abuse of Black Men under American Slavery." *Journal of the History of Sexuality* 20, no. 3 (September 2011): 445–464.

Foster, Thomas A. *Rethinking Rufus: Sexual Violations of Enslaved Men*. Athens: University of Georgia Press, 2019.

Foucault, Michel. *Abnormal: Lectures at the Collège de France 1974–1975*. Translated by Graham Burchell. New York: Verso, 2003.

Foucault, Michel. "Confinement, Psychiatry, Prison." In *Politics, Philosophy, Culture: Interviews and Other Writings 1977–1984*, edited by Lawrence D. Kritzman, 204–246. New York: Routledge, 1988.

Foucault, Michel. *Discipline and Punish: The Birth of the Prison*. Translated by Alan Sheridan. New York: Vintage Books, 1995.

Foucault, Michel. *Society Must Be Defended: Lectures at the Collège de France 1975–76*. Translated by David Macey. New York: Picador, 2003.

Foucault, Michel. *The History of Sexuality Volume One: An Introduction*. Translated by Robert Hurley. New York: Vintage Books, 1990.

Foucault, Michel. *The History of Sexuality, Vol. 3: The Care of the Self*. Translated by Robert Hurley. New York: Vintage, 1988.

Fox-Genovese, Elizabeth. *Within the Plantation Household*. Chapel Hill: University of North Carolina Press, 1988.

France, Margaret E. "Cutting Edge Courtship in Eighteenth-Century London." *ABO: Interactive Journal for Women in the Arts, 1640–1830* 10, no. 1 (2020): 1–19. https://digitalcommons.usf.edu/abo/vol10/iss1/1.

Frederickson, Mary E., and Walters, Delores M., eds. *Gendered Resistance: Women, Slavery, and the Legacy of Margaret Garner*. Urbana: University of Illinois Press, 2013.

Freud, Sigmund. *A General Introduction to Psychoanalysis*. Translated by G. Stanley Hall. New York: Boni & Liveright, 1920.

Freyre, Gilberto. *The Masters and the Slaves: A Study in the Development of Brazilian Civilization*. Translated by Samuel Putnam. Berkeley: University of California Press, 2022.

Fuentes, Marisa J. *Dispossessed Lives: Enslaved Women, Violence and the Archive*. Philadelphia: University of Pennsylvania Press, 2016.

Garrison, William Lloyd. "Is the Cause Onward?" *Independent*. January 14, 1869. https://archive.org/details/sim_independent_1869-01-14_21_1050.

Gaspar, David Barry, and Hine, Darlene Clark, eds. *More Than Chattel: Black Women and Slavery in the Americas*. Bloomington: Indiana University Press, 1996.

Gates Jr., Henry Louis. "Who Was the Real Dido Elizabeth Belle?" *The Root*, August 26, 2014. Accessed February 6, 2016. www.theroot.com/articles/history/2014/05/did_belle_really_help_end_slavery_in_england.html.

Gilmore, Ruth Wilson. *Golden Gulag: Prisons, Surplus, Crisis, and Opposition in Globalizing California*. Berkeley: University of California Press, 2007.

Gilroy, Paul. *The Black Atlantic: Modernity and Double Consciousness*. New York: Verso, 1993.

Glymph, Thavolia. *Out of the House of Bondage: The Transformation of the Plantation Household*. New York: Cambridge University Press, 2003.

Goodell, William. *The American Slave Code in Theory and Practice*. 3rd ed. New York: American and Foreign Anti-Slavery Society, 1853.

Gould, Eliga. "Zones of Law, Zones of Violence: The Legal Geography of the British Atlantic, circa 1772." *William and Mary Quarterly* 60, no. 3 (July 2003): 471–510.

Halberstam, Jack. *Wild Things: The Disorder of Desire*. Durham: Duke University Press, 2020.

Haley, Sarah. *No Mercy Here: Gender, Punishment, and the Making of Jim Crow Modernity*. Chapel Hill: University of North Carolina Press, 2016.

Hammonds, Evelyn. "Black (W)holes and the Geometry of Black Female Sexuality." *Differences* 6, no. 2–3 (1994): 126–145.

Hammonds, Evelyn M. "Toward a Genealogy of Black Female Sexuality: The Problematic of Silence." In *Feminist Theory and the Body: A Reader*, edited by Janet Price and Margrit Shildrick, 93–104. Edinburgh: Edinburgh University Press, 2022.

Hanser, Robert D., and Trulson, Chad. "Sexual Abuse of Men in Prisons." In *Sexual Assault: The Victims, the Perpetrators and the Criminal Justice System*, edited by Frances P. Reddington and Betsy Wright Kreisel, 149–166. 2nd ed. Durham: Carolina Academic Press, 2009.

Haraway, Donna. *Staying with the Trouble: Making Kin in the Chthulucene*. Durham: Duke University Press, 2016.

Harris, Carissa. "A History of the Wench." *Electric Literature*, June 3, 2019. https://electricliterature.com/a-history-of-the-wench/.

Harrold, Stanley. *Border War: Fighting over Slavery before the Civil War*. Chapel Hill: University of North Carolina Press, 2010.

Hartman, Saidiya V. *Scenes of Subjection: Terror, Slavery, and Self-Making in Nineteenth-Century America*. New York: Oxford University Press, 1997.

Hartman, Saidiya. "The Belly of the World: A Note on Black Women's Labor." *Souls* 18, no. 1 (2016): 166–173.

Hartman, Saidiya. "The Dead Book Revisited." *History of the Present: A Journal of Critical History* 6, no. 2 (2016): 208–215.

Hartman, Saidiya. "Venus in Two Acts." *Small Axe* 12, no. 2 (2008): 1–14.

Hartman, Saidiya. *Lose Your Mother: A Journey Along the Atlantic Slave Route*. New York: Farrar, Straus, and Giroux, 2007.

Hartman, Saidiya. *Wayward Lives, Beautiful Experiments*. New York: Norton, 2019.

Haughn, Sarah. "Life Expectancy: Antiblackness, Gestational Violence, and the Poiesis of Antagonism." PhD Dissertation, University of California, Davis, 2022.

Hellerstein, Erica. "Letter from Germany: A Strange and Enduring Love Affair with the Antebellum South." www.codastory.com/rewriting-history/uncle-toms-cabin-germany/.
Hernton, Calvin. *Sex and Racism in America*. New York: Grove Press, 1966.
Heward, Edmund. *Lord Mansfield*. London: Barry Rose Publishers Ltd., 1979.
Hine, Darlene Clark. "Rape and the Inner Lives of Black Women in the Middle West," *Signs* 14, no. 4 (Summer 1989): 912–920.
Hofmann, Bettina. "Uncle Tom's Cabin in Germany: A Children's Classic" *Zeitschrift für Anglistik und Amerikanistik* 53, no. 4 (2014): 353–368.
Holland, Sharon Patricia. *Raising the Dead: Readings of Death and (Black) Subjectivity*. Durham: Duke University Press, 2000.
The Hollywood Reporter Staff. "Vera Farmiga to Sarah Paulson: I Wanted Your '12 Years a Slave' Role." *The Hollywood Reporter*, May 21, 2014. accessed February 28, 2022. www.hollywoodreporter.com/news/general-news/vera-farmiga-sarah-paulson-i-706160/.
hooks, bell. *Black Looks: Race and Representation*. Boston: South End Press, 1992.
Human Rights Watch. "No Escape: Male Rape in U.S. Prisons." *Human Rights Watch*, 2001. www.hrw.org/reports/2001/prison/report.html.
Ibrahim, Habiba. *Black Age: Oceanic Lifespans and the Time of Black Life*. New York: NYU Press, 2021.
Jackson, George. *Soledad Brother: The Prison Letters of George Jackson*. New York: Coward-McCann, 1970.
Jackson, Zakiyyah Iman. "Suspended Munition: Mereology, Morphology, and the Mammary Biopolitics of Transmission in Simone Leigh's *Trophallaxis*." *Parse* 12 (2020): 1–19.
Jackson, Zakiyyah Iman. "Theorizing in a Void: Sublimity, Matter, and Physics in Black Feminist Poetics." *The South Atlantic Quarterly* 117, no. 3 (July 2018): 617–648.
Jackson, Zakiyyah Iman. *Becoming Human: Matter and Meaning in an Antiblack World*. New York: New York University Press, 2020.
Jacobs, Harriett. *Incidents in the Life of a Slave Girl*. Boston: Thayer & Eldridge, 1861.
Jaleel, Rana. *The Work of Rape*. Durham: Duke University Press, 2021,
James, Joy. "Searching for a Tradition: African-American Women Writers, Activists, and Interracial Rape Cases." In *Black Women in America*, edited by Kim Marie Vaz, 131–158. Thousand Oaks, CA: Sage Publications, 1995.
James, Joy. "The Womb of Western Theory: Trauma, Time, Theft, and the Captive Maternal." *Carceral Notebooks* 12 (2016): 253–296.
Johnson, E. Patrick, and Henderson, Mae G., eds. *Black Queer Studies: A Critical Anthology*. Durham: Duke University Press, 2005.
Johnson, Jessica Marie. *Wicked Flesh: Black Women, Intimacy, and Freedom in the Atlantic World*. Philadelphia: University of Pennsylvania Press, 2020.
Johnson, Michael P. "Smothered Slave Infants: Were Slave Mothers at Fault?" *Journal of Southern History* 47, no. 4 (Nov 1981): 493–520.
Jones, Gayl. *Corregidora*. Boston: Beacon Press, 1987.
Jones, Norrece T. *Born a Child of Freedom, Yet a Slave*. Middletown, CT: Wesleyan University Press, 1990.

Jones-Rogers, Stephanie E. *They Were Her Property: White Women as Slave Owners in the American South*. New Haven: Yale University Press, 2019.

Judy, Ronald A. T. *(Dis)Forming the American Canon: African-Arabic Slave Narratives and the Vernacular*. Minneapolis: University of Minnesota Press, 1993.

Kaan, Heinrich. *Psychopathia Sexualis*. Edited by Benjamin Kahan, translated by Melissa Haynes. Ithaca: Cornell University Press, 2016.

Kaba, Mariame. *We Do This 'Til We Free Us: Abolitionist Organizing and Transforming Justice*. Chicago: Haymarket Books, 2021.

Kahan, Benjamin. *The Book of Minor Perverts: Sexology, Etiology, & the Emergences of Sexuality*. Chicago: University of Chicago Press, 2019.

Kaplan, Sara Clarke. *The Black Reproductive: Unfree Labor and Insurgent Motherhood*. Minneapolis: University of Minnesota Press, 2021.

Karera, Axelle. "Blackness and the Pitfalls of Anthropocene Ethics." *Critical Philosophy of Race* 7, no. 1 (2019): 32–56.

Keeling, Kara. *The Witches Flight*. New York: Duke University Press, 2007.

Kermode, Mark. "Belle Review—A Ripe Costume Drama with Teeth." *The Guardian*, June 15, 2014. www.theguardian.com/film/2014/jun/15/belle-review-costume-drama-teeth-slavery.

King, Tiffany Lethabo. *The Black Shoals: Offshore Formations of Black and Native Studies*. Durham: Duke University Press, 2019.

Kohn, Denise, Meer, Sarah, and Todd, Emily B., eds. *Transatlantic Stowe: Harriet Beecher Stowe and European Culture*. Iowa City: University of Iowa Press, 2006.

Krafft-Ebing, Richard von. *Psychopathia Sexualis*. Translated by F. J. Rebman. New York: Medical Arts Agency, 1922.

Lacan, Jacques. "L'Étourdit." *The Letter: Irish Journal for Lacanian Psychoanalysis* 41 (Summer 2009): 31–77.

Lacan, Jacques. "The Deconstruction of the Drive." In *The Four Fundamental Concepts of Psychoanalysis*, edited by Jacques-Alain Miller, 161–173. Translated by Alan Sheridan. New York: Norton, 1998.

KPCC.org, "Actress Lupita Nyong'o Talks about Her Role in '12 Years a Slave.'" *KPCC*. November 18, 2013. www.kpcc.org/show/take-two/2013-11-18/actress-lupita-nyongo-talks-about-her-role-in-12-years-a-slave.

Lavater, John Caspar. *Essays on Physiognomy*. Edited by Thomas Holcroft. London: William Tegg and Co., 1878.

Lorde, Audre. "Age, Race, Class, and Sex: Women Redefining Difference." In *Sister Outsider: Essays and Speeches*, 114–123. Berkeley: Crossing Press, 2007.

Lyotard, Jean-François. "Emma: Between Philosophy and Psychoanalysis." In *Lyotard: Philosophy, Politics and the Sublime*, edited by Hugh J. Silverman, 39–62. New York: Routledge, 2002.

MacKinnon, Catharine A. "Feminism, Marxism, Method, and the State: Toward Feminist Jurisprudence." *Signs* 8, no. 4 (Summer 1983): 635–658.

MacKinnon, Catharine A. "#MeToo Has Done What the Law Could Not." *New York Times*. February 4, 2018. www.nytimes.com/2018/02/04/opinion/metoo-law-legal-system.html.

Manning, Chandra. *What This Cruel War Was Over: Soldiers, Slavery, and the Civil War.* New York: Alfred A. Knopf, 2007.
Marriott, David. "Inventions of Existence: Sylvia Wynter, Frantz Fanon, Sociogeny, and 'the Damned.'" *CR: The New Centennial Review* 11, no. 3 (Winter 2011): 45–89.
Marriott, David. "On Decadence: Bling Bling." *E-Flux Journal* 79 (February 2017): 1–10.
Marriott, David S. *Lacan Noir: Lacan and Afro-pessimism.* Cham: Springer International Publishing, 2021.
Marriott, David S. *On Black Men.* Edinburgh: Edinburgh University Press, 2000.
Mbembe, Achille. "Necropolitics." Translated by Libby Meintjes. *Public Culture* 15, no. 1 (January 2003): 11–40.
Mbembe, Achille. *Necropolitics.* Translated by Steve Corcoran. Durham: Duke University Press, 2019.
McDowell, Deborah E. "In The First Place: Making Frederick Douglass and the Afro-American Narrative Tradition." In *African American Autobiography: A Collection of Critical Essays*, edited by William L. Andrews, 36–58. Englewood Cliffs: Prentice Hall, 1993.
McKittrick, Katherine. *Demonic Grounds: Black Women and the Cartographies of Struggles.* Minneapolis: University of Minnesota Press, 2006.
McLaurin, Melton A. *Celia, A Slave.* New York: Avon Books, 1993.
McSheffrey, Shannon, and Pope, Julie. "Ravishment, Legal Narratives, and Chivalric Culture in Fifteenth-Century England." *Journal of British Studies* 48, no. 4 (Oct., 2009): 818–836.
McQueen, Steve, dir. *12 Years a Slave.* 2014; Beverly Hills, CA: Fox Searchlight Pictures. DVD.
Mehren, Elizabeth. "A Haunting Death Inspires 'Beloved': Novelist Morrison Writes of Families, Freedom and Slavery." *Los Angeles Times*, October 14, 1987. www.latimes.com/archives/la-xpm-1987-10-14-vw-9326-story.html.
Micucci, Marcela. "'Another Instance of That Fearful Crime:' The Criminalization of Infanticide in Antebellum New York City." *New York History* 99, no. 1 (Winter 2018): 68–98.
Moore, Wendy. "Love and Marriage in 18th-Century Britain." *Historically Speaking* 10, no. 3 (June 2009): 8–10.
Moraga, Cherríe L., and Anzaldúa, Gloria E., eds. *This Bridge Called My Back: Writings By Radical Women of Color.* Latham: Kitchen Table Women of Color Press, 1983.
Morgan, Jennifer L. "*Partus sequitur ventrem*: Law, Race, and Reproduction in Colonial Slavery." *Small Axe* 22, no. 1 (March 2018): 1–17.
Morgan, Jennifer L. *Laboring Women: Reproduction and Gender in New World Slavery.* Philadelphia: University of Pennsylvania Press, 2004.
Morgan, Jennifer L. *Reckoning with Slavery: Gender, Kinship, and Capitalism in the Early Black Atlantic.* Durham: Duke University Press, 2021.
Morrisey, Marietta. *Slave Women in the New World: Gender Stratification in the Caribbean.* Lawrence: University Press of Kansas, 1989).
Morrison, Toni. "The Site of Memory." In *Inventing the Truth: The Art and Craft of Memoir*, edited by William Zinsser, 83–102. 2nd edition. Boston: Houghton Mifflin, 1995.
Morrison, Toni. *Beloved.* New York: Vintage Books, 2004.
Morrison, Toni. Interview by Bill Moyers, 1990. https://billmoyers.com/content/toni-morrison-part-1/.

Moten, Fred. *In the Break: The Aesthetics of the Black Radical Tradition*. Minneapolis: University of Minnesota Press, 2003.

Murillo III, John. *Impossible Stories: On the Space and Time of Black Destructive Creation*. Columbus: Ohio State University Press, 2021.

Musser, Amber Jamilla. "The Queerness of Blackness." In *The Cambridge History of Queer American Literature*, edited by Benjamin Kahan, 567–580. New York: Cambridge University Press, 2024.

Musser, Amber Jamilla. *Sensational Flesh: Race, Power, and Masochism*. New York: New York University Press, 2014.

Musser, Amber Jamilla. *Sensual Excess: Queer Femininity and Brown Jouissance*. New York: New York University Press, 2018.

Myers, Scott. "Interview [Part 2]: Misan Sagay, Screenwriter, 'Belle.'" *Medium*. Accessed January 21, 2016. https://gointothestory.blcklst.com/interview-part-2-misan-sagay-screenwriter-belle-7df4dd679a95.

Nash, Jennifer. *Rethinking Black Feminism: After Intersectionality*. Durham: Duke University Press, 2019.

Natanson, Hannah. "Two Centuries Ago, University of Virginia Students Beat and Raped Enslaved Servants, Historians Say." *Washington Post*, October 6, 2019. www.washingtonpost.com/history/2019/10/06/two-centuries-ago-university-virginia-students-beat-raped-enslaved-servants-historians-say.

Neary, Janet. *Sight Unseen: Contemporary Visual Slave Narratives*. New York: Fordham University Press, 2017.

Newland, Courttia. "And Me . . ." In *Safe: 20 Ways to be a Black Man in Britain Today*, edited by Derek Owusu, 61–69. London: Trapeze, 2019.

Nietzsche, Friedrich. *The Genealogy of Morals*. Translated by Horace B. Samuel. New York: Boni and Liveright Publishers, 1923.

Noble, Safiya Umoja. *Algorithms of Oppression: How Search Engines Reinforce Racism*. New York: New York University Press, 2018.

Olagbaju, Yétúndé, and Brandon, Taylor. "Revisiting the Archive: Mildred Howard, 'Crossings' (1997)." *Berkeley Art Center*, June 2021. www.berkeleyartcenter.org/revisitng-the-archive-crossings.

Owens, Ianna Hawkins. "Still, Nothing: Mammy and Black Asexual Possibility." *Feminist Review* 120, no. 1 (2018): 70–84.

Oyěwùmí, Oyèrónkẹ́. *The Invention of Women: Making an African Sense of Western Gender Discourses*. Minneapolis: University of Minnesota Press, 1997.

Palmer, Tyrone S. "Otherwise than Blackness: Feeling, World, Sublimation." *Qui Parle* 29, no. 2 (2020): 247–283.

Pasierowska, Rachael. "All Aboard the *King George* and *Happy Captive*: European Shipnaming Practices in the Trans-Atlantic Slave Trade, 1750–1755." *International Journal of Maritime History* 34, no. 1 (February 2022): 183–195.

Pateman, Carole. *The Sexual Contract*. Stanford: Stanford University Press, 1988.

Patterson, Orlando R. *Slavery and Social Death: A Comparative Study*. Cambridge, MA: Harvard University Press, 1982.

Petitjean, Clément. "Prisons and Class Warfare: An Interview with Ruth Wilson Gilmore." *Verso*, August 2, 2018. www.versobooks.com/blogs/news/3954-prisons-and-class-warfare-an-interview-with-ruth-wilson-gilmore.

Philip, M. NourbeSe. *Zong!* Toronto: The Mercury Press, 2008.

Puar, Jasbir K. "Abu Ghraib and U.S. Sexual Exceptionalism." In *Terrorist Assemblages: Homonationalism in Queer Times*, 79–114. 10th anniversary edition. Durham: Duke University Press, 2017.

Ramos, Steve. "'Truth Is Truth:' Steve McQueen on Making '12 Years A Slave,'" *Fast Company*, October 25, 2013. www.fastcompany.com/3020648/truth-is-truth-steve-mcqueen-on-making-12-years-a-slave (accessed August 5, 2020).

Randall Williams, Caroline. "You Want a Confederate Monument? My Body Is a Confederate Monument." *New York Times*, June 26, 2020. www.nytimes.com/2020/06/26/opinion/confederate-monuments-racism.html.

Reid-Pharr, Robert F. *Black Gay Man: Essays*. New York: NYU Press, 2001.

Reid-Pharr, Robert. Introduction to *The Interesting Narrative of the Life of Olaudah Equiano, or Gustavus Vassa, The African* by Olaudah Equiano. New York: Random House, 2004.

Reinhardt, Mark. *Who Speaks for Margaret Garner?* Minneapolis: University of Minnesota Press, 2010.

Ricks, Omar. "Of Ambivalence: The Help, Obama, and the Ultimate Slave Remix." *The Feminist Wire*, February 27, 2021. https://thefeministwire.com/2012/02/of-ambivalence-the-help-obama-and-the-ultimate-slave-re-mix/.

Riggs, Marlon. *Ethnic Notions*. 1986. https://newsreel.org/transcripts/ethnicno.htm.

Riggs, Marlon, dir. *Ethnic Notions*. 1987; San Francisco, CA: California Newsreel. Kanopy.

Roberts, Dorothy. "The Paradox of Silence and Display: Sexual Violation of Enslaved Women and Contemporary Contradictions in Black Female Sexuality." In *Beyond Slavery: Overcoming Its Religious and Sexual Legacies*, edited by Bernadette J. Brooten, 41–60. New York: Palgrave Macmillan, 2010.

Ross, Marlon B. *Manning the Race: Reforming Black Men in the Jim Crow Era*. New York: NYU Press, 2004.

Ross, Marlon B. "Race, Rape Castration: Feminist Theories of Sexual Violence and Masculine Strategies of Black Protest." In *Masculinity Studies and Feminist Theory: New Directions*, edited by Judith Kagan Gardiner, 305–343. New York: Columbia University Press, 2002.

Ross, Marlon B. *Sissy Insurgencies: A Racial Anatomy of Unfit Manliness*. Durham: Duke University Press, 2022.

Roth, Sarah N. "'The Blade Was in My Own Breast': Slave Infanticide in 1850s Fiction." *American Nineteenth Century History* 8, no. 2 (2007): 169–85.

Salaam, Yusef. *Better, Not Bitter: Living on Purpose in the Pursuit of Racial Justice*. New York: Grand Central Publishing, 2021.

Sawyer, Charles C. "When This Cruel War Is Over," 1863. Song.

Scarry, Elaine. *The Body in Pain: The Making and Unmaking of the World*. New York: Oxford University Press, 1985.

Schafer, Judith K. "Sexual Cruelty to Slaves: The Unreported Case of *Humphreys v. Utz*." *Chicago-Kent Law Review* 68, no. 3 (1993): 1313–1427.

Scott, Darieck. *Extravagant Abjection*. New York: NYU Press, 2010.
Sexton, Jared C. *Amalgamation Schemes: Antiblackness and the Critique of Multiracialism*. Minneapolis: University of Minnesota Press, 2008.
Sexton, Jared. "Afro-Pessimism: The Unclear Word." *Rhizomes* 29 (2016).
Sexton, Jared. "People-Of-Color-Blindness: Notes on the Afterlife of Slavery." *Social Text* 28, no. 2 (Summer 2010): 31–56.
Sexton, Jared. "Race, Sexuality, and Political Struggle: Reading *Soul on Ice*." *Social Justice* 30, no. 2 (2003): 28–41.
Sharpe, Christina. *In the Wake: On Blackness and Being*. Durham: Duke University Press, 2016.
Sharpe, Christina. *Monstrous Intimacies: Making Post-Slavery Subjects*. Durham: Duke University Press, 2010.
Sharpley-Whiting, T. Denean. *Black Venus: Sexualized Savages, Primal Fears, and Primitive Narratives in French*. Durham: Duke University Press, 1999.
Simpson, Audra. "The State Is a Man: Theresa Spence, Loretta Saunders, and the Gender of Settler Sovereignty." *Theory and Event* 19, no. 4 (2016): 1–30.
Singh, Anita. "Belle Authors in Bitter Feud over Writing Credit." *The Daily Telegraph*, August 3, 2014. Accessed January 21, 2016. www.telegraph.co.uk/culture/film/11008121/Belle-authors-in-bitter-feud-over-writing-credit.html.
Sithole, Tendayi. "Meditations on the Dehumanisation of the Slave." In *Decolonising the Human: Reflections from Africa on Difference and Oppression*, edited by Melissa Stevyn and William Mpofu, 130–42. Johannesburg: Wits University Press, 2021.
Smith, Andrea. *Conquest: Sexual Violence and American Indian Genocide*. Durham: Duke University Press, 2005.
Smithers, Gregory D. *Slave Breeding: Sex, Violence and Memory in African American History*. Gainesville: University Press of Florida, 2012.
Snorton, C. Riley. *Black on Both Sides: A Racial History of Trans Identity*. Minneapolis: University of Minnesota Press, 2017.
Somerville, Siobhan B. *Queering the Color Line: Race and the Invention of Homosexuality in American Culture*. Durham: Duke University Press, 2000.
Sorentino, Sara-Maria. "Mistresses as Masters?: The Textual Pleasures of the Plantation Present." *differences: A Journal of Feminist Cultural Studies* 32, no. 2 (September 2021): 69–93.
Spillers, Hortense. "'All the Things You Could Be by Now If Sigmund Freud's Wife Was Your Mother': Psychoanalysis and Race." In *Black, White and in Color: Essays on American Literature and Culture*, 376–427. Chicago: University of Chicago Press, 2003.
Spillers, Hortense J. "Mama's Baby, Papa's Maybe: An American Grammar Book." *Diacritics* 17, no. 2 (1987): 65–81.
Spillers, Hortense J. "Notes on an Alternative Model—Neither/Nor." In *Black, White, and In Color: Essays on American Literature and Culture*, 301–18. Chicago: University of Chicago Press, 2003.
Stanley, Amy Dru. *From Bondage to Contract: Wage Labor, Marriage, and the Market in the Age of Slave Emancipation*. Cambridge: Cambridge University Press, 1998.

Stanton, Mary Olmsted. *A System of Practical and Scientific Physiognomy*. Philadelphia: F. A. Davis, 1890.

Sublette, Constance, and Sublette, Ned. *The American Slave Coast: A History of the Slave-Breeding Industry*. Chicago: Lawrence Hill Books, 2016.

Tallbear, Kimberly. *Native American DNA: Tribal Belonging and the False Promise of Genetic Science*. Minneapolis: University of Minnesota Press, 2013.

Taylor, Grant, and Taylor, Melinda. *This Cruel War: The Civil War Letters of Grant and Malinda Taylor*. Edited by Ann Blomquist and Robert A. Taylor. Macon, GA: Mercer University Press, 2021.

Taylor, Nikki Marie. *Driven Toward Madness: The Fugitive Slave Margaret Garner and Tragedy on the Ohio*. Athens: Ohio University Press, 2016.

Taylor-Guthrie, Danille, ed. "A Conversation: Gloria Naylor and Toni Morrison." In *Conversations with Toni Morrison*, 188–219. Jackson: University Press of Mississippi, 1994.

This Cruel War. https://thiscruelwar.wordpress.com.

Thomas, Greg, and Wynter, Sylvia. "PROUD FLESH Inter/Views: Sylvia Wynter." *Proud Flesh*, no. 4 (2006).

Troupe, Margaret Porter. "An Interview with Mildred Howard." *Black Renaissance/Renaissance Noire* 6, no. 3 (Spring 2006): 80–170.

Turner, Felicity M. *Proving Pregnancy: Gender, Law, and Medical Knowledge in Nineteenth-Century America*. Chapel Hill: University of North Carolina Press, 2022.

Van Cleve, George. "Somerset's Case and Its Antecedents in Imperial Perspective." *Law and History Review* 24, no. 3 (Fall 2006): 601–646.

Vann, Marian. "Sirens of the Sea: Female Slave Ship Owners of the Atlantic World., 1750–1870." *Coriolis: Interdisciplinary Journal of Maritime Studies* 5, no. 1 (2015): 22–33.

Vaziri, Parisa. "Blackness and the Metaethics of the Object." *Rhizomes* 29 (2016). https://doi.org/10.20415/rhiz/029.e16.

"Voices of Slavery: 'They Were Saving Me for a Breeding Woman'." *This Cruel War*, August 25, 2016. https://thiscruelwar.wordpress.com/2016/08/25/voices-of-slavery-they-were-saving-me-for-a-breeding-woman/.

Walker, Alice. *In Search of Our Mothers' Gardens: Womanist Prose*. San Diego: Harcourt Brace Jovanovich, 1983.

Walker, Christine. *Jamaica Ladies: Female Slaveholders and the Creation of Britain's Atlantic Empire*. Williamsburg, Virginia: Omohundro Institute of Early American History and Culture, 2020.

Walters, Delores M. "Re(dis)covering and Recreating the Cultural Milieu of Margaret Garner." In *Gendered Resistance: Women, Slavery, and the Legacy of Margaret Garner*, edited by Mary E. Frederickson and Delores M. Walters, 1–23. Urbana: University of Illinois Press, 2013.

Walvin, James. *The Zong: A Massacre, The Law, and The End of Slavery*. New Haven: Yale University Press, 2011.

Warren, Calvin. "Afro-pessimism, Gay Nigger #1, and Surplus Violence." *GLQ: A Journal of Lesbian and Gay Studies* 23, no. 3 (June 2017): 391–418.

Warren, Calvin. "Onticide: Afropessimism, Queer Theory, Ethics." *Ill Will*, November 18, 2014. https://illwill.com/onticide-afropessimism-queer-theory-and-ethics.

Warren, Calvin. *Ontological Terror: Blackness, Nihilism, and Emancipation*. Durham: Duke University Press, 2018.

Weinbaum, Alys Eve. *The Afterlife of Reproductive Slavery: Biocapitalism and Black Feminism's Philosophy of History*. Durham: Duke University Press, 2019.

Weiner, Mark S. "New Biographical Evidence on Somerset's Case." *Slavery and Abolition* 23, no. 1 (2002): 121–36.

Weld, Theodore Dwight. *American Slavery as It Is: Testimony of a Thousand Witnesses*. New York: American Slave Society, 1839.

Wells, Ida B. *Southern Horrors: Lynch Law in All Its Phases*. New York: New York Age Print, 1892. www.gutenberg.org/files/14975/14975-h/14975-h.htm.

White, Deborah Gray. *Ar'n't I a Woman: Female Slaves in the Plantation South*. New York: Norton, 1985.

White, E. Frances. *Dark Continent of Our Bodies: Black Feminism and the Politics of Respectability*. Philadelphia: Temple University Press, 2001.

Wilderson III, Frank B. "Grammar & Ghost: The Performative Limits of African Freedom." *Theatre Survey* 50, no. 1 (2009): 119–25.

Wilderson III, Frank B. "Gramsci's Black Marx: Whither the Slave in Civil Society?" *Social Identities* 9, no. 2 (June 2003): 225–240.

Wilderson III, Frank B. "The Vengeance of Vertigo: Aphasia and Abjection in the Political Trials of Black Insurgents." *InTensions* 5 (2011): 1–41.

Wilderson, Frank B. "Social Death and Narrative Aporia in 12 Years a Slave." *Black Camera: Newsletter of the Black Film Center/Archives* 7, no. 1 (Fall 2015): 134–49.

Wilderson, Frank B. *Red, White, and Black: Cinema and the Structure of U.S. Antagonisms*. Durham: Duke University Press, 2009.

Withers, Josephine, and Saar, Betye. "Beyte Saar: Art." *Feminist Studies* 6, no. 2 (Summer 1980): 336–341.

Wollstonecraft, Mary. "A Vindication of the Rights of Woman." In *A Vindication of the Rights of Woman*, edited by Eileen Hunt Botting, 19–228. 2nd edition. New Haven: Yale University Press, 2014.

Broeck, Sabine. *Gender and the Abjection of Blackness*. Albany: State University of New York Press, 2018.

Wynter, Sylvia. "Beyond Liberal and Marxist Leninist Feminisms: Towards an Autonomous Frame of Reference." *CLR James Journal* 24, no. 1/2 (2018): 31–56.

Wynter, Sylvia. "Beyond Miranda's Meanings: Un/silencing the 'Demonic Ground' of Caliban's 'Woman.'" In *Out of the Kumbla: Caribbean Women and Literature*, edited by Carole Boyce-Davies and Elaine Savory, 355–372. Fido. Trenton, NJ: Africa World Press, 1990

Wynter, Sylvia. "On How We Mistook the Map for the Territory, and Re-Imprisoned Ourselves in Our Unbearable Wrongness of Being, of Désêtre: Black Studies Toward the Human Project." In *Not Only the Master's Tools: African-American Studies in Theory and Practice*, edited by Lewis R. Gordon and Jane Anna Gordon, 107–169. Boulder: Paradigm Publishers, 2006.

Wynter, Sylvia. "Rethinking 'Aesthetics': Notes Towards a Deciphering Practice." In *Ex-iles: Essays on Caribbean Cinema*, edited by Mbye Cham, 237–279. Trenton, NJ: Africa World Press, 1992.

Wynter, Sylvia. "Unsettling the Coloniality of Being/Power/Truth/Freedom." *CR: The New Centennial Review* 3, no. 3 (2003): 257–337.

Yuan, Jada. "Lupita Nyong'o on *12 Years a Slave*, Getting Into Character and 'Imposter's Syndrome.'" *Vulture*, October 2, 2013. www.vulture.com/2013/10/lupita-nyongo-on-12-years-a-slave.html.

Zietlow, Rebecca E. "Slavery, Liberty, and the Right to Contract." *Nevada Law Journal* 19, no. 2 (Winter 2018): 447–478.

Index

Abel, Marco, 235
abolition: as world-making, 269; abolitionism, 268–69; abolitionist literature, 31, 40
abortion, 76, 102
ab-sens, 146–47, 149–50, 152
affect theory, 119–20
Africa, 111, 161–63, 196, 239, 292n52; African mother, as imagined, 110; as generalized space, 110; as maternal, 110
African Americans, 3, 173, 288n102
Africanness: as fictive kinship, 110
afro-pessimism, 10–11, 145, 147, 151, 153, 169–70, 182–83, 290–91n20; Black positionality, 105; female slave, 107; gender, 106; slavery, as structural positionality, 149–50
Agamben, Giorgio, 47
agency, 65; of female slaves, 67; sexual consent, 7
Alabama, 39–40
Allan, William T., 30–31, 34–36, 38–40, 59
American Slave Code in Theory and Practice (Goodell), 30, 35
American Slavery as It Is: Testimony of a Thousand Witnesses (Weld, Grimké, Grimké), 30–31
Anderson, William J., 41–43
Andrews, Kehinde, 238, 246
antiblack differentiation, 37
antiblack misandry, 197

antiblackness, 10, 13, 15, 72, 93, 126, 149–50, 156, 162, 168, 179, 198, 216, 246, 255, 258–59, 265, 271n17; antiblack psyche, 173–74; Black women, 106–7; criminalization, 266; and gender, 114; of mammy figure, 123; of maternal absence, 132; sexual violence, 174. *See also* white racial violence
anti-miscegenation laws, 96, 138
aphasia, 57–58, 112, 115, 120, 152, 205. *See also* dysrationalia
Arbery, Ahmaud, 287n92
archive, 15–17, 28, 41, 49, 59, 77, 96, 99, 114, 140, 216; as continued project, 53; gruesome content of, 101; historical, 29, 68, 261; as imaginative project, 122; irrational nature of, 46; legal, 51; misclassification, 65; objectification of, 10–11; return to, 231; sexual violence in, 29; of slavery, 2, 11, 18, 30, 39, 46, 53, 62, 64–65
Are Prisons Obsolete? (Davis), 267
artificial intelligence (AI), 263, 305n3
Asante, Amma, 23, 233, 237–38, 247
Asia, 161–62
Auld, Thomas, 223, 225, 227
Aunt Jemima, 20–21, 126, 131, 286–87n86, 287n92, 287n93, 288n104; as archetype, 127; as asexual, 123; iconography of, 127–29; iconography of the mammy, American fixation with, 123–24;

Aunt Jemima (*Continued*)
  lawsuits over, 124, 286–87n86; smile of, 123; as symbol, 124
Australia, 163
Autobiography of an Ex-Colored Man (Johnson), 109

Baartman, Saartjie, 159–60
Bad Education: Why Queer Theory Teaches Us Nothing (Edelman), 146–47, 151
Baldwin, James, 22–23, 209, 211, 257, 297n21
Bamboozled (film), 127
Barbados, 196
Barrett, Lindon, 207
BDSM, 37
Belle (film), 23, 233–34, 237, 241–43, 245, 249–51, 303n20; Blackness in, 239, 244, 247; class, and psychosis of whiteness, 246; narrative arc, 238–39; as white redemption story, 240; *Zong* ruling, rewriting of, 247–48
Belle, Dido Elizabeth, 236–51
Belle, Maria, 236, 250
Beloved (Morrison), 61, 98–99, 101; critical response to, 282n12
Benjamin, Walter, 17
Berkeley Arts Center, 262, 264
Berlant, Lauren: cruel optimism, 118–20
"Beyond Miranda's Meanings" (Wynter), 78, 279–80n21
Bibb, Henry, 52
biocentrism, 113–14, 186–87
biopolitics, 43–45, 47, 52
biopower, 43–45
Black abjection, 256
Black affect, 119
Black captivity, 213, 265, 304n41; psychic hold of, 126
Black differentiation, 13
Black disability studies, 286n81
Black dispossession, 257
Black engendering, 94–95

Black eunuchs: as bedroom guard, 215; sexual disempowerment, as signifier of, 214–15
Black family structure, 3
Black female, 83; as "hyperbolically sexual," 107; violable, 4
Black female sexuality, 130–31
Black feminism, 5, 8, 19–20, 22, 71, 79, 91–95, 101, 103, 105, 107, 109, 112, 145, 191, 198–99, 208–9, 231–32, 297n19; Black male slave sexual harms, obscuring of, 205; double bind, 4; dualistic thinking, 6; female slaveness, 77; womanhood, 73–74. *See also* feminism, white feminism
Black feminist historiography, 4, 7, 64
Black feminist theory, 18, 20, 66, 68, 73, 92–96, 98, 110, 208; Black manhood, 199–200; motherhood, 99–100; womb in, 113
black femme, 75–77
Black gender, 23, 80–81, 83, 92–93, 113, 120, 126, 187, 231, 238, 250, 285m58, 299n66; Black gender theory, 94–95; as "mother-like," 108; peculiarities of, 84, 131; as repressed potential, 181; sexual force, relationship between, 233. *See also* gender
Black Lives Matter, 54; uprisings, 126, 287n92
Black male studies, 22, 197, 199, 232, 297n19; misogyny embedded in, 231
Black manhood, 203, 207, 215, 231; Black feminist theory, 199–200; castration, 213–14, 223; as category of dispossession, 198; as entrapment, 199; fungibility of Black sexual status, 212; household, focus on as autonomous space, 204; inter-racial same-sex violation, 205; lactification, desire for, 198–99; and masculinity, 214; as oxymoronic, 212; sexual violability, 208; violation, 216–17. *See also* manhood, slave manhood

Black matriarchy, 3
Black men, 4, 7, 22, 90–91, 131, 137–40, 142, 174, 195, 200, 232; castration, 211–15, 222; convict leasing, 295n108; cultural fantasies of, 197; derivational form of manhood, 141; "manly autonomy," 203; negative tropes, 198; objectification, 207; oppression of, 196; phallus, 210–14, 222; rape, 180; rape fantasy, 206–7; as rapists, myth of, 206–7; sexual harm, perpetrators of, 205, 207; as sexual objects, 209; as sexually violable, 206; sexual violation of, 206–7, 214–15; sexual violence, relationship between, 199, 206, 212; suffering of, 197; as victimizers of women, 170; vulnerability, 197–99, 206–7; white males, sexual fantasies of, 209, 211–13; white women, and oppression of, 196, 208
Black mothers, 110; absence of, 107–8; Black maternal death, 108–9; as creator, 111; erasure, 108
Blackness, 2–3, 9–10, 17, 24, 32, 44–45, 55, 72, 75, 83, 86, 88–90, 131, 133, 142–43, 149, 157, 161, 170, 176, 198, 200–201, 219–20, 228, 233–35, 240, 243–44, 247, 250, 255–56, 259–60, 264, 267, 270, 290–91n20; ability and incapacitation, 286n81; as agender, 82; "Black persons," 153; "Black persons," as situatedness, 155; embodiment, 54; as empty and itemizable, 222–23; engendering of, 13; erasure of, 238; as formlessness, 120; as fungible, 14, 16, 84, 94, 107, 151, 223; and gender, 81–82; as gendered substance, 92; Human, as genre of, 229; Human kinship, 91; Humanness, emptied of, 222; manhood, relationship between, 208; mass incarceration, 268; and nativeness, 134; as ontological plasticity, 74, 282n12; political onotology of, 199; as quaquaversal, 82; queerness, 21–22, 147, 150, 152–56; queer theory, 145–46; rape theory, 8; sexual bifurcation of, 130; sexual captivity, 7; sexual violation, 174–75; slaveness, equating with, 27–28, 70, 137; slavery, 4, 185; as social death, 11; stain of, 239; and suffering, 236; thingification, 223; transness of, 107, 109; violence against, 105–6, 222–23; visual objectification of, 301–2n3

Black Panther Party, 126
Black queer theory, 9, 22, 208–9, 232, 297n19, 299n66
Black Reconstruction in America (Du Bois), 25–26
Black River (Jamaica), 240
Black sex, 88, 91, 159, 162, 168; Black sexuality, as immoral, 130; Black sexual violability, as fungible, 2; as mindless drive, 153–54; predation and openness, 156; violent cultural fantasies of, 130
Black speech, 196; under violent coercion, 297n15
Black studies, 81, 145, 151, 155, 169–70, 290–91n20, 299n66
Black suffering, 95, 154, 256, 268
Black transness, 107; as possibility, 109
Black trans theory, 9, 232
Blackwell, Luce Stone, 98
Black wildness, 156–57
Black womanhood, 71, 73, 75, 82–83, 93, 113–14, 129, 131, 186, 238, 285n58; as essence of female slave, 72; heroic image of, 65; problem space, 230–31. *See also* womanhood, white womanhood
Black women, 3–4, 8, 19–20, 58, 65, 69, 71, 74, 76, 78, 82–83, 87, 93–95, 121, 187, 194–95, 233, 236–37, 247, 249, 285n58; antiblackness, 106; Black womb/belly, 112–13, 131; as condition, 114; cult of secrecy, 72; erasure, 106; interiority, 6; as primordial figures, 5; rape, 7, 215; as revolutionary actors, 5; secrecy, as self-protection, 72–73; sexual violence, 77; suffering of, 68, 92; as superhuman saviors, 75, 77
Bloch, Iwan, 292–93n61

bondage, 65, 101, 110, 137–38, 141, 178, 227, 230, 238; of Blackness, 133; disempowered, 137; maternal, 136; sexual, 41, 234, 301n116
Boston (Massachusetts), 54
Boyce-Davies, Carole, 279–80n21
Brazil, 88, 292n52
breeding, 20, 26–27, 42, 190, 202, 270; breeding woman, 114–18; instability of, 120; as negative pregnant condition, 136; as objective vertigo, 117
Brent, Linda, 222
Brison, Susan, 115
Britain, 246. *See also* England
Broeck, Sabine, 185
Brooks, Gwendolyn, 102–3
Brown, Henry Box, 56
Brown, Kimberly Juanita, 124
Brownmiller, Susan, 171–72, 175, 294n96
Burke, Tarana, 194–95
Butler, Judith, 145, 285n58
Butler, Octavia E., 120, 122
Butterwood Nan, 21, 132, 134–36; Mrs. Butterworth, similarity to, 288n104; as signifying figure, 133

Cahill, Ann J., 171, 173, 175–76, 294n96; interracial rape, 174; "stumbling block," 172, 174
capitalism, 8, 267–69
Canada, 133
Caribbean, 26, 196
Cartwright, Samuel A., 221
castration, 22–23, 201, 209, 217, 221; as act of domination, 211; antiblack, 212, 222; Black castration, 215; Black manhood, 223; double-blind effect, 215; as emasculation, 213; fear of, 214; homoerotic act of, 213–14
Celia (slave), 48–52
Central Park Five, 156, 291n33
Child, Lydia Maria, 57–58
Christian, Barbara, 129, 282n12
Civil War, 25, 114

Cleaver, Eldridge: Black Eunuch, 214–15
Clough, Patricia, 119
Cobb, Jasmine, 301–2n3
colonialism, 43, 83, 93, 196–97
Combahee River Collective, 5
Conagra Brands, 288n104
contract theory: racial slavery, 181–82
convict leasing, 179–80, 295n108
Cooper, Brittney, 191
Cooper, Cecilio M., 81–82; "black descensus," 87
corporeal death, 41
Corregidora (Jones), 19–20, 88–91
Covey, Edward, 22–23, 223–29
COVID-19 pandemic, 287n92
Creation of Patriarchy, The (Lerner), 183
crip theory, 284n36
Crossings (Howard), 262; transatlantic slave trade, rendering of, 263–64
cruel optimism, 118–20
Cruz, Ariane, 37
Cumberbatch, Benedict, 259
Curry, Tommy J., 197–202, 208–14, 216, 222–23, 297n21, 297n30; aphasia, 205
Cuvier, Georges, 159–60

Darwin, Charles, 159–60, 163, 292n52; fusion, theory of, 164–65
Davis, Adrienne, 134
Davis, Angela Y., 3–5, 7–8, 226–27, 230, 267, 271n2
death drive, 209, 269
de Beauvoir, Simone, 285n58
debt peonage, 179–80
Deleuze, Gilles, 190
Descent of Man, The (Darwin), 159
disability studies, 284n36
(Dis)Forming the American Canon: African-Arabic Slave Narratives and the Vernacular (Judy), 147–48
dissemblance, 72; politics of, 73–74
Dixon, Turner, 58
Douglass, Frederick, 22–23, 49–50, 56, 230, 274n23, 301n116; Covey, violent

encounters with, 223–29; manhood, as recurring theme, 224; master and slave, reworking of, 226–27; slave, as universal signifier of political reason, 224
drapetomania, 221
Du Bois, W. E. B., 25–26, 37, 108, 196
duCille, Ann, 67–68
dysrationalia, 205. *See also* aphasia

Edelman, Lee, 145–49, 151–53, 155
Egypt, Ophelia Settle, 114
Ejiofor, Chiwetel, 23, 251
Ellis, Havelock, 292–93n61
emancipation: marriage contracts, 180
England, 141, 303n34; English common law, 136–37, 142. *See also* Britain
Equiano, Olaudah, 56, 147–48
erasure, 9, 45, 53–54, 65–66, 83, 87, 92, 108, 205, 218, 228, 249, 284n56; Black erasure, 81, 93, 106, 108, 114, 155–56, 205–6; epistemological, 134; genocidal, 135; ontological, 10, 80; of slave mothers, 281n2
eunuchs, 215. *See also* Black eunuchs
Europe, 45–46, 76
Evans, Larnell, 286–87n86

Falconbridge, Alexander, 161
Fanon, Frantz, 2–3, 10, 105, 117, 152, 156, 167, 207, 209, 228–29, 231, 266, 290–91n20, 297n15; corporeal schema, 84; duality of recognition between slave and Blackness, 264
Farley, Anthony P., 304–5n50
Farmiga, Vera, 256–57
fascism, 94
Fassbender, Michael, 251
featurism, 85
Federici, Silvia, 43–44
Felton, Tom, 240
female slaves, 4–7, 19, 72, 108, 111–12, 132, 187, 192–93, 258, 259, 301n116; afro-pessimism, 107; agency of, 67; as Black woman, 68–69, 71, 74; as breeders, 96,

103, 114–18; capitalized womb, 190; class, 184; fighting back, 76; in forced relation to master and mistress, 186; impregnation of, and slave economy, 190; infanticide, 98, 101, 104; as mammy, 96; objecthood, 77; as political actor, 75; rape, 294n96, 294n98; as rapeable, 176; sexual contract, 180–81; sexual violence, 177–78, 261; as slave mother, 96–97, 100, 104–5; superhuman resiliency, figure of, 75; as unknowable, 64; unrapeable status of, 66–67; as wench, 62–63, 65; womb, as organ of slavery, 191
feminism, 78, 173, 185, 269; autonomous, 279–80n21. *See also* Black feminism
feminist theory, 67, 69
Fielder, Brigette, 284n31; childless mother, 103; "kinfullness," 103
Floyd, George, 287n92
Foster, Thomas A., 7, 35, 139, 202–5
Foucault, Michel, 9, 29, 44, 157–59, 163; biopolitics, 47; biopower, 43
Fox, George, 62
Freud, Sigmund, 147
Freyre, Gilberto, 25
Fugitive Slave Act, 98

Gabon, 239
Gaines, Archibald, 98
Garner, Margaret, 20, 96–97, 101, 239, 282n11, 282n13, 283n21; as figure of motherhood, 103; infanticide, 98–100, 103–4, 265, 284n31; in liminal space, 98; motherhood, and sexual violence, 104; as slave mother, 104–5
Garrison, William Lloyd, 178
gender, 8, 9, 17, 19, 67–68, 72, 85–86, 94, 96, 105, 107, 139, 143, 145, 175, 188, 192–93, 199–201, 205, 216, 232; antiblackness, 114; as becoming, 285n58; cartography of, 181; as coffle, 2; injury, 22; myth of femininity, 3–4; as ontological, 189; racialized, as form of positive knowledge, 78; racial violence, 77; and sex,

gender (*Continued*)
69; sexual difference, 73; and sexuality, 11, 16, 22; sexual violence and rape, 70; slavery, 4; social death, 9, 106; as structural making, 74; structural positionality, 140. *See also* Black gender
Gender and the Abjection of Blackness (Broeck), 185
gender violence, 22, 74, 84, 186, 197, 205, 208, 269
genocide, 133
Genovese, Eugene, 184
Georgia, 179–80
Gilmore, Ruth Wilson, 267–68
Gilroy, Paul, 226, 230
Ginger Pop (slave), 222–23, 227, 229; sexual violence and torture of, 219–21
Glymph, Thavolia, 187–88
"Going to Meet the Man" (Baldwin), 22–23, 209–13, 222
Goodell, William, 30, 34–35, 42
Goode, Matthew, 23, 239
Gordon, Sarah, 241, 242
Gramsci, Antonio, 80
Gregson v. Gilbert, 239–40, 247–49
Grimké, Angelina, 30–33
Grimké, Sarah Moore, 30–31
Guattari, Félix, 190

Halberstam, Jack, 145, 156
Haley, Sarah, 179–80
Hammonds, Evelyn M., 5–6, 72–74
Haraway, Donna, 286n75
Harrington, Anna Short, 124, 286–87n86
Hartman, Saidiya V., 14, 41, 48, 51, 106, 109–11, 143, 175–76, 200–202, 217, 239, 245, 274n23, 276n60, 287n96, 294n98
Hawkins Owens, Ianna, 131–32
Hegel, G. W. F.: master-slave dialectic, 226–28
Hemings, Sally, 58
Hernton, Calvin, 214
Hine, Darlene Clarke, 19, 73; dissemblance, 72

History of Sexuality, Vol. 1 (Foucault), 157
HMS *Beagle*, 160, 292n52
Hoffman, George, 58
Holland, Sharon, 99
homoeroticism, 208–9, 213
hooks, bell: "eating the other," 67
Howard, Mildred, 262–64
hypodescent, 25. *See also* one-drop rule
Hudgins v. Wrights, 21, 132–33, 135–36
Humanness, 30, 34, 229; historical present, 119; social body of, 119
Humphreys, George W., 219, 227
Humphreys, John C., 219–20, 227
Humphreys v. Ute, 22–23, 201, 218–19, 223; genital mutilation and castration, example of, 217
Hunter, D. W., 286–87n86

incapacitation, 267–68
Incidents in the Life of a Slave Girl (Jacobs), 57
indentured servitude, 140
infanticide, 20, 76, 97–98, 103, 105, 265, 283n18, 284n31; as act of insurgency, 104; heroism of, 104; insurgent potential, 101–2; as mother-love, 99
In Search of Our Mothers' Gardens (Walker), 111, 279n20
installations, 263
Interesting Narrative of the Life of Olaudah Equiano, or Gustavus Vassa, the African (Equiano), 147; Black speech in, 148
intersectionality, 208
Invention of Women, The (Oyewumi), 69
Irigaray, Luce, 78

Jackson, George, 3, 271n2
Jacobs, Harriet, 56–57
Jackson, Zakiyyah Iman, 131, 282n12; black-female, 113; ontological plasticity, 74–75; trophallaxis, 113
Jamaica, 303n34
James, Joy, 238
Jefferson, Thomas, 58–59

Jim Crow, 94, 179
Johnson, Charles, 114
Johnson, James Weldon, 109
Johnson, Jessica Marie, 75
Jones, Gayl, 19–20; genital fantasies, 88, 91–92
July, Ronald, 147–49

Kaan, Heinrich, 158–63, 169, 292–93n61
Kaba, Mariame, 266
Kahan, Benjamin, 158, 292–93n61
Kaplan, Sara Clarke, 101, 124, 286–87n86
Karera, Axelle, 154
Keeling, Kara, 234
Key, Elizabeth, 136–37
King, Tiffany Lethabo, 54
kin, 109, 117, 286n75; and kinship, 36
Kindred (Butler), 120–23
kinfullness, 103–4
King, Martin Luther Jr., 126
kinship, 11, 76, 91, 98, 100, 103, 109, 111, 120–21, 124, 186, 189, 192, 204; Black kinship, 180; and kin, 36; loss of, 122; nuclear, 203; social death, 101
Krafft-Ebing, Richard von, 163–64, 166–68, 292–93n61

labor contracts, 180
Lacan, Jacques, 42, 297n15; ab-sens, concept of, 146–47; afro-pessimist project, 290–91n20; sexuation, 278n2
Lavater, Johan Caspar, 84–85
Lee, Spike, 127
Lerner, Gerda, 183, 188–89
liberalism, 265
"Liberation of Aunt Jemima" (Saar), 126–28, 131–32
Lindsay, Sir John, 236
Little, Maya, 54
Lorde, Audre, 273n29
Lose Your Mother: A Journey along the Atlantic Slave Route (Hartman), 109
Louisiana, 217, 219
lynching, 2, 206, 210, 212–13

MacKinnon, Catharine A., 171–72, 175
Malabou, Catherine, 148–50
male slaves, 141–42, 178, 189, 225, 230; autonomous intimacy with female slaves, 204; manhood, 204–5; mayhem, classification of, 217; physical torture, 203; rape, 200–201; self-making, 224; sexual violation of, 7, 139, 201–5, 216–17; sexual vulnerability, 140; West African manhood, traditions of, 203
"Mama's Baby, Papa's Maybe: An American Grammar Book" (Spillers), 191
mammy, 124, 126, 128, 287n92; antiblackness of, 123; as asexual, 130–31; as breeder and caregiver, 131; as desexualized figure, 130; as docile, 129; figure of, 123; as hypersexualized, 129–30; and Jezebel, 130
manhood, 216; animality of, 223; as becoming, 230; as form of integrity, 223; masculinity, and infantilism, 230; respectable Humanity, 224. *See also* Black manhood, slave manhood
"Man-Not," 199; concept of, 197–98
Man-Not, The: Race, Class, Genre, and the Dilemma of Black Manhood (Curry), 197–99, 200, 206–7, 209, 212, 297n19
Mansfield, Lady, 239, 250
Mansfield, Lord Chief Justice (William Murray), 236–37, 239–40, 242, 247–50, 303n34
Marriott, David S., 82, 197–99, 222, 265, 290–91n20, 297n21
marronage, 76
Marshall, James, 282n13
Martin, David, 236
Marxism, 269
mass incarceration, 94, 268; incapacitation, 267; slavery, linkage between, 267
master/slave dichotomy, 229–30, 267, 301n110
Maryland, 21, 28–29, 116, 137–42, 289n128
masochism, 21–22
Mbatha-Raw, Gugu, 23, 233

Mbembe, Achille, 47–48, 275–76n50, 276n60
McDade, Toni, 287n92
McDowell, Deborah E., 224, 301n116
McInnis, Maurie D., 58
McKittrick, Katherine, 83, 193
McQueen, Steve, 23, 233, 252–53, 257–58, 304n42
memorialization, 53–54
memory, 29, 53, 55, 60–61
#MeToo movement, 194–95
Middle Passage, 61, 153, 189–90, 192, 261–62, 264
Milano, Alyssa, 194
misogynoir, 195, 197
misogyny, 197, 231
Mississippi, 116
modernity, 65–66, 69, 110, 143, 176
Morgan, Jennifer L., 28–29, 76–77, 288n118
Morrison, Toni, 56–58, 60–61, 98–100, 239, 250, 282n12
Moten, Fred, 274n23
"mother, the" (Brooks), 102–3
motherhood, 20–21, 66, 97, 99–100, 104–5, 107–8, 110–13, 142; as figment of imagination, 103
mothering, 281n2
Moynihan, Daniel Patrick, 3
Moynihan Report, 3
Murillo, John, 121
Musser, Amber, 145, 152, 164
mutilation, 217, 221; genital fantasies, 91–92
"My Body Is a Confederate Monument" (Williams), 53–54, 58

Narrative of the Life of Frederick Douglass, The (Douglass), 224
nation-state, 43
Native Americans, 134–35; Native genocide, 177
necropolitics, 47–48, 275–76n50
negative pregnant: as term, 135–36
Newland, Courttia, 22, 194–97, 199, 231

New Orleans (Louisiana), 75
New World, 21, 43–44, 76, 79, 92, 96, 142, 144, 160, 168, 185, 190, 275n45; sexual violence of, 134–35
Northrup, Solomon, 23–24, 233, 251–55, 258–61, 304n42
Norton, James, 244
"Notunda" (Philip), 248
Nyong'o, Lupita, 23, 233, 257–58

objecthood, 65, 77, 138, 258
"Occult of True Black Womanhood, The" (duCille), 67–68
Oduye, Adepero, 258
one-drop rule, 25. *See also* hypodescent
onticide, 45
ontology, 10, 84, 93–94, 222–23; ontological plasticity, 74–75, 282n12
Oyewùmí, Oyèrónké, 69

Palmer, Tyrone, 119
partus sequitar ventrem, 21, 29, 132, 135–36, 139, 143, 177
Pateman, Carole, 181–86, 188–90, 192–93; original contract, 185
patriarchy, 4, 175, 185; patriarchal kinship, 32; racial particularities of, 180; sexual contract of, 181; white heteropatriarchy, 269
Patterson, Orlando, 182, 230
Paulson, Sarah, 251, 255–57
Pearl Milling Company, 123, 287n92
Philip, M. NourbeSe, 248
Philippines, 163
phrenology, 85
physiognomy, 84–86
Pierce, Charles Sanders, 128
Pitt, Brad, 260
plantation economy, 44; binary gender, 181; sexual contract, 180
plantation mistresses, 184; as slaveholders, 187–88
Polynesia, 163
power movements, 67

prison-industrial complex (PIC): abolitionist movement, 24, 266–67
Psychopathia Sexualis (Kaan), 158, 161, 292–93n61

Quaker Oats, 20, 124, 286–87n86, 287n92
queerness, 21–22, 147; Blackness, 150, 152–56; and slavery, 148
queer theory, 21, 170, 198; Blackness, 145–46; slavery, 145

racialization, 14, 27, 175
racial othering, 86–87
racial sexuation, 12–13, 17–18, 20, 27–28, 32, 33, 36–38, 46, 54, 76, 91–92, 105, 130–31, 144, 175, 192, 268; entombing nature of, 15; as modern predicament, 14; paradigm of 15, 24, 51, 116; as predicament of absent life, 52
racial slavery, 69, 136, 176, 184; contract theory, 181–82
racial violence, 65, 77, 195, 198
racism, 195, 246
Rainbow Center, 126
rape, 7, 22, 65, 69–70, 115, 117, 173, 180, 186, 195, 210, 215; Black female body, 200; Black male rapist, myth of, 141; common law definition of, 200; female slave, 294n96, 294n98; as force and crime, 172; of male slaves, 200–201; Native genocide, 177; plantation life, 3; as political, 171; rape theory, 8, 171, 174, 176; ravishment, 170–71, 177, 183, 191; as signifier of race, 207; sexual consent, 14; and slavery, 201; of slaves, not an offense, 66. *See also* sexual violence
reciprocity, 227–28, 239
Reconstruction, 25–26, 94, 108
Red, White, and Black: Cinema and the Structure of U.S. Antagonisms (Wilderson), 105, 148
Reid-Pharr, Robert, 148
Reid, Sam, 240
replication, 26

reproductive capacity, 27, 29
reproductive violence, 177
Rethinking Rape (Cahill), 171, 294n96
Rethinking Rufus: Sexual Violations of Enslaved Men (Foster), 174–75, 202–4
Ricks, Omar, 123
Roberts, Dorothy, 130
Roberts, Ned, 50
Ross, Marion B., 212–13

Saar, Betye, 126–29, 131–32, 287n92
Sagay, Misan, 236–37
Saussure, Ferdinand de, 128
Scarry, Elaine, 36
Scenes of Subjection: Terror and Self-Making in Nineteenth Century America (Hartman), 200, 202, 276n60, 294n98
Schafer, Judith, 217–18
Scone Palace, 236
scopophilia, 38
Scott, Darieck, 215; violation, as pain and pleasure, 216
Scott v. Sanford, 40
Selection in Relation to Sex (Darwin), 159
self-making, 78, 92, 224
sexology, 155
Sex and Racism in America (Hernton), 214
Sexton, Jared C., 48–49, 214–15, 238, 276n60, 278n2; borrowed institutionality, 302n10
Sexual Contract, The (Pateman), 181, 183–86
sexual death drive, 51
sexual mutilation, 180, 217, 220, 227
sexual violence, 1–2, 3, 16, 19, 23, 27, 42, 49, 55, 58, 63, 70, 73, 76, 93, 116, 118, 121, 195, 215, 219, 234, 265; antiblackness, 6, 174; Black women, 77, 179; female slaves, 177–78; of former slaves, 179; gender, 5; as gendered, 84; interracial, 53; of New World, 134–35; silence of, 57; under slavery, 5–6, 8–9, 17–18, 24, 38–39, 65–66, 91, 201; value, metaphor of, 17; and violability, 87

sexuation, 60, 75, 82, 121, 272n27, 278n2; antiblack, 269; paradigm of, 122; of slaves, 6, 15, 27, 51, 55, 204, 269; world-making, 134-35. *See also* racial sexuation

Shakespeare, William, 19-20, 78

Sharpe, Christina, 91, 282n11, 283n21, 296n144

signification, 50, 129, 261

Simpson, Audra, 133

"Site of Memory, The" (Morrison), 56, 60

Slave Codes, 275n45

slave films, 234-35, 257-58; as genre, 24

slave jubilee, 48

slave manhood, 224-25

slave mothers, 18-20, 96, 98, 104-5, 108-9, 112, 136, 270; erasure of, 281n2

slave narratives, 55-57, 115-16, 147-49

slaveness, 191, 230

slave rape, 55, 200

slave resistance, 35, 46, 56, 60, 76, 122; fantasy of, 51; romanticization of, 49; sexual violence and refusal, 49-50

slavery, 2, 9-12, 14, 16-17, 21, 24, 30, 56-58, 64-65, 72, 83, 92-93, 96, 98, 101, 106, 120-23, 128-30, 136, 138-39, 152, 170, 179, 197, 199, 205, 212-13, 216, 224, 227, 239, 247, 249, 257-58, 262, 268, 275n45, 304n41, 304n42, 304-5n50; abolition of, 178; aestheticization of, 23, 233; Blackness, 185; captive nature of, 131; death drives, 32-33, 40-41, 43-44, 46-47; in cinema, and plantation, 250; end of, 303n34; epochal rupture of, 110; as event of the past, 256; gender, 3, 180-81, 238; as institution, 26, 47; mass incarceration, linkage between, 267; mothers, 111-12; normation of death and sexual violence, 52; queerness, 148; queer theory, 145; racial schematization, 45; racial sexuation, 144; racial violence, 77; and rape, 201, 215; "rape-colored skin," 54-55; rape theory, 176; reproductive language of, 143-44; sexual bondage, 41; sexual captivity, 13; sexual and gendered terror of, 246, 269; sexual violence under, 5, 26, 49, 53, 59-60, 114-15, 234, 254, 260-61, 264-65, 267, 270; sexual(ized) violations, 71; as social death, 105, 183, 192-93, 230, 260; structural dimension of, 117; structural positionality, 149-50; violence of, 1, 74, 105, 116-17, 228; violence, as ordinary and routine response, 100; as visuality, 235; white women's violence, 188

slaves, 16, 47, 66, 73-74, 107, 224, 233, 253, 259, 262, 275n45; antiblack fantasy, 45-46; aphasic relationship to sexual violence, 58; bios, devoid of, 52; Blackening of, 175; Blackness of, 1, 268; as breeders, 117; death drive, 269; deathliness of, 46; as degraded workers, 182; *durante vita* of, 139, 142-43; former slaves, in labor market, 178, 179; as gendered, 9, 70-71, 143-45, 183; household, as autonomous space, 204; hypervisibility, erasure, and redress of, 228; ideological solidity, 28; labor contracts, 180; lived experiences of, 117; master dialectic, 226-28; as metaphor for woman, 183-84; mothers, 111; motility and resistance, 43; mutilation, 15; nonexistence, 268-69; non-Human status of, 117, 134-35; objecthood, 11; ontological incapacitation, 268; personhood, loss of, 182; as reasonless object, 1; replicability of, 26; as sex personified, 257; sexual captivity, 1; as socially dead, 182; sexual fecundity, 28; sexualized violence, as method of control, 220-22; as sexually open, 1, 269-70; sexual suffering, 236; sexual violability, 2, 53, 77, 266; sexual violation, 25, 29, 61, 122-23, 139, 176, 235-36, 260-61, 264, 268-69; sexuation of, 6, 15, 27, 51, 55, 204, 269; slave sex, 42; social death, 109; as source of power, 227; suicidal imperative, 276n60; theft of body, 190;

torturers, sado-masochistic relation between, 36; as unthought, 142; violation of, 151; violence, as central scope of, 251; as women, 184–85. *See also* female slaves, male slaves
Smith, Andrea, 176–77
Snorton, C. Riley, 109; absent Black mother, 107–8
Snyder, Alonzo, 220
social contract, 188–89
social death, 11, 90, 103, 105, 108–9, 260, 272n19, 275–76n50; Black fungibility, 107; gender, 106; kinship, 101; slavery, 183, 230
sociality, 48
sociodicy, 70; of feminist frameworks, 71; of Human gender, 17; violence of, 71
Somerset, James, 303n34
Somerset v. Stewart, 249, 303n34
Somerville, George, 62, 64
Somerville, Siobhan B., 86
Soul on Ice (Cleaver), 214
Spillers, Hortense J., 4, 9, 87, 101, 106–8, 110–11, 131, 188–89, 191, 245, 288n102, 290–91n20, 303n20; oceanic, 192; theft of body, 190
Stanton, Mary Olmstead, 85–86
State of Missouri v. Celia, a Slave, 48–49, 51–52
statues: toppling of, 53–54
Steinberg, Ron, 260
Stewart, Charles, 303n34
Stowe, Harriet Beecher, 165–66
subjectivity: objectification, movement between, 155

Tallbear, Kim, 133
Taney, Roger B., 40
Tardieu, Auguste Ambroise, 292–93n61
Tarnowsky, Benjamin, 292–93n61
Taxil, Léo, 164
Taylor, Alan, 58–60
Taylor, Breonna, 287n92
Taylor, Nikki M., 283n18

Tempest, The (Shakespeare), 19–20, 80–84, 86–87, 90; as allegorical, 78–79
Temple, Robert, 135–36
theoretical politics of dissemblance, 19, 72; woman-man-slave relation, 73–74
thingification, 48, 223
Third Wave feminisms, 67
"This Cruel War" (website), 114–18
Thomas, Alan, 59
torture, 26–27, 42–44, 46, 203, 219–21; public spectacle, disappearance of, 45; sado-masochistic relation between torturer and slave, 36; as structure of sexual impulses, 45; from symbolics of blood to analytics of sexuality, 45
trans theory, 198
Turner, Felicity M., 281n5
12 Years a Slave (film), 23, 233–34, 261, 304n42; Blackness in, 255–56, 259–60; Patsey (character), sexual violation of, 251–55, 257–58

Uncle Tom's Cabin (Stowe), 165–66
Unilever, 288n104
United States, 1, 10, 25–26, 126, 133, 138, 267, 304n41; anti-miscegenation laws, 96; black and white bodies, policing boundary between, 86; confederate and colonial monuments, 54
University of North Carolina, Chapel Hill: Silent Sam statue, 54
University of Virginia, 58–59
Unwritten History of Slavery (Egypt and Johnson), 114
Up from Slavery (Washington), 109
Utz, Henry, 219–23, 227, 229

Vindication of the Rights of Women, A (Wolstonecraft), 185
violence: sociodicy of, 71
Virginia, 132, 137–39, 141–42, 303n34
Virginia Act XII (1662), 28–29, 136–37, 143, 288n118
virtual reality, 305n3

Walker, Alice, 111, 279n20
Walvin, James, 247
Warren, Calvin, 45, 152–53, 155, 281n2; distorting similes, 154
Washington, Booker T., 109
Watson, Emily, 239
Weinbaum, Alys Eve, 101
Weld, Theodore Dwight, 30–31
Wells-Barnett, Ida B., 206
wench: as racial gender marker, 62
Werley v. State, 201
West Indies, 26
White, E. Francis, 159, 292n52
white feminism, 83. *See also* Black feminism, feminism
white gender theory, 170
whiteness, 138–39, 186–87, 211, 228–29, 245; psychosis of, 246
white patriarchy, 203
white power, 141
white racial violence, 198. *See also* antiblackness
white settlers, 133
white supremacy, 80, 179
white violence, 207
white womanhood, 79, 131, 138–39, 142, 256; longue durée, 185; marriage, 140–41; power of, 140; violence of, 188, 208. *See also* Black womanhood, womanhood

Wilderson, Frank B. III, 10, 16, 105–6, 148–50, 153, 156, 182, 259–60, 281n2, 290–91n20, 297n15, 301n110, 304n42; absent Black mother, 107–8; objective vertigo, 117
wildness: Black criminality, 156
Wilkinson, Tom, 239
Williams, Caroline Randall, 53–55; historical silence, 58
Wollstonecraft, Mary, 185
womanhood, 68, 94, 112, 170, 175, 177, 181, 185–86, 188, 201–2; Black feminism, 73–74; care and violation, scales of, 184; femaleness, 70, 107; as ontological, 69, 189; for white women, 106; woman: as property, 69–70. *See also* Black womanhood, white womanhood
womanism, 279n20; feminism, split between, 78
woman-man-slave relation, 73–74
Works Progress Administration (WPA), 202
world-building, 102, 265
Wynter, Sylvia, 19–20, 70, 78–80, 82–83, 86–87, 240, 246, 279–80n21, 299n66

Zoffany, Johann, 302n4
Zong (slave ship), 239–40, 242, 247–48
Zorgue (ship). See *Zong* (slave ship)

Inventions Black Philosophy, Politics, Aesthetics
Edited by David Marriott

Le véritable saut consiste à introduire l'invention dans l'existence—the real leap consists in introducing invention into existence. Among this and other demands for a thought, a blackness of thought that is itself an act of liberation, for Frantz Fanon, the critical task of any aspirational black philosophy is its ability to tell apart blackness from its mirages and impossibilities in science, art, and European history and philosophy. Is it still possible to pursue this goal today, within the ongoing reaches of anti-blackness? And what could this "leap" be, given the undecidability of blackness as a concept, feeling, or figure? The premise of the series is that blackness cannot be subsumed under the prevailing forms of philosophy, politics, or aesthetics without putting into question what this leap could be, or mistaking invention for their presuppositions, and so losing sight of what this invention could be *in its very difference*. To that end, *Inventions* seeks to publish works that set the agenda for what this leap would look like or be.

Anteaesthetics Black Aesthesis and the Critique of Form
Rizvana Bradley

Of Effacement Blackness and Non-Being
David Marriott

The authorized representative in the EU for product safety and compliance is:
Mare Nostrum Group
B.V Doelen 72
4831 GR Breda
The Netherlands